A CULTURAL HISTORY OF TRAGEDY

VOLUME 2

A Cultural History of Tragedy
General Editor: Rebecca Bushnell

Volume 1
A Cultural History of Tragedy in Antiquity
Edited by Emily Wilson

Volume 2
A Cultural History of Tragedy in the Middle Ages
Edited by Jody Enders, Theresa Coletti, John T. Sebastian, and Carol Symes

Volume 3
A Cultural History of Tragedy in the Early Modern Age
Edited by Naomi Liebler

Volume 4
A Cultural History of Tragedy in the Age of Enlightenment
Edited by Mitchell Greenberg

Volume 5
A Cultural History of Tragedy in the Age of Empire
Edited by Michael Gamer and Diego Saglia

Volume 6
A Cultural History of Tragedy in the Modern Age
Edited by Jennifer Wallace

A CULTURAL HISTORY OF TRAGEDY

IN THE MIDDLE AGES

VOLUME 2

*Edited by Jody Enders, Theresa Coletti,
John T. Sebastian, and Carol Symes*

BLOOMSBURY ACADEMIC
LONDON • NEW YORK • OXFORD • NEW DELHI • SYDNEY

BLOOMSBURY ACADEMIC
Bloomsbury Publishing Plc
50 Bedford Square, London, WC1B 3DP, UK
1385 Broadway, New York, NY 10018, USA
29 Earlsfort Terrace, Dublin 2, Ireland

BLOOMSBURY, BLOOMSBURY ACADEMIC and the Diana logo are trademarks of
Bloomsbury Publishing Plc

First published in hardback in Great Britain 2020
This paperback edition 2023

Copyright © Jody Enders, Theresa Coletti, John T. Sebastian, Carol Symes,
and contributors, 2020

Jody Enders, Theresa Coletti, John Sebastian, Carol Symes, and contributors have
asserted their right under the Copyright, Designs and Patents Act, 1988, to be
identified as Authors of this work.

For legal purposes the Acknowledgments on p. xi constitute an extension of this
copyright page.

Series design by Raven Design

Cover image: Giotto, Lower Church Assisi, *The Massacre of the Innocents*
01 © ART Collection / Alamy Stock Photo

All rights reserved. No part of this publication may be reproduced or transmitted
in any form or by any means, electronic or mechanical, including photocopying,
recording, or any information storage or retrieval system, without prior
permission in writing from the publishers.

Bloomsbury Publishing Plc does not have any control over, or responsibility for, any
third-party websites referred to or in this book. All internet addresses given in this
book were correct at the time of going to press. The author and publisher regret
any inconvenience caused if addresses have changed or sites have ceased to
exist, but can accept no responsibility for any such changes.

A catalogue record for this book is available from the British Library.

A catalog record for this book is available from the Library of Congress.

ISBN: HB: 978-1-4742-8790-6
       HB set: 978-1-4742-8814-9
       PB: 978-1-3504-1676-5
       PB Set: 978-1-3504-1692-5

Series: The Cultural Histories Series

Typeset by RefineCatch Limited, Bungay, Suffolk
Printed and bound in Great Britain

To find out more about our authors and books visit www.bloomsbury.com
and sign up for our newsletters.

CONTENTS

LIST OF ILLUSTRATIONS	vi
NOTES ON CONTRIBUTORS	vii
SERIES PREFACE	ix
GENERAL EDITOR'S ACKNOWLEDGMENTS	xi
Introduction: Miscarriages of Justice *Jody Enders*	1
1 Forms and Media *Carol Symes*	15
2 Sites of Performance and Circulation *Christopher Swift*	27
3 Communities of Production and Consumption *John T. Sebastian*	49
4 Philosophy and Social Theory *Antonio Donato and Erith Jaffe-Berg*	65
5 Religion, Ritual and Myth *John Parker*	81
6 Politics of City and Nation *Hannah Skoda*	99
7 Society and Family *Theresa Coletti*	113
8 Gender and Sexuality *Karen Sullivan*	127
NOTES	141
BIBLIOGRAPHY	181
INDEX	213

LIST OF ILLUSTRATIONS

CHAPTER 1

1.1	Euripides' *Helen*: ancient fragmentation and medieval mediation.	16

CHAPTER 2

2.1	*The Castle of Perseverance* stage plan (*c.* 1440).	29
2.2	Mappa Mundi, *De natura rerum* (*c.* 1055–74).	30
2.3	Wheel of Fortune with Christ Enthroned in Judgment (1230).	37
2.4	*Danse Macabre* mural, Parish Church of Kermaria-an-Isquit (1490).	41
2.5	*Ad Mortem Festināmus*. Llibre Vermell de Montserrat (*c.* 1399–1400).	43
2.6	*Passio Christi* stage plan. Ordinalia (1425).	46

CHAPTER 3

3.1	Fortune and her wheel from the opening of Book II of John Lydgate's *Siege of Troy*.	53
3.2	The beginning of Seneca's *Hercules furens*, with interlineated commentary by Nicholas Trevet.	55
3.3	Eve prevented from performing penance in the Jordan by the devil disguised as an angel from *La Penitance Adam*.	59
3.4	York Minster, Great East Window: The Expulsion of Adam and Eve.	61

CHAPTER 4

4.1	*Philosophy Consoling Boethius and Fortune Turning the Wheel*, about 1460–70. Coëtivy Master (Henri de Vulcop?).	73
4.2	Masters of Dirc van Delf, "The Lamentation."	77

CHAPTER 5

5.1	Illumination of virtues and vices in Prudentius' *Psychomachia* as Roman gladiators.	89
5.2	Chastity slays Lust in Prudentius' *Psychomachia*.	90
5.3	Death of St. Cassian in Prudentius' *Liber Peristephanon*.	92
5.4	Mask-wearing slave and prostitute from Terence's *Hecyra*.	95
5.5	Thomas Kyd, *The Spanish Tragedy* (London, 1633). Woodcut from title page showing the hanging of Horatio.	98

NOTES ON CONTRIBUTORS

Theresa Coletti is Professor of English and Distinguished Scholar Teacher Emerita at the University of Maryland College Park. She has published widely on medieval drama, medieval women's literary and religious cultures, Chaucer, and medievalism. Her essays have appeared in numerous edited collections and in journals such as *Speculum, Exemplaria, ELH, Studies in Philology, Journal of Medieval and Early Modern Studies,* and *Studies in the Age of Chaucer.* She is the author of *Naming the Rose: Eco, Medieval Signs, and Modern Theory* (1988) and *Mary Magdalene and the Drama of Saints: Theater, Gender, and Religion in Late Medieval England* (2004), and editor of *The Digby Mary Magdalene* (2018).

Antonio Donato is Associate Professor of Philosophy at Queens College, CUNY. He specializes in medieval and Renaissance philosophy. He is the author of *Boethius' "Consolation of Philosophy" as a Product of Late Antiquity* (2013). His essays have appeared in the *British Journal of the History of Philosophy, Classical World,* and *Traditio.*

Jody Enders, Distinguished Professor of French at the University of California, Santa Barbara, is the author of four books on the medieval theater: *Rhetoric and the Origins of Medieval Drama* (1992), winner of the inaugural Scaglione Prize from the Modern Language Association, *The Medieval Theater of Cruelty* (1999), *Death by Drama and Other Medieval Urban Legends* (2002), winner of the Barnard Hewitt Prize from the American Society of Theatre Research, and *Murder by Accident* (2010); plus two books of performance-friendly literary translations destined for medievalists, historians, theater practitioners, and classic comedy lovers: *The Farce of the Fart and Other Ribaldries* (2011) and *Holy Deadlock and Further Ribaldries* (2017). A past editor of *Theatre Survey* and Guggenheim fellow, she has published numerous essays on the interplay of rhetoric, medieval literature, performance theory, and the law.

Erith Jaffe-Berg is a professor of Theatre at the Department of Theatre, Film and Digital Production at the University of California at Riverside. Her research focuses on the *commedia dell'arte* and performances by minority groups in Early Modern Italy. She is the author of *Commedia dell'Arte and the Mediterranean: Charting Journeys and Mapping "Others"* (2015) and *The Multilingual Art of Commedia dell'Arte* (2009). She has published essays on early modern performance in various journals and anthologies, including the Bloomsbury *Cultural History of Theatre in the Middle Ages* (2018). Abiding research interests include the Jewish contribution to sixteenth- and seventeenth-century theater in northern Italy.

John Parker is Associate Professor of English at the University of Virginia. He is the author of *The Aesthetics of Antichrist: From Christian Drama to Christopher Marlowe* (2007), among several book chapters, articles, and reviews. His primary interests include drama from antiquity to the Renaissance, the New Testament, Christian theology, and continental philosophy. He received a Federal Chancellor Scholarship from the Alexander von Humboldt Foundation (1999–2000) and was awarded the Rome Prize in medieval studies from the American Academy in Rome (2008–9). Before coming to Virginia he taught at Macalester College and Harvard University.

John T. Sebastian is Vice President for Mission and Ministry and Professor of English at Loyola Marymount University in Los Angeles. He is, with Christina M. Fitzgerald, general editor of the *Broadview Anthology of Medieval Literature* and its spinoff volumes, including an edition of English morality plays. He is also the editor of the TEAMS edition of the Croxton *Play of the Sacrament*. In addition to his editing work, he has published chapters on medieval drama, the devotional poetry of John Lydgate, and medievalism in video games.

Hannah Skoda is Associate Professor in History at St John's College, Oxford. She is the author of *Medieval Violence: Physical Brutality in Northern France, 1270–1330* (2012). She has also co-edited *Legalism: History and Anthropology* (2012) with Paul Dresch, and *Legalism: Property and Ownership* (2018) with Georgy Kantor and Tom Lambert. She has wide-ranging interests and has published on the history of nostalgia, medieval student misbehavior, Dante studies, and histories of physical impairment.

Christopher Swift is an associate professor of Theater in the Humanities Department at New York City College of Technology, City University of New York. His research focuses on medieval theater technologies, devotional objects, Holy Week processionals, and public performances of penance. His writing has appeared in the *Journal of Religion and Theatre*, *Preternature*, *TDR*, and *Theatre Journal*. Dr. Swift has been a fellow on a number of grants from the National Endowment for the Humanities aimed to develop interdisciplinary curricula among humanities and STEM fields.

Karen Sullivan is Irma Brandeis Professor of Romance Culture and Literature at Bard College. She is the author of *The Interrogation of Joan of Arc* (1999); *Truth and the Heretic: Crises of Knowledge in Medieval French Literature* (2005), which won the Modern Language Association's Aldo and Jeanne Scaglione Prize for French and Francophone Literature; *The Inner Lives of Medieval Inquisitors* (2011); and *The Danger of Romance: Truth, Fantasy, and Arthurian Fictions* (2018), which was supported by a John Simon Guggenheim Memorial Foundation Fellowship; as well as numerous essays on Old French and Occitan literature. Much of her work concerns the intersection of history and literature, including in medieval accounts of Eleanor of Aquitaine.

Carol Symes is Professor of History, Theatre, and Medieval Studies at the University of Illinois, Urbana-Champaign. Educated at Yale and Oxford, she subsequently trained at the Bristol Old Vic Theatre School and pursued an acting career while working toward the PhD at Harvard. Her book, *A Common Stage: Theatre and Public Life in Medieval Arras* (2007), has won four awards, including the Herbert Baxter Adams Prize of the American Historical Association and the John Nicholas Brown Prize of the Medieval Academy of America. She is the co-editor, with Caroline C. Goodson and Anne E. Lester, of *Cities, Texts, and Social Networks: Experiences and Perceptions of Medieval Urban Space, 400–1500* (2010); co-author of a bestselling college textbook, *Western Civilizations*; and founding executive editor of *The Medieval Globe*, the first academic journal to promote a global approach to medieval studies. She has published many articles on the medieval reception and transmission of ancient texts.

SERIES PREFACE

A cultural history of tragedy faces a daunting task: how to address tragedy's influence on Western culture while describing how complex and changing historical conditions have shaped it over two and a half millennia. This is the first study with such an extensive scope, investigating tragedy's long-lived cultural impact and accounting for its material, social, political, and philosophical dimensions.

Since antiquity, tragedy has appeared in a myriad of forms, reinvented in every age. It has been performed as opera, dance, film, and television as well as live theater. From the beginning, concepts of tragedy have also surfaced in other literary genres such as narrative poetry and novels, as well as in non-literary forms, including journalism, visual art, and photography. Tragedy never appears in a vacuum: the conditions of performance and production and its communal functions always affect its form and meaning. Tragedy has never belonged solely to elite culture, and who creates and consumes these forms of tragedy also makes a difference. Not only has the status of tragedy's producers—the writers, actors, artists, and performers—evolved over time, but so has the nature of the audiences, viewers, and readers as well, all significantly affecting tragedy's aesthetic and social impact.

Tragedy also does more than simply represent or perform human catastrophe or suffering; it is a mode of thought, a way of figuring the human condition as a whole. Philosophers and social and cultural theorists from Plato to Lacan have long pondered the idea of the tragic, while in turn literary models have influenced philosophy, social thought, and psychoanalysis. Tragedy has always had a complex relationship with religion and ritual practices, both complementing and conflicting with religious orthodoxies concerning fate, the power of the gods, and the meaning of suffering. At the same time, since its earliest staging in fifth-century Athens as a civic as well as religious event, tragedy has both echoed and challenged relationships of power and political events in societies experiencing conflict or change.

While tragedy in all its versions has thus profoundly tapped into broad social, intellectual, and political movements, it has often represented those themes through individual experiences, ranging from the titanic sufferings of princes to the sorrows of ordinary men and women. While tragedy's themes of ambition, authority, transgression, and rebellion are grounded in religion and politics, its plots often play out through family relationships that both mirror and conflict with social and political norms. When tragedy thus engages familial and personal themes, it often involves tensions of gender and sexuality. Sexuality is a powerful driver of tragic catastrophe, when desire is granted its own kind of fatal power.

As with other *Cultural History* series, here the story of tragedy writ large is divided into volumes covering six historical periods from antiquity to modernity. Although the boundaries between those time are necessarily fluid, the volumes are divided as follows: 1. Antiquity (500 BCE–1000 CE); 2. Middle Ages (1000–1400); 3. Early Modern Age (1400–1650); 4. Age of Enlightenment (1650–1800); 5. Age of Empire (1800–1920), and 6. Modern Age (1920–present). While such a history naturally focuses on Western culture and history, at the end it also touches on tragedy's later post-colonial adaptations, which put its fundamentally Western concerns in a global context. Each volume has its own introduction by an editor or co-editors presenting an original and provocative vision of tragedy's manifestations in one historical era. Each volume also covers the same eight topics as the others in the *Cultural History*: forms and media; sites of performance and circulation; communities of production and consumption; philosophy and social theory; religion, ritual, and myth; politics of city and nation; society and family; and gender and sexuality. Readers may thus follow one topic over a wide historical span, or they may focus on all dimensions of tragedy in one period. Either way they read, they will be able to appreciate the power of tragedy to shape our understanding of human experience, and in turn, how tragedy has changed over time, both reflecting and challenging historical conditions.

Rebecca Bushnell, University of Pennsylvania, General Editor

GENERAL EDITOR'S ACKNOWLEDGMENTS

The original vision for this volume was Claire Sponsler's. Claire courageously shouldered the task of imagining a cultural history of tragedy in the Middle Ages, although many critics would say there was no such thing. She also recruited many of its eminent contributors and shaped the framework for their essays. However, her inspiring work was cut short by her horrid sudden death on July 29, 2016. The death of this brilliant scholar and kind friend was deeply mourned by everyone involved in this project and by the world of medieval scholarship at large.

In the face of this catastrophe, Claire's friends and collaborators stepped up to make sure that her critical legacy would be honored in this volume of the *Cultural History of Tragedy*. Four of the contributors—Jody Enders, Theresa Coletti, John Sebastian, and Carol Symes—volunteered to serve as editors of individual essays. I am so grateful to them for their spirited collaboration, excellent advice, and close attention to every aspect of this work. I am especially indebted to Jody Enders, who not only encouraged me from the very beginning of this undertaking, but who also took a lead role in navigating us through a series of crises we encountered. We simply could not have completed this volume without Jody's wisdom, energy, and strong will to get it done. In the end, everyone dedicated themselves to the work of writing about medieval tragedy because this is such an important story to tell, but they also did it for Claire.

Introduction

Miscarriages of Justice

JODY ENDERS

The machine is in perfect order; it has been oiled since time began, and it runs without friction. Death, treason, and sorrow are on the march; and they move in the wake of storm, of tears, of stillness. Every kind of stillness. The hush when the executioner's axe goes up at the end of the last act. The unbreathable silence when, at the beginning of the play, the two lovers, their hearts bared, their bodies naked, stand for the first time face to face in the darkened room, afraid to stir. The silence inside you when the roaring crowd acclaims the winner—so that you think of a film without a soundtrack, mouths agape and no sound coming out of them, a clamor that is no more than a picture; and you, the victor, already vanquished, alone in your desert of silence. That is tragedy.

—Jean Anouilh[1]

Having issued multiple threats of violence, the husband raises his hand and lands the blow. It is brutal enough to shatter his wife's nose, after which he punches her in the back, on the sides, and about the face, straddling her, choking her as she pleads that he spare her vital organs: "No kidney punches! Help! Murder!"[2]

The audience laughs.

Somewhere else in medieval Europe, the sounds of domestic violence are loud enough to raise the dead and to create the unborn. A pregnant Alice is beaten to death; another wife is "beaten so severely by her husband that her child [is] born dead."

Some neighbors intervene; others do not.[3]

Yet elsewhere, innocent babies are ripped from their mothers' wombs and slaughtered alive: "Dame, show me thy child there; he must hop upon my spear. And it any pintel [penis] bear, I must teach him a play."[4] A saintly woman is bound to a spit before her tongue is removed with red-hot pincers, all as a mysterious figure appears to direct the unspeakable proceedings before onlookers.[5] By a king's justice, a messiah is tortured for hours, for days, his living body used as a punching bag or dartboard until such time that, of violence, He is reborn.[6]

A spectator gasps; a reader meditates on an image of devotion; a theatergoer weeps.

A beautiful maiden is raped again and again on a bed of soft petals. "Let's play a game," he says, "I'll make you a woman." "He pulled up my little shift," she says, and "broke into my little fortress with his erect spear."[7] A chambermaid who has formerly sold a consecrated Host to a Jew finds herself pregnant after a sexual assault by the master's valet. She murders her newborn and buries the dead child "in a dung heap, a most bitter thing." Burned at the stake, she is "no true mother / Who would ever destroy the fruit of her womb like that."[8] Another chambermaid is "heavy as a cow with child" by her master while the mistress is away on pilgrimage.⁹ And yet another pregnant chambermaid gives birth all alone while the household sleeps: "the poor wretch, beside herself, took it by the feet and hit it against a wall, and killed it. And, having done that, she threw it into a well." Some ten days later, she too is burned at the stake.[10]

A troubadour sings; an actor plays; a monarch forgives; an audience guffaws; a chronicler records.

And, faced with the above montage of sources of unjust legal deserts spanning the twelfth through the fifteenth centuries, the cultural historian looks and listens: for the text, for the past, and, for purposes of this series, for a theory and practice of tragedy that was foundational enough to have informed almost two millennia of thought.

A farce, a legal record, a song, a Passion play, an image, a letter of remission, a religious drama, another farce, a chronicle. And what about a morality play, a fool's play, a saint's life, an epic, a romance, or an allegory? An expiatory procession, a charivari, a gynecological treatise, a conduct manual? A political proclamation, a siege poem, a trial, a prayer, a sermon, a crusade? Some events, genres, or media move piously toward the piteous beauty of rape, abuse, and martyrdom, others impiously toward the cheerful horror of rape, abuse, and martyrdom. Some move toward the sure and certain hope of release from earthly pain, others toward the big joke that is brutality. Although the term "tragedy" turns up nowhere in our opening montage, there can be little doubt that we are in its presence. But tragedy as what? A literary genre or mode? A subset of theater? A performance practice? An aesthetic? A worldview? A medium that is its own message?[11] Is tragedy a branch of philosophy, folklore, theology, politics, law, or ethics? Do we simply—or not so simply—know it when we see it? Hear it? Feel it? And, if so—or, if not—how *do* we know? Is it a measure of the intentions of an author, actor, or actant? Does it exist only in the eye of the beholder? In the successful elicitation of tears or laughter? Does it depend on proportion? All or none of the above?

It is the premise of this Introduction and of the eight distinguished essays here assembled that, once we make room for a wide range of social performances, a new vision of a vital and influential medieval tragedy is possible. Indeed, the pieces of a vast cultural puzzle have already started to come together in the era's relentless obsession with the justice and injustice associated with death and dying, birth and rebirth, the born and the unborn, the stillborn and the never born. Prone to apocalyptic thinking in literature, art, theology, and philosophy, medieval people shared with their forebears an abiding preoccupation with the nature of lives that seemed doomed from the start, lived or unlived in pain, with or without the hopeful comfort of an afterlife. A legend of 460 BCE, for instance, had it that, in ancient Greece, the Furies had made so dramatic an entrance in Aeschylus' *Eumenides* that terror-stricken "women aborted, children died, and several spectators were struck by madness."[12] But, in the 1300s, it was no legend when "the Parisian parish of Saint-Maur-des-Fossés witnessed multiple tragedies in the household of an English artisan called Richardus: he murdered his mother-in-law, and his wife was then found guilty of infanticide."[13] Nor was it legend when a legal regulation of 1501 in Mons denied pregnant women admission to the theater (along with children and "senile old people"), lest such terror be repeated.[14] Tragedy was a matter of life and death; so too is its historiography. But we cannot locate its cultural history until coming face to face with the unparalleled influence of a truism that has inadvertently silenced discussion: namely, that there was no such thing as medieval tragedy.

Largely gleaned from George Steiner's *Death of Tragedy*, the truism in fact derives from the rhetorico-aesthetic imagination of I.A. Richards (1893–1979), the important philosopher, rhetorician, and speech-act theorist. In a trenchant but oft decontextualized insight, Richards posited that "the least touch of any theology which has a compensating heaven to offer the tragic hero is fatal."[15] In other words, for a faith-based Middle Ages, the advent of a Christian afterlife hastened no Nietzschean "birth" but, rather, the "death of tragedy" (or, at best, a messy medieval afterbirth). I contend, however, that, if anything has proved "fatal," it is the Anouilh-like silencing of a powerful medieval medium.

Suffice it to insist from the outset that reports of the death of medieval tragedy have been greatly exaggerated. Like Saint Erkenwald of fourteenth-century hagiography, who "turns to the tomb and talks to the corpse" of a pagan man of laws, we might thus bid of medieval tragedy: "in this sepulcher stay in your silence no more."[16] By analogy to the literally foundational trope of liturgical drama, the *Visitatio sepulchri* or *Visit to the Sepulcher*, we might ask a version of the question aligned with the alleged birth ex nihilo of medieval theater itself sometime between the seventh and the eleventh centuries. Instead of *Quem quaeritis in sepulchro, o Christicole?* ("Whom do you seek in the sepulcher of Jesus?"), we might ask: *Quem quaeritis in sepulchro tragoediis? What do you seek in the sepulcher of tragedy?* Medieval Christians heard each Easter that Christ was no longer in His tomb for He had risen; contemporary readers will see throughout this book that a medieval tragic practice might also rise from the ashes.[17]

Midway through life's journey between the purported artistic apogees of classical antiquity at one end and the Renaissance on the other, there lies, per its name, the *medium aevum* or "Middle Age" (c. 500–1500). Over the millennium that witnessed the massive social shifts of feudalism, urbanization, and the rise of humanism, had tragedy truly slumbered until its literal sixteenth-century rebirth? If anything, it is infinitely more plausible that, as is the case for Claire Sponsler, the luminous thinker and original editor of this volume, tragedy is the great absent presence in medieval literary history. It is that absence which is not one.[18] Even so, its silence is deafening. From time to time, medievalists' attention has been captured by an article or book chapter on the subject; but, to this day, the sole book-length study remains Henry Ansgar Kelly, *Ideas and Forms of Tragedy* (1993).[19] Otherwise, we must await an explosion of studies often drawing inspiration from the early modern period: to name but a few, Donald Stone's *French Humanist Tragedy* (1974), Jonathan Dollimore's *Radical Tragedy: Religion, Ideology, and Power in the Drama of Shakespeare and his Contemporaries* (1984), Francis Barker's *Culture of Violence* (1994), Terry Eagleton's *Sweet Violence: The Idea of the Tragic* (2003), or Blair Hoxby's remarkable *What Was Tragedy?* (2017). In France, Raymond Lebègue starts the history of tragedy per se in 1514 with the relatively pallid imitations of Greco-Roman tragedy by the likes of Etienne Jodelle (1532–73) and Robert Garnier (1544–90); in England, its arrival is forestalled until 1561 with Thomas Norton's and Thomas Sackville's *Gorboduc*.[20] But, as early as 1315, the Italian Albertino Mussato (1262–1329) had authored the tragedy of *Eccerino*, a Latin-verse adaptation of Seneca's *Thyestes*. And, for all the sixteenth-century creators of "tragicomedy," exemplified by such a work as the *Celestina* (1499) by Fernando de Rojas, the tragic side of the so-called hybrid must certainly have been known.[21] Surely, there must be another way into our subject; it is the goal of this Introduction to propose one.

In reality, medieval commentators pondered tragedy repeatedly, among them such keen observers as Boethius (c. 480–524/25), Isidore of Seville (c. 570–636), Remigius of Auxerre (841–908), William of Conches (c. 1080–1154), Averroës (1126–98), Hermann the German (thirteenth century), Nicolas Trevet (1258–1328), who is highlighted in John Sebastian's Chapter 3, and Dante (1265–1321). They did so even though their knowledge of that art form was sometimes as imperfect as Isidore's use of the imperfect tense when he implied that tragedy was a lost art of a distant past.[22] But, whether it be the infanticide of *Medea*, the medieval *Massacre of the Innocents*, an actual infanticide of 1495, or the haunting *ataxia* of Neil Labute's *Medea Redux*: tragedy belongs to a long, pan-European Middle Ages. Its scope extends from the Middle East to what Claire Sponsler termed the "ritual importation" of medieval Passion plays to such far-flung destinations as Oberammergau, Germany and Black Hills, New York.[23] Writ and performed large along a coherent historical continuum, it must accommodate, as John Parker does in Chapter 5, history and pseudohistory, metahistory and "mythistory," legendry and Gospel truth.[24] Expansive and ubiquitous, influencing and influenced by culture, medieval tragedy is part of Richards' whole: "tragedy is still the form under which the mind may most clearly and freely contemplate the human situation, its issues unclouded, its possibilities revealed."[25] It is so daunting in scope that it is difficult to know where to begin; but begin we must, for there is an urgency with which tragedy clamors aesthetically to speak and to be heard. It must speak what cannot be spoken, even as others—representatives of a variety of hegemonies—threaten to impose silence, in art as much as in life.

Even our rapid initial foray into a panoply of primary sources has imparted a medieval metareflection on the beginning of the end and the end of all beginning, incarnated by the gestational image and reality of the dead baby and the very breath of life. There is something physiological about tragedy: something that leaves its audiences literally and metaphorically gasping for air as it moves inexorably toward the universal confrontation with unbreathable, unspeakable death. Once we give medieval tragedy some breathing room, we may better understand that it embodies a key theme of medieval romance and of Theresa Coletti's Chapter 7: the terrifying prospect of the loss not only of life, lineage, and the future but of *all* futures. An early edition of the *Princeton Encyclopedia of Poetry and Poetics* features a definition of tragedy as astute as it is succinct in its eloquence: "After comedy and most other literary forms, life goes on. But *tragedy stops history*; it is a summit or end stage, always concerned with problems of value; it is human life seen in an ultimate perspective."[26] In this Introduction, it need in no way stop *literary* history. The end of all beginning need not signal the historiographical beginning of the end of medieval tragedy.

To borrow the eminently appropriate Platonic lexicon of maieutic, the Socratic, dialogic "birthing" of ideas, medieval tragedy has had a difficult labor; but all its alleged rebirths, resurrections, and renaissances assist us immeasurably in reassessing a number of genealogies, medieval and modern.[27] So I proffer three sections dedicated to midwifing the medieval tragic: "Genre Trouble," "Historiography Trouble," and a preliminary, speculative conclusion on "Audience Trouble." In the first section, "Genre Trouble: Tragedy, Comedy, and the *Confusion des genres*," we turn to what medieval thinkers actually said about tragedy. Thereupon, we notice that, like Aristotle before them in *Poetics* (chaps. 2–5), they frequently refer to tragedy in the same breath—if not necessarily the same *breadth*—as comedy. This makes for what T.S. Eliot presciently called a "*confusion des genres*,"[28] a "confusion" that may be dispelled when we revisit the single greatest obstacle to our recuperative efforts. The second section, "Historiography Trouble: That Absence Which is Not One," takes up the critical misappropriation of I.A. Richards via George Steiner, the better to redress a number of unsustainable genealogies. Finally, in "Audience Trouble: Catharsis and Social Control," I conclude (all too briefly) that tragedy oscillates between liberation and repression, chaos and order in philosophical ways evocative of the theater itself. Regardless of medieval access to Aristotle at any given moment, the period belies a relentless but productive tension between the purgative, cathartic release of *Poetics* 1449b and the Platonic social orchestration exemplified in the *Laws* by an anarchic "theatrocracy," a social disorder which, as we shall see, counterintuitively models both submission and resistance.[29] Notwithstanding the limitations of any definition, and as our examples of living and dying have already hinted, there emerges a working definition of our subject. Like tragedy itself, it encompasses a cultural history of the just and unjust which has been rehearsed by historiographies just and unjust: *Tragedy is a social metareflection about justice: a mode more than a genre, manifesting in multiple forms and media as an aesthetic, affective, rhetorical, historical, political, theological, philosophical, and legalistically construed embodiment of the pain and pleasure that inform a justice-driven yet unjust end*. And to that end, we begin.

GENRE TROUBLE: TRAGEDY, COMEDY, AND THE *CONFUSION DES GENRES*

From antiquity through the Middle Ages and beyond, and as Kelly's wealth of evidence handily demonstrates, tragedy and comedy have perpetually defined one another. In pain and pleasure, rhetoric and law, philosophy and theology, theirs is a history of communion, separation, and reconciliation. As early as the second century CE, Lucian of Samosata sought to distinguish not comedy from tragedy but both *together* from *saltatio*, a multimedia form of music, gesture, and dance (which was by no means limited to the "display of a single activity" as was "tragedy's mummery or comedy's buffoonery").[30] Later, the *comoedus* and the *tragoedus* would reappear together alongside "musicians, actors, mimes and dancers" in Isidore of Seville's *Etymologies*, one of the premier reference works of the European Middle Ages. "Writers of comedy (*comoedi*)," Isidore explained, "would recount in word and gesture the deeds of common people, and their plots would represent the defiling of virgins and the love affairs of courtesans"; whereas "[t]ragedians (*tragoedi*) are those who would sing for the audience in poetry about the ancient deeds and lamentable crimes of wicked kings."[31] Glending Olson reminds us that, for Albert the Great, "comedies and tragedies were intended to provide a rest for the spirit after intense study and thus belong to the genus of play."[32] And tragedies, states Remigius in his commentary on Boethius, "describe ludicrous and monstrous things (*res ludicras et monstruosas*)."[33] But so too do the comedies that were oftentimes performed by one and the same medieval troupe. By the 1530s, for instance, Jean Bouchet characterized the maker of farce as one who aims to "declare by *grave tragedy*, rude satire, and *feigned comedy*, the good of the good and the evil of the wicked."[34] And, by 1599, the Bishop of Esne indicted the lot of them when complaining to his local government that actors had been granted permission to play "*farces, comédies et tragedies*."[35] One can only wonder how it came to pass that postmedieval critique tore asunder what—even in service of antitheatrical polemic—the Middle Ages had so clearly brought together.

Our wonder is but compounded by the claim of Thomas Sébillet (1512–89) that, in France, it was the morality play, a theatrical debate between embodied allegorical figures, that took the place of tragedy *and* comedy: "For us, *moralités* stand in for tragedies and comedies alike."[36] And yet, toward the end of the sixteenth century, a neologism was necessary: "tragicomedy" (*tragicocomoedia*), from *tragicus* + *comoedia*. On one hand, the very philology of a hybrid bespeaks an almost proto-humanist coincidence of opposites that would come to the fore with the influential Renaissance philosopher, Nicholas of Cusa, or, for Kenneth Burke (1897–1993), the philosopher of rhetoric and contemporary of

I.A. Richards, a pre-Hegelian "consubstantiality" in which seemingly irreconcilable concepts, genres, or media cohere.[37] In fact, comedy and tragedy seem conjoined in ways akin to the Augustinian commingling of Christian and carnal love (*caritas* and *concupiscientia*) which, avers D.W. Robertson, typically did *not* "conform to a pattern of conflict and synthesis" and did *not* "merge to form a new position compounded of their diversity."[38] On the other hand, Pierre Corneille would go on to dub *Le Cid* a *tragicomédie* (1637) and, his hagiographic *Polyeucte* (1642), a "Christian tragedy" or *tragédie chrestienne*: the very entity denied post hoc to the Middle Ages. Likewise, by the time the little known Belgian Denis Coppée penned a *Sanglante et pitoyable tragédie de nostre Sauveur et Rédempteur Jésus-Christ* (1624), the "bloody and piteous" Passion itself had become precisely what so many now exclude from medieval thought: a tragedy. For Henri Dupont, Coppée had at last resolved the unacceptable generic confusion. While "a far cry from a tragedy in the classical sense of the term," at least, he announced with apparent relief, it was "not a mystery play," the massive cyclical, days-long community extravaganza that dramatized the life of Christ. No, said, Dupont, it possessed "none of the elements that precipitated the decline of the mystery plays: the admixture of *tragic episodes with grotesquely comic scenes*, the atrocity of tortures, etc. . . . ."[39] Then again, it wasn't exactly a play either. Coppée reconceived the entire tragic medium for the page as a "speaking picture" (*peinture parlante*).

In his "Dialogue on Dramatic Poetry," T.S. Eliot famously imagined a medieval spectator who was incapable of separating religion from aesthetics and who thereby suffered from a *confusion des genres*. Eliot's hypothetical congregant was "satisfied by the Mass, precisely because he was not interested in the Mass, but in the drama of it."[40] That self-same confusion has long undergirded the aesthetic critique of medieval literature, as when the nineteenth-century theater historian Eugène de Lintilhac bemoaned the medieval "commingling of species to the extent of excluding the possibility of distinct genres, and the titles themselves bear witness to that confusion in the mind of the authors."[41] Postmodern though such indeterminacy might appear, medieval culture routinely celebrated the order in chaos and the chaos in order. After all, during the "long Middle Ages," supposedly unshakable political and theological hierarchies were regularly answered by carnivalesque reversals of class or gender as citizens of every stripe celebrated and sneered, screamed, and snorted.[42] But one does well to question whether "reversal" is truly the proper term. Already in 1910, Frank Ristine had postulated that "while tragedy and comedy, the recognized main divisions of dramatic composition, are theoretically of antipodal emotional effect, the one is constantly blending with the other. . . ."[43] Elisabeth Lalou concurred that, "in reality, the medieval theater presents an almost ontological mixture of the tragic and the comic," as did Charles Mazouer that "we must get rid of the dichotomy that has haunted our theatrical culture since the Renaissance, that of the comic and the tragic."[44] Or hear now the alcoholic professor Frank when educating his lower-class charge in Willy Russell's *Educating Rita*: "The sort of thing you read in the paper that's reported as being tragic, 'Man Killed by Falling Tree,' is not a tragedy." Says Rita: "It is for the poor sod under the tree."[45] At stake, throughout this volume is the uneasy but no less natural mix of comic and tragic, in proportion and disproportion, harmony and disharmony, consonance and dissonance. Says Rita to Frank: "It's fun, tragedy, isn't it?"[46] Yes, it is.

In *Poetics* 1448a, Aristotle had once ventured a character-based distinction between tragic men who are better than we are and comic ones who are worse. For William of Conches, the generic distinction was plot-based, turning on the presence or absence of a happy ending: "Tragedy is a writing dealing with great iniquities, which begins in prosperity and ends in adversity. And it is contrary to comedy, which begins with some adversity and finishes in prosperity."⁴⁷ But, from *The Jackass Conjecture* to the *Second Shepherd's Play* to the Dutch *Lippin*, medieval comedy is gleefully beset by the cyclical despair of ubiquitous pummeling, insults, subjugation, and subjection. Invocations to the saints abound, as do clerical figures galore, in whom no trace of true Christian charity is to be found. Instead, there is a hopelessness at the end of hundreds of medieval comic pieces, a denial of salvation when, almost à la Northrop Frye's genealogically cast *mythos* of spring, cycles of violence tend to renew themselves.⁴⁸ Is it not tragically unjust when, with a great laugh of recognition, a wife returns to the status quo of domestic abuse, when a valet is beaten, or when a chambermaid is coerced into sex with her master? One of the most tragic medieval plays ever written boasts a Pontius Pilate-like figure who washes his hands of the ill-advised plan of two foolish wives to have their sexually non-performant husbands refashioned in a Bell Maker's magic oven. In an exceptionally lyrical set piece on the duality of human nature, the craftsman obliges, all the while cautioning the women about their tragic flaw of insatiability: "it's against my better judgment. I wash my hands of it. . . . I can only wonder what you'll make of the finished product when it comes out." After a lengthy scene in the oven—almost impossible to stage in a post-Holocaust era— the two men emerge from their makeover as venal, wife-beating brutes. It was inevitable. The machine had been set into motion. But *Extreme Husband Makeover* (*Les femmes qui font refondre leurs maris*) is a farce.⁴⁹ And the Conchian "prosperity" with which it ends is domestic violence.

Germane to our inquiry is an early assertion by Walter Kerr about comedy and tragedy; so is its converse. Where Kerr intuited that "[c]omedy at its most penetrating derives from what we normally regard as tragic,"⁵⁰ I submit that *tragedy* at its most penetrating derives from what we normally regard as *comic*. Aristotle notoriously gave short shrift to spectacle when enumerating the constitutive parts of tragedy as plot, character, thought, diction, song, and spectacle. "Spectacle," he wrote, "while highly effective, is yet quite foreign to the art and has nothing to do with poetry. Indeed, the *effect of tragedy does not depend on its performance by actors*, and, moreover, for achieving the spectacular effects the art of the costumier is more authoritative than that of the poet."⁵¹ That history elucidates Olson's indication that Mussato "was crowned poet (not playwright) laureate; and even though his play [*Eccerino*] was performed, both it and Mussato's commentary on Seneca show more interest in the literary than the theatrical aspects of tragedy."⁵² Still, as any theater historian knows full well, and as Christopher Swift shows in Chapter 2, performance changes everything and need not be limited to the theater. Thus, for Hoxby, "*tragedy is a theatrical rather than a poetic art*."⁵³ As we shall see, once the body gets into the act, it regularly transforms the religious into the sacrilegious, the sublime into the grotesque, the tragic into the comic—and in ways that multiply as exponentially as authors, actors, actants, and readers. "Parody easily overtakes [tragedy]," affirms Richards, "the ironic addition paralyses it; even a mediocre joke may make it look lopsided and extravagant."⁵⁴ In its infinite enactments and reenactments of what is just and unjust, medieval tragedy is indeed "confused" in the most positive sense of the term. A generic version of Paul Zumthor's *mouvance*, it has always been a shape-shifter.⁵⁵

To follow the paths of medieval tragedy, therefore, is ever to be off course. It is to see and to be blind, to hear and to mishear, to get it right and to get it wrong, even as the trap door opens beneath our feet or the gong ejects us from the stage. Above all, it is to struggle to find our footing, lest we trip over comedy. For any era, the distinctions are not so easy to draw, which is very much the paradox set forth by Kerr when seeking out the import of comedy: "I found myself forced, in the end, either to try to come at comedy through tragedy or to *stand silent* before this perpetual ambiguity. That is why what follows has at least as much to do with tragedy—and with tragedy *first*—as it does with comedy."[56] In this volume, the converse obtains anew: what follows has at least as much to do with comedy—and with comedy *first*—as it does with tragedy. And, needless to say, "standing silent" might supply an exquisite metaphor of the tragic to an Anouilh or a Kerr; but it is no way to write the cultural history of medieval tragedy. And, to write it, we must turn to what silenced it in the first place.

HISTORIOGRAPHY TROUBLE: THAT ABSENCE WHICH IS NOT ONE

And so it goes: "the least touch of any theology which has a compensating heaven to offer the tragic hero is fatal."[57] From that point onward, the rest was logical. The medieval period was dominated by the Church; *ergo*, no tragedy was possible. The eleventh-century epic *Song of Roland* could not have been a tragedy because, after much terrestrial pain and suffering, a valiant soldier is carried to Heaven in the arms of the Angel Gabriel. Likewise for Hrotsvitha's tenth-century *Fall and Redemption of Mary* (analyzed by Karen Sullivan in our Chapter 8), for the late-medieval Mulhausen *Play of Saint Catherine*, and for the hagiographic tales of Jacob de Voragine's *Golden Legend* (compiled *c*. 1260): none of them were tragic in that their martyred heroes and heroines rejoined their Savior in a glorious afterlife. An eleventh-century Saint Nicolas play depicting the murder of three students (*Tres Clerici*) was no tragedy either; nor was the relentlessly unjust persecution and despair of the fourteenth-century Dutch *Esmoreit*; nor the redemptive plot of a fourteenth-century Perugian *Harrowing of Hell*; nor, for that matter, a seventeenth-century Ukrainian one. And we can forget about the non-Christian performances such as the cheery violence of Ibn Dāniyāl's thirteenth-century Arabic shadow plays. Or can we? Plus, unless we're inclined to dispense with the entire Old Testament, we would also exclude a Croatian *Judith* play by Marko Maruli'c (1450–1524), a fifteenth-century Florentine *Representation of Abraham and Isaac* by Feo Belcari (1410–84), and at least two massive French Old Testament cycles. We would similarly deny any tragic status (or stature) to the Spanish *auto sacramental* or to the mutilation of a sacred Host in the Croxton *Play of the Sacrament*— just as we would to the tortured gaming of crucifixions and pseudo-crucifixions from fifteenth-century Wales, Chester, Mons, Paris, Benediktbeuern, or St. Gall to twenty-first century Filipino reenactments of the same.[58] Or would we?

A host of ideological difficulties arise almost immediately: Was there nothing tragic in all the murders and forced conversions of all the *Roland*'s Moorish "unbelievers," the target, moreover, of contemporaneous Crusade propaganda? Was the Anglo-Saxon epic *Beowulf* a tragedy because its hero was not Christian? What about the rape of Thamar in a series of Old Testament plays? Or the anti-Semitic race-baiting by angry mobs of Passion-play Jews urging that Christ be crucified? When Judas, goaded by Despair, hangs himself in Day 3 of Arnoul Gréban's *Mystère de la Passion*, was that a happy ending? Would it have made a difference if the actor playing Despair had eventually hanged himself? Or that despair was the principal cause of suicide in the Middle Ages?[59] And what are we to make of the lyrical pathos of Marian lamentation? Cuckolded Joseph was a bona fide laughing stock: *Poor, stupid Joseph: he just doesn't get it!* But no one has seriously suggested that medieval audiences were meant to be thinking: *Poor, stupid Mary: she just doesn't get it!*

Although such examples might be multiplied ad infinitum, this much is clear: it is incongruous to pronounce that one and the same work of art is or is not a tragedy solely by dint of its theology. It is equally incongruous to insist that the compensating Heaven of Christianity is the *sine qua sic*, as it were, of medieval tragedy. For one thing, not everyone in the Middle Ages was Christian. For another thing, one of the most widely cited passages in the history of medieval drama establishes the *coexistence* of tragedy with a compensating heaven. In *De tragoediis* (c. 1100), Honorius Augustodunensis characterized the priest reciting Mass as a tragedian (*tragicus*) who represents for the faithful a dramatic Christian struggle: "It is known that those who recited *tragedies* in the theaters represented to the people, by their gestures, the actions of conflicting forces. Even so, our tragedian [*sic tragicus noster*] represents to the Christian people in the theater of the church, by his gestures, the struggle of Christ, and impresses upon them the victory of his redemption."[60] Consequently, any so-called death of medieval tragedy compounds the problem of an illogical genealogy with an illogical historiography. As we have already seen, medieval genres resist neat categories; but, once we return to Richards' own words, a more coherent vision of tragedy may follow.

Fascinatingly enough, Richards articulated his famous idea not in the context of the Middle Ages and not even in the specific context of tragedy. Instead, he was reflecting upon the ways in which the aesthetic imagination responds, with "discordant impulses," to "*great and sudden crises in experience*" (and, granted, the Middle Ages had more than enough of those to go around.) For Richards, the singular distinction of the pity and terror of tragic catharsis—and "whether Aristotle meant anything of this kind or not"—was the "*balance or reconciliation of opposite and discordant qualities*" and the bringing together of "a welter of disconnected impulses into a *single ordered response*." Pity, he continues, or "the impulse to approach, and terror, the impulse to retreat, are brought in Tragedy to a *reconciliation* which they find nowhere else, and with them who knows what other allied groups of equally *discordant impulses.*"[61] On first glance, that reconciliation of conflicting emotions appears evocative of Hegelian thesis-antithesis-synthesis (regardless of Richards' curious use of a passive voice that obscures the origin of that "single ordered response" in author, audience, or text). Obscurity notwithstanding, though, he alludes to an ability to hold simultaneously two seemingly contradictory impulses in our heads—and hearts— without necessarily synthesizing them into a third position. The cathartic mindset more closely resembles Nicholas of Cusa's coincidence of opposites or Kenneth Burke's "consubstantiality" mentioned above. But there is something else too; and Richards sounds more like a psychotherapist when he tells us about it.

Tragedy awakens these conflicting impulses instead of suppressing them, rendering tragedy writ large a matter of sublimation and suppression: "This is the explanation of that sense of release, of repose in the midst of stress, of balance and composure, given by Tragedy, for there *is no other way in which such impulses, once awakened, can be set at rest without suppression.*" What is unique to tragedy—and what compels Richards to prefer *Lear* to *Romeo and Juliet* and to relegate most of Greek tragedy and "almost all Elizabethan tragedy" to the category of "pseudo-tragedy"—is the *absence* of our usual "suppressions and sublimations."[62] It is well worth reproducing this passage at length:

> It is essential to recognise that in the full tragic experience *there is no suppression*. The mind does not shy away from anything, it does not protect itself with any illusion, it stands uncomforted, unintimidated, alone and self-reliant. The test of its success is whether it can face what is before it and respond to it without any of the innumerable

subterfuges with which it ordinarily dodges the full development of experience. *Suppressions and sublimations* alike are devices by which we endeavour to avoid issues which might bewilder us. *The essence of Tragedy is that it forces us to live for a moment without them.* When we succeed, we find, as usual, that there is no difficulty; *the difficulty came from the suppressions and sublimations.* The joy which is so strangely the heart of the experience is not an indication that "all's right with the world" or that "somewhere, somehow, there is Justice," it is an indication that all is right here and now in the nervous system. Because Tragedy is the experience which most invites these subterfuges, it is the greatest and the rarest thing in literature, for the vast majority of works which pass by that name are of a different order.[63]

Interestingly and perhaps unintentionally, Richards' tragedy is a rendition of the *pons asinorum*, literally, the untranslatable "bridge of asses" of medieval philosophy. Technically, it denoted the middle premise of a syllogism that bridged premise and conclusion; but, in common parlance, it referred to the fool who sees obstacles there where there are none because he confuses the obstacle with the solution. Like the stubborn ass of *The Jackass Conjecture*, the first text cited in this Introduction, he foolishly fears the bridge when the *river* is the true obstacle for which the bridge is the solution. For our own part, it might not be so foolish to consider the putative death of medieval tragedy not the solution but the obstacle. Richards solves the problem of subterfuge by removing "justice" from the emotional equation (although, in Section 3 below, I am inclined to retain it). And, when he posits an affect-driven tragic experience, it is as if the inevitable solitude of the tragic conflict of laws were being transferred from a sociopolitical construction of justice to an individual rather than a community psyche. But, if catharsis is the cessation of suppression—and if the *presence* of tragedy is the *absence* of suppression—then it is nothing if not unjust (or at least tragically ironic) that Richards' tantalizing theory about the quieting of suppression would itself have quietly suppressed the literary history of tragedy in the Middle Ages, to which he turns in his next breath.

Only after that extensive foray into catharsis, sublimation, suppression, and the nervous system does Richards make his influential statement, pointing toward the dualistic religious sect that emerged in the Middle East in the third century and which once attracted the attention of the likes of Augustine and Abelard: "Tragedy is only possible to a mind which is for the moment agnostic or Manichean. The least touch of any theology which has a compensating Heaven to offer the tragic hero is fatal. That is why *Romeo and Juliet* is not a Tragedy in the sense in which *King Lear* is."[64] But what if we were to focus not just on the second part of the statement about the compensating heaven but also on the first part about "for the moment?" And even on the allusion to "*any* theology?" What if we were to shift our focus from the Manichean coexistence of seemingly discordant impulses to the *momentary nature* of the duality and suppressions? "*For the moment* agnostic or Manichean," said Richards, which is as much about theologies as about the *confusion des genres* as about keeping "discordant impulses" alive at the same moment in time. Even if we were to take the Richards truism at face value and accept that, "because Christianity offers a promise of redemption and an afterlife, its world view is not tragic," Donald Stone suggests a more nuanced reassessment. "Hope," Stone counters, "may be immediately realized or endlessly awaited. Also the portrait of the saved does not exclude the horror of the castigation of the damned."[65] In all matters literary, time is of the essence, as when Rebecca Bushnell meditates on a tragedy that "engages us in a sense of a present 'thick' with past and future when it stages a crisis: a moment of decision in which everything changes."⁶⁶ It is no coincidence that Classicism reinterpreted Aristotelian tragedy's aesthetic needs as the "unity of time" (with that of action and place). Nor is it a coincidence that another one of Anouilh's master tropes is *Antigone*'s ticking tragic clock. I submit that it is this question of time and timing that takes us to the heart of tragedy and that this has everything to do with performance *in time*.

As noted above, and as Carol Symes documents in Chapter 1, performance changes everything. It does so all in its own good historical, historiographical, and dramaturgical time. Whether it be the protracted wait for the eternal bliss of heaven or for the palliative cessation of farcical violence, it remains unsustainable to assert that, after lives of violence, sin, and noisy desperation, a Passion play, a saint's life, and a miracle play would *not* qualify as tragic but the sure and certain hope of comedy's renewal of violence *would*. Religion is part of context but it does not unilaterally determine context. Christianity cannot tell the whole story of a literary genre any more than can an ever-ephemeral performance. Nor can the essence of medieval tragedy be distilled into the pseudohistorical equivalent of the old adage that *comedy = tragedy + time* in favor of a correspondingly preposterous adage according to which *tragedy = polytheism + time*. There must somehow be a way that concomitantly accounts for performance-wrought changes but which simultaneously *relieves* performance of the full burden of the ontology of tragedy. If we keep to the time (and timing) of the mental and physical presence of contradiction and coexistence in *eternal suspense*, we stand to discover a way by which to reject the false binaries that medievalists now eschew (learned vs. popular, urban vs. rural, Christian vs. secular, Christian vs. pre-Christian) at the same time that we adopt a more holistic paradigm of tragedy: Christian, pre-Christian, *and* non-Christian; comedy *and*—Kerr was right— tragedy. Such a paradigm may then bring us full circle to the vast cultural legacy of medieval pleasure and pain in the face of what is just or unjust—just *and* unjust—over time.

AUDIENCE TROUBLE: CATHARSIS AND CONTROL

Long before Umberto Eco ever conceived the exquisite monastic murder mystery of the *Name of the Rose* in which the birth of laughter is the death of religion, observers in late-medieval York had reported that the beating of Fergus in the Corpus Christi cycle "used to produce more noise and laughter than devotion" (*magis risum & clamorem causabat quam deuocionem*).⁶⁷ They were not alone. One Pierre des Essarts was led giggling to his own execution in 1413 as onlookers wept "so piteously that you would never have heard tell of greater sobbing for the death of a man—all the while that he alone was laughing."⁶⁸ By the 1530s, the humanist Juan Luis Vives (b. 1492) was critiquing the frivolity with which Passion plays were received: "here they laugh at Judas . . . There the disciples flee policemen in hot pursuit, not without a big yuck on the part of both the players and spectators alike."⁶⁹ And, when Clément Marot (1496–1544) eulogized the popular comic actor Jean de Serre, he offered that "the whole point is they laugh so loud / That tears well up inside the crowd. / They cry for him with laughter deep / Just as in laughing, so they weep."⁷⁰ Comic relief? We might just as well say comic catharsis. And, even though Richards made little room for it, we have come to expect it in the midst of tragedy. So too did medieval citizens, whose tearful frivolity was typically matched by frivolous tears. When negotiating violence, disease, despair, injustice, repression, servitude, or poverty, they laughed until they cried and cried until they laughed, prompting the distinguished historian Natalie Zemon Davis to notice that the "mixture of laughter and horror was hardly foreign to the sixteenth century."⁷¹ Nor was it foreign to the Middle Ages, when farce's Blotto the Cobbler might well have said it best: they were "laughin' one minute and cryin' the next, both at the same time."[72] Davis was moved to confess that, when confronting "accounts of bloodshed, which may often have left sorrow, terror, and regret in their wake, *I found I was sometimes laughing.*" Could it be heartlessness or *Schadenfreude?*, she mused.[73] To which I would add, quoting Dana Carvey's beloved comic character from *Saturday Night Live*, the Church Lady, could it be Satan? Could it be tragedy?

Throughout the cultural history of tragedy, perhaps no single concept has held greater sway than Aristotle's purgative, psychomedical release of catharsis which, through the manipulation of pity and fear, grants "relief to these and similar emotions" (*Poetics* 1449b). As early as the fourth century, Saint Augustine had agonized in his *Confessions* over the seductive power of stage plays to convert pain into pleasure. "What is the reason," he asked, "that a spectator desires to be made sad when he beholds doleful and tragical passages (*vult dolere luctuosa et tragica*), which [he] himself could not endure to suffer? Yet for all that he desires to feel a kind of passionateness, yea, and *his passion becomes his pleasure too* (*et dolor ipse est voluptas eius*)."[74] Certainly, by the time the Crucifixion was staged all over fifteenth- and sixteenth-century Europe, pain was so pleasurable—and pleasure so painful—that the French corpus routinely paired *lier* (to tie up or bind) with *liesse* (joy), and *batre* (to beat) with *ebatre* (to enjoy, to take pleasure, sexual or other).[75] Richards carefully reframed the corporeal joy of the tragic as "an indication that all is right here and now in the nervous system;"[76] but the admixture of pleasure and pain was also a principle of the legal system.

Once upon a time, Plato had likened lawmakers to the "authors of a tragedy" (*tragoidias*) and the law itself to "a representation (*mimesis*) of the fairest and best life, which is in reality, as we assert, the truest tragedy."[77] Duty-bound to "persuade people that their notions of justice and injustice are illusory pictures," the Platonic man of laws appears to have turned to his own version of catharsis: "When men are investigating the subject of laws, their investigation deals almost entirely with *pleasures and pains*, whether in States or in individuals." His strategy was to habituate citizens to be "pleased and pained" in conformity with the law, and Plato called that *mousike*. Nowadays, we would be more likely to call it *tragedy*, a collective, affective modeling of values and an aesthetic version of sociopolitical "orchestration."[78] Plato was so disturbed, for instance, by the disorderly behavior of audiences during the celebration of the Dionysian liturgy that he coined a term for their "unmusical illegality": an anarchic *theatrocracy* that posed a powerful threat to a civilized polis. The life and death of a community is illuminated by a living, breathing—but also stifled, dying—theatricality as Plato's theatrocracy returns us to the interplay between speech and silence with which we began.

Ignorant as both poets and audiences were of "what was just and lawful in music," Plato complained, "the theater-goers became *noisy instead of silent*, as though they knew the difference between good and bad music, and in place of an aristocracy in music, there sprang up a kind of base theatrocracy."[79] But there was a solution; and it bears a surprising resemblance to Richards' tragic subversion, sublimation, and suppression. The better to bring unruly citizens around to the values of the community—the canonical function of the tragic chorus—Plato championed strict penalties for the disobedient: "it was a rule made by those in control of education that they themselves should listen throughout *in silence*, while the children and their ushers and the general crowd were kept in order by the discipline of the rod."[80] And, lest Plato strike the reader as too far removed, any number of episodes—including those presented by Antonio Donato and Erith Jaffe-Berg in Chapter 4—bring into focus a distinctly medieval manifestation of such tragic discipline.

In England, community members could be compelled to participate in religious processions or pay a fine; and the British *Tretise of Miraclis Playinge* has been much studied for its hellfire-and-brimstone godliness.[81] In France, where medieval bishops were empowered to force men to accept Christ through flogging, expositor after expositor bade Passion-play audiences to "shut up," potentially in full view of such bishops.[82] More dramatically still, legislation from 1486 in the city of Angers authorized the use of military personnel to impose silence "under threat of prison or other penalty."[83] It all took place linguistically, moreover, in Latin and in multiple European vernaculars in which the word for Lord (*senior, sendra, seigneur, señor, signore*, etc.) was the same word that denoted the feudal overlord. Hegemonic messages of quiet obedience were organic to medieval life, especially in a performance culture that, for the historian Jacques Le Goff, was ever wont to "act itself out."[84] And, as humankind endured the slings and arrows of an outrageous fortune explored by Hannah Skoda in Chapter 6, "acting out" was as hospitable to the expressional efficacy of pathetic lamentation as to mime as to farcical guffaws. In terms of genre, politics, and the affect of reception, the liveliness of comedy might readily metamorphose into the deadliness of tragedy, and the deadliness of comedy into the liveliness of tragedy. They were two sides of the same coin, such that the real tragedy for the Middle Ages would be—and has been—the unjust insistence on denying one in favor of the other, a historiographical miscarriage of justice.

Tragedy is about orthodoxy as it pertains to a communal experience of justice and injustice; comedy, it seems, with its every breath, is about unorthodoxy as it pertains to that self-same experience. By analogy, however, to the ways in which censorship can amplify rather than diminish subversion, if a tragic theatrocracy was associated with affective unorthodoxy, it could also serve to instantiate more orthodox feelings. Tragedy incarnates both the threat to the sociopolitical order and the means by which to bring disorder back under control. Or see it rebel anew. Faced, therefore, with the power of performance to change tears to laughter and back again, we might prefer to take our cue from a learned but playful Middle Ages and stand ever poised to embrace an instability that is as much about affect as it is about justice or genre.

When Saint Alexis of eleventh-century hagiographic fame flees his honeymoon chamber to dedicate his life to God by living under a staircase, was that too met by laughter? Could audiences have cried when the silly nuns of Antonia Pulci's *Play of Saint Theodora* battle it out over the costumes and makeup for the devotional drama they are about to stage?[85] What if the Virgin Mary's crown falls off while she saves a sinner in a miracle play; or when an unhappy wife's lament is sung in a jaunty major key?[86] Or when Marie de France's young romantic hero struggles to carry a chubby princess up a mountain in the *Lai des Deux Amans*, to which the boys of *Monty Python's Previous Record* would indubitably have exclaimed: "Why not? She's a fuckin' princess!"[87] When hubris prevents the exhausted lad from imbibing the very philter concocted to sustain him, his untimely end eerily anticipates Anouilh's tragic unbreathability and Kerr's stifled silence. So too does a Passion play of 1437 during which the actor playing Christ was left hanging so long that he almost suffocated.[88] So too does a revival of farce on London's West End in 2012 that occasioned one reviewer to remark that he "feared he might stop breathing because he was laughing so much. It's this sense of helplessness—that laughter is controlling us rather than the other way around—that is the special pleasure of farce, the fear that it may not only be pratfalling actors who need attention from paramedics."[89] And why not the special pleasure of tragedy too? At the end of the *lai*, the hero dies—tragically?—his paramour by his side. But a tree of life rises up from their common grave, standing in metaphorically for death and renewal, for life's breath and dying breaths.

Laughing and crying, living and dying. Tragic time is now.[90] Over the shifting sands of the politics of reception, in a millennium-long encounter with the tragic, medieval artists worked tirelessly toward a deep cultural understanding of the ways in which individuals played out their relationships with the order and chaos that informed their lives. To come full circle to our opening montage, medieval tragedy finds itself along a continuum of birth and death, breathless rebellion and stifled silence, orthodoxy and unorthodoxy, laughter and tears, beginnings and endings . . . and new beginnings. Once we reanimate the indeterminacy of tragic catharsis, once we have freed ourselves from the anxiety of historiographical influence, we are in a far better position to do justice to our subject. Medieval tragedy gives voice to a culture's pain; and its future is now. But to give voice, it must speak, and to speak it must breathe. It is from the dynamic interaction between the first breath of life and the last dying breath that medieval tragedy draws its own life's breath.

CHAPTER ONE

Forms and Media

CAROL SYMES

For centuries, understandings of tragedy's medieval reception have been based on a false narrative of ignorance, misappropriation, and loss. According to this narrative, ancient theatrical genres, especially tragedy, were universally condemned and successfully suppressed by Christian authorities. As a result, the people of western Christendom had little knowledge of tragedy's "true" purposes and meanings. In the eastern Roman Empire (Byzantium), meanwhile—where nearly all extant classical Greek texts were preserved—tragedy was allegedly confined to the classroom. Medieval ideas and forms of tragedy were, accordingly, either aberrations unworthy of the name or pale imitations of the eradicated originals. It was only in the fifteenth century that humanist scholars, first in Italy and then elsewhere in Europe, restored tragedy to its proper (Aristotelian) form and its proper (theatrical) medium.[1]

In reality, medieval intellectuals ensured tragedy's survival by copying and disseminating the available texts of ancient dramas and by mobilizing tragedy as a richly productive concept. Without the efforts of these scribes and commentators, and the cultural contributions of medieval artists and communities, there would be very little tragedy to study or emulate today. Consider the pair of images in Figure 1.1. On the left is a fragment of papyrus found in a Greco-Roman garbage dump at Oxyrhynchus in Upper Egypt. It was once part of a scroll conveying the text of Euripides' tragedy *Helen*, copied around the second century BCE. On the right is a page from the only surviving manuscript of the entire tragedy, a parchment codex copied in Constantinople (now Istanbul) more than 1,500 years later, in the early fourteenth century CE. If we didn't have the latter, based on older sources, we'd have only a fragile remnant of the former.

Not only is the medieval suppression of classical tragedy a myth, it is unreasonable to hold medieval forms of tragedy to an impossible, anachronistic standard of "authenticity." No other period of human endeavor is expected to remain in stasis; what we value about the tragic dramas of the early modern period, or the manifestations of tragedy in modern arts, are their newly vibrant interpretations of ancient traditions. When medieval uses of tragedy are allowed the same latitude, the entire cultural history of tragedy will be transformed. For, as all of the chapters in this volume demonstrate, it was in the Middle Ages that tragedy underwent the dynamic metamorphosis that has made it useful in so many contexts and for so many social, intellectual, spiritual, and aesthetic projects. In its heyday, tragedy was fostered by state-sponsored civic rituals, which occurred on particular occasions in specific spaces. In the fourth century BCE, its parameters were restricted by a singularly influential critic, Aristotle, after which certain selected texts of tragedies became fossilized. Thereafter, the term "tragedy" was unmoored from these classic texts and used to describe a range of entertainments, which were condemned as decadent by pagans and Christians alike. But in the Middle Ages, tragedy became liberated.

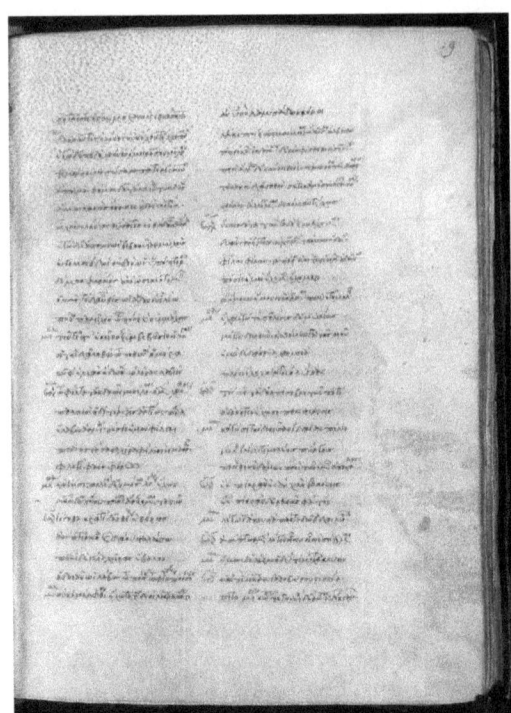

FIGURE 1.1: Euripides' *Helen*: ancient fragmentation and medieval mediation.

Left: Oxford, Ashmolean Museum, Pap. Ox. XXII 2336 (v. 630 ff.). Courtesy of the Egypt Exploration Society and the University of Oxford Imaging Papyri Project.

Right: Florence, Biblioteca Medicea Laurenziana, Conventi Soppressi 172, fol. 19r (vv. 610–69). Courtesy of MiBAC.

This chapter accordingly tells a very different story about tragedy's medieval mediation during the first thousand years after the legal establishment of Christianity in the fourth century CE. It begins with a brief account of tragic drama's documentation and dwindling relevance in the Greco-Roman world. It then offers a sketch of the ways that the medieval heirs of tragedy's legacy applied their received understandings to an array of didactic, aesthetic, and political projects. In Greek-speaking Byzantium, where the surviving canon of Athenian texts was actively sustained, tragedy was integral to elite education and a catalyst for new literary and performative genres, including devotional drama, public displays of rhetorical persuasion, and historiography. In western Christendom, tragedy's cathartic potential, moral arc, and explanatory power informed Latin and vernacular poetics, historical writing and storytelling traditions, pedagogy, biblical exegesis, popular entertainments, and many aspects of religious worship—including the theory and enactment of the Eucharist. Common to both was tragedy's proliferation in a plethora of forms.

ANCIENT TRAGEDIES AND MEDIEVAL MEDIA

The oldest manuscript of Euripides' *Bacchae* is a fourteenth-century codex now divided into two parts and preserved in two different Italian libraries; it is therefore the crucial mediating link in a tenuous chain of transmission that stretches back to the time of this tragedy's debut at the Athenian Dionysia in 405 BCE.[2] We don't really know to what extent even this original performance reflected the poet's intentions, since it was produced after his death. We also don't know when, or how accurately, that performance was eventually captured by a text.[3] Tragedies and other poetic performances usually circulated orally in their heyday, and even Aristotle relied partly on oral traditions when he dictated the terms of tragic poetics in the middle of the fourth century BCE.[4] The canonization of certain tragic poets in this era was prompted, not by the needs of performers, but by the erosion of Athens' political and cultural hegemony in the Greek world; in order to counter this, texts representing these esteemed works were deposited in the polis archive as artifacts of a halcyon past. Thereafter, whenever one of these classics was officially revived, it was held up as a paradigm of excellence—not entered into competition.[5]

As the public and private reading of these tragedies became fashionable, so did their citation in political and popular rhetoric, making them touchstones of moral and cultural authority. Of this select group, the few classic Athenian tragedies to survive today are those that found currency in the wider Hellenistic world, where they were amended by actors according to their own preferences or glossed by schoolmasters and readers.[6] In some locales, they were performed in the local vernacular or farced with interludes of the kind explicitly condemned by Aristotle.[7]

In the Roman territories of the ancient world, meanwhile, theatrical entertainment was driven by profit or patronage, not by state- or privately-sponsored festivals. Moreover, theatrical impresarios and performers were usually slaves or men of low birth, not the free citizens of a polis; when they adopted the terms or plots of tragedy, they tainted it with populism.[8] As the (pagan) Roman Emperor Julian "the Apostate" (r. 361–3 CE) observed, in a letter to the (pagan) High Priest of Roman Asia, "these licentious theatrical shows" (τοῖς 'ασελγέσι τούτοις θεάτροις) had so demeaned the tastes of audiences for centuries that it was impossible to restore the "pure offspring" (καθαρὰ γενόμενα) of Dionysius. He accordingly ordered that no (pagan) priests should be seen attending the theater or consorting with entertainers.[9] The "pure" tragedies valued by Greco-Roman elites were not those to be seen in public theaters but those which resided on library shelves as talismans of good breeding. When new tragedies were composed by intellectuals such as Seneca (d. 65 CE), they paid homage to the classics but were dramaturgically distinct: designed for small, private audiences and often performed by a single skilled reader. Solo performances of tragic speeches also remained in vogue. In his *Confessions*, the Christian bishop Augustine of Hippo (354–430 CE) proudly recalled the successes he often scored with his favorite selection, "The Flying Medea."[10]

Centuries before the birth of Christ (c. 30 CE), therefore—and well before the acceptance of Christianity as a legal religion three centuries later—the canon of ancient Greek tragedy had been narrowed to the texts we have now. These texts were then assiduously preserved and copied in the eastern Roman Empire, where new scribal technologies—miniscule cursive, word separation, punctuation, and pedagogical commentary—made them staples of the educational curriculum and the *lingua franca* of all elites, including many women. These texts, in turn, became the exemplars used in the great copying campaigns of the Paleologan Renaissance, after Emperor Michael VIII recaptured Constantinople from the Venetians in 1261 and attempted to reverse the devastation wrought by the crusades. Part of this project involved safeguarding the cultural legacy of cities seized by the Ottoman Turks, by rescuing the contents of many monastic and private libraries. After the fall of Constantinople in 1453, a year or two before Johannes Gutenberg pioneered a new publication medium, a diaspora of Greek-speaking elites brought the resulting manuscript witnesses of tragedy to Italy, where they became the basis for the first printed editions.

But even if we had the text of Euripides' *Bacchae* in a form close to that posthumously produced in ancient Athens, we must still recognize that no written medium is an adequate vehicle for tragedy's visual, sonic, and emotional affects; or its civic, social, religious, and political messages. Similarly, the existence of these texts means little without a nuanced understanding of what tragedy signified, and the kind of work it did, in the medieval world. To gain this understanding, we need to move well beyond the denunciations of pagan entertainments by early Christian teachers, which have been radically decontextualized to be used as evidence for a specifically Christian animus against theater. These negative comments were, as I noted above, part of a larger critique of popular culture on the part of elites across the religious spectrum.[11]

In practice, early Christian leaders could only succeed if their own forms of theater were as compelling and competitive. When Archbishop John "Golden Mouth" Chrysostum (*c*. 349–407) has to remind his Constantinopolitan audience that his church is not a theater, he is betraying the fact that people flocked there precisely because he was such a charismatic performer.[12] His contemporary, Bishop Gregory of Nazianzos (*c*. 329–89/90), reports that John's preaching was regularly greeted with applause.[13] Meanwhile, impassioned debate over the role of music in the early Church (which has also been misinterpreted as a sign of Christian hostility toward tragedy) "testifies more strongly than any pagan source to the intense appeal of the solo songs of the ancient theatre," according to Edith Hall. These songs continued to be performed by prominent clergy (e.g., Augustine) and they deeply informed the musical styles of Christian composers.[14] Even after the Emperor Justinian (r. 527–64) cut state funding for the training of professional singers—he also shut down the academies of Athens and the venerable *gymnasia* of his realm—their talents found performative outlets in the music of Christian worship. The embodied, living knowledge of how a choral ode should be performed or a great lyric passage delivered—the most affective, even essential, attributes of tragedy—thus influenced the development of the liturgies of both the Orthodox and Roman Churches.[15]

Justinian himself, as his misguided policies testify, had not benefited from the Christian-infused classical pedagogy which kept the ancient Hellenic past alive in New Rome. Born into a Latin-speaking family of low status, he probably nursed an inferiority complex vis-à-vis his cultivated predecessors and clerical contemporaries. These men, for whom the koiné of the New Testament was painfully vulgar, actively promoted a *paideia* that included the texts of classical tragedy and comedy. When the pagan emperor Julian briefly banned the instruction of this classical curriculum by those not aligned with its core tenets, in an edict of 362, he was explicitly challenging the hypocrisy of Christians who prided themselves on their sophisticated education while professing to follow the gospel of Christ.[16] Some early Christian leaders, like Bishop Athanasios of Alexandria (d. 373), did become supporters of the new monastic movement—which *was* anti-intellectual and unworldly. But Athanasios himself was a prolific and learned man whose condemnations of pagan culture were penned in elegant Attic Greek and laced with literary allusions and turns of phrase borrowed from favorite pagan authors. As Anthony Kaldellis puts it: "Hellenism was complicit with the ordering of Christian rhetoric and identity in so many ways that it could not be cut away."[17]

FORMS OF TRAGEDY IN THE EMERGING LATIN WEST

For the territories of the western Roman Empire, far less urbanized than Byzantium and undergoing slow fragmentation into a constellation of medieval "barbarian" kingdoms, we also need to recontextualize the antitheatrical rhetoric of Latin elites. As Donnalee Dox has documented, talking about pagan theater was actually a way of talking about problematic aspects of Christian ritual and belief.[18] Classical dramatic genres were not perceived as threatening in themselves. Rather, tragedy and comedy were becoming key elements of a common cultural vocabulary. In fact, this can be proven via a quantitative and qualitative analysis of all references to *tragoedia/tragedia* and its grammatical variants in the digitized *Patrologia Latina*: a nineteenth-century compendium of Latin texts dating from the time of the early Church to the advent of written European vernaculars around 1200.[19] My analysis of these texts yields four hundred discrete instances of tragedy's situated usage in theological, social, and political discourses over a thousand years. The meanings attached to it can be sorted into five main categories:

- value-neutral references to tragedy as an ancient Athenian theatrical genre: 130 (33%)
- negative references to tragedy as a pagan practice: 92 (22%)
- tragedy as a metaphor for division or dissent within the Church: 82 (21%)
- tragedy as a disruptive event in the history of a family or community, or a narrative framework for telling such stories: 71 (18%)
- tragedy as vehicle for commenting on contemporary (medieval) performance practices: 25 (6%).

The second category is not as statistically significant as it appears. Nearly all of these negative references to tragedy can be traced to Tertullian (*c.* 155–230), a Christian theologian and activist who lived through a time of increased imperial persecution in his native Carthage; the remaining handful date from the very first decades of Christianity's institutionalization in the mid-fourth century and, as such, testify to theologians' anxieties about the blending of Roman and Christian values. The most prominent of these is the rather weird statement that "Whole tragedies of Euripides are nay-sayings against women" (*Totae Euripidis tragoediae in mulierum maledicta sunt*),[20] a sentiment which St. Jerome (347–420) probably learned from his teacher, the grammarian Ælius Donatus, who clearly preferred the comedies of Terence.[21] When Jerome's judgment gained currency again in the twelfth century, it was quoted either by notorious misogynists[22] or by the authors of satire.[23]

St. Augustine of Hippo, whose perspective on theater was particularly well developed and influential—he mentions it over two hundred times—only refers to tragedy on seven occasions: once in a nostalgic comment on his youthful love of "sorrowful and tragic things" (*luctuosa atque tragica*);[24] twice to comment on the tragic human condition;[25] three times as a simile for a sorrowful event;[26] and once in his commentary on the Sermon on the Mount (Matthew 6:2-5), in which Christ himself had mentioned tragic actors.

> *Thus, when you give alms*, He said, *sound no trumpet before you, as the actors* (hypocritae) *do in the synagogues and in the streets, that they may be praised by men.* No one, He said, should wish to become as notorious as actors. Moreover, it is obvious that actors not only present lying fronts to the eyes of men but also to sway the heart.

> Such men are like actors, just as if they were playing the characters of other people, as in theatrical plays (*theatricis fabulis*). This doesn't only apply to someone who acts the part of Agamemnon, saying his words in a tragedy, or to anyone else who enacts a story or play: any man who dissembles himself is called an actor (*hypocrita*).[27]

For Augustine and his audiences, the word *hypocrita* retained its primary meaning, "actor." The bishop therefore needed to explain why Christ had condemned shows of piety using this familiar term. But for later commentators on this same passage, the term *hypocrita* had taken on its current colloquial meaning and, as such, no longer required explanation. Only one medieval author, Rabanus Maurus, accordingly cites Augustine in his discussion of this same biblical passage, thereby lending his commentary an antiquarian flavor.[28]

Far more significant than these references to tragedy in negative contexts are those in the first category, amounting to one-third of the total references, which occur when medieval authors discuss tragedy as an artistic product of ancient Athens. In so doing, they display their classical credentials and make favorable comparisons between their own times and the distant past, so as to place themselves within an historical continuum shared with the ancients. For example, Cassiodorus (c. 485–c. 585) depicts the Emperor Theodoric, a Byzantine-educated Goth, as eager to rebuild the theater of Pompey because tragedies had been mounted there.[29] Elsewhere, he likens the eloquence of two Greek theologians, Basil the Great and Gregory of Cappadocia, to that of Homer and the tragic poets.[30] Augustine's mentor, Ambrose of Milan (c. 338–97), compares the inscription of King David's psalms to the written preservation of classical tragedies and comedies, all of which were—as he rightly observed—genres "to be sung on stage (*in scena*)."[31] A similar comparison is made by the Northumbrian monk Bede (673–735) in his treatise *De arte metrica*:

> [Poetry] is dramatic, or active, when speaking characters are introduced without the interruption of the poet, as [the Greeks] did in their own tragedies and plays (*fabulae*). [A]nd among us, this is the form in which the *Song of Songs* is written, where the alternating voice is of Christ and the Church—even if this is not made plainly obvious by the intervention of the scribe.[32]

Like Ambrose, Bede elevates a genre of Christian poetry by comparing it to classical poetics. Also like Ambrose, he is alive to the challenge of conveying the dynamism of performance in writing, placing even more emphasis on the difficulty of communicating the mimetic effects of dramatic arts through textual media.

In short, when we focus on how and why Latin-literate intellectuals discuss tragedy—rather than assuming their stupidity or animosity—we find that most considered it to be an important part of their own heritage, even though they had no way of accessing the texts of classical exemplars. Very few could read any Greek, and yet information about tragedy was commonly shared cultural knowledge. The generations of schoolboys raised on Priscian's Latin grammar, as redacted by Rabanus Maurus (d. 856), were taught that "comedy differs from tragedy because in tragedy heroes, leaders, and kings are brought to the fore; but in comedy it is humble and even private matters. In one [there is] sorrow, banishment, and bloodshed; in the other love-affairs and the abduction of virgins."[33] Although this definition doesn't capture tragedy's moral or political commitments, other ways of talking about tragedy show that it was well understood to have those dimensions. The historian Gregory of Tours (c. 538–94) underscores the cruelty of Nero by reporting that he sang "tragedies" while Rome burned.[34] In a treatise "In Praise of Virginity," the

Anglo-Saxon abbot Aldhelm of Malmesbury (c. 640–709) describes the martyrdom of Christians as a Roman moral tragedy.[35] And Hugh of Fouilloy, in an early twelfth-century bestiary, compares Ulysses' sailors, stricken by the sirens' seductive songs, to those "who are ravished by the delights of the world, by pomp and theatrical pleasures, indulging in tragedies and comedies."[36]

In addition to understanding tragedy as an ancient genre, my analysis reveals that it constantly informed narratives of Judeo-Christian history, where it signaled the dangers of schism and heresy, especially the original "heresy" of the Jewish people. The chronicler Freculf of Lisieux (fl. 825–52), who displays a detailed knowledge of tragedy's genesis in Athens, continues to trace its development alongside events of the Old Testament and then uses it to describe the "lamentable tragedy" (*luctuosa tragoedia*) of the Jews, as related by their historian Josephus (c. 37–c. 101 CE).[37] Tragedy's heightened metaphorical meaning thus coincides exactly with the momentous change in the human condition brought about by the sacrifice of Christ: the tragedy of this new age is played out by those who reject him. Hence "the tragedy of John the Baptist" (*haec tragoedia de Joanne*) was the aboriginal instance of Jewish violence against Christians, according to Abbot Paschasius Radbertus of Corbie (c. 790–860), since Herod's stepdaughter Salome had "demanded, as a prize for her tragedy," the head of the prophet.[38] For earlier commentators, too, Salome's "tragic" dance highlighted the dysfunctionality of Herod's incestuous and adulterous household, which clearly bore a family resemblance to that of Oedipus or Agamemnon.[39] In his commentary on the story of Joseph's rejection of Potiphar's wife (Genesis 39:1-20), Rupert of Deutz (c. 1075–1129) moves from that specific "tragic" event to depicting all Jews as tragic temptresses "because the Synagogue lusts to be with Christ, and when unable to have what she wants for herself she is sorrowful and betrays Christ to her governor."[40] As "the most prolific of all twelfth-century writers,"[41] Rupert was especially influential in casting the history of the Jews in a tragic mold. In one treatise, their role in the crucifixion of Christ is an act of *hubris* punished by the *deus ex machina* of the Temple's destruction, as foretold by the Jews' own "oracles."[42]

Rupert and his predecessors also saw tragedy in the Christian divisions and schisms of their own times.[43] The equation of heresy with tragedy can be traced back to Pope Leo I (r. 440–461), who railed against "the whole Manichean tragedy" threatening the unity of the Roman Church and who regarded any thwarting of his apostolic authority as a "woeful tragedy."[44] On the one hand, tragedy could denote the unjust deposition of a bishop from his see;[45] on the other, it could signal the abuse of episcopal authority.[46] Cassiodorus calls doctrinal disputes "tragedies"[47] and also uses the term for crimes committed within a family.[48] Indeed, tragedy as a crisis within the Christian community is the driving plot of many chronicles.[49] For historians reporting on secular events, "tragedy" was also the framework for describing the far-reaching consequences of civil unrest.[50] When William of Malmesbury (d. c.1143) recounts the untimely death of England's promising young royal prince in a shipwreck, he underscores the fact that this tragedy precipitated a succession crisis and even more tragic civil wars. These events are even narrated in a tragic mode by William's avatar within the history: the only surviving member of the ship's crew to have "lived to perform the entire act of the tragedy."[51]

Not only did contemporary historians know that tragedy revolves around a sudden reversal or violation of the social contract, they knew that its mimetic power lay in the manner of its performance. The historian, like the tragedian, could elicit horror and pity through the skillful practice of his craft. For some historians, indeed, this was to be avoided as unnecessarily inflammatory. One chronicler omitted certain events from his text to avoid the charge that he was performing a tragedy.⁵² Another refrained from enumerating "many very unfortunate things that happened" in his monastery "because it is enough that such tragedy is sung in the theater of the world."⁵³ The prolific Anglo-Norman historian Orderic Vitalis (1075–c.1142) bases his very claim to authority on the avoidance of *pathos* and unseemly exhibitionism, dismissing tragedy as a style detrimental to rigorous inquiry: "I value neither the accolades brought in by tragedy's fabrications nor the loud guffaws the groundlings give to comedy's chatter, but the more truly profound understanding of ever-changing events by careful readers."⁵⁴ Yet even these historians' distrust of emotive language and poetic hyperbole calls to mind ancient models, including Thucydides, who noisily rejected the lies of poets while artfully deploying the structure and dialogue of tragedy.

MEDIEVAL MODES OF CONVEYANCE

If, as I noted above, many aspects of classical Hellenic culture were preserved and cultivated in Byzantium, why weren't tragic dramas ever staged? We have no evidence that they weren't. In 692, the Trullan Synod of Constantinople repeated several earlier, failed attempts to outlaw certain types of entertainment tied to pagan ritual: probably a veiled reference to theatrical performances, and certainly an admission that these prohibitions weren't working. In any case, essential elements of tragedy were already being channeled into liturgical music and devotional poetry. And while overtly realistic representations of the sacred were unacceptable in the Orthodox Church, other kinds of dramatic representation continued even during the controversy over the veneration of icons that divided Byzantine society during the eighth century. Men schooled in classical oratory staged highly charged and competitive performances in a variety of venues to which the term *theatra* (θέατρα) was applied: the pulpit, the classroom, and the political assembly. Those who excelled were capable of enacting multiple roles in a single scene, and even religious homilies were expected to feature the direct speech of holy characters. Public orators and preachers alike drew on the skills they had learned in the "spoken-word" (*ethopoiia*) exercises that were an integral part of their schooling and in which students composed and delivered speeches of imaginary characters in dramatic situations: "What Death might have said in reaction to the raising of Lazarus" or "What a sailor might have said seeing Ikaros flying high."⁵⁵

Some of these performers may have read the surviving book of Aristotle's *Poetics*, but it is more likely that Aristotle's views on tragedy were conveyed through commentaries or epitomes like the remarkable "Tractatus Coislinianus" (Paris, Bibliothèque nationale de France MS Coislinianus 120 [C], fols. 248v–249v), which appears to be a digest of the (now lost) second book devoted to comedy. Copied in the tenth century, probably at the monastery of Great Lavra on Mt. Athos, the "treatise" was based on an exemplar from the sixth century and appears alongside a number of texts associated with Aristotle and his late antique commentator, Porphyry the Phoenician (c. 234–c. 305). Materials in this epitome are also found in an introductory preface to the comedies of Aristophanes, which survives in several other manuscripts dating from the late eleventh century to the end of the fifteenth.⁵⁶ This evidence suggests that many other such epitomes once existed, and that knowledge of the *Poetics* circulated in a variety of forms. For example, the author of the Tractatus assumes that his readers have a common knowledge of Aristotle's doctrine of *catharsis*, and he applies it equally to tragedy *and* comedy. Tragedy "takes away the soul's fearful passions through compassion and awe" (ὑφαιρεῖ τὰ φοβερὰ παθήματα τῆς ψυχῆς δι' οἴκτου καὶ δέους) and is born of pain: "it has sorrow for a mother" (ἔχει δὲ μητέρα τὴν λύπην). Comedy, too, "accomplishes the purifying of the same passions [as tragedy] through pleasure and laughter; it has laughter for a mother" (δι' ἡδονῆς καὶ γέλωτος περαίνουσα τὴν τῶν τοιούτων παθημάτων κάθαρσιν. ἔχει δὲ μητέρα τὸν γέλωτα).[57]

This tantalizing text provides a context for understanding another extraordinary witness to the Byzantine rejuvenation of tragedy: the *Christos Paschon* (Χριστὸς πάσχων, "Suffering Christ"), usually dismissed as a "closet drama."[58] Profoundly influential in its own time, it survives in multiple manuscript copies and was often attributed to the fifth-century theologian Gregory of Nazianzos, although it was more plausibly composed in the late eleventh or twelfth century.[59] One of its earliest manuscripts describes it as the Passion gospel "according to Euripides" (κατ' Εὐριπίδην).[60] Its author was clearly inspired by the cento ("patchwork") tradition of poetic pastiche, in which a classic work would be unstitched and re-woven to create a new one, whether in parody or homage. In this case, Christ's broken body is stylistically rendered by the author's artful dismemberment of the still-living verses of Euripides. The full impact of this sacramental drama, which sanctifies and sublimates the cruelty of the original in a thoroughly Dionysian manner, would have depended on the audience's shared familiarity with those verses in their original context. Its protagonist, the Blessed Virgin, calls to mind not only the suffering mothers of Euripides (Agave, Hecuba, Andromache) but the Aristotelian metaphor of tragedy's birth in the epitome I just cited: Christ, like tragedy, "has sorrow for a mother."

In western Christendom, where classical tragedies could not be so directly engaged and recycled, understandings of tragedy's capacity to stimulate profound emotional and spiritual responses nevertheless made it central to the critique and creation of many contemporary performative media, including preaching, singing, the celebration of the Eucharist, and the recitation of vernacular romance. Jerome invokes tragedy in this sense when commenting on a salient passage from Ezekiel 33:31-32: "And lo, you are to them like one who sings love songs with a beautiful voice and plays well on an instrument, for they hear what you say, but they will not do it."[61] This, he says, reminds him not only of audiences who take pleasure in the tragedies of the theater, but those attracted to charismatic preachers who "are carried away with applause, and cry out, and throw up their hands, and yet who pay no heed to good works."[62]

We catch some rare glimpses of the techniques that could inspire such responses in a journal kept by an anonymous Franciscan friar who was active in Italy for over two decades in the late fifteenth century, more than a millennium after Jerome warned against tragic theater disguised as evangelism. This itinerant preacher kept detailed notes of his daily successes and failures, recording the lengths of his sermons (which could run from one to four hours), where they took place (accompanied by a play on at least one occasion), and appraisals of his own performance and the audience's responses: "not as passionate as a sermon on this subject as it should have been" (*non fuit fervens sicut debebat et requierebat materiam*)—"really boring and badly preached" (*cum magno tedio et male predicatus*)—"it was the best and most effective sermon, [delivered] with passion and in a ringing voice" (*fuit optimus et utilissimus sermo cum fervore et optima voce*)—"it was a devout sermon and they burst into tears" (*fuit devotus sermo et ad lacrimas proruperunt*). His *tour de force* was reserved for Passion Sunday, when he "held up a dead man's skull" (*[m]onstrati caput mortui*).[63] A century later, an absentee student from Martin Luther's *alma mater* of Wittenberg would make the same tragic gesture at a graveside in Denmark (*Hamlet* 5.1).[64]

Whereas the austere Jerome had expressed distaste for such showmanship, the urbane Cassiodorus—writing a couple of generations later—favorably compares the stichomythia of "salubrious psalmodies" to that of "tragic scenes" in order to praise the emotional affects of the former.[65] Many medieval commentators made similar comparisons. Agobard of Lyons (c. 779–840), a notorious critic of the theatrical techniques embraced by contemporary proponents of the Carolingian Renaissance, railed against "those young men" who regarded the chanting of sacred song as an opportunity for showing off their beautiful, expressive voices "in the manner of tragedians." Church was not the place for "theatrical little rhythms"; rather, sacred song should be raised "in fear, in workmanship, in the knowledge of the Scriptures."[66] Agobard's own voice would be drowned out by the swelling chorus of those who advocated for more and more virtuosic and captivating performances. By the twelfth century, the concordance of canon law attributed to Gratian quotes Agobard's remarks only to footnote prevailing trends, ruling that deacons serving at Mass should be excused from singing and psalmody "lest, while concentrating on modulating their voices, they neglect the ministry of the altar."[67] Sicard of Cremona (d. 1215) went so far as to link the liturgical roles played by Christian clergy with those of their ancient counterparts, the "comedians, tragedians, historians."[68]

Tragedy's assimilation into the doctrines and rituals of the Roman Church is most explicitly revealed in the hugely influential *Gemma animae* (Jewel of the Soul) by the theologian Honorius Augustodunensis (1075/80–c. 1156), who likens the enactment and effect of the Eucharist to that of a classical tragedy:

> It is well known that those who used to perform tragedies in theaters displayed to people, through their actions, the deeds of warriors. So our tragedian [the celebrant of the Mass] performs, through his actions, the battle of Christ for Christian people in the theater of the church, and impresses on them the victory of His redemption. So when the priest says, "Pray," he imitates Christ who underwent trials (*agonia*) on our behalf, as when he exhorted the apostles to pray. In the mystic rite of silence [during the consecration of the Host], he signifies Christ as a lamb without a voice, being led forth as a sacrificial victim. By spreading out his hands, he indicates the outstretched arms of Christ on the cross. By the singing of prefatory prayers, he imitates the cry of Christ, hanging on the cross.... Through [the passing of] the Peace and the [sharing of Communion,] he signifies the peace granted after the Resurrection of Christ and the sharing of joy. In concluding the sacrament, peace is granted to the whole community by the presiding priest; because our opponent has been overthrown by our champion [*agonotheta*] in this duel, peace is proclaimed to the people by the judge, and they are summoned to a feast. Thus everyone is commanded to return to his own affairs with joy by the *Ite missa est*, to which he should shout "thanks be to God," and return home rejoicing.[69]

In this extended metaphor, Honorius explains how the components of the Mass work to produce a Christian form of catharsis.[70] Although the Eucharist had long been crucial to the sacramental program of the Roman Church, it was only in the twelfth century that it was promoted as important to lay spirituality. Indeed, Honorius' vivid description came to undergird the program of pastoral care and public outreach promoted by the Fourth Lateran Council of 1215, whose canons defined the parameters of Catholic orthodoxy until the Counter Reformation.[71] It became even more widely accessible through vernacular translations and adaptations.[72] Like the *Christos Paschon*, it amounts to a transubstantiation of Greek tragedy, with the dismembered body of the tragic hero becoming the regenerative Body of Christ.

By choosing tragedy as *the* explanatory paradigm for the Mass, Honorius reveals that there was a common, widespread understanding of this concept which was not confined to clerical discourses. In the late eighth and ninth centuries, the Carolingian revival of classical learning had increased dissemination of information about ancient dramatic genres, as well as their renewal. In the tenth century, the hagiographer of Archbishop Bruno of Cologne (brother of Emperor Otto the Great) was unabashedly frank about his saintly protagonist's love of "buffoonery and play-acting," which he and his courtiers indulged through the performance of "comedies and tragedies enacted in parts," in an atmosphere of commingled enjoyment and scholarship.[73] One youthful participant in these revels was the future canoness Hrotsvit of Gandersheim (935–1001/2), whose Terence-inspired tragicomedies are among the first surviving examples of a popular medieval genre.[74] Meanwhile, the countless denunciations of such pastimes by more ascetic clergy are an index of their ubiquity: Peter the Venerable, abbot of Cluny (1092–1156), zealously policed the behavior of his monks—and yet they still loved reading comedies aloud, weeping over tragedies, and other "stupidities" (*stultitiae*).[75] And there were many other abbots much less austere, including the poet and dramatist William of Blois (fl. 1167), whose lost "tragedy about Flaura and Marcus" may have been composed in his native French vernacular and who also authored at least one surviving Latin comedy.[76] His brother Peter of Blois (c. 1153–c. 1203) was a prominent cleric and diplomat known for "writing comedies and tragedies"[77] which were also probably couched in vernacular verse, like the *romans* of his contemporaries Chrétien de Troyes and Marie de France.

For Peter, indeed, tragedy's appeal made it the perfect vehicle for capturing the attention of audiences far beyond the cloister and the court, and for cultivating the virtues of compassion and contrition at the same time. In a treatise on the sacrament of Confession—which, like the Eucharist, was being newly promoted to the laity in the twelfth century—Peter teaches his readers how to turn any popular romance into an opportunity for reflection on repentance.

> Often in the tragedies and other songs of the poets, or in jongleurs' ballads, some distinguished man is described: handsome, strong, beloved and approved by everyone. It is told, then, how that same man is cruelly afflicted by pressing trials and injuries, as in the stories of Arthur and Gawain and Tristan, the tales the actors recreate, which in the hearing shake to compassion the hearts of the audience, who are moved even to tears. Therefore, anyone you rouse to pity through the telling of tales, or if you should hear anything about God's righteous justice that wrenches tears from you, isn't this because you are able to convey that meaning through the love of God? Anyone you make compassionate for God, you also make compassionate for Arthur.[78]

Peter preaches compassion for the heroes of popular romance as a form of spiritual training, opening the heart to the knowledge of God's mercy and the love of one's fellow man. In so doing, he makes the worldliest of performing arts media for redemption. Honorius had conflated the Christian priest and the pagan tragedian; Peter suggests that even a humble jongleur can be an instrument of divine salvation.

This radical perspective on tragedy's potential differs significantly from that of the Cistercian abbot Ælred of Rievaulx (1109–1167), who warned his monks against attaching any meaning whatsoever to the passions aroused by Arthurian romance or the equally passionate—but potentially hypocritical—shows of piety in the performance of monastic prayer.[79] Peter's more populist view reflects not only the Roman Church's outreach to the laity but the changing media landscape of twelfth-century Europe: the rise of written vernaculars and the concomitant increase of lay literacy, the burgeoning of long-distance trade and travel, and the emergence of cosmopolitan urban centers—all of which challenged the hegemony of Latin and the papacy's ever more insistent claims to supremacy. If the clergy were going to be effective transmitters of the Church's message, the tragedy of the suffering Christ had to be made at least as compelling as that of Lancelot or Tristan. As one observer put it, in a rueful Latin sermon preached in northeastern France during the thirteenth century:

> When in the voice of the jongleur, sitting in the public square, it is recited how those errant knights of old, Roland and Olivier and the rest, were killed in war, the crowd standing around is moved to pity, and oftentimes to tears. But when in the voice of the Church the glorious wars of Christ are daily commemorated in sacrifice—that is to say, how He defeated death by dying, and triumphed over the vainglory of the enemy—where are those who are moved to pity?[80]

Just as the Fathers of the early Church had appropriated tragic modes and discourses to suit the needs of their times, so the clerical elites of the later Middle Ages had to communicate through the popular narrative forms and media that had become the contemporary conveyances for tragedy: hence the bravura Passion Sunday performances of skull-wielding preachers.

CONCLUSION

In his influential study of *The Ideas and Forms of Tragedy from Aristotle to the Middle Ages*, Henry Ansgar Kelly celebrated "the more enlightened views of twelfth-century writers" whose knowledge and use of tragedy redeemed those "totally in the dark" at the "low points" of tragedy's medieval reception. Although his book's stated goal was to evaluate "what authors of the past meant by the word [tragedy] as a literary or dramatic term," Kelly invariably measured the capacious medieval meanings of tragedy against the narrow definition of the *Poetics* or the later achievements of Dante, Chaucer, and Shakespeare.[81] My very different goal has been to show that the invocation and use of tragedy were never confined to a "rather limited number of writers in the Middle Ages," nor was it "an obsolete genre," as Kelly claimed. The very opposite is true. In western Christendom, tragedy was received as an important part of the classical heritage claimed by medieval intellectuals and kept alive by the practices of Christian worship, the narrative conventions of history, the moral teachings of theologians, and all forms of performative storytelling from the chanting of the Psalms and the celebration of the Mass to the jongleurs' lyric songs and the reading of chivalric romance. In Byzantium, surviving ancient tragedies were preserved and transmitted in textual forms while contemporary tragedies informed an array of spiritual, cultural, and social projects. In both cases, tragedy was released from the bondage of Aristotle and the limitations of the Roman theater to become a creative force across a wide range of media.

CHAPTER TWO

Sites of Performance and Circulation

CHRISTOPHER SWIFT

As the saying goes (and as evoked by Jody Enders in her Introduction), "humor is tragedy plus time." We instinctively understand the formula—loss and misfortune have the potential for ironic retelling only once the memory of trauma fades to nostalgia. But in another sense, the opposite is also true; humor is tragedy *minus* time. Staged tragic dramas are longer plays, even when playwrights adhered to the neoclassical Unity of Time, which restricted dramatic time to a 24-hour period. Pierre Corneille's most celebrated tragic play, *Le Cid* (1636), exceeds this rule and is also his longest in performance. A number of other examples bear out the point. During the Dionysian festival in Ancient Greece, trilogies of full-length tragedies were performed on a single day; the median length of a Shakespeare tragedy is 3,244 lines, while his comedies are nearly one thousand lines less; and in the twentieth century, the tragedies of Arthur Miller and Eugene O'Neill regularly run over three hours in performance. While tragic dramaturgies and subjects are unique to every culture, it is often the case that the cruel machinery of tragedy requires narrative complexity and chronological intensity to allow protagonists to undergo a complete cycle of crisis and ruination. In cultures across the world, the falls of deities that foreshadow the eventual dissolution of humankind (as in the Sanskrit epic Mahābhārata and the Passion and *descensus* of Christ) occur at a deliberate pace so that the weight of spiritual agony is fully experienced by its witnesses. As Terry Eagleton explains, "tragic art highlights what is perishable, constricted, fragile and slow-moving about us. . . . It stresses how we are acted upon rather than robustly enterprising."[1]

In the theater arts, deliberativeness is expressed spatio-temporally: place and time function symbiotically to elevate tragic stories beyond the mundane world and into cosmic domains. Epic tragedies occur across epic distances. One manner by which a theater audience may experience a sense of transcendental time is through the depiction of capacious space: distant regions of the world and supernatural regions where threats are encountered and truths are revealed. The histories and tragedies of Shakespeare— which owe a large debt to the poetics and staging of medieval drama—are exemplary. King Lear's madness is presented on the open, disorienting primeval heath. The errors in communication that propel Juliet and Romeo towards their ends occur outside Verona, in plague-ridden Mantua, and by the fifth act, liminal spaces (monastery and graveyard) command the stage.

The same crises of dislocation are evident in dramatic representations produced prior to the Reformation and the classical revival. A number of medieval morality and Passion dramas follow the trials, sorrows, and existential terrors of protagonists on their paths towards death, and similar to the examples of Western tragedies mentioned above, they embrace cosmic time and space. The form of staging most frequently mentioned in medieval texts is *locus* and *platea* staging, which uses an open, undifferentiated playing area surrounded by scaffolds. Unlike the proscenium arrangement of space that dominated theater in the West from the seventeenth century, audience space and performance space were not clearly delimited in the medieval outdoor theater. Onlookers could potentially move between various *loca* across the *platea*, as evidenced in the mention of "stytelers"—stage assistants who helped corral and reorient the attention of audiences—in the fifteenth-century *Castle of Perseverance*. *Perseverance* and the contemporary East Anglian *Mary Magdalene* were spectacles of great physical size that reflected a Christian worldview in staging practices. In *Perseverance*, Humanus Genus (Mankind) risks spiritual corruption and damnation by journeying away from his immutable castle at the center of the *platea* and onto the five scaffolds at the margins (World, Devil, Flesh, Covetousness, and God), "So that I be lord of toure and toun, / Be buskys and bankys broun. / . . . . I wyl folow thee / Be dale and every towne" (lines 569–74).[2] The position of God is in the east, not unlike the typical position of the chancel of medieval churches that oriented the gaze of parishioners in the direction of Jerusalem. As Alexandra Johnston writes, the "frenetic activity by the wicked" at the margins of the world was contrasted thematically with the "calm stillness of good" in the center in art and literature in the late Middle Ages, providing "English playwrights the underlying theological principle around which to build their dramaturgy."[3] Additionally, theatrical intermingling of spiritual and pedestrian realms would have enhanced the experience of the otherworldliness for performers and audiences alike.

As a number of scholars have written, the unique stage plan for *Perseverance* (Figure 2.1) re-inscribes the orientation of *mappae mundi*—an ideological schematization of the world—onto the page and into social space.[4] Medieval Christian and Muslim astronomers and philosophers based their mathematical calculations on the distances and orbital relationships of heavenly bodies on Ptolemy's planetary model, and mapmakers illustrated this arrangement by positioning the earth at the center of embedded concentric spheres. The outermost circle provided a dwelling place for God. Bede's *Mappa Mundi* incorporates the standard ideological model of a tripartite Christian world (the T-O map) into this quasi-scientific system of spheres (Figure 2.2). From 1250 through the Renaissance, most educated Europeans were familiar with this model.[5] More detailed renderings of T-O maps depicted images of headless men and fantastical monsters at the periphery of the world. *Locus* and *platea* staging cohered to this general ideology of space: the phantasmagoric and extraterrestrial characters (God, ghosts, vice characters, and demons) occupied platforms on the outer scaffolds, while the earthbound home of the protagonist (in life and death) was staged at the central focal point of the *platea*. In T-O maps, Jerusalem sat at the nexus of the three continents, the axial position of the world.

It is likely that this configuration informed the staging of burial sites at the center of the action in medieval ritual and theater. The first liturgical enactments in medieval churches in the tenth century—the *visitatio sepulchri*—were performed at the main altar, where the Three Marys encountered an angel at the mouth of Jesus' now empty tomb. The miraculous raising of Lazarus from the dead, the central event in the vita of Mary Magdalene, was another opportunity from the Bible for theatrical lamentation. The scene accrues special significance in the staging of the Digby *Mary Magdalene*. The sprawling *Magdalene* encompasses the saint's *vitae eremitica*, *apostolica*, and *evangelica* in thirty-

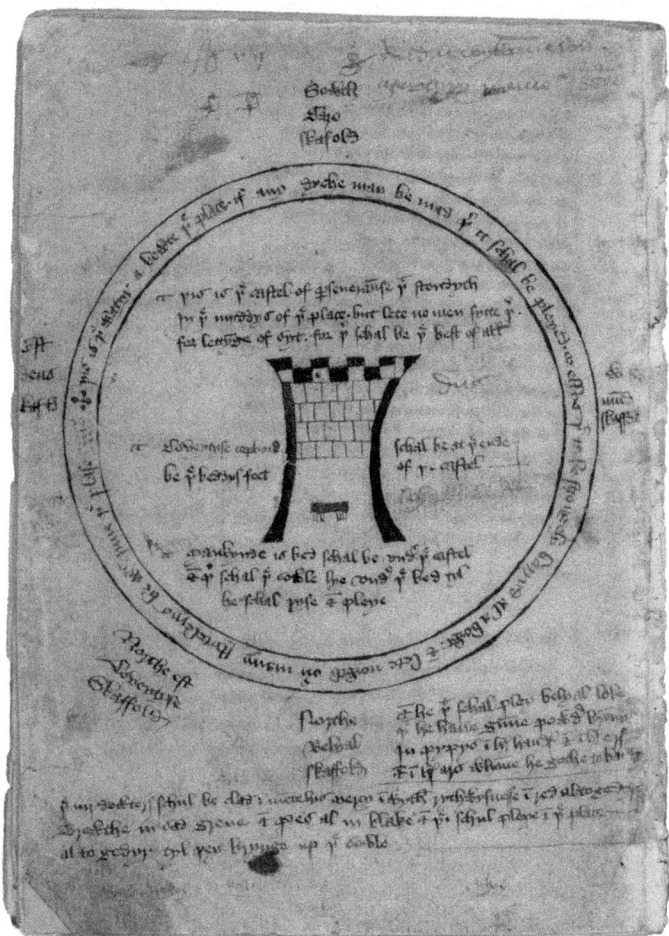

FIGURE 2.1: *The Castle of Perseverance* stage plan (*c.* 1440), V.a.354, 191v. Courtesy of the Folger Shakespeare Library under a Creative Commons Attribution-ShareAlike 4.0 International License.

seven real and allegorical locations, from Hell to Jerusalem and nearly everything in between, a geographical/ideological admixture that expands imaginative space beyond the known world.[6] In the play, Mary's journeying away from her father's home in Jerusalem symbolically underscores her downfall into a state of lechery. Two burials bookend Magdalene's fall, her father's and her brother's, the second of which localizes her first meeting with Jesus and the beginning of her rise to sainthood. Given the theological and emotional weight of Lazarus' burial and resurrection, the tomb of Lazarus (which presumably doubled as the tomb of her father and of Christ) was likely positioned next to Mary's castle in the middle of the *platea*. Beginning with Greek tragedy, the theatrical primacy of tombs highlights the moment of anagnorisis in the plot, a geographical sign expressing liminality, danger, and madness, as epitomized in Sophocles' *Antigone*. Creon—the symbolic embodiment of Theban polity—encounters the unburied bodies of his niece and son in a tomb-like cave in the wilderness, an inversion of civilization and

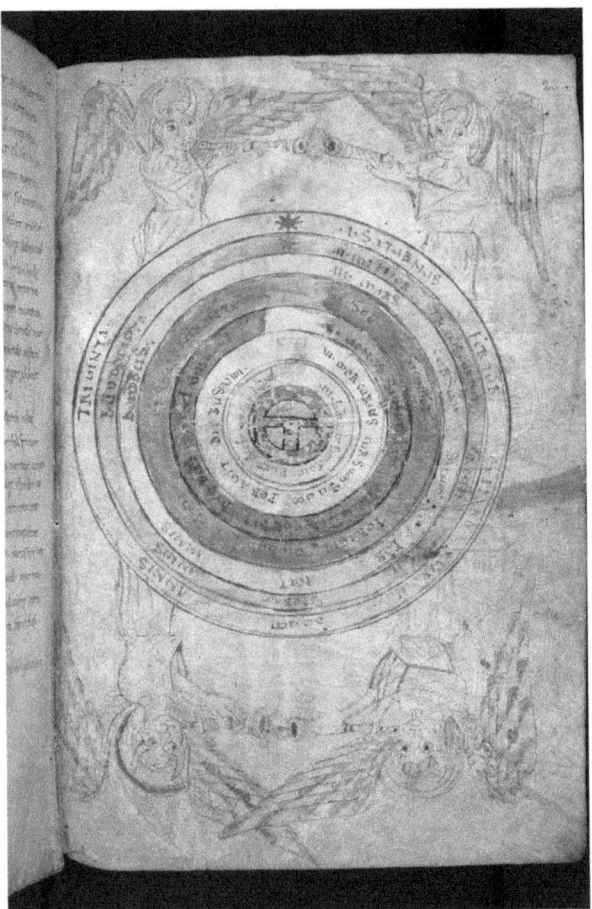

FIGURE 2.2: Mappa Mundi. *De natura rerum* (c. 1055–74), MS. Canon. Misc. 560, 23r. Used by permission of the Bodleian Libraries, University of Oxford.

harmony in spatial terms. What occurs on the edges of civil society in the dramatic narrative gets primary focal attention on the Greek stage.

Tragic protagonists transgress social norms by reifying the value of peripheral spaces (Hamlet in Yorick's grave, for instance) or by violating central, hegemonic places (Hamlet at court). The irrational, antisocial impulses that propel the protagonist into distant realms at the periphery (where one might encounter vice) are the same impulses that create irreconcilable conflicts at home. If we concur with scholars of medieval theater that the *platea* mirrors the metaphysics of the Christian universe, with the space of peaceful domesticity at the center, then the dramaturgical logic of staging the threshold moment between life and death at the center of the world is clear. Within this semiotic system, tragic themes were mapped theatrically onto a specifically medieval concept of space.

Uncommonly capacious in spatio-temporal terms, performances of East Anglian morality plays and saint's plays accrued a sense of the tragic from Christian metaphysics of sin, death, and resurrection, but also from the monumental, emblematic performance conditions. Lengthy extravaganzas like *The Castle of Perseverance*, *Mary Magdalene*, and the Cornish *Ordinalia* were anomalies in medieval English theater, since they required extensive work and resources to mount and were likely preserved in manuscripts because the productions themselves were so lavish. Shorter plays were far more commonly performed.[7] The circular arena stages of East Anglia and Cornwall, and others on the continent, exemplify Henri Lefebvre's sociological concept of *absolute space*: "mythical and proximate, it generates times.... It has no place because it embodies all places, and has a strictly symbolic existence.... It consecrates, and consecration metaphysically identifies any space with fundamentally holy space: the space of sanctuary *is* absolute space."[8] Here, the tragic aspects of medieval performance flow from the sense of sacred space projected onto theatrical place, embracing and implicating the audience into the world and grand design of the plot. *Locus* and *platea* arrangements provided sites that could accommodate the breadth of biblical and hagiographic histories, as well as the large crowds that undoubtedly attended.

As explained by Carol Symes, the word "tragedy" was most often, but not exclusively, used to describe ancient pagan practices through the medieval period.[9] Augustine (c. 354–430) wrote of the "pernicious pleasure" he felt when "beholding doleful and tragical things" in Roman amphitheaters, which led him away from true Christian compassion.[10] Isidore of Seville's (560–636) widely read *Etymologies* contained descriptions of theaters from the Roman past, which, according to him, accommodated a wide range of performance forms: dance, mime, juggling, and comic and tragic poems and songs.[11] Although medieval drama is distinctly non-generic—gamboling among comic, tragic, pastoral, spectacular, didactic, and festive modes—strains of tragic themes were expressed in textual, architectural, and choreographic forms. Passion plays, allegorical drama, and the Dance of Death (and the theatrical spaces in which they were performed) are embodied actions that exhibit these qualities. These spectacles cannot be abstractly conflated into a broad category of "tragedy," of course. However, they do share narrative and thematic elements common to tragic drama in the West: judgment, decline, reversal of fortune, bodily mortifications, and the supernatural. Significantly, these forms also stage microcosmic space in dynamic ways, suggesting a spatio-temporal link between the semi-sacred spaces of ancient Dionysian tragedy and the "unworthy scaffolds" (Prologue, *Henry V*, Shakespeare) that projected entire worlds into the confining platforms of Elizabethan public theaters.

The case studies in this essay include dance-music dramas about the dissolution and the inevitability of death from the late medieval period. On the Iberian Peninsula, the *Song of Sybil* was uniquely staged around the choir in the nave. Songs from the *Llibre Vermell* manuscript from Montserrat and the widely practiced Dance of Death demonstrate embodied encounters with the specter of death. In East Anglia, *The Castle of Perseverance* engaged a poetics of tragedy, spatially and ritually. Finally, the *Passio Christi* play from the Cornish *Ordinalia* is a single example of a Passion play among a multitude that contemplate the affective life of the tragic protagonist. Before discussing the stagings of these performances, I propose a provisional poetics of medieval tragedy, explicating the links between tragic misfortune, scapegoating, and death, on the one hand, and, on the other, the Judeo-Christian conception of sin and redemption. In order to highlight the "lively discourse surrounding modes of performance"[12] of tragedy, I trace the dissemination of tragic themes and stories in manuscript drawings, frescos, and ritual architecture. Two graphic configurations that were common among the staging practices of each of the examples emerge: the circle and the threshold.

TOWARDS A POETICS OF MEDIEVAL TRAGIC PLACE

In *De spectaculis*, written around the turn of the third century, Tertullian (155–240) railed against the polluting influences of the theatrical tradition in the Roman city of Carthage.[13] In the treatise, the Church Father most well-known for his condemnations of Roman games and drama directed Christians to turn away from theatrical contests and focus their attention on the conflicts between moral forces.

> Would you have fighting and wrestling? Here they are—things of no small account and plenty of them. See impurity overthrown by chastity, perfidy slain by faith, cruelty crushed by pity, impudence thrown into the shade by modesty; and such are the contests among us and in them we are crowned.[14]

Tertullian contemplates the allegorized figures of impurity, chastity, perfidy, and faith as antidotes to pagan spectacle, foreshadowing theatrical presentation of allegories a millennium later in works such as Hildegard von Bingen's *Ordo Virtutum* (1151) and three centuries after that in English morality plays. In the seventh century, Isidore of Seville used the word *theatron* ("seeing place") to describe theatrical architecture, recalling a performance tradition that had long since ended. Isidore described the Roman theater as semicircular with standing room for spectators and containing a "scene":

> The scene was a place within the theater built like a house with a stage, and the stage was called the orchestra.... The orchestra was the platform of the scene, where the dancer could act, or where two persons could hold a disputation. For it was the orchestra that the comedic and tragic poets ascended for their competitions, and while they were singing, others made gestures.[15]

It is not clear from Isidore's description if he was working from an understanding of Roman theater alone or Greek performance practices as well. He may have been relying on the Greek for his definition of orchestra ("dancing-place") or perhaps from Livy's account of the origins of Roman theater. Henry Ansgar Kelly points out that Isidore's use of the term *scena* (*scaena*, in Old Latin) to refer to the large, roofed structure behind the platform stage (*pulpitam*) was accurate.[16] It is also very likely that the seventh-century encyclopedist encountered Roman theaters in the provinces around Seville, and this may have informed his descriptions.[17] Similar to early folk performance practices that the Church translated into liturgical festivals of the Christian calendar, memories of ancient games and tragic drama endured in the writings of reforming bishops and in the ancient spaces of performances left in the footprint of the Roman Empire. These material presences facilitated associations between pre-Christian violence and sacrifice and the theater of Christ's Passion.

Despite the fact that the Roman tragic performance tradition was feeble by the third century and only an artifact of history after the fifth, Roman theaters and amphitheaters populated the geography of medieval Western Europe, Byzantium, and the Ottoman empire. The remains of hundreds of Roman theaters in Christian and Islamic kingdoms—from England to Alexandria, Cádiz to Palestine—were in better condition than they are today, existed in greater numbers, and, like Roman basilicas, aqueducts, and roads, constituted a material presence in the daily life of medieval people. It is not clear to what extant Roman theaters in western Christendom, or Greek amphitheaters in the east, were repurposed in the medieval period for new forms of religious plays or secular spectacle, dance, and disputation. It seems quite possible they were used for oratory, poetic recitation, and song since the raked, cave-shaped architecture of the amphitheater offered excellent acoustical environments, sight lines, and ample seating. William Tydeman suggests that a number of medieval towns on the continent—Bourges, Saumur, Orange, Nimes, and Arles—used the remnants of their local Roman amphitheaters for performances.[18] In a document from 1497 there is record of religious plays being staged in the ruins of the Colosseum in Rome.[19] Although it might seem improbable that a structure once used for the public persecution of early Christians would be repurposed for performances of plays based on Bible stories, it should be remembered that when Christianity became the official religion of the Roman Empire at the end of the fourth century, Constantine initiated the construction of churches modeled on Roman civic architecture.

In the Middle Ages, elements of Roman architecture accrued symbolic meanings specific to medieval structures of belief, related to original Roman architectural semiotics but reformulated allegorically for Christianity. For instance, the Roman triumphal arch was formally incorporated into the design of church entrances, legible to devotional communities as the triumphal second entry into paradise. The Doric, Ionic, and Corinthian columns that suggested trees in Roman society were resignified as human bodies in churches and cathedrals: two rows of twelve columns supporting church choirs represented the twelve apostles and twelve prophets upon which the "universal church" was carried.[20] Likewise, the remains of imperial Roman amphitheaters documented a history of pre-Christian games, dances, and tragic and comic song that could be repurposed for medieval performance. In Cornwall, two open-air amphitheaters, or rounds (in Cornish, *plen an gwary*), survive, one at St. Just-in-Penwith and the other near Perranporth (the Perran Round), each approximately 120 feet in diameter. Archeological evidence suggests the existence of sixteen others, some of which may have been adapted from pre-historical earthworks. An engraving from the eighteenth century shows Perran Round with raised earth banks, *vomitoria*, and a *platea* encircled with a trench. The extant Roman amphitheaters in western England may have inspired the designs of *plen an gwary*.[21]

Evidence of the significance of Roman theatrical architecture and drama in medieval culture is also preserved in the visual arts. Literary scholar Rosa María Rodríguez Porto claims that the iconography of the Greco-Roman tragic repertoire arose in the absence of classical texts in the medieval period, undergoing "a process of Christianization and medievalization which brought new layers of meaning to Greek sources."[22] The image of a semicircular stage occupied by actors and a chorus serves as the frontispiece illustration to a manuscript containing Nicholas Trevet's gloss upon Seneca's *Hercules furens* (c. 1330s). The image demonstrates that the fourteenth-century illustrator was aware of some elements of classical iconography, depicting Hercules wearing a lion skin and the Furies seated in the midst of flames.[23] The tenth-century ivory carving on the Veroli casket (held at the Victoria and Albert Museum, London) depicts Bellerophon and Iphigenia at Aulis and is attributed to a Constantinopolitan workshop. It includes figures from classical mythology and history, such as the sacrifice of Iphigenia and a Dionysian procession. The popular medieval romance *Roman de Troie* and a Castilian translation of the work commissioned by Alfonso XI in the fourteenth century, the *Cronica Troyana*, were both presented in richly illustrated manuscripts offering oral and visual means for the transmission of classical mythology. The images of extreme violence and matricide in *Cronica Troyana* and the sacrifice of Iphigenia on the Veroli casket attest to the fact that the medieval notion of the tragic was informed by classical mythology, and representations of sacrifice and death in Christian contexts invite us to consider "the obstinate presence of ancient tragedy in the folds of medieval culture."[24] It is quite possible that a hybrid concept of Christian tragedy developed through citations to ancient culture in sacred spaces and associations between death, violence, and sacrifice in Christ's Passion and various forms *ars moriendi*.

Parallel to the active assimilation of classical stories, images, and ideas—and quite distinct from their Roman and Greek forebears—medieval theater practitioners physicalized stories of decline and death in the naves, aisles, and altars of churches, the squares and streets of towns, graveyards, and the outdoor play spaces. In some cases, these spaces were inscribed with specific emblematic representations of the cosmos, biblical history and revelation, and death. In other cases, the sense of spiritual decay and rejuvenation was accessed through the gestural movement of performers in places containing little symbolic information—such as the *platea*—where audiences might experience affective transcendence in empty space. The twentieth-century theater director and theorist Peter Brook elucidates such an abstract, otherworldly space in his definition of "Holy Theatre":

> it could be called The Theatre of the Invisible-Made-Visible: the notion that the stage is a place where the invisible can appear has a deep hold on our thoughts. We are all aware that most of life escapes our senses: a most powerful explanation of the various arts is that they talk of patterns which we can only begin to recognize when they manifest themselves as rhythms or shapes.[25]

In her performative reading of the Croxton *Play of the Sacrament* (1461), Donnalee Dox applies Brook's idea to medieval playing, writing that the "space of imagination offers a conception of space that links performance space directly with belief in God in a way that two-dimensional iconography, nonmimetic performance (such as public preaching), statuary, and even liturgy could not."[26] What Brook and Dox are suggesting is that figural representations of theological and ethical concepts are phenomenologically potent when explored in nonfigurative, nondescript spaces. When theatrical action is framed in abstract space, the audience is encouraged to engage their imaginations to envision a realm beyond the pedestrian. For example, the monumental spaces of gothic cathedrals offer evocative environments that produce affective awe for worshipers. Although Christian emblems populate cathedral niches, tympana, lintels, aisles, shrines, and choir stalls, the sense of enormity of God's creation and the heavens could be accessed by communities of faith in vast vacancies above naves, where the exterior immensity of place is coextensive with the internal experience of universality. Like-minded devotees participating in prayer and ritual would have enhanced this affective engagement with space. As Gaston Bachelard explains, the phenomenology of space is linked to human occupation: "[i]n the dynamic rivalry between house and universe, we are far removed from any reference to simple geometrical forms. A house that has been experienced is not an inert box. Inhabited space transcends geometrical space."[27]

Locus and *platea* staging provided devotional communities with opportunities to explore the Christian universe; nowhere in particular and everywhere at once. The voided central performance area was defined simply by the action that took place there, and the co-presence of empty space was a meaningful frame for exploring metaphysical concepts and allegories. In the Croxton *Play*, themes of materialism, Jewish doubt, and the commodification of the Eucharist were projected against the empty space of the *platea*. Despite the presence of spectacular and grisly effects, the theme of absence weaves together the text and play space of the drama: absence of belief, a disembodied hand, the substitution of Eucharistic bread for a bleeding Jesus, and the eradication of Jewishness in the converted Jew. Catherine Belsey illuminates this point: "[i]n the symbolic order being implies the possibility of non-being, presence and the possibility of absence. Not to know difference is not to know God: but to know God is to know separation from the world."[28] The *platea* staged an experience of the universe beyond the physical senses of sight and sound. Props, set pieces, and costumes, recognizable as everyday and earthbound, were allegorized to the status of ubiquity. In the Croxton *Play*, the image of the bleeding child is a phantasmagoric analogy for the Eucharist. The castle in *Perseverance* is an analogy for "safety" during the battle for the soul: a fortress for the army of virtues, the sacred center of the world. The castle, with a bed upon which Mankind is born and returns to die, also symbolizes a threshold for the movement of the soul away from the body and into the regions beyond.

In addition to providing a neutral space for the engagement of the imagination, the outdoor playing space of sacred, didactic theater also performed a countervailing role in a cast of allegorical figures. Several medieval theater scholars have taken note of the effective juxtaposition of the unmarked *platea* with the rich imagery and emblematic language of allegorical drama: "large-scale plays with numerous *loca* (scaffolds or raised stages) are conducive to multiple presentations of time and place, thereby reminding the audience of the universality of the themes on display and of God's unique, eternal perspective on them."[29] The morality play *Everyman* (c. 1510–25) explores the subject of avarice (represented by the character Goods) in narrative and thematic depth, where the conflict between material and spiritual realms is heightened in performance. God and Death compel the protagonist to commence a pilgrimage, rendered in performance as "walking and wending" through the diverse scaffold locations. Meanwhile, the withdrawal of Everyman's companions Fellowship, Kindred, and Cousin from the playing area emphasize the void. In their absence, Everyman seeks out an old comfort, Goods, who because of Everyman's haste, cannot be seen:

> Who calleth me? Everyman? What, hast thou haste?
> I lye here in corners trussed and pyled so hye,
> And in chestes I am locked full fast,
> Also sacked in bagges, thou mayste se with thyne eye.
> I cannot stere, in packes low I lye.
> What wolde ye have? Lyghtly me saye.
>
> —lines 393–8[30]

While the description of Goods' stuffed bags and money chests could serve as internal instructions for the pageant-master to supply properties, it is more likely that Goods' elaborate narration about the objects obviates the need for real props. Goods invites the audience to produce the images of excess in their minds: "thou mayste se with thyne eye." The message carried in the *mise en scène* is clear: Everyman's search for worldly plentitude is futile since, in fact, riches are not there. Where he seeks goods for his accounting, he finds only their absence. For Walter Benjamin, allegorical performance was the paradigm of existence-in-absence "bodied forth in the dance of represented ideas" and elevated the tragic arts in particular to sublime knowledge and experience. In Benjamin's estimation, allegories derive their power "from the very fact of their pointing to something else, a power which makes them appear onto a higher plane, and which can, indeed, sanctify them."[31]

Pre-modern philosophers recognized the symbolic link between the worldly stage and tragic theater. John of Salisbury crafted the topos *theatrum mundi* in *Policraticus* (1159) long before Shakespeare allegorized the Globe theater and Caldaron composed *Gran*

Teatro del Mundo. Salisbury wrote that "[a]lmost the entire world, according to the opinion of our friend Petronius, is seen to play the part of actor to perfection.... It is surprising how nearly coextensive with the world is the stage on which this endless, marvelous, incomparable tragedy, or if you will comedy, can be played: its area is in fact that of the whole world."[32] For medieval spectators, the metaphor functioned in the opposite direction as well—the stage as cosmos in the figure of Fortune's Wheel, one of the most popular literary and artistic topoi of the Middle Ages. In the narrative, poetic, visual, and dramatic arts, humans were carried in a circular manner on the path to inevitable doom. The genealogy of Fortune's Wheel can be traced to Boethius' widely read *Consolation of Philosophy* (524), which itself was based on classical philosophy and formative concepts of Revelation during the early patristic period.[33] Fortune's Wheel and the related allegories of Vice and Virtue bound together religious doctrine, popular belief, and the machinery of tragic inevitability and were widely disseminated in the visual and performing arts, poetry, and exegesis. Based on the extant evidence, Fortune's Wheel first appeared as a stage object in a *ludus* about St. Catherine at Dustable, Bedroddshire (c. 1110). As an allegorical stage persona, Fortune appeared in the thirteenth century in Adam de la Halle's *Jeu de la Feuillée*.

In the same tradition, Giovanni Boccaccio's *De casibus virorum illustrium* (c. 1355–60) collects stories told in the first person about victims of disaster. *De casibus* influenced Geoffrey Chaucer's *Monk's Tale* and set the pattern for a form of literary tragedy into the early modern humanist period. Instances of creative amalgamation between Fortune's Wheel and Christian theology appear in religious sermons, as both subject matter and rhetorical strategy. In a thirteenth-century miniature in a Carmina Burana manuscript, Lady Fortune is replaced by the figure of Christ at the center of the wheel, sitting in judgment of the humans that roll past (Figure 2.3). The miniature contains essential characters of the Fortune's Wheel motif: an image of a king at the top of the wheel followed by, in clockwise direction, stages of his fall from greatness. As art historian Mitchell Merback has convincingly argued, in addition to cosmological meaning and religious symbolism of Fortune's Wheel and the Crucifix in this and other iconographic images, the wheel and the cross suggested punitive justice to the medieval spectator.[34] The "breaking wheel" was the instrument of St. Catherine's martyrdom (which, legendarily, broke when she touched it) and was used as a method for punishing criminals in spectacular and painful fashion throughout the medieval and early modern periods. The victim was strapped to the turning wheel and beaten, the weight of his shifting, stretched body causing bones to crack between the spokes. The graphic semiotics of sin and punishment in the Wheel corresponded to the circular staging of allegorical drama, where themes of vice and damnation spun out actions and events.

As an instrument for Christian instruction, the leitmotif of Fortune's Wheel added a layer of ethical didacticism to the medieval construction of tragic plot, particularly in morality plays. The allegorical wheel mechanically turning its victims towards death brings *every man* into the centripetal force of its rotation. In morality plays, the pivotal event for post-performance introspection is the moment Mankind crosses the threshold between death and judgment. Having witnessed correct and incorrect choices, spectators leave the performance contemplating their positions on the cosmic wheel and, perhaps, the means for their salvation.

What is notable about the various literary and artistic iterations of Fortune's Wheel, in the late medieval period especially, is that unlike the cause-and-effect dramaturgy prescribed by Aristotle and exemplified in Oedipus' *hamartia* of pride and willful blindness, reversal of fortune of the lives of medieval souls has a sense of inevitability.

FIGURE 2.3: Wheel of Fortune with Christ Enthroned in Judgment. *Codex Buranus*, 1230. BSM, Clm 4660, 1r. Used by permission of the Bavarian State Library under a Creative Commons Attribution-ShareAlike 4.0 International License.

Embodied by the female figure of Fortuna, the force of (mis)fortune is indifferent and relentless as she churns her victims under the wheel. The lack of retributive justice in the medieval tragic arts may also relate to the construction of Jesus as a scapegoat in various literary texts and in Passion theater. For Terry Eagleton, to have a socially ameliorative effect, a scapegoat's death must be a wasteful act, without culpability or reason:

> Jesus was left only with a forlorn faith in what he called his Father, despite the fact that this power seemed now to have abandoned him. But it is precisely this bereftness, savoured to the last bitter drop, which in a classically tragic rhythm could then become the source of renewed life. . . . Only by being "made sin" in the Pauline phrase, turned into some monstrous, outcast symbol of inhumanity, can the scapegoat go all the way through that condition to emerge somewhere on the other side.[35]

The often spectacular violence rendered on the body of Christ during his trial, tortures, and crucifixion provided spectators with a compelling reminder of their own mortality, both theatrically and *actually*, as in self-mortification rituals imitating the Passion of Christ or the many real episodes of pain suffered by actors playing the role of Jesus in Passion dramas.[36]

In his monograph on mythopoetics and ritual structure in medieval religious drama, Rainer Warning elaborates on the archetype of the scapegoat embodied in the sacrifice of Jesus in Passion plays. Warning argues that Christ's passivity in the face of ferocious cruelty in the French Arras Passion, Arnould Greban's Passion play, and scenes of torment in episodes from English plays, adds a dimension of pagan ritualism to religious theater. The stoic resignation of Christ recalls certain ancient rites of sacrifice where the victim (or god) is masked and immobile: "in the Adam play the Christian tradition is not represented purely. The Christian-figural level of what takes place in the *loca* is associated with a pre-Christian ritualistic element on the level of what takes place in the *platea*."[37] While Warning does not attribute archetypal figures to an unmediated folkloric substratum in the plays, his argument that the emotional and symbolic investments in violence exhibit an "epochal longing for scapegoats" is convincing, and links *imitatio Christi* to the social function of ancient drama.[38] The connection between ancient ritual affect and Christ's Passion was observed by medieval writers themselves, Remigius in the tenth century and Honorius Augustodunensis in the twelfth, among others.[39]

For Warning, pre-Christian mythological typologies become more apparent in the embodied act of playing, impulses that are in conversation, and sometimes at odds, with the doctrinal elements of biblical drama. For instance, in some liturgical plays the climax of the Passion occurs at the *descensus* episode, while the body of Jesus (the actor playing Jesus) remains on the cross, suggesting that "the Redemption is in large measure detached from its specifically Christian background. The cardinal function has passed from the moral event of the Crucifixion to the mythologeme of the descent into hell."[40] Postponement of the doctrinal function of the Resurrection also occurs in the Cornish *Ordinalia*, a three-day event that covers episodes from biblical history, apocrypha, and folkloric traditions, as described in more detail below.

During the peak of Passion devotion in the late medieval period the public expression of remorse and sadness was essential and often expressed in tearful acts of contrition. Grief, of course, is the core emotion of tragic drama, both for the characters who mourn loss on stage and audiences who respond sympathetically (or, in medieval terms, with co-passion). The ancient practice of performative lamenting and mourning in funeral rites was active through the Middle Ages. As it was rehearsed in liturgical drama and English Mary plays, mournful wailing would have contrasted dramatically with the stoicism of Christ in his role as the scapegoat, both occupying the mythological stratum. Yet, in other regions of Europe like Spain, public weeping was integrated into devotional practices in the Stations of the Cross, Holy Week processions, and other Passion enactments. From the thirteenth century forward, the lay population participated more directly in the celebrations of the body of Christ. In *imitatio Christi*, ritual actors somatically delineated the tragic suffering of Christ across spaces, mimetically reviving the Son of God's painful journey to Golgotha. Related to the prerogatives of sincere confession, the spectacle of violence and suffering in penitential processions partook in a wider culture of public crying and tearful contrition.[41]

In summary, medieval tragedy bodied forth "absolute space" where the fall of man and god *as* man were lamented. In the final section, I analyze dramatic iterations of this theory by observing correspondences between the dramaturgical patterns of tragedy and the mythopoetic journey of the soul, and how these trajectories were enacted in specific spaces of performance. The examples are limited by the availability of evidence for staging, the scope of my areas of expertise, and the editorial constraints of this collection. A more comprehensive list might include processionals and private devotional acts that would produce additional areas for analysis and contrasting propositions.

THE *SONG OF SYBIL*, CASTILE AND CATALONIA (THIRTEENTH THROUGH SIXTEENTH CENTURIES)

The *Song of Sybil* was a paraliturgical music-drama popular in Catalonia and Castile, and is still performed (albeit in a less theatrical manner) in Spanish churches today. Developed from the liturgical, Latinate *Ordo prophetarum*, the *Song of Sybil* related a vision of the Apocalypse and was performed on Christmas Eve. Enactments included a procession of Old Testament prophets presaging the coming of Jesus, followed by the Sybil's prophecy of the end of the world. The Sybil was dressed as an angel and occupied a raised platform above the action in order to supervise the procession of prophets. The play resided at the cusp of two Christian liturgical seasons and contained thematic elements of both—the somber, penitential Advent season and joyous Christmastide with its carnivalesque features. The play employs allegorical characters to remind the lay population of the ultimate role the Son of God will play on earth at the very beginning of His life's story. By linking historical Old Testament prophecies of the birth of Jesus to the prophecy of the Second Coming, the *Song of Sybil* staged the intersection of past and future, signifying cyclical time and engendering a sense of timelessness.

The music dramas were performed in cathedrals and churches in Catalonia and Castile, and due to the unique architectural design of many Romanesque and Gothic churches in Spain, the plays were staged in the center of the nave, with parishioners viewing the scenes from all sides. Between the thirteenth and sixteenth centuries, choirs were installed at a distance from the main altar in the naves of the cathedrals of Toledo, Barcelona, Oviedo, Mallorca, Tortosa, and elsewhere. In many ways, liturgical dramas staged at the pulpit of the choir, in the transept, and the antichoir (between the choir and the chancel) involved a greater participation of the laity than in music dramas staged in churches where the choir was situated behind a rood screen in the chancel. Eduardo Carrero Santamaría points out that the unique position of the choir among the laity provided a natural arrangement for procession and greater stage visibility for larger audiences in the antichoir, nave, and north and south transepts. The "theater-in-the-round" setting for various feasts plays, including the *Song of Sybil*, included highly theatrical stagings and spectacular effects to enhance miraculous, supernatural, and apocalyptic visions: temporary scaffolds and platform stages (including planked bridges linking the high altar and the choir); ornate costumes; angels wielding swords and torches; biblical characters, doves, and burning axes flown in from the ceiling; lightning and thunder effects; groups of musicians; and, in the cathedral of Burgos during the first and second vespers of Pentecost, live chickens and geese let loose into the playing area.[42]

FARSA DEL JUEGO DE CAÑAS, TALAVERA LA REAL (1554)

Evidence about the staging of the *Song of Sybil* is also available in the play *Farsa del juego de cañas* (the Farce of the Game of Canes), written by the parish priest of Talavera la Real, Diego Sánchez de Badajoz. Performed inside the church at Christmastide, the *Farsa* frames the traditional *Song of Sybil* liturgy with dramatic dialogue between the Sybil and two shepherds, beginning with a scene in which the Sybil conjures a procession of Old Testament prophets for the entertainment and edification of the pastoral characters. Only the shepherd, the shepherdess, and the Sybil are in view of the audience; Adam, Noah, Abraham, Moses, David, Isaiah, and Jeremiah sing their roles offstage. To the traditional dramaturgy of the *Song of Sybil*, Sánchez de Badajoz adds to the drama a staged "game of canes," a mock battle with sticks between the seven Virtues and seven Vices. Perhaps to increase the sense of surprise for the shepherd, shepherdess, and audience in the nave, sound effects from battle were produced from a location hidden from view. As in the widespread Peninsular tradition of *La Sibilia*, the Sybil "settles into a chair, to be placed in a section above so that she subjugates everyone and everyone sees her, in front of which will be a candle or burning ax with a thread of iron, with a metal sheet on top, made with skill so that it seems to be in the air."[43] The Sybil sat on a rotating seat in a supernatural realm above the nave, directing and judging the singing and battling a cast of characters. Similar stage arrangements were used to perform Sánchez de Badajoz's *Farsa de la Muerte*, a short comic sketch about the inevitability and unexpectedness of death that conforms to the pan-European Dance of Death tradition.

DANCES OF DEATH, PAN-EUROPEAN (FIFTEENTH AND SIXTEENTH CENTURIES)

The Dance of Death (or *danse macabre*) was a theme in literature, the visual arts, and performance culture that developed in the fourteenth century. Similar to the allegorical forms discussed above, the Dance of Death was a confrontation of the living with allegories of Death, often illustrated as human skeletons or ghostly post-mortem figures. As in the visual and textual representations of Fortune's Wheel, the men and women who were pulled into the dynamic force of mortality came from every station in society. Direct and indirect evidence for embodied representations and dances on the theme are extant. For instance, the conventions of the German *Totentanz* appear to have developed from a deathbed monologue into a dialogue song form between the dying and the allegorical figure of Death. Also, the music from the *Totentanz* tradition incorporates elements from popular dances of the period. Death also appears as a character in performance forms other than dance, such as *tableaux vivants*, court entertainments, and biblical plays, such as the N-Town *Death of Herod*. Death is a staple character in morality plays, one example among many of animated skeletons that cajole and threaten in the visual, sculptural, and performance arts. As an allegorical form that "plays" with heightened emotional commitment to fear and sorrow, the Dance of Death discloses medieval poetics of tragedy. As Walter Benjamin wrote, allegories of death that constitute the ancient roots of tragedy are especially potent because "the allegorization of the physis ... can only be carried through in all its vigour in respect of the corpse."[44]

Elina Gertsman argues that a coherent and recognizable embodied dance practice of the *danse macabre* existed in many regions of Europe in the fifteenth and sixteenth centuries, and the dance was conducted in the presence of spectators. She writes that Death's dance

> appears as a tool for differentiation between the immoral, supernatural, demonic, and chaotic domain of death and the ordered world of the living that death disrupts. This dancing, moreover, is performed for the sake of the spectator, the viewer of the Dance of Death, who is not (yet) performing the dance, but is invited to contemplate it.[45]

A number of medieval theater historians have recommended restraint when examining works of art as evidence in the theater arts. As Clifford Davidson has shown, theater was experienced within a larger culture of images, and this broader culture informed the reception of iconographic figures metonymically.[46] The large murals of the Dance of Death painted and carved into interiors and exteriors of church naves and tympana, cloisters,

FIGURE 2.4: *Danse Macabre* mural, parish church of Kermaria-an-Isquit. 1490. Courtesy of Elina Gertsman.

charnel houses, and graveyard walls offer another way of thinking about late medieval art and theater. Processional narratives in mural form need to be analyzed in the context of the spaces they inhabit; the standard uses of those spaces must also be considered. Church naves, aisles, and yards were commonly used for processions, dances, and enactments. Graveyards, of course, were the endpoints of funerary processions. Murals painted on the walls surrounding these spaces required viewers to walk alongside the painted surfaces to appreciate the full picture, as in the 60-meter long mural painted on the walls of a Dominican cemetery in Basel. Or they required circular movement around the inner circumference of a church nave, as in the parish church of Kermaria-an-Isquit, France, and the *Danse Macabre* mural (*c.* 1490) within (Figure 2.4) or cloister (such as the painted cycle on the walls of the enclosed burial ground of Old St. Paul's Cathedral in London, where John Lydgate's English translation of Dance of Death verses was inscribed [*c.* 1430]). The dioramic images functioned like stage objects that invited interaction from ritual actors. Paintings were sites "for active spectatorship" that played "a crucial role in the construction of meaning as well as its reception," particularly since the format and the size of the murals required the physical movement of viewers through space.[47]

LLIBRE VERMELL, MONTSERRAT (*c.* 1399–1400)

The ten songs from the *Llibre Vermell* were written for pilgrims worshiping a statue of the Blessed Virgin Mary of Montserrat at a Benedictine monastery high in the mountains surrounding Barcelona. Nine of the ten songs (verses in Latin, Occitan, and Catalan) are Marian, and the last falls squarely within the *ars moriendi* tradition and may have influenced the composition of songs from the Castilian *Dança general de la muerte* manuscript from the same period. A miniature of a skeleton illustrates the stanzas and verses of the last song, *Ad Mortem Festināmus* ("We Hasten Towards Death") (Figure 2.5). The placement of this song at the end of the cycle, with its thematic shift away from the main subject of the other songs, suggests that it served as punctuation to the nightly festivities. The style of music of the entire collection, in fact, is unique for the region and the time period, supporting the idea that the songs were written for a very specific purpose in a specific location. Kevin Kreitner concludes that since the songs are uniquely popular in tone—contrasting the self-conscious service music found in other contemporary Peninsular church manuscripts—the inscription on folio 22 can be trusted as evidence for staging in the plaza outside the monastery:[48]

> Because sometimes the pilgrims holding night vigil in the church of Santa Maria of Montserrat wish to sing and dance, and also by day in the plaza, and only decent and devout songs are allowed there, the songs above and below are written. And these must be used decently and sparingly, not disturbing those who continue in their prayers and devote contemplations . . .[49]

The eleventh-century Romanesque monastery is still standing, however it is difficult to determine the dimensions of the plaza with any degree of certainty since the majority of the current architectural elements in the complex were built after the medieval period. Still, because the shrine was a popular pilgrimage destination at the time, the plaza would have been sizable in order to facilitate the activities of a large number of unruly celebrants, as the inscription implies. The forms and styles of the songs are remarkably diverse. Prominent among them is the Iberian popular dance form, the *virelai*. The *virelai* is a round dance, and the clear melodies and simple, even rhythmic patterns of the song lend themselves to devotional dancing and singing.[50]

The boisterous cadence of the *virelai* form contrasts with the somber verse of *Ad Mortem Festināmus*:

Ad mortem festinamus:	We hasten towards death:
peccare desistamus.	sin we must end.
Peccare desistamus.	
Scribere proposui de contemptu mundano,	I write about the contempt of the world
ut degentes seculi non mulcentur in vano;	so this degenerate age will not pass in vain;
iam est hora surgere a sompno mortis pravo.	now is the hour to rise from the evil sleep of death.
A sompno mortis pravo.	
Vita brevis breviter in brevi finietur,	Life is short, and shortly it will end,
mors venit velociter quae neminem veretur,	death comes quickly and respects nobody,
omnia mors perimit et nulli miseretur.	it destroys everything and has no mercy.
Et nulli miseretur.	
Ni conversus fueris et sicut puer factus	If you do not turn back and become like a child,
et vitam mutaveris in meliores actus,	And transform your life into good deeds,
intrare non poteris regnum Dei beatus.	And change your life for the better,
Regnum Dei beatus.	You will not be able to enter blessed into the Kingdom of God.

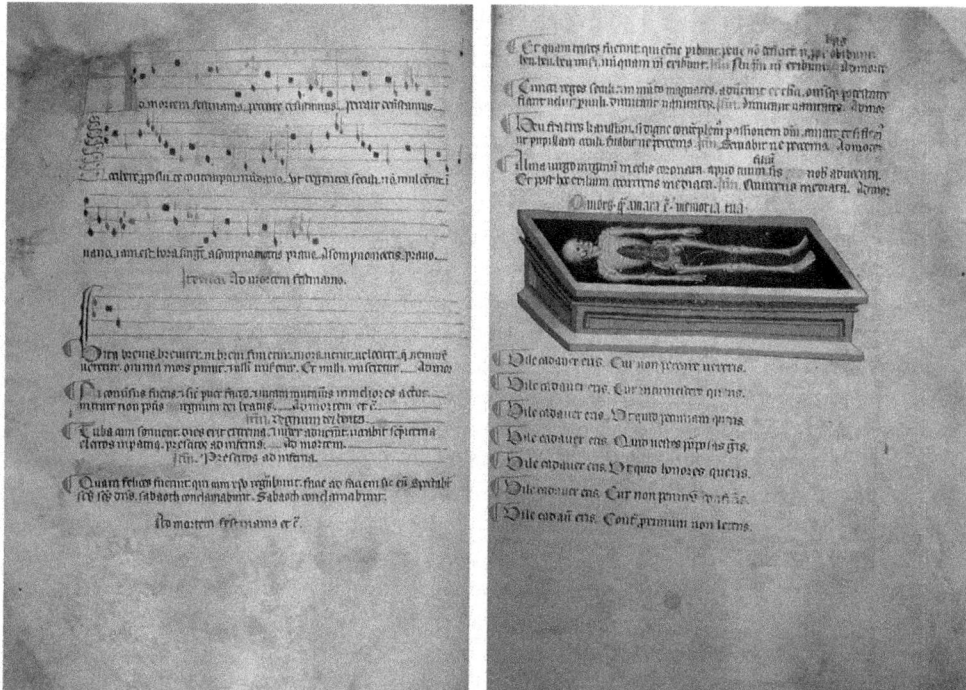

FIGURE 2.5: *Ad Mortem Festinãmus*. Llibre Vermell de Montserrat (c. 1399–1400). 26v–27r. Courtesy of the Biblioteca de Montserrat.

What is striking to the modern reader, perhaps, is the expression of themes on death in a festive dance. However, a treatment that might seem irreverent or frivolous to our ears had far more complex meanings in late medieval culture. The sense of mortality, particularly after the Black Death in the mid-fourteenth century, was ever-present. *Ars moriendi* was a creative means for reconciling the nearness of death. The phenomenon of dying, and the ways in which this phenomenon was expressed somatically in dance, "was viewed both as a destructive phenomenon and a possible gateway to eternal recompense," inviting a "flood of ambiguities, including the liminal nature of the Dance protagonists: the deadened state of the living and the enlivened state of Death."[51] Choreographed in the form of a round dance, the presence of death in the pilgrim song enters into a rehearsal of celestial circularity. Burdened with maladies that hastened them towards their deaths, worshipers entreated the Mother of God to heal their illnesses (as is expressed in the seventh song from the collection, *Mariam matrem virginem*). Having recently completed a journey and strenuous climb to the mountaintop shrine, the pilgrims sought a means for expressing their thanks and love for the Virgin of Montserrat in voice and movement, and to receive the comfort and restoration She provided. The songs of the *Llibre Vermell* offered a way for worshipers to embody the ambiguities experienced at the threshold of death, resolving difficult emotions through familiar round dances in sacred/secular space in the sky.

DANÇA GENERAL DE LA MUERTE (COMPOSED *c*. 1392, COPIED *c*. 1460–80)

Descriptions of choreographies of the Dance of Death are also found in the Castilian *Dança general*. For instance, as part of one narrative, a preacher introduces the dance from a raised platform (not unlike the church platform for the *Song of Sybil*) as a procession of members of various estates forms in a circle below. Michelle Hamilton's work on the fifteenth-century Hebrew *aljamiado* (Arabic transcriptions of European-language texts) copy of the manuscript (MS Parm. 2666) also points to a performance tradition specific to Peninsular Muslim and Jewish cultures. What distinguishes this text from those of the popular northern European tradition of Dance of Death are the figures of a rabbi and a Muslim judge partaking in the processional dance, as well as a figure of Death which more closely resembles the Semitic Angel of Death (Mal'ak ha-Mavet) and Angel of the Resurrection (Israfil) than it does the skeletal image common in other regions of Europe. The choreographies suggested by Parm. 2666 do not exclude a courtly milieu (such as *entremeses* and coronation rituals) and also strongly imply ancient Mediterranean funerary rites among Jews, Muslims, and Christians. These include accounts of pantomimes in which gravediggers wore skeleton costumes and depicted Death leading all humankind in a dance to the grave. Both the *Dança general* and its Hebrew copy allude to musical instruments, and the works are written in dialogue form.[52] Further, the dance may have had a performative function in Jewish and *converso* funerals, and in the Jewish Diaspora the themes would have highlighted theological aspects of Yom Kippur and Rosh Hashanah: transgression, repentance, sin, and forgiveness.[53]

Two conclusions can be drawn from these Iberian examples. First, unique interfaith relationships in Iberian communities reveal practices that occurred at and around gravesites (dance performances by grave-digger guilds were a tradition long before the fourteenth century), and in circular choreographies that resonate with other medieval tragic forms discussed above.[54] Second, the evidence shows that the exploration of tragic affect—fear, sorrow, and contrition—were not exclusive to Christian communities, and additional research on Jewish and Islamic exegesis and funeral rituals and other forms of public lamentation might reveal strains of mythopoetics of tragedy in these cultures.

THE CASTLE OF PERSEVERANCE, EAST ANGLIA (*c*. 1440)

The stage diagram of *The Castle of Perseverance* (Figure 2.1) plots a comic-tragic-action/ adventure journey for the soul of Humanum Genus (Mankind), embodying not only the circular pattern of Christian revelation, atonement, and redemption, but also the didactic metaphor of Fortune's Wheel. The *platea* illustration in the Macro manuscript exemplifies a microcosmic geography according to a cardinal orientation with spiritual dimensions: God in the east, Flesh to the warm south, World opposite paradise in the west, and the devil's scaffold in the north. In *Perseverance*, Mankind physicalizes this cosmic motion in a peregrination around the scaffolds on the perimeter of the playing space, where he experiences some success, but more often failure, in his pursuit of his goals. A war for the soul of Mankind is the centerpiece of the drama, a tragic *agôn* in the most basic sense, that which "stages conflicts where the contesting characters are given ample opportunities to present their reasons for wanting to act in a certain way before their disputes culminate in the obliteration of the world that they live in through these actions."[55]

The resolution of *Perseverance* is unlike all other extant English morality plays (except for the fragment *The Pride of Life*) since the protagonist dies in a state of sin, and rather than proceeding to heaven, he is summarily beckoned to hell where he is repeatedly beaten by devils. Fortunately for Mankind, and in the nick of time, the Four Daughters of God plead for this undeserving soul—who, in 3,649 lines of text prior to salvation mostly fails to resist the Vices—and he is retrieved from Hell and brought to God's scaffold. As Clifford Davidson points out, the progression of Mankind through the scaffolds does not suggest a sense of pilgrimage towards a transcendental goal.[56] Although the eventual salvation of Mankind is doctrinally sound, the action leading up to this point suggests a tragic downfall culminating in Mankind's exhortation to the audience, "takythe example at me./ Do for yourself whyl ye han spase" (2,839). The ultimate reconciliation with God, then, emphasizes the theological point that good deeds and penance are not enough to save one's soul; ultimately, salvation depends on God's mercy. This typology fits into the poetics of medieval tragedy described above: a lack of control over one's destiny, with suffering along the way. The last line of the play encourages the audience to meditate on the end of life and the end of history itself: "Thynke on youre last endynge" (3,648). More than other English moralities, then, the emotional trajectory of the soul follows the path of the Psychomachia, buffered by a chance act of mercy that sends the protagonist back up the other side of fortune's wheel.

The appearance of Belyal (Satan) recalls another trope familiar to the audience of *Perseverance*: the Dance of Death. Belyal mentions bones a few times in the play (the typical depiction of Death in the *danse macabre* is a skeleton), and during battle he dances to the sounds of bagpipes, "gunne-pwder brennyn In pypys in his handis and in his eris, and in his ers":

> What, for Belyalys bonys,
> Whereabowtyn chyde ye?
> Have don, ye boyes, al at onys.
> Lasche don these moderys, all three.
> Werke wrake to this wonys.
> The vaunward is grauntyd me.
> Do these moderys to makyn monys.
> Youre dowty dedys now lete se.
>   Dasche hem al to daggys.
> Have do, boyes, blo and blake
> Wirke these wenchys wo and wrake.
> Claryouns, cryeth up at a krake,
>   And blowe your brode baggys!
>
> —2,186–98

The iconography of the Dance of Death is rehearsed again in a speech near the end of the play when Justice says of Mankind "that he schulde a levyd ay,' Tyl Deth trypte him on hys daunce...." (3,424–5)[57] The inducement of Death into playful circumstances was a familiar theme in a variety of art forms, and in this network of associations a sense of tragic doom was made present for audiences. In the microcosmic place and scaffold of the fifteenth-century morality, Death marked for the viewer the tragic threshold for the soul's pilgrimage in real time and space.

ORDINALIA, CORNWALL (LATE FOURTEENTH CENTURY)

Like *The Castle of Perseverance*, the staging plan in the compendious fourteenth-century Cornish *Ordinalia* symbolically connects the emblematic force of space with the iconography of misfortune, downfall, and death. Of the four plays in the Bodley 791 manuscript, three are structured on a composition of biblical and extra-biblical events: *Ordinale de Origine Mundi*, *Passio Domini Nostri Jhesu Christi*, and *Ordinale de Resurrexione Domini*. Each play is around three thousand lines in length and thematically linked to the others by the defeat of the Devil and Redemption, from the Fall to the Resurrection. The tremendous size and scope of the plays, which included music and an invitation at the end of the fourth play in the manuscript (*Beunans Meriasek*) to dance and drink, indicate that they must have been performed on occasions of some importance, perhaps Corpus Christi.[58] In addition to the plan from the manuscript, remaining physical evidence provides information about the staging of the *Ordinalia*. The plays were staged on Cornish rounds (*plen an gwary*), permanent playing spaces built out of earth and held by stone retaining walls in an amphitheater arrangement. The diagram for staging the second play of the trilogy, the *Passio Christi* (Figure 2.6), indicates locations for the principal characters of the play (clockwise from the east): Celum, Centurio, Cayphas, Princeps Annas, Herodes, Pilatus, Doctores, and Tortores.

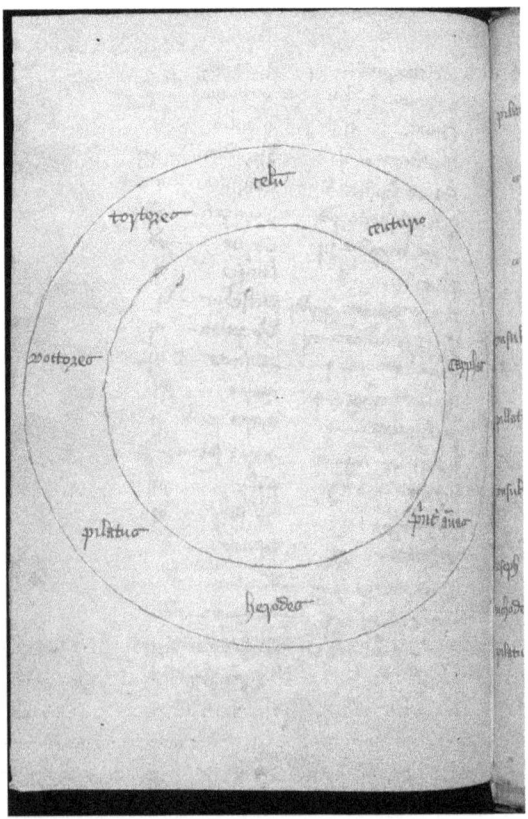

FIGURE 2.6: *Passio Christi* stage plan. Ordinalia (1425). MS Bodley 791, 56v. Used by permission of the Bodleian Libraries, University of Oxford.

Two elements of the second play relate to the subject of tragedy. The *Passio Christi* includes various events from Christ's ministry and ends with two non-biblical scenes and the deposition, after which Nicodemus addresses the audience directly, calling on them to reflect on the events of the Passion. The Resurrection play was performed on the third day, which provided an interval in which the audience could fully explore affective sorrow in response to the death of God's son. The Three Marys, Harrowing of Hell, Death of Pilate, and the Ascension are held in abeyance. As such, the arc of the *Passio Christi* reaches its nadir at the most sorrowful scene of Christian history, prior to the positive sign of resurrection in the *visitatio* or the victorious Harrowing of Hell. Old Testament prophecies remain unfulfilled in *Passio Christi* and death is thematically triumphant. The audience is left to lament the violent end of the protagonist without an optimistic resolution or hope for salvation. The scapegoat becomes an empty vessel in which witnesses to the sacrifice may pour their emotions.

Like the Passion episodes expressed in the English pageants and on the continent, the physical trials of Christ in the *Ordinalia* are particularly violent. The instruments of the Passion receive strong emphasis: Christ's brain is pierced by the crown of thorns and he is stretched, pierced, and tortured on the cross. The nails used in the crucifixion are the subject of a non-biblical mini-episode all of their own. In contrast to this intensity of mortal violence, which is germane to tragic drama prior to, and after, the Middle Ages, Jesus remains silent and impassive throughout, fully embodying the ritual scapegoat function of pre-Christian ritual.

CONCLUSION

Unlike the Aristotelian linear diagram of exposition, rise, climax, fall, and denouement, the medieval circular trajectory of tragic action was repetitive, open to changing outcomes, and ultimately unresolved for the audience. Likewise, life on earth for medieval Christians was a pause more than it was a trajectory—an interregnum between the First Advent and the Second Advent, lived between unknown periphery and spiritual center in Jerusalem. Only upon the threshold of death does Fortune's Wheel come to a stop, and even when this moment is staged in choirs, *platea*, and graveyards, the ultimate destiny of mankind remains a terrible unknown for the future to determine. The theatrical processions, dance forms, morality dramas, and saint's plays that rehearsed the spatiality of Christian cosmos did not resolve these paradoxes by ending in social stasis, but rather challenged audiences with compelling questions that required resolution only after the crowds had dispersed, within the soul's encasement.

CHAPTER THREE

Communities of Production and Consumption

JOHN T. SEBASTIAN

There is no such thing as medieval tragic drama. So goes the conventional wisdom. According to this tradition, in deploying the term *tragedie* English writers of the later Middle Ages either invoke the specter of an ancient and alien curiosity—the lurid performances of the Roman *theatrum* long associated by Christian moralists with excess—or the more current literature on the misfortunes of the powerful, of which Boccaccio's *De casibus virorum illustrium*, Chaucer's *Monk's Tale*, and Lydgate's *Fall of Princes* (an English versification of Boccaccio's work via Laurent de Premierfait's French intermediary) serve as well-known examples. Chaucer's ignorance of an ancient dramatic tradition determines his own definition of this latter species of tragedy as "a certeyn storie . . . / Of hym that stood in greet prosperitee, / And is yfallen out of heigh degree / Into myserie and endeth wrecchedly" (*Monk's Tale* 1,973, 1,975–7).[1] For Chaucer, tragedy is fundamentally a narrative genre, a certain kind of story, one that operates by attributing calamity to the inexorable workings of Fortune on the deserving and undeserving alike rather than to the misguided choices of flawed individuals in any Aristotelian sense.[2]

This official narrative poses a challenge to the author of an essay on the communities that produced and consumed tragedy in the Middle Ages. How does one write about the persons who make and enjoy a thing that is not supposed to exist? Yet as Carol Symes demonstrates in her own contribution to this collection and in a series of recent essays repeatedly invoked throughout this volume, the rumors of tragedy's death at the end of antiquity have been greatly exaggerated by a handful of Christian polemicists, Tertullian and Augustine chief among them, whose passing comments are too often decontextualized by modern scholars and unduly treated as representative of widespread medieval attitudes toward the tragic. Such critiques reflect the eagerness of their authors to distance a still-young Christian faith from the decadence of the Roman culture which had first conferred status upon it.[3] Symes has persuasively argued not only that tragedy continued to maintain a cultural presence during the thousand years between Rome's collapse and the sixteenth-century revival of classical theatrical modes and Aristotelian dramatic theory but also that the previous richness and diversity of Greek tragedy had already been largely circumscribed by the Greeks themselves in their efforts to establish a dramatic canon.[4] In any event, medieval scribes participated in the preservation of tragedy by copying ancient texts, which in turn continued to serve as staples of schoolroom instruction throughout the ensuing millennium, while the tragic drama of the past remained a vivid context for understanding the undeniably performative elements of the Christian liturgy and other devotions.⁵ For Symes, the quest for "authenticity"—for medieval tragedies that imitate what the Greeks composed and performed—also fails to take proper account of the variety of creative and Christianized adaptations of the form in subsequent centuries. Symes has therefore observed that even "when medieval texts described as 'tragedies' do survive, they have tended to be overlooked or openly derided by scholars because they are not obviously laid out like modern plays and tend to transgress Aristotelian conventions."⁶

Of course it is arguably the purpose of markers of genre like "tragedy" to forestall this sort of confusion or mislabeling. It is, furthermore, a critical commonplace that genre functions to establish a set of ground rules that govern interactions between tragedy's producers (authors, copyists, and performers) on the one hand and its consumers (spectators and readers) on the other. Take, for instance, the claim of Robert Hodge and Gunther Kress in their seminal study of social semiotics that the system of rules implied by genre "control[s] the behaviour of producers of such texts, and the expectations of potential consumers." Hodge and Kress define genres as "socially ascribed classifications of semiotic form" but classifications that are meaningful only insofar as "a social group declares and enforces the rules that constitute them."⁷ Within this model, producers provide—and are rewarded for providing—a desired commodity while consumers derive pleasure from having their expectations satisfied by that commodity. Genre thus serves to guarantee meaning and to ensure pleasure.

Yet it is precisely tragedy's seeming refusal to function in the Middle Ages as a genre—that is to say, as a contract—and its inability to regulate interactions between producers and consumers that has rendered it such a problematic form for literary and theater historians. Responding to this resistance, Alfred Hiatt labels medieval tragedy an "ungenre," calling it "the spanner in the works, the stone in the shoe, the grit in the eye: an impediment to categorization, order, function." As ungenre, tragedy "represents a 'breach of contract' between author and audience that brings system, and systematic understanding, to a halt."⁸ Julie Orlemanski similarly invokes medieval tragedy's inability to structure the relationship between consumers and producers—in other words its failure as genre—when she observes that, despite its being

> one of the most venerable topics in the history of genre criticism, in the Middle Ages the "goatish song" was at the margins of literature—a category in search of texts, a classifying gesture without much to order, the vestige of a literary sensibility that no medieval writer or reader quite shared.⁹

But Orlemanski's characterization of medieval tragedy also reveals the nature of the impediment for literary histories incapable of contending with the disruption caused by tragedy, namely, the assumption that ancient tragedy's alterity fundamentally renders it an inaccessible and undesirable commodity in the Middle Ages. In commenting on English literary genres, Hiatt asserts that tragedy "is deployed in Middle English writing as an alien genre."¹⁰ Rooted, indeed trapped, in an alien past, ancient tragedy appears fundamentally incompatible with the expectations of medieval consumers and beyond the abilities of medieval playwrights to reproduce.

By contrast, and in the spirit of Symes' reappraisals of tragedy's post-classical fortunes, this essay seeks to reclaim medieval tragedy as a meaningful and meaning-making category at the nexus between producers and consumers, actors and audiences, playwrights and play-readers. I contend that we can productively recover a medieval tragic hermeneutic operative in late-medieval vernacular drama that serves to structure a contractual relationship between producers and consumers even in cases where the surviving texts do not explicitly identify themselves as tragedies. By recovering this hermeneutic we can gain insight into the exchange between those who produced medieval drama (playwrights, copyists, and performers) and those who consumed it (spectators and readers). Thus, rather than attempting a broad survey of communities of production and consumption of medieval tragedy, this essay pursues two case studies organized around readings of theoretical and dramatic texts that reveal how tragedy serves as an instrument of moral reform within a medieval Christian framework.[11] I begin by examining the definition of tragedy advanced in the fourteenth century by the Dominican Nicholas Trevet. Trevet's commentaries on the plays of Seneca highlight tragedy's invitation to its audience to engage in what Trevet calls ethical interpretation of dramatic texts for the purpose of reforming individual behavior. Influenced by Trevet's tragic hermeneutic, I then turn to two late-medieval English biblical plays that portray the Expulsion of Adam and Eve from Paradise. A striking lyrical lamentation by Adam serves as the climax in each of these scenes and provides an entry point for interrogating the attempts of playwrights and performers to regulate the emotional reaction of their audiences to the tragedy enacted by the first parents. This chapter thus focuses not on communities of actual persons responsible for producing and consuming dramatic tragedy in medieval England, although something will be said in passing about the circumstances surrounding the production of the plays discussed. Rather, in keeping with the series' general approach to tragedy as an expression of culture, this essay instead identifies the tragic as facilitating the moral reform of spectators and readers, who in turn are hailed by dramatic texts as the descendants of Adam, that is, as tragedy's heirs.

NICHOLAS TREVET, *TRANSLATOR STUDII*

The persistence of the myth that tragedy died—or, to borrow Symes' provocative image, was murdered[12]—at the start of the Middle Ages has had regrettable consequences, not the least of which has been scholars' failure to recognize medieval tragedy for what it is not only in the variety of adapted forms cataloged by Symes but even when it has been hiding in plain sight. Such is the case with the voluminous commentaries on the tragic dramas of Seneca authored by the fourteenth-century Dominican Nicholas Trevet, commentaries which have received little notice from scholars of the drama of medieval England.

Born in the middle of the thirteenth century and dead by about 1334, Nicholas Trevet was educated at Oxford by the Dominicans, of whose order he was a member.[13] He pursued advanced theological studies at Paris before returning in 1314 to Oxford, where he spent most of his ensuing academic career. Although what little is known of Trevet's intellectual formation seems typical enough of late thirteenth- and early fourteenth-century academic friars, his modern biographers have been quick to point out that Trevet's scholarly preoccupations were unique in comparison with the intellectual pursuits of his fellow scholastics.[14] Among the most notable of his surviving works, then and now, is the commentary on Boethius' *De consolatione philosophiae*, which survives in more than one hundred manuscript copies[15] and which had become by the time Chaucer drew on it either directly or indirectly in preparing his English translation of it the most popular commentary on the *De consolatione*. But Trevet's engagement with antiquity extended well beyond Boethius, as Beryl Smalley has shown, to commentaries on Augustine's *De civitate Dei*, Virgil's *Eclogae*, Livy's *Ab urbe condita*, the *Declamationes* of the elder Seneca, and Seneca the Younger's tragedies, each of which represents the first known effort to compile a commentary on that particular text.[16] Indeed, Trevet's reputation as a skilled interpreter of classical literature resulted directly in a commission from Cardinal Nicholas of Prato, Bishop of Ostia, to take up the tragedies, which he did, completing his commentary on them probably around 1317.[17]

Trevet had previously encountered the idea of tragedy in Boethius' writings. Prior to delving into Seneca's plays, Trevet's conception of ancient tragedy, like that of many of his contemporaries, derived ultimately from Isidore of Seville. In the eighteenth book of the *Etymologiae*, Isidore describes tragedians as those "who would sing for the audience in poetry about the ancient deeds and lamentable crimes of wicked kings [*qui antique gesta atque facinora sceleratorum regum luctuosa carmine spectante populo concinebant*]."[18] In her study of the idea of theater in Latin Christian thought, Donnalee Dox cautions that in his explanations of features of the ancient theater, Isidore "takes sources out of context, conflates information, comments without analyzing, and ignores inconsistencies" and that these decontextualized explanations are consequently "wildly inaccurate."[19] Despite such misrepresentation, Isidore's cataloging of pre-Christian culture achieved a level of authority such that Trevet's own glossing of *De consolatione philosophiae* paraphrases Isidore's statement as filtered through Trevet's fellow commentator William of Conches: "Tragedy is a song of great crimes beginning in prosperity and ending in adversity [*Tragedia est carmen de magnis iniquitatibus a prosperitate incipiens et in adversitate terminans*]."[20] Chaucer in turn preserves Trevet's gloss in his own English translation of Boethius when he notes that tragedy "is to seyn a dite of a prosperite for a tyme, that endith in wrecchidnesse."[21] Henry Ansgar Kelly has argued that the very idea of tragedy as a genre was subjected to continuous reinterpretation throughout the Late Middle Ages, culminating in the figurative and non-dramatic form established by Chaucer in the *Monk's Tale* and especially *Troilus and Criseyde*, which subsequently exercised a profound influence on subsequent writers.[22] Among the inheritors of this tradition was the prolific Benedictine poet John Lydgate, who echoes and characteristically amplifies Chaucer in an oft-quoted passage in his *Troy Book*:

> tragedie, whoso list to knowe,
> It begynneth in prosperité
> And endeth in adversité;
> And it also doth the conquest trete
> Of riche kynges and of lordys grete,
> Of mighty men and olde conquerouris,
> Whiche by fraude of Fortunys schowris
> Ben overcast and whelmed from her glorie.[23]

The image of Fortune's wheel adorning the opening of Book II of *Troy Book* (Figure 3.1) in a lavishly illustrated copy of the poem from the middle of the fifteenth century points to the persistent association by English poets of tragedy with Boethius and his glossators.

Trevet had already written his commentary on Boethius prior to the arrival of Nicholas of Prato's commission for the Seneca. Reading actual exemplars of classical tragedy appears to have led him to revise and expand his thinking about tragedy, which he began to understand as a didactic genre intended to provide moral exempla for instructing its audience in ethical reading and proper moral behavior. The circumstances surrounding Nicholas of Prato's commission to Nicholas Trevet are explained by surviving letters sent between the two Dominicans. This correspondence reveals that within their order Trevet was already a well-regarded scholar thanks in no small part to his work on Boethius' *De*

FIGURE 3.1: Fortune and her wheel from the opening of Book II of John Lydgate's *Siege of Troy* (i.e., *Troy Book*). Manchester, University of Manchester Library English MS 1, f. 28v. Courtesy of Getty Images.

consolatione. In fact, his relationship with Nicholas of Prato would eventually result in the wider dissemination of his commentaries and probably in a further commission from Pope John XXII for Trevet's Livy commentary.[24] Nicholas the cardinal was well acquainted with the commentative achievements of Nicholas the scholar and held out hope that his fellow Dominican might next set his interpretive sights on Seneca's tragedies. As Ruth J. Dean has shown, even intellectuals like Nicholas of Prato, who found himself equally at ease talking papal politics and Boethian philosophy, quailed before the ancient poets at the pre-dawn of European humanism and thus turned to men like Trevet to serve as *translator studii*, a conduit of ancient learning to the present. In his letter to Trevet, Nicholas of Prato emphasizes the obscurity of the fables that Seneca stitched together to produce his tragedies, which he described as "a book full of so many obscurities, connected by so many holes, and interwoven and entwined with so many fables, that it immediately scares off with its obscurity anyone tempted to read it [*liber tantis … obscuritatibus plenus, tantis connexus latebris, tantisque contextus et implexus fabellis, ut statim temptantem se legere obscuritate sua deterreat*]." Cardinal Nicholas continues with a touch of literary flair all his own: "if your skills are up to the task, we ask that you might make a home for us and for all those who flee that sea of troubles and that you might give us a swimmable path [*si facultas vobis suppetit, rogamus ut faciatis nobis domesticum et omnibus qui tamquam teterrimum pelagus ipsum fugitant, natabilem perviumque reddatis*]."[25] The cardinal sought from Trevet not literary criticism but literal explication of the plays' more obscure references and allusions, the value of which Nicholas of Prato recognized but the meanings of which were impenetrable to him. Trevet's task was to produce not an appreciation of Roman poetry but a guide to ancient culture and to render that culture accessible to new generations of consumers.

Trevet's first order of business was to produce a working theory of tragedy. It is not clear whether Trevet knew Hermannus Alemannus' thirteenth-century translation of Averroes' commentary on Aristotle's *Poetics*, and in any case the Dominican does not, as we shall see, discuss tragedy in terms consonant with those set forth by Aristotle. Trevet instead turns to the intellectual apparatus of scholasticism in addressing the problem of Seneca's tragedies, which, for Trevet, were simply without precedent. Trevet expends much of his commentative energy on lexical interpretation, mythological explanation, and, in the case of *Hercules furens* particularly but also elsewhere, on astronomical explication. As Valentino Fabris has observed with disapproval, "[l]'interpretazione ... è del tutto scolastica [the interpretation is thoroughly scholastic]" in that it consists almost exclusively in literal explication.[26] Trevet's relentless pursuit of the literal across hundreds of pages commentary is all the more remarkable given that his subject matter included shockingly violent scenes of fratricide, filicide, mariticide, uxoricide, regicide, and suicide. The commentary on *Medea* offers an illustrative take on Trevet's detached approach to glossing the tragedies. Toward the end of that play Medea's filicidal rage is briefly forestalled by the unexpected appearance of the shade of Absyrtus, the brother whom Medea has killed and whose hacked-up remains she has scattered in order to delay her pursuing father and make fast her escape with Jason. Medea wonders at this apparition: "Whose shade approaches ill-defined with limbs dispersed? It is my brother, he seeks amends [*cuius umbra dispersis venit / incerta membris? frater est, poenas petit*]."[27] On the phrase *membris dispersis*, Trevet comments:

> that is, representing scattered limbs. When they appear, the shades of the dead should show themselves in the likeness of how they were killed; and therefore this one appeared dismembered, because Medea in the course of killing him scattered his body.
>
> [*id est representans membra dispersa. Vmbre enim mortuorum quando apparent solent se ostendere cum ymagine facti quo interfecti sunt; et ideo iste apparuit cum dispersis membris, quia Medea ipsum occidendo membratim dispersit.*][28]

Trevet passes over the enormous monstrosity that is his subject matter here, instead constraining himself rather prosaically to the exercise of explaining how and why one might present dismemberment to an audience. Grace G. Wilson observes that the commentaries' "greatest strength lies in supplying synonyms and paraphrases, with many an 'id est' and 'scilicet.'"[29] But Trevet's dispassionate and meticulous exposition, as illustrated by the running interlinear commentary crammed between lines of text in a manuscript copy of *Hercules furens* preserved in the Biblioteca Civica Guarneriana, serves to bridge the interpretive gap between Seneca and his would-be latter-day admirers, including Nicholas of Prato, by rendering ancient culture less opaque (Figure 3.2).

And it is not just the store of myths and astronomical lore that Trevet needs to translate for Seneca's fourteenth-century readers. Trevet also addresses the claims that tragedy itself as a marker of genre makes on behalf of the texts to be glossed and on those who read them. In the *accessus* to his commentary on *Hercules furens*, the first in order of the plays as he arranges them, Trevet observes the following about the nature of tragedy:

> From what has been said, therefore, it is clear that there are four causes of this tragedy, of which the efficient cause was Seneca; the material cause is the madness of Hercules

FIGURE 3.2: The beginning of Seneca's *Hercules furens* with interlineated commentary by Nicholas Trevet. Courtesy of Biblioteca Civica Guarneriana MS 75, f.3r, San Daniele del Friuli.

in which he kills his children and wife; the formal cause pertains to the mode of writing, which is "dramatic," as they say, and ordered by parts, which will be seen in the exposition; the final cause is the delight of the people listening; or to the extent that certain things deserving of praise are narrated here, and others worthy of blame, this book can be treated in some way ethically, and then the final cause is the correction of behaviors through the examples here supplied.

[*Ex dictis autem patent quatuor cause huius tragedie, quia causa efficiens fuit Seneca, causa materialis est furia Herculis in qua interfecit filios et uxorem; causa formalis consistit in modo scribendi, qui est dragmaticus, ut dictum est, et ordine partium, qui patebit in expositione; causa finalis est delectatio populi audientis; vel in quantum hic narrantur quedam laude digna, quedam vituperio, potest aliquo modo liber hic supponi ethice, et tunc finis eius est correctio morum per exempla hic posita.*][30]

Trevet's explication of tragedy as a genre according to its four causes (efficient, material, formal, and final) represents a unique contribution to medieval literary theory. He articulates tragedy in terms that his own readers could understand and appreciate. Moreover, he does so in a way that foregrounds the relationship between producer—Seneca the efficient cause of tragedies—and consumer—the *populi audientis* whose delight and moral correction are tragedy's final cause. In pursuing the literal meaning of Seneca's plays, in other words, Trevet does not deny the prospect of allegorical reading; rather, he provides the framework within which such interpretive moves can be made by readers steeped in the literary theory of the fourteenth century.

Trevet briefly models the practice of reading tragedy for its ethical content and effects in his exposition of one of the chorus's songs in *Hercules furens* in which Hercules' descent to hell is narrated and his fall foreshadowed:

it pertains to the tragic poet to describe the sorrowful falls of great men, and since there ought to be many rumors concerning such [falls] among the people and diverse judgments bandied about, Seneca in his tragedies therefore introduces the chorus to sing about such things and to represent such rumors and such judgments of the people. . . . First, then, on that occasion on which Hercules went to hell, it [the chorus] teaches that all men naturally tend that way; second, because Hercules fell from such supreme glory into madness, it teaches that it is safer to live in little fortune than in great.

[*ad poetam tragicum pertinet describere luctuosos casus magnorum virorum, solent autem de talibus multi esse rumores in populo et diversa ferri iudicia, ideo Seneca in suis tragediis, ad representandum tales rumores et talia iudicia populi, interpolatim introducit chorum de talibus canentem. . . . primo enim, occasione illa qua Hercules ivit ad infernum, docet quod omens homines naturaliter tendunt illuc; secundo, quia Hercules a tanta excellentia glorie cecidit in furiam, docet quod securius est vivere in parva fortuna quam in magna.*][31]

Hercules, viewed through Trevet's hermeneutic lens, emerges here as a stand-in for fallen humanity, an exemplary figure whose missteps are a warning to perspicacious readers. Trevet thus reminds the readers of his commentaries that tragedy depends for its meaning on the interpretive capacities of its consumers, who must be prepared to read for the moral messages contained in tragedy's generic code.

TRAGEDY'S ORIGIN: THE FALL OF ADAM

What, then, if anything can we say about the influence of Trevet's Senecan commentaries on medieval thinking about tragedy's ethical final cause? As Richard Rouse has demonstrated, copies of the tragedies were available in England and France at least as early as the early thirteenth century.[32] Among known or assumed readers of the Senecan commentaries we can name Boccaccio, who seems to have come across them in the early 1360s just prior to beginning work on *De genealogia deorum gentilium*; Dante's son Pietro Alighieri; maybe Robert Holcot, Trevet's fellow Dominican, who did know Hermannus Alemannus' translation of Averroes on the *Poetics*; maybe Ranulf Higden and perhaps John Trevisa independently of Higden; and the English Benedictine chronicler Thomas Walsingham.[33] John Lydgate may also have been aware of the commentaries, even if perhaps he never read them or not much of them. At the very least we do know that a copy of the tragedies themselves was available by the thirteenth century in Bury, Lydgate's spiritual home but also the intellectual center of East Anglia, where roughly one-third of all surviving vernacular English play scripts were produced in the fourteenth, fifteenth, and sixteenth centuries. Lydgate frequently bolsters his discussion of the calamitous falls from grace of princes by citing the *auctoritas* of Seneca in his guise as the author of tragedies, some of which Lydgate mentions by name. Whether or not Lydgate directly knew the Senecan commentaries, Trevet clearly helped secure the status of Seneca as an *auctor* based on his tragic writings for future generations of poets, even if the very idea of Senecan tragedy continued to be misunderstood and underappreciated.

To be clear: I do not argue here for the direct influence of Trevet on any of the mostly anonymous authors of vernacular drama in England, only that Trevet's idea of tragedy as a didactic genre aimed at the moral improvement of its audience allows us to identify similarly intended "tragic" moments in surviving plays. Specifically I argue that the authors of dramatizations of the Expulsion of Adam and Eve from Paradise and those who performed them strived to evoke particular emotional responses from their audiences for their delight—Trevet's *delectatio populi*—and for the sake of their instruction. Expulsion plays provide a particularly apt site for exploring the tragic workings of medieval drama, moreover, since tragedy arguably has its origins with the fall of Adam and Eve.[34] In her survey of occurrences of *tragedia* and its related forms in the writings of Latin authors collected in the *Patrologia Latina*, Carol Symes records a pair of twelfth-century abbots, Wolberus of St. Pantaleon and Henry of Marcy (also known as Henry of Albano), who liken Adam's fall to tragedy.[35] In particular Henry, sometime abbot of Clairvaux, papal legate of Gregory VIII, and propagandist for the Albigensian crusade, in his allegorical exposition of the meaning of Septuagesima in his *Tractatus de peregrinante civitate Dei*, notes the edifying qualities of the story of the fall: "Not only should it be read but it is even more beneficial that it be imprinted on human hearts, a tragedy to be lamented in its singing [*Non solum legitur, sed et ut cordibus humanis utilius imprimatur, etiam cantando tragoedia eadem deploratur*]."[36] For Henry, it is appropriate that the readings for the pre-Lenten season begin at the beginning, that is, with Genesis, so that faithful Christians may come to understand how they have arrived at their present state through the sin of Adam and may learn from his failings to amend their own ways ("*ut dum ex his homo cognoscit unde quo devenerit, quo etiam ei redeundum sit, per hoc admoneatur*").

Indeed, the legendary lives of the first parents were a favorite subject for didactic and devotional embellishment during the Middle Ages. The earliest apocryphal lives of Adam and Eve are recorded in a number of languages, but it is the loose collection of related texts commonly referred to as the *Vita Adae et Evae* and their numerous retellings in verse, prose, and drama across the range of European vernaculars that are most relevant here.[37] A common stock of interpolated episodes unifies the textual descendants of the Latin *Vita Adae et Evae* tradition and includes, among others, scenes of starvation and hardship; of penances undertaken in the expectation of regaining entry to Paradise and frustrated by further diabolical temptations; and Seth's quest to relieve the suffering of his parents.[38] The surviving derivatives, even limited just to those in English, are too many to survey adequately here,[39] but the prose version of the *Vita* appended to the end of some versions of the fifteenth-century *Gilte Legende*, the English translation of Jacobus de Voragine's *Legenda aurea* via Jean de Vignay's intervening French version, illustrates the extent to which Adam's tragic credentials were amplified in the texts.[40] The Expulsion opens with the couple newly cast forth from Paradise and traveling west of Eden. They eventually construct a tabernacle, wherein they remain for seven days, passing their time with "wepenge, louringe and crienge in moost tribulacioun."[41] Continuous lamentation soon gives way to intense hunger, yet despite his efforts, Adam fails to find adequate sustenance, and his mind turns darkly to thoughts of self-harm: "howe might it be that I might slee my flesshe?"[42] Adam nevertheless perseveres in his pursuit of his next meal, but he and Eve can find "nat such as thei had in paradis" but only food suitable for beasts.[43]

In her desperation, Eve ingenuously invents the Christian concept of penance as a means of placating their angry God and eventually relieving their suffering. "My Lorde," Eve asks of her husband, "what is penaunce or howe shuld we doo penaunce, lest happelie þat we take on vs that we mai not fulfille, and oure praieris be nat herde and God turne his face from þou so?"[44] Adam responds that each of them should take a stone and stand upon it in a river, Adam in the Jordan and Eve in the Tigris, in neck-high water for forty days—Adam vows to remain for forty-seven, the extra week an acknowledgment of the time it took God to bring forth all of creation—where they are also to observe silence in recognition of their unworthiness even to praise God because of the defilement of their lips.

Adam, however, cannot help but to ignore his own advice, and upon mounting his rock in the Jordan, he begins to lament:

> I seie to the, Iordan, gedre togidir thi wawes and alle living beestis within the and com about me and make sorowe [with] me, but for youreselff make ye noo sorowe but alle for me, for ye haue nat synned, but I wickidlie ayenst my Lorde haue synned; nothir ye did noo defaute, ne ye were nat begilid from your sustenaunce ne from youre meetis ordained for you, but I am begilid fro my sustenaunce the whiche was ordained for me.[45]

Adam's appreciation for the consequences of his actions is notably limited: his preoccupation with whence his next meal will come distracts him from the far more serious matter of his moral failure. And while Adam's misprision of the grievousness of his predicament veers uncomfortably towards the comic for the reader of the *Gilte Legende*, his sorrow over the potential consequences of that failure, including the likelihood of his starving, is genuine. The narrator describes Adam's outpouring of anguish as a "lamentacion with sighynge and sorowefulle teeris."[46] Adam's wailing further compels all living things, those that go on land as well as those surrounding him in the waters of the Jordan, to still themselves and then join him "in making sorowe."[47] In the short term, Adam's sorrow, as well as the sorrow of the creatures that make common cause with him, draw unwanted attention from the fiend, who, again donning the guise of an angel, assays once more to tempt Eve, this time by convincing her that her own penance performed in the Tigris suffices to offset her sin and to earn her alimentary relief. Adam, upon discovering this latest ruse, drops to the ground "and his sorowe was doubled."[48] Distraught, Adam begs the fiend for some explanation of his relentless pursuit of the first couple's destruction, upon which the devil discloses his envy at having been displaced by Adam, who learns of his own creation in God's image and likeness as a replacement for the fallen angels (Figure 3.3). The *Gilte Legende* narrates further the travails of postlapsarian existence, including those that accompany Eve's discovery of her pregnancy, although Adam's steadfastness in performing penances eventually leads to succor in the form of an angelic visitation at the time of her delivery and the passing on of knowledge of how to work the land. Nevertheless, the *Legende*'s reliance on the diction of sorrow in narrating the travails of Adam and Eve reminds us that the story of their exile is fundamentally a tragic one. In response to the tragedy of Genesis, and with attention to

FIGURE 3.3: Eve prevented from performing penance in the Jordan by the devil disguised as an angel from *La Penitance Adam* translated from Latin into French by Colard Mansion. Paris, Bibliothèque de l'Arsenal MS 5092 réserve, f. 5v. Courtesy of the Bibliothèque Nationale de France.

the embodiment of sorrow through the attendant acts of lamenting, sighing, and weeping, the *Gilte Legende* stages a performance of penitential behavior for the benefit of the reader in direct response to Eve's request for a demonstration of penance. Adam's response to his tragic undoing instructs his reader in the proper performance of repentance through the expression of sorrow. Indeed, where Adam fails to grasp the long-term significance of his disobedience for re-charting the course of human history, readers of the *Gilte Legende* who choose to perform their own sorrow in imitation of that of their progenitors do so as ethical actors more fully cognizant of the stakes.

Dramatic retellings of the Expulsion from York and Chester have much in common with the performance of sorrow as an appropriate response to tragedy modeled by Adam in the *Gilte Legende*'s version of the afterlives of the first parents.[49] Both of these scripts feature Adam bemoaning his and Eve's fallen state, and in both pageants this monologic act of lamentation stands out from the surrounding dramatic dialogue and functions as a form of direct address to the audience. Both also offer, moreover, opportunities for the kind of "ethical" interpretation proposed by Trevet as appropriate to dramatic tragedy and for uncovering the plays' strategies for eliciting emotional responses from their consumers.

The York Armourers' portrayal of the Expulsion stands as a distinct episode among the more than four dozen pageants performed by the members of York's craft guilds between at least 1376, from when the earliest record of the spectacle survives, and its final performance in 1569.[50] This creation-to-doom cycle of biblical plays was the pinnacle of the city's annual celebration of the still relatively young Feast of Corpus Christi, which had become part of the ritual year of the universal Church only in 1264. Each pageant traced a path through the city stopping at a series of preassigned stations that varied from year to year. At each station the pageant was performed anew for York's citizens who filled the streets, excepting those wealthy enough to rent a view from seats on scaffolds erected for the occasion.[51]

Little can be said definitively about the anonymous authors of the York pageants. Likely they were several in number, although it is just as likely that a single editor revised many of the plays at a later moment. The scripts survive in a lone copy, the so-called York Register, probably compiled in the 1460s and 1470s for a very specific use: the Register was kept by the city clerk, who tracked each performance to ensure that the annual event conformed to the civic authorities' expectation, with notes in the manuscript in the hand of the clerk hinting at occasional departures from the official script.[52] Discreet pageants were staged by members of York's craft guilds, whose responsibilities for supporting the annual production were carefully regulated by the city's ruling class. Scholars have long recognized the potential for well and lavishly executed pageants to elevate the social reputation of individual corporations within York's competitive guild hierarchy; as Nicole R. Rice and Margaret Aziza Pappano have observed, "the phenomenon of civic religious drama evolved in tandem with artisanal organization and status in the urban centers of premodern Chester and York."[53]

York breaks the Genesis account into several distinct episodes, not unlike the episodic rendering of the creation of the world and of humankind in the stained-glass program of the Great East Window in York Minster (Figure 3.4). The play of the Expulsion commences with the Angel announcing the first couple's recent reversal of fortune and emphasizing the woe into which they have willfully plunged themselves. Indeed, to drive the point home, the Angel employs *woo* or *wa* in end rhymes no fewer than five times in this relatively short 168-line scene (lines 4, 22, 57, 71, and 167).[54] Following the Angel's

FIGURE 3.4: York Minster, Great East Window: The Expulsion of Adam and Eve. Courtesy of Alamy.

relentless upbraiding and threats of perpetual sorrow—another word that appears frequently in this pageant, as it did in the *Gilte Legende*'s account—Eve ceases rehashing the past events that precipitated their exile and looks instead to the future: "Allas, for doole, what shall Y doo? / Now mon I neuer haue rest ne roo" (75–6). Adam replies with the longest speech in the pageant (lines 77–122), which amounts to more than a quarter of the scripted text. Adam notably dwells throughout his speech not on his alienation from God on account of his sin but rather on his separation from the material abundance and total obedience that distinguished life in Paradise. "For putte we were to great plenté/ At prime of þe day," mourns Adam. "Be tyme of none alle lost had wee" (89–92). "Alle bestis were to my biddyng bayne," he wails, "And nowe is alle thynge me agayne / Þat gois on grounde" (94, 97–8). Like his counterpart in the *Gilte Legende*, this Adam takes a short-sighted view of his new predicament, while the citizens of York, who in many cases would have shared Adam's preoccupations with material prosperity and earthly dominion, are challenged by the performance to see the bigger picture. After all, Adam had no moral exemplars and no tragic forebears from whom to learn ethical behavior; the same cannot be said of his descendants.

The York pageant signals this invitation to identify with, lament alongside of, and ultimately choose differently from Adam through a striking shift in the structure of the play's verse form at this point. Adam's speech is noteworthy and otherwise unique within this play for the concatenation that connects the last word or phrase of each stanza to a repetition of or variation on that word or phrase in the first line of the succeeding stanza:[55]

> Nay, lo, swilke a tole is taken me too
> To trauaylle tyte;
> Nowe is shente both I and shoo,
> Allas, for syte.
>
> Allas, for syte and sorowe sadde,
> Mournynge makis me mased and madde,
> To thynke in herte what helpe Y hadde,
> And nowe has none.
> On grounde mon I neuyr goo gladde,
> My gamys ere gane.
>
> Gone are my games . . . .
>
> —77–87

And so on. Adam's lamentation is thus formally marked and differentiated from the dialogue that surrounds it. These formal shifts in the play signal the importance of Adam's speech for the audience, especially given that the act of the Expulsion itself proceeds with minimal fuss; Adam's lamentation is the pageant's dramatic highpoint.

In an effort to bring the work of historians of emotion to bear on literary study, Sarah McNamer has explored how texts can elicit emotion from their audiences by building on Stanley Fish's concept of "affective stylistics" as a means to account for a performative text's production of emotion. To the question "how do texts make *feeling*?" McNamer points to "literary techniques of many kinds—emplotment, rhythm, repetition, imagery, narrative pace, and so on—[that] manifestly invite attention for the way they can generate feeling."[56] If genre serves to structure a contract built on mutual expectations between producers and consumers, then feelings serve as the currency of that transaction and are elicited through the kinds of conspicuous literary devices—a long monologue featuring direct address to the audience, concatenated stanzas, the diction of sorrow and sorrowing—deployed uniquely at this moment in the pageant.

The York playwright arguably presents Adam as a tragic figure who, like Trevet's version of Seneca's raging Hercules, functions to caution spectators against taking their good fortune for granted and who might have benefited from having less good fortune in the first place. Adam steps outside the bounds of human history but also of salvation history: his fall is, of course, fortunate in that it sets up the inevitable redemption to be wrought by Christ in the fullness of time, but as a tragic figure he also invites "ethical" response from the audience. Adam emerges from the pageant not as original man but as everyman: his fall generates what McNamer calls "affective dissonance," whereby "a text elicits opposing emotions [that] can expose the way it functions *cognitively*, producing a desire to resolve affective conflict through new ways of thinking." By inviting the audience to identify with Adam, the play moves its witnesses to engage in their own performances of penitential sorrow in acknowledgment of past transgressions, for, as McNamer avers, affective dissonance can "operate as a progressive force in history."[57]

Adam reprises his role as tragic figure in the *Play of Adam and Eve* performed by the Drapers of Chester. Like the York Corpus Christi play, the Chester cycle of biblical dramas witnessed regular performance beginning not later than the first half of the fifteenth century and continuing until 1575, when, through pressure from Puritans recently returned to England from their Marian exile to the Continent, the staging of biblical plays in Chester was discontinued.[58] As is similarly true for York, the circumstances surrounding the composition of individual pageants in Chester cannot be securely ascertained, notwithstanding the surviving banns erroneously proclaiming the author to be one of Chester's most famous fourteenth-century literary citizens, the Benedictine Ranulf Higden. The citizens of Chester performed their pageants during Whitsuntide, the three days of celebration accompanying the midsummer feast of Pentecost.

Chester embeds the Expulsion within a longer pageant that commences with Creation and concludes with Cain's murder of Abel. Adam's lament follows upon God's pronouncement of the threefold punishment of the serpent, Eve, and Adam and just before God drives the sinners from Paradise. While Chester compresses Adam's lamentation, the playwright, not unlike his counterpart from York, signals a shift at this moment in the script, in this case by means of a Middle English stage direction indicating that "Adam shall speake mourninglye" (s.d. 344+) a monologue directed not to the other characters in the pageant but to the audience:

> Alas, now in longer I am ilente!
> Alas, nowe shamely am I shente!
> For I was unobedyente,
> of weale now am I wayved.
> Nowe all my kynde by mee ys kente
> to flee womens intycemente.
> Whoe trusteth them in any intente,
> truely hee is disceaved.
>
> My licourouse wyfe hath bynne my foe;
> the devylls envye shente mee alsoe.
> These too together well may goe,
> the suster and the brother.
> His wrathe hathe donne me muche woe,
> hir glotonye greved me alsoe.
> God lett never man trust you too,
> the one more then the other.
>
> —345–60[59]

Chester's Adam, like York's, fails to recognize the stakes: his preoccupation with punishment distracts him from the grim consequences of alienation from God. And even more explicitly than Adam in the York pageant, he offers himself as a cautionary tale so that all his "kynde" may be "kente" by his example. His speech ultimately and regrettably devolves into the familiar tropes of medieval antifeminist discourse as he lays the blame for his fall at the feet of his wayward helpmate, but the moral of the story is more broadly stipulated: never trust those who are out to deceive you. The playwright minimizes the enormity of original sin and its consequences for human salvation in favor of pedestrian marital advice about "lickourouse" wives. Yet, the final cause, to return to Trevet, remains "the correction of behaviors through the examples here supplied." Adam's story thus functions both universally and domestically as a tragedy.

CONCLUSION

This essay has sought to illuminate the ways in which tragedy functions as a viable generic category in the Middle Ages at the intersection of its producers and consumers. Nicholas Trevet's commentaries on the tragedies of Seneca adumbrate a form of ethical interpretation influenced by scholasticism and aimed at uncovering the moral meaning of ancient stories for late-medieval readers, while contemporary dramatizations of the Expulsion figure Adam as humanity's forefather and through him stage lessons in the performance of penitential sorrow suitable for imitation by the Christian citizens of England's cities. Together these texts suggest that tragedy remains a viable category for interrogating and understanding the culture of the Middle Ages long before its supposed rebirth in the sixteenth century. To be sure, we are a long way from the Greeks or Shakespeare—and even, indeed, from Seneca. But if we take medieval ideas about genre on their own terms, we can begin to uncover cultural forces that shaped the production of tragic texts and the expectations of the communities who consumed them.

CHAPTER FOUR

Philosophy and Social Theory

ANTONIO DONATO AND ERITH JAFFE-BERG

What happened to tragedy in the Middle Ages? The traditional scholarly answer is that, during this period, tragedy entered a long, dark phase which ended only with the Renaissance.[1] The plays of Aeschylus, Euripides, and Sophocles were almost forgotten, according to this narrative, and there was only a vague understanding of Athenian drama. The word *tragoedia* (and its cognates) was often surrounded by an aura of confusion and obscurity and the term was used in a great variety of senses which seem to have little in common with one another. Moreover, the decline and near disappearance of Athenian drama was the result of a broader cultural phenomenon: the Christian rejection of classical culture.

More recently, scholars have successfully challenged this bleak account.[2] They have argued that, during this period, tragedy underwent not a decline but a transformation. In this view, the medieval departure from the classical Athenian ways of understanding and performing tragedy should be construed not as a betrayal of its essence, but a development in the history of its continuous transformations. Tragedy had never been static: already in the third century BCE tragedies were no longer conceptualized and performed in the ways they had been just a century before. Followers of this new reading also urge us to consider medieval tragedy in its own right and to individuate its features, instead of assessing its value in terms of its departure from its classical origin as most scholars had done traditionally. These current studies have predominantly examined this topic by reconsidering the medieval meanings of *tragoedia*, tracing the transmission of classical plays, and investigating dramas characteristic of the medieval period.

There is, however, a further source of information that scholars have mostly neglected so far: philosophical analyses. The benefit of considering tragedy through the prism of what medieval philosophers had to say about it is not merely that of adding yet another piece to a very intricate puzzle. It also allows us to recognize the conceptual framework in which the modifications of tragedy took place, understand the theoretical motivations behind such changes, and identify the common threads that connect the various senses of *tragoedia* developed during the Middle Ages. Indeed, the examination of these philosophical accounts reveals not only what philosophers did for tragedy, but also what it did for them: these theoretical reflections led medieval thinkers to develop new ways of conceptualizing human life. The influence of philosophy on tragedy and of tragedy on philosophy, however, can be fully appreciated only when we also examine the capacious role of performance in the Middle Ages. During this period, the social function of theater was all pervasive—it was a means of marking occasions; a mechanism for coping with suffering, loss, sorrow, and conflict; as well as a force for communal cohesion and a way of marking differences and thereby solidifying religious and cultural identity, be it Christian, Muslim, or Jewish.[3] As Kathleen Ashley has recently written: "The sheer volume and variety of medieval performances make any single generalization about social functions problematic."[4] Acknowledging this, we begin by discussing medieval theories of tragedy and their transformation and then, in the final section, we highlight a few important ways in which medieval ideas of tragedy found expression in theatrical forms, in both Christian and non-Christian communities.

I. THEORIES OF TRAGEDY IN LATE ANTIQUITY

Scholars agree that late antiquity was a time of intense debate about tragedy. Followers of the traditional view focus almost exclusively on the vehement criticisms formulated by Christian thinkers;[5] those who adopt the new perspective offer a more balanced picture by showing how both pagan and Christian intellectuals developed negative as well as positive evaluations.[6] Both interpretations, however, miss a crucial feature of these late antique assessments of tragedy. Although this debate was a response to specific historical and cultural transformations, it was also a reformulation of a much older dispute which had arisen in tandem with tragedy's development in the fifth century BCE. Late antique authors often borrowed their arguments from Plato and Aristotle and, just like their classical predecessors, considered tragedy contentious because of its ethical, pedagogical, political, and religious implications. Thus, we need to ask why late antique authors followed their classical predecessors so closely in their evaluations of tragedy. Why, indeed, did this type of drama provoke such strong reactions from its very inception until late antiquity?

Although a full assessment of this issue is far beyond the scope of this analysis, one element seems to stand out. In antiquity, tragedy was not simply a form of entertainment; it was an incredibly powerful and influential cultural force which aimed to awaken people's minds to all sorts of moral, political, and religious issues. While Aeschylus, Euripides, and Sophocles did not explicitly articulate a philosophy, a political ideology, or a theology, each of them conveyed a distinct and original worldview. Perhaps the most controversial contribution of all these dramatists was the pedagogical model they proposed. From Socrates and the Sophists onwards, the philosophical education propagated in classical Athens was characterized by the dialectical method, i.e., the careful, rational examination of competing claims to assess the truth. By contrast, the tragedians offered a "sentimental education" in which learning occurred via the emotional experience of witnessing a tragic performance—an experience that constituted a pathway to knowledge about human agency, society, and the nature of gods. Moreover, classical tragedy's focus on human emotions was often perceived to be at odds with the classical ideal of self-restraint as a key moral virtue.

Tragedy's significant cultural role in ancient Athens naturally made it a force to contend with for philosophers, intellectuals, and religious leaders. If we limit our attention to Plato and Aristotle, we see that, in spite of their differences, they agreed that philosophy needs to take tragedy very seriously, whether to reject or integrate it. They believed that tragedy's strength comes from two sources. One is its ability to have a transformative effect on people's characters and behavior by affecting their emotions; the other is its capacity to articulate a compelling account of reality. Plato famously regarded tragedy as a dangerous and deleterious competitor for philosophy.[7] Aristotle saw in it an ally which fulfills the same, fundamental human desire that philosophy also tries to satisfy: curiosity.[8]

In light of our analysis, it is not surprising that the rise of Christian tragedy re-engendered this intense debate. The new religion could not overlook a genre of performance and poetry which, though changed over time, still conveyed ethical values, views of the divine, a pedagogical model and, more generally, a worldview. Tragedy was not a problem because it was pagan; it was a problem since it offered a particular way of conceptualizing reality—one that even ancient Greek thinkers had difficulty integrating with their mindset. Christian thinkers had managed to assimilate (at least in part) classical philosophy by adopting its methodology, arguments, language, etc. However, when it came to tragedy, their reactions were mostly negative. But what aspects of tragedy did Christian thinkers find so problematic?

Christians often rejected tragedy for reasons that were not too dissimilar from Plato's and, in fact, they often employed watered-down versions of his arguments. Moreover, Christians agreed on the value of self-restraint that featured so prominently in the Greco-Roman moral outlook. Thus, we should not be surprised to find out that Christian thinkers were very concerned that the extreme emotions that people regularly experienced when attending tragedies could affect their psychological balance and lead to erratic, if not dangerous, behaviors. For example, Tertullian (c. 155–c. 240) warns his readers of the dangers of tragedy by mentioning the case of a woman who experienced such emotional distress after watching a performance that she became completely insane and died soon after.[9] Similarly, in the *Confessions*, Augustine (354–430) regards watching tragedy as a form of madness since it amounts to exposing oneself to negative emotions that one would never want to experience in real life.[10] In the *Republic*, Plato is driven by the same concern when he bans tragic poetry from the ideal state. He worries about the effects that strong emotions can have on young individuals as well as people in whose souls rationality is not fully developed.[11] Christian thinkers, just like many pagan intellectuals, promoted a pedagogical model according to which a person's character is formed and maintained by limiting the type and the intensity of the emotions to which he is exposed. By contrast, poets and dramatists, both in the classical and late antique eras, suggested that the pedagogical value of their works consisted in guiding people to improve their characters by accessing their emotions and developing them in refined ways. Augustine's famous disdain towards his own youthful emotional reaction to reading of Dido's suicide in the *Aeneid* is indicative of this response.[12] Augustine argues that he should have worried about his own troubles instead of sympathizing with the Carthaginian queen, and his comment appears to deny that poetry can help us to become more mature and humane individuals by teaching us the depth and complexity of human emotions.

Christian philosophers also borrowed from Plato the argument that tragedies are dangerous because they portray deplorable actions.[13] For example, Augustine criticizes tragedies for depicting human beings behaving in despicable ways instead of showing positive examples of how men should act. Yet the most insidious feature of these plays, he adds, is that they do not just *describe* people who act in immoral ways but, worse, they make us empathize with individuals who do not deserve our pity.[14] It appears that both Plato and Augustine were concerned with the potential moral ambiguity of the human beings portrayed in tragedies. They seem to argue that when, for example, we empathize with characters who commit atrocious acts, our own sense of right and wrong is overridden. The problem with this critique is that it attributes to tragedies a kind of moral relativism when, in fact, they aim to show that true moral character consists not only in distinguishing right from wrong but also in being capable of feeling empathy even for the wicked.

A further concern was tragedies' ability to influence people. For example, the Christian teacher Lactantius (*c*. 250–*c*. 325) opined that the refined verbal skills of poets bewitch our minds into focusing on the lascivious things portrayed onstage instead of the truths revealed by God.[15] Similarly, Tertullian observed that tragedies divert people from reading the Bible through the captivating beauty of their music and words.[16] These arguments were not new in late antiquity. Plato's contemporary, the sophist Gorgias, warned his readers of language's power to control people's minds and compared poetry to a drug and a magic spell.[17] Plato, in book seven of the *Laws*, suggests that tragic plays are dangerous because they have the capacity to sway people's minds.[18] Hence, Christian thinkers' attack on tragedy was only superficially a new fight arising from the clash between Christian and pagan ideals. It was, in fact, an old fight conducted with old arguments, and it was sparked not so much by religious differences but, as it had been in Plato's time, by the enormous cultural power of tragedy and the message it conveyed. It was, above all, tragedy's underlying assumption that true character is developed only when a person fully confronts and explores his emotions that all of these thinkers, from Plato onwards, found so problematic.

Hitherto, a focus on the evaluations of Christian thinkers has prevented scholars from considering the more positive analyses of tragedy formulated by Neo-Platonists. The great cultural significance of this philosophical school was due, in part, to its widespread popularity throughout the Mediterranean world: its main centers were in Apamea (Syria), Alexandria, Athens, and Rome. The influence of Neo-Platonism was also due to its attempted synthesis of the entire philosophical tradition of the Greco-Roman world. When it came to tragedy, Neo-Platonists faced the challenge of reconciling Plato's radical rejection, in the *Republic*, with Aristotle's qualified defense in the *Poetics*. In his commentary on the *Republic*, for example, the Athenian Neo-Platonist Proclus (412–85) follows Plato in rejecting tragedy, but with some telling exceptions.[19] He repeatedly observes that tragedy is particularly dangerous for the young, leaving room for the possibility that mature and well-balanced people may be able to enjoy it without suffering its deleterious effects.[20] Even more significantly, Proclus is willing to concede that tragedy has moral and pedagogical value, but only for those who are not capable of studying philosophy. He argues that tragedy is an inferior kind of poetry (i.e., mimetic poetry) since it portrays the material and not the intelligible world; but it plays a crucial role in the moral education of less intellectually gifted individuals by familiarizing them with the complexity of human nature.[21]

Olympiodorus (495–570), one of the leading figures of the Neo-Platonic school of Alexandria, is even more explicit about the moral value of tragedy. In the *Life of Plato*, he shows tragedy's positive role in forming a person's character by making clever use of a famous episode from the philosopher's life. Plato's pursuit of a career as tragic poet in his youth, before he gave it up for philosophy,[22] is taken to suggest that acquaintance with tragedy is an important, though preliminary, step in a person's education. Olympiodorus' argument seems to reflect a common practice in Neo-Platonic schools, in which students were first exposed to literature, including tragic plays, before approaching the study of philosophy.[23] The rationale of this pedagogical system was that tragedies helped young people to recognize and educate their emotions. The most explicit defense of Greek tragedy is found in the work of the Syrian Iamblichus (245–325) whose *On the Egyptian Mysteries* stresses the cathartic effects of watching tragedies as well as comedies.[24] He argues that the purification of extreme emotions brought about by attending dramatic performances has the moral value of helping a person attain the balanced psychological state necessary for conducting a virtuous life.

Although the qualified defenses of tragedy formulated by Neo-Platonic thinkers were not very detailed and had limited cultural impact, a decisive theoretical contribution to the debate on tragedy came from Boethius' *Consolation of Philosophy* (henceforth *Consolation*). In this, his last work, this Roman statesman (d. 524) offers a powerful integration of philosophy and, not just tragedy, but poetry in general. The *Consolation* is a dialogue in which the personification of philosophy (*Philosophia*) consoles the character Boethius[25] by conveying her ideas in both prose and in poetry. In the initial part of the dialogue, she distinguishes "bad" from "good" poetry.[26] The first consists in indulging and fueling our negative emotions; the second in guiding us to overcome them. *Philosophia* also notes that, while bad poetry simply conveys emotions, the good integrates them with reason. The poems she composes thus place the prisoner's emotional distress within the broader framework of her philosophical worldview.

The *Consolation*'s distinction between good and bad poetry constitutes a distinctive advancement in the debate on tragedy since it offers a convincing way out of the clash between Platonic rejections and qualified Aristotelian defenses. The strength of this solution consists in shifting the focus of the discussion from the considerations of the effects of poetry to that of its intent. According to Boethius, any poetry is good so long as it is composed not to fuel emotions but to overcome them by integrating them within a philosophical perspective. Boethius' elegant theory also provided Christian authors with the ideal justification—and tools—for making tragedy acceptable and even compatible with the Christian liturgy, as we will see in section two. In some cases (*e.g.*, Honorius Augustodunensis), the integration of tragedy within Christian liturgy went as far as comparing the church to a theater and conceptualizing the Mass as a tragic play that portrays Christ's Passion. The goal of this unique type of performance was considered to be the promotion of community identity and the attainment of collective catharsis.[27]

The power of the *Consolation*'s integration of philosophy and poetry, combined with the extraordinary influence that this work had throughout the Middle Ages, led to the virtual disappearance of the debate about the dangers of tragedy from Christian Latin literature in all genres, including that of music. It may be easy for us to forget that Athenian tragedies were (mostly) musical events,[28] but this was not lost on late antique philosophers whose analyses of tragedy belonged to the broader context of their discussion on music, which was not distinguishable from poetry. Neo-Platonists' views on tragedy reflected their more general attitude towards music: they were aware of its extraordinary capacity to transform the human soul, for better or for worse. Indeed, Neo-Platonists devoted much more attention to the examination of music than to the study of tragedy.[29] Neo-Platonic schools went as far establishing strict rules as to what types of music were allowed and which types of melodies should be played at different times of the day.[30] In the initial pages of his treatise *On Music*, Boethius offers a short but effective overview of these theories, focusing particularly on the capacity of certain types of music to create and maintain balance and harmony in the human soul.[31] Like his *Consolation*, *On Music* had great influence throughout the Middle Ages. Since music was one of the seven medieval liberal arts that any educated person was expected to learn, Boethius' treatise became one of the standard reference texts. In *On Music*, medieval thinkers found an effective theoretical demonstration of music's spiritual value of music. In practice, moreover, music came to play a crucial role in the religious and civic functions of medieval society.

II. THE LEGACIES OF LATE ANTIQUE THEORIES OF TRAGEDY IN MEDIEVAL MUSICAL PRAXIS

Developments in musical practice during the Middle Ages reveal how emotive performance fulfilled tragedy's social function of expressing suffering, providing solace, reinforcing community, and performing conflict in various religious and cultural communities. Vocal and instrumental performance traditions in various religious and cultural contexts range from Mozarabic/Visigothic, Gregorian, and Jewish chants to the complex melodic and lyric structures of thirteenth-century polyphony and the lamentations of late medieval Italian *laudesti*. In all these cases, musical expression was a vehicle for collectively sharing intensely individual feelings, cultivating and establishing what Barbara H. Rosenwein has termed "emotional communities."[32]

Just as late antique philosophers worried about overly emotional performances, so authorities in both Jewish and Christian communities strove to balance the desire for the expression of strong emotions within the liturgy with the need for their control. One significant result of this was the policing and suppression of texts recording these traditions, which appear to emerge only in the ninth and tenth centuries (in both contexts) but are really much older practices. Within the Jewish context, liturgical poems or *piyyutim*, in both Hebrew and Aramaic, were often sung or chanted during religious services. Their development in the fourth and fifth centuries is often overlooked, yet this period corresponded to the emergence of Christian liturgical poetry and reveals many shared elements, notably an especially pronounced degree of heightened and even theatrical expression.[33] For example, the Avodah *piyyut*, which dates back to the fourth to seventh centuries, was recited during the Yom Kippur service (day of repentance/atonement) and contains very physical and heightened elements, which may explain why the service was heavily monitored and, at times, supressed by rabbinical authorities. Much as Carol Symes has argued that Bishop Æthelwold of Winchester's "Concordance of Rules" for monastic performance in Anglo-Saxon England is "not the beginning of a performance practice; it is an attempt to put an end to one," the usual narrative of the *piyyutim*'s development in connection with the more fulsome Andalusian poetic expression of the ninth and tenth centuries is misleading and belies its emergence many centuries earlier.[34]

The Avodah *piyyut* enacts a performance in which "the congregation would call, 'perform our sacrifice.'"[35] During the service, the leader of the *piyyut* (a hazan/cantor or even the *payetan*/composer himself) would accordingly prostrate himself, along with the congregation, reciting a song in praise of God. It is possible that a chorus of singers would then respond.[36] These are surprising elements to find in the Jewish service because the prostration foregrounded an implicit performativity and an overt emotionality. As Michael Swartz and Joseph Yahalom put it: "[t]his service, with its unusual prostration, its detailed discourse on sacrifice, and its historical sweep, is unique in the liturgy of the synagogue. To modern Jews, it has been the subject of attraction – consternation."[37] Despite their repeated rabbinical suppression, the *piyyutim* were preserved among Jewish communities throughout the Middle East and the Mediterranean, and were accepted and flowered in the later period of Sephardic (Iberian/Andalusian) *piyyutim* of the eleventh and twelfth centuries with the work of well-recognized poets such as Yehudah ha-Levi (Judah ha-levi) and Solomon Ibn Gabirol. Ha-Levi and Ibn Gabirol are known for their poems of longing and suffering in the face of exile and physical pain, to which we will return.

In the Christian context, hymns, psalms, and other liturgical elements served a similar emotive function. As Symes has shown, the genres of tragedy, song, drama, and psalmody are often interchangeable in the writings of influential medieval commentators.[38] Indeed, Bruce Holsinger has suggested that Christianity's emphasis on embodiment was reflected in discourses on music as a mediator between the human and the divine, as in the case of Hildegard of Bingen (1098–1179).[39] In extreme cases, the "musicality of the body in pain provided a mode of direct identification with the sounds of Christ's suffering," as in the songs that accompanied the processions of flagellants during the Black Death.[40] Holsinger thereby reveals the central paradox of musicality as both a source of comfort and expression of physical anguish. "A 'psalm' represents the antithesis of violence. A psalm by its very nature heals, reconciles, and erases social difference" and yet, at the same time, "music and bodily violence coexisted intimately in the religious culture of the Christian Middle Ages, so much so that in many cases music is violence."[41] In late medieval Italy, for example, groups of lay confraternities, known as *laudesti*, developed processional musical compositions as a means of expressing communal solidarity, rage, and suffering in the face of adversity and urban conflict.[42] Eventually, performances of these *laude* incorporated dramatic elements (*lauda drammatica*) connected with the development of Italian vernacular theater, a practice documented in the fourteenth century but almost certainly much older.[43]

Meanwhile, music as a means of performing and even resolving conflict was inherent in the performance of polyphony: multi-vocal musical compositions which captured and harmonized seemingly incompatible melodic and lyric lines. First documented in the bustling urban centers of Paris and Arras, the polyphonic motet can be considered "a dialogue of voices" but it is also, as Alex Novikoff has shown, an embodiment of disagreement or disputation (*disputatio*).[44] Another musical genre that replicates disagreement and resolution is the dialogical *jeu-parti*, "a vernacular genre of sung debate in which two or more singers argued for and against a given question."[45] The hundreds of *jeux-partis* surviving from the Franco-Flemish city of Arras were also expressions of potential class warfare performed by minstrels, clerics, citizens, and aristocrats and can be seen as musical forms of conflict resolution.[46]

In these ways, in various religious communities, music made possible tragedy's social function as an expression for both sorrow and solace. In other musical expressions, the presence of conflict is marked when music provided an opportunity for engaging in disputations and disagreements. In the next section, we turn to the social functions of tragedy in Byzantium.

III. TRAGEDY AND SOCIETY IN BYZANTIUM[47]

In Byzantium, tragedy did not attract the attention of philosophers in ways comparable to developments in the Latin West, but it did play a crucial role in the conscious revival of Hellenism which, from the eleventh to the thirteenth century, led to the development of a new cultural and political identity among elites in the eastern Roman Empire.[48] Tragedy was central to Byzantine education; around the tenth century, grammarians identified the tragedies that needed to be part of the permanent curriculum. They were known as the "Triads": three plays for each of the three great Greek tragedians (*Prometheus Bound, Persians, Seven against Thebes* by Aeschylus; *Ajax, Electra, Oedipus the King* by Sophocles; and *Hecuba, Orestes, Phoenician Women* by Euripides). The study of these plays was supposed to help young men, aspiring to hold high political office, to become fluent in the sophisticated and highly literary language of the imperial court and familiar with the cultural tradition and values of the society they intended to serve. The general preference for Euripides—to the point that he was simply called "the Tragedian"—was motivated by a preference for his elegant language, especially vis-à-vis Aeschylus' more difficult style.

But the Byzantine interest in tragedy was not simply pedagogical. Although theoretical analyses of the emotional impact of tragedies are not comparable to those of the Neo-Platonists, John Tzetzes (c. 1110–80), in his commentary on Aristophanes' *Frogs*, reflects on how lamentation songs by Euripides can move people to tears. Michael Psellus (c. 1018–78) also highlights the emotional power of Euripides' plays by reporting that they caused many Athenians to cry.[49] The Euripidean *Christos Paschon* is one of the most compelling examples of tragedy's contribution to shaping a cultural identity which integrated Hellenism with Christianity. This play is a Christian drama which tells the story of Christ's Passion and Resurrection by threading together verses taken from seven plays of Euripides (*Hecuba, Orestes, Medea, Hippolytus, Trojan Women, Rhesus*, and *Bacchae*). Its re-appropriation of these tragedies in the service of sacred history is one of the author's explicit goals: "I shall recite the world-saving Passion in Euripides' style."[50] The *Christos Paschon* is therefore a testimony to the great familiarity with Greek tragedy on the part of the audience, and some of its more climatic moments assume the audience's ability to identify the origin of the verses cited. For example, the moving scene of Christ's body being battered loses much of its power if the audience is unable to recognize that some of the verses employed are taken from the famous passage of the *Bacchae* which depicts the dismemberment of King Pentheus.[51]

Tragedy had an impact on the Byzantine world that was as decisive as the one it had on the classical world and the Latin Middle Ages. It helped the Byzantines to define and articulate their Greek identity by giving them a common language and conceptual landscape. However, it also provided them with essential linguistic and intellectual tools to integrate their Greek identity with their Christian one.

IV. THEORIES OF TRAGEDY IN THE LATE MEDIEVAL WEST

The hallmark of later medieval analyses of tragedy is the proliferation of the meanings attached to the word *tragoedia* (and its cognates). During this period, as Symes has shown, tragedy is used to refer to the poetic and performative genre of classical antiquity, divisions within the Church, dramatic changes in the life of a community, a way of conceptualizing and narrating historical events, and a way of talking about various types of performance.[52] However, a crucial question remains to be addressed: What explains the development of these numerous and diverse senses of *tragoedia*? An overview of contemporary philosophical analyses of tragedy helps to explain this proliferation.

Medieval philosophers did not formulate assessments of tragedy comparable in depth and complexity to those of their late antique predecessors since, due to the re-interpretations of its meaning and goals formulated by late antique thinkers such as Boethius and Honorius Augustodunensis, it was no longer perceived to be as controversial as early Christian thinkers believed. However, central to the investigations of those who do discuss the concept is the reception of two philosophical texts: Aristotle's *Poetics* and Boethius' *Consolation*. Boethius' last work not only formulated the distinction between good and bad poetry we have studied above; it also contains a brief reference to tragedy that was destined to become very influential: "What else does the cry of tragedies lament if not the downfall of happy kingdoms brought about by the unpredictable blows of fortune?"⁵³ Boethius thus defines tragedy by alluding to what Aristotle regarded as one of its key features: *peripeteia*, the dramatic change of circumstances which takes a character or a community from one condition to its opposite (e.g., from happiness to despair).⁵⁴ Medieval readers, however, understood Boethius' remark not only as a definition of tragedy but also as a way of conceptualizing a specific type of human experience. In other words, Boethius' learned gesture to Aristotle became the starting point for the development of the idea of tragedy.

But how could this interpretation be possible at all? The answer lies in the context of Boethius' analysis. In this section of the *Consolation*, the personification of the Roman goddess Fortuna tells the character Boethius that his fall is not an exceptional event since it is a common, though unpleasant, occurrence in human affairs. It is because it is so common, she adds, that these losses feature so prominently in tragic plays. Here, Boethius illustrates Fortuna's workings with an image that was common in his time, the "wheel of fortune" (Figure 4.1).⁵⁵ According to this image, life is compared to a wheel that is constantly spinning and on which a human being sits precariously: one moment he is a king, another in ruin. He has no control over the movement of the wheel because it is operated by the goddess herself.

In the light of this vivid imagery, it was not such a stretch for later medieval readers to turn a passing reference to tragedies into a theory of what counts as tragic. This creative reading of the *Consolation* was, perhaps, facilitated by the late antique practice of using the term *tragoedia* to describe terrible events in the lives of people or communities.⁵⁶ However, what distinguishes the idea of tragedy later inspired by the *Consolation* is its very specific scope. "Tragedy" does not indicate a horrible event in a broad sense; it means a sudden, unpredictable, and often underserved loss of "external goods" (i.e., wealth, power, health, friends, family, etc.) brought about by misfortune. As we shall see in section five, this account of tragedy was central to many late medieval literary works and performances. And its popularity may be perceived as surprising since the idea that fortune controls individual destiny seems at odds with Christian beliefs in God's

FIGURE 4.1: *Philosophy Consoling Boethius and Fortune Turning the Wheel*, about 1460–70. Coëtivy Master (Henri de Vulcop?) (French, active about 1450–85). The J. Paul Getty Museum, Los Angeles. Reproduction by permission of the Getty through its Open Content Program.

omnipotence and man's free will. Indeed, medieval philosophers struggled to integrate pagan Fortuna within a Christian framework.[57] However, the view that life is tragic because of fortune's unpredictable actions remained very popular in a wide variety of medieval genres; its enduring success was, perhaps, its ability to capture people's lived experiences.

The idea of tragedy extrapolated from the *Consolation* thus gave rise to what may be called "Boethian tragedies" which depict individuals who suffer extreme, negative changes of fortune. We cannot, however, understand this understanding of tragedy becoming so central without considering late medieval philosophical commentaries on the *Consolation*. In spite of their variety, two lines of interpretations stand out amongst these exegetical works. One was introduced by the philosopher William of Conches (1090–1154), who observed that:

> Tragedy is a writing that describes great crimes; it begins in prosperity and ends in adversity. . . . It is called "tragedy" because its writers were awarded a goat[58] to indicate the baseness of the vices it portrayed.[59]

William changes the meaning of Boethius' words in one crucial way. He states that tragedies deal with the crimes and deeds of wicked people because such changes of fortune can be seen as a deserved punishment for evil behaviors. In William's perspective, fortune is a moralizing force which rights people's wrongs. By contrast, the *Consolation* made it very explicit that what makes Fortuna so terrifying is her moral neutrality: she gives and takes without any consideration of people's moral conduct. William's radical departure from the text may have been motivated by an attempt to integrate Boethius' account with Christianity theology. If the goal of Fortuna is to punish the wicked, then it is not difficult to place her within God's providential plan. Several later commentators (e.g., Nicholas Trevet, the Pseudo Aquinas, William Wheatley) adopted William's interpretation,[60] but its influence went far beyond the confines of learned discussions of Boethius, since it was the foundation of such works as the morality plays discussed in section five.

The *Consolation*'s account of tragedy was also interpreted in a way that remained more faithful to Boethius' meaning. In his influential vernacular commentary, Jean de Meun (c. 1240–c. 1305) defines tragedy as a work which shows how fortune, understood as a morally neutral force, racks the lives of human beings.[61] Geoffrey Chaucer (c. 1342/43–1400) adopted this reading which is, for example, the premise of his *Monk's Tale*:

> I will lament in the manner of tragedy
> The misfortune of those who stood in high degree,
> And fell so that there was no remedy
> To bring them out of their adversity.
> For there is no doubt that, when Fortune desires to flee,
> No man can keep her from leaving.
> Let no man trust on blind prosperity;
> Take head of these examples true and old.[62]

This passage offers a very explicit example of how a philosophical theory about tragedy shapes a literary work. Chaucer does not only report Boethius' view, but most of his stories in the *Monk's Tale* are "Boethian tragedies" illustrating the *Consolation* as interpreted in the manner of Jean de Meun.

So far, a common aspect of the exegeses of Boethius' comment on tragedy do not situate his remark within the broader context of the *Consolation*. Although, in book two, he does claim that the loss of external goods is a cause of despair, in book four he shows that this is only a partial truth and formulates a more complex view. He argues that true unhappiness does not consist in the sudden loss of external goods but in adopting the mistaken mindset that equates happiness with the possession of such goods. On this view, this loss is not a cause of despair because it *reveals* what happiness is ultimately about, i.e., the care of one's soul. In the later Middle Ages, this more complex reading of Boethius led to the development of a new kind of "Boethian tragedy," examples of which can be found in some of the stories contained in Dante's *Inferno* (e.g., Pier delle Vigne, Count Ugolino). These stories *appear* to be tragedies since they depict sudden terrible, material losses. However, when these stories are examined from the broader perspective of the entire poem, it turns out that what makes them tragedies is that they portray characters who consider happiness to depend on the possession of such goods.

The second philosophical text whose influence, or absence, shaped late medieval accounts of tragedy was Aristotle's *Poetics*. Although this work proposes a notoriously narrow account of tragedy, it does contain a very sophisticated philosophical analysis of its features. However, the *Poetics* became available in the Latin world relatively late, when compared to other Aristotelian works, and then only at second hand. In 1256, Hermannus Alemannus (d. 1272) completed a partial Latin translation of the Arabic version by Averroës (1126–98), which had a wide circulation. By contrast, a translation made from the Greek by William of Moerbeke in 1278 was little known and had hardly any contemporary influence. Although this has been described a "missed opportunity,"[63] the scarce diffusion of Aristotle's work gave late medieval thinkers the freedom to articulate various creative ways of thinking about tragedy. If the *Poetics* had been more widely received, Aristotle's authority could have confined the discussion of tragedy as, in fact, it did in the case of other philosophical debates. From this view, the limited impact of the *Poetics* was one of the main reasons why late medieval intellectuals could transform tragedy and conceptualize it in such diverse and original ways.

Although the impact of the *Poetics* on the Latin West was negligible, the influence of Alemannus' translation of its commentary by Averroës played a decisive role.[64] The Arabic philosopher took "tragedy" to mean *madīh* which was then translated into Latin as *encomium*, i.e., a praise song. Averroës thus understood tragedy to be a celebratory poem delivered by a performer in a sophisticated style. In this view, the distinctive feature of tragedy is not its plot but its style. In *On the Eloquence of the Vernacular Tongue*, Dante expanded on this new view by describing tragedy as a high style befitting the social distinction of its characters (e.g., nobles, kings, queens, etc.) and its topics (i.e., arms, virtue, and love).[65] In this analysis, it became possible to regard as tragedies works that differed widely in subject matter and which had never been classified in this way before. For example, Dante regarded certain classical poems as tragedies[66] (e.g., Virgil's *Aeneid*) as well as a specific type of vernacular poetry, the *volgare illustre*.[67] Over a century earlier, Peter of Blois (*c.* 1130–*c.* 1211) had also considered works as diverse as Arthurian romances and the accounts of Christ's Passion to be tragedies.[68] The identification of tragedy with a style or a mode not only broadened the scope of this genre, it also laid the foundation for the development of the modern understanding of tragedy.

During the later Middle Ages, therefore, we witness the development of new and original meanings of *tragoedia* which broadened the scope of tragedy to encompass works as diverse as epic poems, vernacular poetry, Arthurian romances, and depictions of

Christ's Passion. The creation of these new varieties of *tragoedia* did not, however, occur by chance. It was, to a significant extent, the result of the creative reception of two influential Greco-Roman philosophical works, Aristotle's *Poetics* and Boethius' *Consolation*.

V. THE USES OF TRAGEDY IN MEDIEVAL COMMUNITIES: CHRISTIAN, JEWISH, AND MUSLIM

In this section we consider three ways in which medieval ideas of tragedy found expression in the theatrical forms of both Christian and non-Christian communities. First, we consider how tragedy informed medieval presentations of suffering, which was especially essential to the evolving Christian dramaturgy, interlacing emotion and devotion in order to cement communal solidarity. Next, we return to tragedy's association with the Boethian trope of "the wheel of fortune," to which we have already referred. Finally, we review how images, in performance, evoked emotions, drawing on what Theodore Lerud has termed "quick images" and on Aquinas' understanding of images' capacity to awaken inner sensations, exploring how these ideas help to explain tragic dramatization as a conductor of emotions in the highly visual cycle and mystery plays of later medieval Europe.[69]

The late antique understanding of tragedy as an exploration of human suffering was taken up in many medieval theatrical forms. In the Christian context, Job's suffering, Christ's suffering, and the suffering of the saints are tragedies conveyed through a variety of media: icons and manuscript illuminations, altarpieces and the liturgy, hymns and epic poetry, saints' lives and morality plays. Thus, the idea of tragedy became capacious, generous, and capable of encompassing all kinds of human sacrifice and suffering, as well upheavals in the lives of institutions, countries, and communities. In Symes' words, drama in the Middle Ages was "something vital to a culture that was 'absolutely theatrical.'"[70] And as Kathleen Ashley states, "live public performances in the Middle Ages had a prominent and visible role in all Western societies and theatricality permeated the ways in which medieval people thought about their world and created their own place in it."[71] Theatricality was an essential means for making sense of life in the context of a broader Christian viewpoint. According to Donnalee Dox: "theatre schooled medieval playgoers to respond emotionally within (and perhaps, without) the ideological framework of Christianity."[72] Moreover, as we have shown, many of these ideas were already debated in late antiquity.

While a central function of tragic enactment was to underscore the Christian communal experience, there was an added importance in distancing non-Christian groups living within Europe. As Claire Sponsler observed, "[t]he cultural functions of these rituals of walking or riding through towns and cities included the tying together as well as the demarcating of spaces, making visible the patterns of inclusion as well as exclusion in the local community."[73] Sponsler reminds us that the affirmation of corporate identity went hand in hand with an exclusionary function of performance. Indeed, Jody Enders has emphasized the ways in which theatrical performances were used as vehicles for unleashing anti-Semitic vehemence, thus demonizing different religious and cultural communities.[74] "Even as the staged conversion of Jewish characters assured Christians of their own salvation," Dox notes, "it reinforced an ideology of religious intolerance."[75]

Performance was also an important conveyor of "affect-driven responses moment by moment, scenario to scenario."[76] In the Christian context, in which bread and wine are consecrated in the Mass and transformed into the blood and body of Christ, and in which the reception of the Eucharist is an act of communion, the life and suffering of Christ themselves became tragic performances, blurring distinctions in time, performer/audience, and place.[77] In the course of the Middle Ages, as V.A. Kolve has shown, representations of Christ shifted earlier, majestic images of Christ as ruler and judge to later images in which "Christ is depicted suffering on the cross, his body broken and bleeding" (Figure 4.2)[78] The latter, according to Katie Normington, inspired empathy and encouraged piety.[79] To insure the indelibility of the message, moreover, Jody Enders has emphasized that spectacle was important in cementing "the memory of Christ's body in pain."[80] For Enders, "violence is reimagined, reenacted, and commemorated" to become a "medieval theater of cruelty."[81] This idea is reinforced by Normington, who has shown the spectacle of the suffering body of Christ was also a means of underscoring the importance of the sacrament during Corpus Christi commemorations.[82]

FIGURE 4.2: Masters of Dirc van Delf, "The Lamentation," miniature of the Lamentation found in a book of hours, probably created in Utrecht in the Netherlands about 1405–10. The J. Paul Getty Museum, Los Angeles. Reproduced by permission of Getty through its Open Content Program.

Presentation of Corpus Christi plays thus became a salient genre within the wider category of late medieval cycle plays, both reinforcing communal identity and mediating collective emotional responses to the spectacle of suffering. The establishment of a feast dedicated to the body of Christ, and to Christians' corporate worship of its suffering, can be traced to the first official articulation of the dogma of transubstantiation in 1215, and was formalized when Pope Urban IV promulgated a holy day devoted to Christ's Last Supper and its celebration in the Eucharist (1264), which was fixed by Clement V to the Thursday after Trinity Sunday (1311). Usually falling in the month of June, this feast had a tremendous effect on the composition and performance of cycle dramas.[83] In their urban settings, the enactment of Christ's Passion touched each audience member; sorrow and tragedy were laid open in an act of communal pain shared by all.[84]

Recent cognitive studies have underscored the transformative potential of performance to induce affective responses. "Kinesthetic knowledge and understanding is at the heart of applied theatre practice where participatory performance is used to 'effect' change (defined variously as 'transformation' or 'transportation') through its 'affect' on participants."[85] Dox has gone so far as to suggest that affect could be an alternative measurement for determining medieval generic categories, enabling "investigations into how theatre schooled medieval playgoers to respond emotionally within (and perhaps, without) the ideological framework of Christianity."[86] Following this approach, we can see how performances of the Crucifixion shaped and reinforced participants' emotions. As Sarah Beckwith reminds us, medieval plays "are extremely interested in the communities formed around a present action." Indeed, in enactments of the Crucifixion it is not the scripted action of the plot or development of character that matter, but "their engagement with the complexities of presence, with the embodiment of forgiveness – and its negation – in the penitential community that is the body of Christ. It is a form of theater that explores theology through the very logic of performance."[87] In her analysis of the Crucifixion pageant from the York Cycle, for example, Beckwith observes that "Christ's body is ritually tortured in an agonizingly extended sequence culminating in the reconstruction on stage of the central icon of the culture – Christ on the cross, dramatically played as both reenactment of the Crucifixion, and a construction of its central representation."[88] In previous pageants, as in this one, the audience witnesses the harrowing agony of Christ's torture, and it is this act of witness which the pageant emphasizes: for when Christ speaks, he does not address his torturers but those watching the action unfold.[89] "What is taking place is not an event long passed to which the action *refers*. Rather, it is happening in a present that exists as a moment of painful and pure communication between Christ and the present audience."[90] It is the very "liveness" of the event, the immediate embodiment of the sacrificial act of Christ, that captivates the audience.[91]

It is significant that many Andalusian philosophers, literary commentators, and translators—Jewish and Muslim—were also physicians. Yehudah ha-Levi (1075–1141), Averroës, Maimonides (1138–1204), and Muhammad Ibn Dāniyāl (1248–1310) were all intimately acquainted with the ravages of body and soul, and their medical and literary commentaries draw upon that intimate understanding. But there are also important distinctions in the representation of tragic events in these works. In addition to the absence of Christian narrative elements, the understanding of tragic suffering as shared by the entire Jewish nation (Maimonides) or tragedy as a praise of virtue (Averroës) are other distinctions.[92] In the Jewish context, tragedy was often connected to persecution, exile, and mass murder, whether in the present or the distant past. As early as the third century BCE Ezekiel of Alexandria's play *Exagoge* had used the framework of Hellenistic tragedy to retell the story of Exodus.[93] By contrast, Joseph b. Judah ibn' Aqnīn (1150–1220), a resident of Morocco, wrote his *Therapy of the Soul* (*Tibb al-nufūs*) in response to the Almohad persecution of Jews in the late twelfth century[94] and the first generation of forced converts, of which he was one, relayed in "doleful tone."[95]

Like Boethius' *Consolation*, the *Therapy of the Soul* is not a historical narrative, but a contemplation of how to cope with trauma which, for Jewish communities, often materialized through cycles of persecution, violence, and expulsion. For this reason, the most important Jewish thinker of his time, Moses Maimonides, focuses on the misfortunes of the Jewish people as a whole, rather than those of an individual. His articulation of fortune as rising or receding (in Hebrew, *Oleh ve yored*) is laid out in the first volume of *The Guide of the Perplexed* (*Moreh Nevuchim*, 1190) as a series of events that literally *befall* a nation, through afflictions that are *descended* upon them.[96] In book 3, Maimonides discusses all human suffering, exemplified by Job, as a means of getting closer to God, recalling the Christian representations of saints' suffering. On the one hand, then, his evocation of waning fortunes recalls the Boethian trope of the wheel and suggests the influence, direct or indirect, of "Boethian tragedy." On the other, the emphasis on seeking a pacifying outlet for suffering through poetry, music, and drama reflect a commonly shared perspective that influenced the performance traditions that evolved across all cultures of the medieval world and that left their influence for centuries to come.[97]

The theatricalization of the cycle of fortune is embedded in the very cyclical nature of the liturgical year, the annual enactments of the cycle plays, and even in the staging of the morality and Corpus Christi plays which were not confined to theaters but which instead cycled through a community (on pageant wagons) or were performed in the round. The wheel of fortune finds a literal embodiment in the Cornish play of *St Meriasek* or *Beunans Meriasek* (1504) based on the legend of Meriasek, a fourth-century Breton saint. Scholars have suggested that the ground plans for the play reveal the stage to be circular, resembling a 13-hour clock.[98] According to Glynn Wickham, "[t]he script is carefully orchestrated to facilitate staging on and within an earthwork 'round' and resembles the Cornish Corpus Christi Cycle in this respect."[99] The famous morality play of the *Castle of Perseverance* (fifteenth century) is even accompanied by a diagram, considered to be a stage plan, which suggests that this play may have also been performed in the round: it shows a crenellated castle positioned in the middle of the acting space, with a circle drawn around it. Morality plays were vibrant mechanisms for teaching both the tenets of good works and necessity of confession.[100] Beckwith writes that they have "the ability to put, as it were, the very functions of the mind and soul on display."[101] Staging in the round could accommodate a larger audience but it also had a symbolic value, as the performance itself embodied circularity and cyclical repetition. An interesting cultural counterpart is found in Arab shadow play genre (*khayāl al-zill*), in which puppeteers either worked behind a screen, with a light source behind the figures they manipulated with rods or, alternatively, shadow puppets could be placed on a turning wooden wheel to create a "moving image" akin to early cinematic experiments.[102] Metaphorically, then, the mechanics of staging were themselves a concretization of the ways in which men's fortunes could literally turn and reverse.

While biases against image-making prevailed in many Muslim and Jewish traditions, and while Aristotle himself may have relegated the element of spectacle to the sixth and least essential element of tragedy, the relationship between exterior representation and interior experience were crucial to all medieval devotional practices and to parallel forms of theatricality. Thomas Aquinas (1225–74) conceived of images as bridges between *sensibilia* (things that could be sensed) and spiritual understanding.[103] He believed that people think by creating mental *phantasmata* or images, which also make it possible to sense the empirical world and to feel emotions.[104] Aquinas believed that images, static or moving, were also avenues through which people could be brought closer to the contemplation of God. In Aquinas' understanding, a performance became a repository of spiritually suggestive images. "Through a process of externalization of interior cognitive concepts, the drama becomes a treasure-store or *thesaurus* of key Christian images that can move the audience toward spiritual knowledge."[105] Performance thus made possible what Lerud has termed "quick images." "Plays, especially the Corpus Christi plays of Christ's Passion, were viewed as 'quick images' or 'quick books' uniquely able to jog the mind to spiritual understanding."[106]

In Judaic and Muslim contexts, although figurative representations are usually forbidden,[107] theatrical representation nevertheless existed simultaneously with these interdictions. In the Islamicate world, theatrical representation through shadow play (or "play of images") was possible because the audience was not looking at an actual figural image but at the shadow of a figure. Furthermore, since the paper or leather puppet often had holes in it, for the insertion of the puppeteer's rods, the image is not "whole" but punctured. The important Andalusian poet Ibn Hazm (994–1064), considered "the poet laureate of Muslim Spain," described human life through the metaphor of a passing shadow play while the literary theorist Al-Jurjānī (1009–1078) emphasized the profoundness of the "vanishing shadow" as a similar metaphor.[108] The philosopher Al Ghazālī (1058–1111), meanwhile, reflected on the operation of divine by invoking the metaphor of the puppet master.[109]

In the shadow plays, too, we find echoes of the traumatic displacement and loss of community familiar from Judaic performative traditions. Li Guo has remarked that most of the well-known writers and performers of shadow plays originated from Mosul (in present-day Iraq), and that their existence in Mamluk Cairo meant that nostalgia and a sense of rootlessness informed their elusive performance techniques.[110] The most famous medieval shadow play writer, Ibn Dāniyāl, lived and worked as an eye doctor in Cairo, far from his homeland of Mosul, Iraq.[111] Physical sacrifice, as shown in the deformed bodies of characters who appear in his shadow plays, among others, is another point of connection with the tragic dramas of medieval Christian Europe.[112] The plays may be bawdy and scatological, but they also represent pain and despair; overtones of suffering, exile, and displacement are omnipresent.

CONCLUSION

During the Middle Ages, Judaic, Muslim, and Christian theories of tragedy led to a variety of performance genres that were often connected and mutually influential. While all would not be considered "tragedies" in purely Aristotelian terms, they expressed common themes of conflict and suffering and enabled audiences to participate in experiential, emotional journeys that were often in concert with their distinctive cultural traditions. These tragic forms relied on analyses of tragedy that were predominantly developed by late antique philosophers which had a profound impact on medieval theorist, artists, and performers.

CHAPTER FIVE

Religion, Ritual and Myth

JOHN PARKER

You sometimes hear that tragedy disappeared from the Middle Ages because Christian theology could not handle the austerity of its premise: "the best of all things is something entirely outside your grasp," went the unthinkable dictum. "Not to be born, not to *be*, to be *nothing*. But the second-best thing for you—is to die soon."[1] Antiquity in Nietzsche's telling had justified meaningless pain by extracting from dramatizations of its inevitability a hidden, abysmal pleasure. Christianity, by contrast—born of oppression in an occupied land and appealing to the wretched—offered at best a weak moralization: you *deserve* to suffer, on account of your sin. Noble resistance in the face of an inescapable fate no longer made suffering beautiful then. Heroics of that sort merely struck a posture, T.S. Eliot explains, "of self-dramatization" that was "the reverse of Christian humility" and precluded any salvific endgame.[2] When high tragedy was reborn in the Renaissance, particularly on the London stage, it helped break the enchantment of the Middle Ages with "a new attitude," which "is modern" and "culminates, if there is ever any culmination, in the attitude of Nietzsche."[3] However much Eliot himself disliked that mindset, he agreed with Nietzsche that it explained the absence of tragedy for more than a millennium.

And yet there are other ways to tell the story—one of them arising from Nietzsche's critique of Christian humility: he knew better than anybody that the early church made a virtue of necessity. What he did not appreciate was its debt to stoicism, how Christians learned from Seneca in particular to value—love, even—the abjection visited upon them by Roman spectacle. I want to argue here that ancient tragedy can be said to disappear in the Middle Ages only because the Middle Ages so thoroughly absorbed, to the point of worship, its aesthetic for glorifying pain. Of all the pagan materials and customs spoliated or otherwise repurposed by the iconoclasm of the early church (its transformation of despised theater masks, for example, into the Trinity's personae),[4] tragedy was an especially alluring genre insofar as it promised audiences the sublime satisfaction of watching a semi-divine protagonist come to horrific grief. Specifically I'll be arguing that elements of the New Testament, liturgy, and lives of the martyrs—three great well-springs of vernacular drama in late medieval Europe—either culminate in or otherwise recall the spectacles of death, so popular in the Roman Empire, that the antitheatrical fathers had claimed to abhor. I mean to show that various retellings and dramatizations of Christ's torture and execution, along with the equally spectacular deaths of the martyrs, eventually replaced among Christians the gladiatorial games and gorier tragedies of Rome, in particular those staged executions where the condemned were given a costume (a crown of thorns, a purple robe), then in point of fact killed.[5] This replacement—or reoccupation, rather, akin to how churches were superimposed on temples that the new faith had ruined—created a permanent renascence in medieval ritual and drama: Christians replayed over and over the loss of tragic decorum to Roman bloodthirst. That is how they restored tragedy proper to a post-classical world.

I. THEATER VS. AMPHITHEATER

Among the copious *miracula* of ancient Rome, Pliny singles out for special consideration the theater of C. Scribonius Curio—a spendthrift politician and lover of games whose particular coup was to devise an edifice that could serve as a theater until the show finished then whirl about on ingenious hinges with the spectators still in their seats to become an amphitheater where gladiators fought to the death.[6] "Here we have the nation that has conquered the earth," Pliny laments, "that has subdued the whole world . . . that dispatches its dictates to foreign peoples, that is heaven's representative, so to speak, among mankind, swaying on a contraption and applauding its own danger! What a contempt for life this showed!"[7] For Pliny, the "commitment to death" on display in Curio's theater augured the coming civil wars, when audience members accustomed to enjoying violence from a safe distance became a version of the conflict they watched.[8] His invention thus helped initiate a sequence of events that would culminate in the assassination of Julius Caesar—outside a theater, because of course.

Curio built this remarkable structure to host the funeral games for his father, following the hallowed and highly competitive tradition of honoring the dead by spilling more blood. Already by the time of Terence in the second century BCE, the Roman enthusiasm for spectacular bloodshed threatened to upstage any attempt to cultivate a more sophisticated drama on the Greek model. The debut of his *Hecyra*, based on a lost original by Apollodorus, was forced offstage by "talk of a boxing match . . . crowds of supporters, general uproar, and women screaming."[9] The second performance had a better start but was interrupted by rumors of a gladiatorial bout: "crowds rushed in, with much confusion, shouting and fighting for place,"[10] and the show again came to an end. Similarly a few years earlier, in 167 BCE, a Roman general named Lucius Anicius had imported musicians and actors from Greece to grace a triumph but grew weary of their artistry and made them fight instead: "The situation as all these groups wrestled with one another was beyond description," reports Polybius. "And as for what I could add about the tragic actors . . . some people will think that I am joking."[11]

Terence's status as a freedman indicates a common denominator between the allure of players, gladiators, and the earliest Christians, all of whom competed for the same audiences: they belonged to social strata—and in the case of Christians, a social movement—that classier Romans reviled yet came to celebrate anyway. "On one and the same account, they glorify them and degrade and diminish them," writes Tertullian—speaking here of the attitude toward gladiators, though elsewhere in this treatise he deals with the actors who inspired similar admiration but were equally subject to discriminatory legislation based on the same disdain: "The perversity of it! They love whom they lower; they despise whom they approve."[12] Tertullian's implicit hope seems to have been that if Romans could admire in the arena what they loathed everywhere else, they might one day extend their appreciation to Christians, as well, since Christians were likewise demonized and yet also presented an inspiring spectacle, especially when crucified. Even while censuring games of all sorts, in other words, Tertullian simultaneously worked to include his fellow believers on the list of protagonists whose public degradation gave cause for joy; whose staged suffering earned them, too, a crown of victory normally worn by sacrificial victims, triumphant playwrights, and, among others, the arena's combatants.[13]

Throughout the corpus of Tertullian, we see again and again an attempt to redeem, as it were, Roman blood sports: the *damnatus ad bestias*, though defeated in the arena, is supposed to find in the afterlife an eternal triumph over his adversaries. Martyrs such as Perpetua (whose *passio* Tertullian may have edited) and those immortalized in Prudentius' *Book of Crowns* [*Liber Peristephanon*] (more on this shortly) corroborated numerous passages from scripture to the effect that Christians would have "to fight the good fight" (1 Tim. 6:12) not only because they were subject to Roman persecution but because God himself had a special appreciation for blood sports: "the living God is the exhibitor of games," writes Tertullian, "the Holy Spirit the trainer;" meanwhile Christ Jesus "has anointed you with his spirit and led you forth to the arena."[14] According to Tertullian, the Lord had provided Rome with all its "cruel and excruciating battles ... in order to inspire us even now" so that on the day of public denigration Christians might suffer "for the truth ... what others out of vanity have eagerly sought for their ruin."[15] There are a number of ways to take this commonplace—it appears throughout late antiquity and the Middle Ages—but in my view the evidence Nietzsche found in Tertullian for the nascent triumph of a slave morality over Roman nobility is best interpreted as the conquest of Rome by its own entertainment industry.[16]

That process of Christianization was made easier by Christians' willingness to adopt (or, at any rate, adapt) pagan customs and to model their thinking on Roman authorities—chief among them Seneca, to whom Tertullian and Jerome both refer as one of "ours."[17] According to Eliot, Senecan stoicism was like the Christianity described by Nietzsche: namely, "a philosophy suited to slaves,"[18] insofar as it trained initiates to face with dignified, if impotent calm the superior forces that determined their fate. It was for this reason also suited to life in close proximity to an imperial power that had been literally deified; with Nero in command *all* citizens were effectively enslaved, or at least began to think they were, especially the aristocrats accustomed to their privileges—perhaps none more so than Nero's erstwhile *magister*, Seneca.[19] He was generally inured for high-brow reasons to the allure of the amphitheater, but he nonetheless saw a paradigm for stoic virtue in the hardened will of condemned entertainers.[20] Even though he wanted to believe that "triumph over the calamities and terrors of mortal life is the part of a great man only,"[21] he knew that great men, as traditionally defined by power and money, experienced too little terror and calamity to test their full grandeur. Their exceptional status exempted them from the barrage of everyday misery that was the sage's special distinction to have mastered: "I judge you unfortunate," Seneca says to his fellow aristocrats, "because you have never been unfortunate; you have passed through life without an antagonist; no one will know what you can do—not even yourself" (*De prov.* 4.3).

The same could not be said for Rome's lowest social orders. They faced all manner of adversity and could therefore teach the leisured classes how to live according to the most severe philosophical tenets. Seneca draws several examples from "the basest kind of men,"[22] such as a Germanic beast fighter—likely a war-trophy, *damnatus ad bestias*, hence forbidden all freedom and privacy, save when relieving himself. One day, before the morning show, he withdrew to the cloaca; alone for the briefest of moments, "he seized the stick of wood, tipped with a sponge, which was devoted to the vilest uses, and stuffed it, just as it was, down his throat ... What a brave fellow! He surely deserved to be allowed to choose his fate!" (Ep. 70:20–1). Such examples were especially edifying for the all-too comfortable patricians who longed to be wise but therefore needed to learn from inferiors that "death can be despised even by the most despised of men" (Ep. 70:23).

This was a lesson from Seneca that Christians also wanted to teach. We owe all of his letters to medieval copyists, plus some that were forged on his behalf to the Apostle Paul, traditionally counted among the most unflappable victims of Roman blood sports—"an athlete of Christ," as Augustine writes, "crucified with him [Gal. 2:20], who gloried in him and who in the theatre of this world, for which he was exhibited as a show before both angels and men [1 Cor. 4:9], fought a mighty fight according to the rules [2 Tim. 2:5] and pressed forward for the prize of his heavenly calling [Phil. 3:14]."[23] By the ninth century, and lasting well into the Renaissance, "the friendship of the philosopher Seneca and the Apostle Paul was accepted as a historical fact, doubted by no one"[24] and further embellished by the occasional proposition (as in Boethius) that Seneca's death had been a "philosophical martyrdom,"[25] if not also, given its setting in a bath, some sort of baptism.[26] These medieval and early modern legends were not entirely without historical basis: Seneca's brother was proconsul of Achaia when some local Jews dragged Paul before him for judgment, though he declined to pass sentence over a matter of mere "words and names" (Acts 18:15). When Paul was arrested again, he appealed directly to "the Emperor" (Acts 25:10)—this would have been Nero—and then traveled to Rome. The Praetorian Prefect at the time—this would have been Seneca's friend, Sextus Afranius Burro—for some reason allowed him to preach under something like house arrest (Acts 28:16; Phil. 1:13), allegedly at the site later occupied by S. Paolo alla Regola, where he is reputed to have met Seneca and, for all we know, actually might have.[27]

At any rate we also owe Seneca's drama to the same medieval copyists who considered him a major pagan forerunner, if not an outright ally, of the coming Kingdom. Although the early Middle Ages often treated the philosopher and tragedian as two different people, tending to embrace the former while neglecting the latter, the neglect was never total and did not last: by the tenth century, quotations from and allusions to the tragedies begin to appear with greater frequency. The earliest codex now extant—the so-called *Etruscus* (eleventh century), currently in the library of S. Marco in Florence—may have been based on a copy at Monte Casino that allowed Eugenius Vulgaris, earlier in tenth-century Naples, to season his letters with borrowings and reminiscences from the plays.[28] Metellus, a mid-twelfth-century monk at Tegernsee, took repeatedly from the tragedies in the same place, at the same time, that the monastery's great *Ludus de Antichristo* also came into being.[29] By the thirteenth century, Seneca's plays had been integrated into the school curriculum and were read through the same Christian lens as his philosophy, both of which were now regularly attributed to one person: the "'theologian and poet' or more briefly, 'theological poet,'" whose plays were subject to "an allegorical conception of poetry, widespread throughout the Middle Ages, as a coded disguise for philosophical-Christian truths."[30]

Taken together, his plays open a unique window onto the place of spectacle in an imperial order that produced much of the New Testament at roughly the same time. His *Trojan Women*, for example, culminates in, and meditates on, two human sacrifices that are "not represented simply as a mythical necessity but . . . above all as an object for the gaze of onlookers who delight in it with relish."[31] The deaths occur in a place shaped like a theater (*theatri more*) and inspire both wonder and pity (*mirantur ac miserantur*) on account of the spiritual fortitude (*animus fortis*) shown by the victims, who stoically face their doom with eyes wide open (*leto obvius*), volunteering for death (*sua sponte*).[32] In this they blazed a trail for the martyred Christian saints—also impotent victims of pagan cruelty and, at the same time, powerful icons of true virtue. When Jerome came to write the life of St. Malchus, for instance, he borrowed lines from *Trojan Women* to illustrate a perfectly Senecan-Christian moral: namely, "that in the midst of swords, and wild beasts of the desert, virtue is never a captive and that he who is devoted to the service of Christ may die, but cannot be conquered."[33] Thanks to Seneca, the martyr here is already a step ahead of the *Übermensch*: what *kills* him makes him stronger.

The martyr's paradoxical strength-in-weakness begins to explain, I think, both the extravagance of hagiography's masochism and the kind of catharsis it promised when enacted as play. From Aristotle's telling forward, as Noah Guynn has shown, no one has been able to say for sure whether the tragic discharge of compassion and terror is supposed to make an audience more or *less* sympathetic and afraid.[34] Evidently, at times, the objective of tragedy was to purge (*kathairein*) its viewers of demeaning emotions, in which case drama (to say nothing of blood sports) must have functioned as an inoculation against pity and fear in the face of pain—something we find in *Trojan Women*, for example, when Hecuba insists that Priam, having been killed before the altar of Jove in the manner of an obscene sacrifice, must not be pitied: "'Blest is Priam,' you should all say" (145), because his defeat at the hands of a Greek was only apparent: under the aspect of eternity he found the ultimate freedom by bearing his throat and welcoming the sword in the manner of a beaten but fearless, and therefore all the more resplendent, gladiatorial combatant.[35]

Unlike gladiatorial combat, however, the fundamental premise—and cathartic promise—of Senecan tragedy, according to a number of scholars, is the artificiality of its carnage. By insisting on a difference between real violence and its fanciful staging, Seneca restores to Roman drama the strictly "aesthetic enjoyment of terror."[36] The calamities of tragedy—to borrow from Marcus Aurelius—have to be synthetically "conjured on stage [ἐπὶ τῆς σκηνῆς ψυχαγωγεῖσθε]"[37] (the word for conjuring here normally entails the ritual spilling of blood) *without* any bloodshed, so that an audience might learn to face the real-world equivalent with more detachment, hence greater pleasure. From the stoic perspective, tragedy creates a movement toward the aestheticization (and, subsequently, the spiritualization) of bloodshed that alone endows it with a philosophically satisfying or even redemptive content: indeed the satisfaction is worth experiencing only to the extent that the bloodshed seems on some level superficial or merely apparent: in a word, *phenomenal*. Tragedy covers the Dionysian terror of noumenal existence, that is, with a terrific, Apollonian surface.[38]

As a result Seneca's drama sometimes implies a parallel between the enjoyment of its contrafactual violence and the pleasure that impassible immortals might take in the ephemera of human pain: "who could not be pleased," asks Hecuba, "by the savage slaughter of a man at the last climacteric of mortal life, and by the gods witnessing the scene, and by a kind of sanctity belonging to fallen kingship?" (51-3).[39] Nietzsche explains this sort of thinking with the argument that humans can bear all manner of suffering so long as it has some meaning. Antiquity's genius was to enhance even the most senseless anguish with a certain intrigue by imagining that it provided entertainment for higher beings: "So as to abolish hidden, undetected, unwitnessed suffering and honestly to deny it, one was in the past virtually compelled to invent gods and genii of all the heights and depths, in short something that roams even in secret hidden places, sees even in the dark, and will not easily let an interesting painful spectacle pass unnoticed."[40] Mere mortals could then catch a glimpse for themselves of the meaning that meaningless agony might hold for divinities by putting the human tragedy on stage, where, for once, it appeared at an unbridgeable distance.

Paul's sense that the persecution of martyrs created "a spectacle to the world, to angels and men" (1 Cor. 4:9) derives from the same worldview. For later Christians, as for

Seneca, the spectacle's importance was also best captured by pretend reenactments—whether in the symbolism of the liturgy or the outright mimesis of the myriad passions of Christ and his martyrs. Medieval performances of violence insist on contrived appearances; they advertise their secondary status as mere representation to teach the faithful to look on the historical adversity faced by earlier Christians as an equally gratifying form of theater. The Christian who, according to Nietzsche, "interprets a whole mysterious machinery of salvation into suffering" thus reaffirms, against the Roman trend, the more ancient tradition of using mimesis to banish pointless misery. Doesn't every medieval passion attempt to justify, through contrafactual artifice, the random butchery from which Christianity sprang, as though the slaughter had been a thing of divine beauty?

II. THE BIRTH OF CHRISTIANITY FROM THE SPIRIT OF TRAGEDY

Herod the Great built the first theater in the Holy Land, together with an amphitheater, a hippodrome, and a temple dedicated to Caesar, after whom he named the city they were meant to adorn.[41] To celebrate the end of construction (about six years before the birth of Christ), he hosted contests in music and athletics and prepared "a great number of gladiators" while purchasing a huge supply of exotic animals that could fight amongst themselves or be set upon the condemned.[42] His imports quickly spread across the region, enraging the natives, to whom "it seemed a glaring impiety to throw men to wild beasts for the pleasure of other men as spectators" (15.274–5). They accused Herod of corrupting "the ancient way of life, which had thitherto been inviolable . . . [since] the use of such buildings and the exhibition of such spectacles have not been traditional with the Jews" (15.267–8). Such spectacles had not been traditional with the Greeks, either, insofar as Roman custom tended to elide the differences between forms of entertainment that were elsewhere distinct: "From the circus to the theater," writes Donald Kyle, "formerly separate elements continued in combination, with violence as the common mortar."[43] Martial, an exact contemporary of the evangelists, tells of a thief costumed as Laureolus (a brigand famous to the point of myth) and forced to reenact his death on stage—though in this case the legendary figure would be "hanging on an unfeigned cross [*non falsa cruce*]" while a genuine bear ripped at his viscera. "What had been fable," says Martial, "became punishment."[44]

It was of course another routine, theatricalized crucifixion of thieves that moved the Roman penchant for spectacular bloodshed—and, not incidentally, for violently flouting Jewish tradition—to the center of medieval Christendom. According to Mark (in all likelihood the earliest of the gospels and a key source for Matthew and Luke), Roman soldiers first mocked Jesus by inflicting on him a royal costume and dramatic role commensurate with his ridiculous pretense, while they themselves played the part of his groveling subordinates: "They struck his head with a reed, spat upon him, and knelt down in homage to him" (Mk 15:19). Violence blends seamlessly here with artificial make-believe, and yet the elision, from the Christian perspective, legitimates the *artifice*. The soldiers may be merely pretending—and pretending badly—but Mark drops the words "as if" so that, as they beat Jesus, they kneel down for real in unwitting "homage." "They also bedecked him with a purple robe," comments Cyril of Jerusalem. "Although they treated him this way for ridicule, it was a prophetic act: for he really was King."[45] According to the gospel, in other words, the truth of Christianity has been articulated in the guise of pagan play-acting. For Mark and his subsequent readers, the phony gestures of non-believers were nothing less than revelatory: when the heathen hailed Jesus with feigned respect for his power, their simulation, from the perspective of heaven, was truer than their contempt.

And truer than their violence. Christians interpreted the brutal humiliation experienced by Jesus not as a sign of shameful weakness but of undying glory. In fact one faction in the early church went so far as to argue that Christ's suffering, along with his humanity, had been a theatrical illusion all along since the omnipotent godhead could not in reality be subject to such denigration.[46] The orthodox rejoinder was somewhat more complex but did not abandon the radical reevaluation of his anguish as a form of exaltation: Jesus had indeed suffered, and died, yet his suffering and death had consequences that were the opposite of real pathos—no defeat, but triumph; no senseless injustice exercised on a frail victim, but the center of all human history and a sacrificial act voluntarily undertaken by the immortal God to provide humanity with the only possible route to eternal life. The ineffectual ugliness of Christ's suffering was thus transformed into a kind of love—and loveliness.

This wholesale appropriation and repurposing of pagan violence so that it worked to the advantage of the church was made easier, according to a number of scholars, by Mark's formal imitation of Greek tragedy and the performative recitation of his storyline in the liturgy.[47] Seen in this light, the episode with the soldiers is not only theatrical, it's a play-within-a-play auguring the innumerable passions of the coming Middle Ages; precisely by *reenacting* the soldiers' buffeting, scourging, and crucifixion of Christ, these later plays tried to elevate the meaning of his death in fulfillment of the soldiers' histrionic pretext: namely, that Christ was king. If medieval Christians could be said for that reason to celebrate or even worship Roman brutality, it's worth stressing that they celebrated it in a strictly ersatz form that forbid death's actual return to pretend reenactments, unless it returned as fiction or, at worst, an accident (hence the urban legend that drama still killed its actors). Thanks to the church, gladiatorial combat was gone; the amphitheaters and theaters were in ruins. The performances taking place in churches, inn yards, and city streets were not "snuff"[48]—as Jody Enders has it—but a more refined "gore-nography."[49] They presented, in place of the old fatal charades, charades pure and simple. Theirs was strictly an *aesthetic* of violence. Persecution and public executions of course remained throughout the Middle Ages (and were sometimes fueled by stage caricatures, of Jews especially), but, as Robert Mills has argued, "capital punishment was not as regular or spectacular an occurrence . . . as is commonly imagined" on the basis of its constant presence in medieval ritual and art.[50] Which is to say that the punitive function of Roman spectacle, after the fall of the Roman Empire, was restricted to comparatively rare, comparatively genuine executions, while the relentless *imitation* of ancient torture invited Christian veneration, but only so long as it excluded real violence. That exclusion, I want to argue, marked a significant change in Western theater: it created Catholic ritual and paved the way for the vernacular saint plays and passions, which effectively return to an earlier vision of tragedy by *representing* blood sports rather than enacting them for real.

We have four medieval versions of Christ's death-by-drama in English, all of them underscoring how the gratuitous, theatricalized violence of the soldiers intimates the future grace effected by the sacraments; how the fake adulation of someone they take to be an imposter portends the worship he deserves from the church; and how his apparent guilt proffers believers a renewal of innocence. All of them further present the soldiers' mock exaltation of Jesus as "a newe play of Yoyll [Yule]"[51]—which is to say, as an early version of celebrating "the lowest in society as 'kyng of chrystmas'"[52] or, alternately, a *rex stultorum*. According to medieval cycle drama, when Romans used ironic play-acting to persecute the marginalized, they unwittingly invented a "newe game"[53] that *correctly* prophesied the Christian reversal of their own values. The first king of fools, in other words, was a Jewish peasant forced to wear a royal costume that forecast revolution. Naturally by the Middle Ages the social leveling promised in the gospels' less temperate moments had not, as yet, come to pass—except at Christmas, carnival, and other seasonal interludes set aside for symbolic inversion. Eventually, maybe, the last really would be first. But for now that could happen, if at all, only through play-acting: the soldiers' accusation that Christ was a low-born nobody pretending to higher station may or may not have been true of Jesus, but it was certainly true of the actor now portraying him, who could take on the role of God only because God was supposed to have assumed "the form of a slave" (Phil 3:8) and then received from unbelievers' mock-royal treatment.

III. THE TRAGEDY OF MARTYRDOM

Theater scholars searching among the fathers for a bridge between the ancient and medieval worlds have traditionally looked foremost to Prudentius (348–405?). A poet from the Iberian peninsula like Seneca, he modeled his work on pagan letters to such an extent that even if Roman tragedy had been completely lost to the Middle Ages, its internalization of ancient blood sports would have lived on in the *Psychomachia* (an allegorical representation of the human soul as a battlefield between virtue and vice [Figures 5.1 and 5.2], in the *Cathemerinon* (a collection of liturgical songs that frequently memorialize pagan violence) and in the *Liber Peristephanon* (stories of the martyrs [Figure 5.3])—all of which provide key models and source-texts for later Christian ritual and drama. This is not to say, however, that the multiple ensuing affinities between pagan and Christian spectacles of suffering created a happy alliance: on the contrary, the most intimate points of contact literally mark the most extreme points of conflict. I will have more to say below about Peter Brown's seminal work on martyrdom but want to begin by noting its chief limitation—namely, the view that "[t]o explain the Christian cult of the martyrs as a continuation of the pagan cult of heroes helps as little as to reconstruct the form and function of a late-antique Christian basilica from the few columns and capitals taken from classical buildings that are occasionally incorporated into its arcades."[54] In reality, a tremendous amount of Christian architecture, in Rome especially, came about through the spoliation of the classical world and the reoccupation of sacred locales, while the liturgical performances that these buildings housed were strategically timed to coincide with the traditional festivities of the pagan world. That is how the church managed to appropriate what it opposed and to display, as tokens of victory, the fragments of a world it meant to destroy.[55] Christians could in other words condemn pagan spectacles even while integrating them into the fabric of their own performance spaces.

Take the allusions to and quotations from Seneca incorporated throughout the *Cathemerinon*, for example when Prudentius speaks of Christ's descent after death into the "darkness of eternal night [*noctis aeternae chaos*]."[56] That phrase is drawn verbatim from Seneca's *Hercules* (610), whose titular hero—attached by Roman convention to gladiatorial combat—made a similar journey to the underworld. In time the parallel between these two figures would appear in iconography while also being performed in the liturgy,[57] so that the very words Prudentius drew from Seneca, later medievals drew from Prudentius as lyrics for the mass.[58] The same phrase makes a passing appearance in Seneca's *Medea*, which also supplied Prudentius with a useful terminology to describe the Slaughter of the Innocents.[59] The *barbarum spectaculum* (*Cath.* 12.117) of Herod's

FIGURE 5.1: Illumination of virtues and vices in Prudentius' *Psychomachia* as Roman gladiators. Bern, Burgerbibliothek, Cod. 264 (*c.* ninth century). Photo: Codices Electronici AG (www.e-codices.ch).

Christmas butchery—the source, according to tradition, of the first Christian martyrs (notwithstanding that the slaughtered infants were unconverted Jews)—became a widespread subject of drama in Latin and the vernacular, as did the sufferings of Christ's other "offerings" [*Christi victima*] (*Cath.* 12.129). Prudentius directly shaped the aestheticized violence of this later hagiography, just as he had been shaped by Seneca.[60] Although you still sometimes hear that "there is no evidence that Seneca's tragedies ever inspired the medieval drama,"[61] the extensive borrowings throughout the *Peristephanon* have led some scholars to see in it (St. Romanus especially) a "Christian tragedy"[62] or, if you prefer—given the conventional reversal, whereby the worst fate imaginable is, to Christians, actually the best—an "anti-tragedy."[63]

The appropriation of Roman blood drama for the purposes of a Christian *passio* is most explicit in the life of St. Hippolytus. Prudentius knew him as a Novatian and

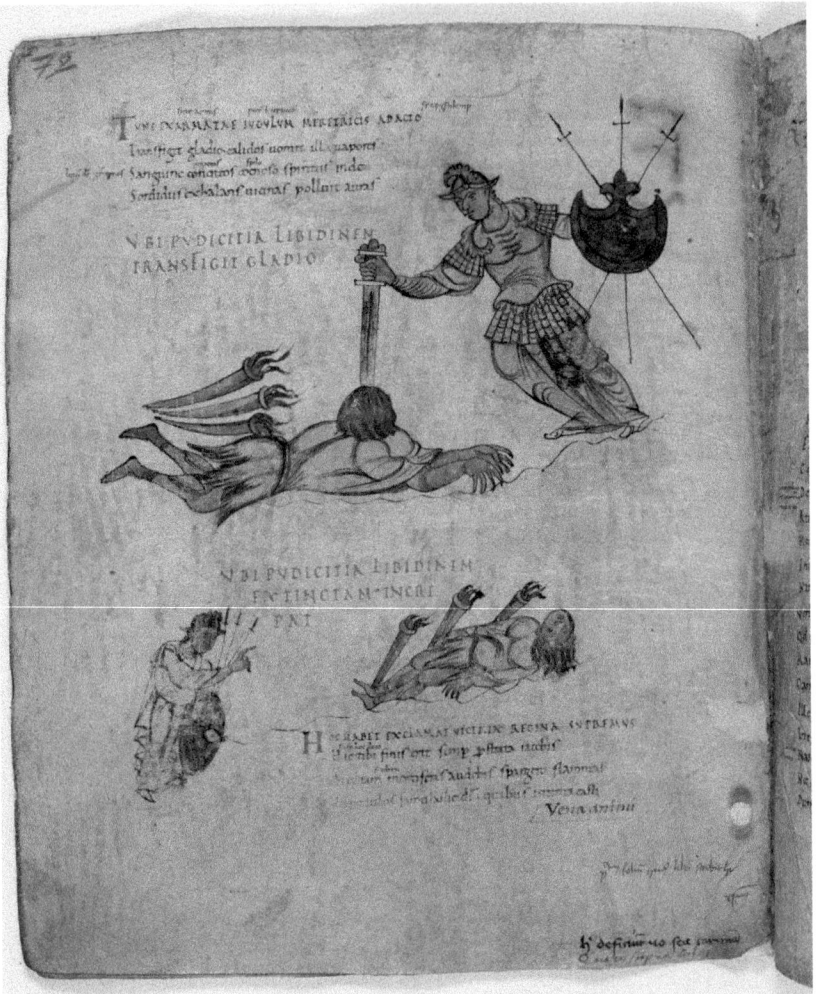

FIGURE 5.2: Chastity slays Lust in Prudentius' *Psychomachia*. Bern, Burgerbibliothek, Cod. 264 (c. ninth century). Photo: Codices Electronici AG (www.e-codices.ch).

schismatic who had had the good sense to recant before being martyred in a gruesome spectacle deliberately modeled on the death of his pagan namesake. The story, which Seneca took from a play by Euripides, called out for Latinization insofar as Hippolytus' favorite pastimes—hunting and chariots—were by then closely associated with contemporary blood sports: the animals that would become a favorite method of executing Christians first appeared in the Forum when Caesar built a special "cynegetic" or hunting-theater.[64] Just as the myth called out for artistic depiction—a Roman sarcophagus featuring Hippolytus in bas-relief was repurposed for a Christian burial under San Clemente[65]—so too did combat with animals, whose savagery, set in mosaic, came to grace certain well-appointed residences.[66] This particular brand of slaughter soon rivaled in popularity the races with their uproarious din, loudest at crashes, that Seneca trained himself to bear with "utmost patience" (Ep. 83:7)—having been inspired by other victims of the arena (some of them possibly Christian) to cultivate mental calm in spite of duress. Like the sage in his study or the martyr in the Colosseum or the charioteer in the circus, Hippolytus too faces death "immune to fear" (*Phaedra* 1054).

After chastity, such courage is Hippolytus' chief virtue, regardless of whether he is pagan or Christian. The story in Prudentius begins with a "mad" emperor engaged in "constant slaying of the righteous" (*Perist*. 11.39, 44) for their refusal to bow before the gods. When an audience gathers round and demands from the judge "a novel punishment," he asks the name of the Christian before him, which becomes the man's sentence: "Hippolytus let him be, then" (*Perist*. 11.87). The future saint is thus doomed to star in the old mythological drama, such that Prudentius can describe the historical event simply by lifting lines from Seneca's *play*: there too the wild-eyed horses "seized the chariot [*rapuere currum*]" (*Phaedra* 1069) and, driven by "fury" (*Phaedra* 1070), tore their rider limb from limb. The Christian Hippolytus dies the same way (*Perist*. 11.111–14), except his "seizure" or "ravishment" by the horses results in a sacred ecstasy: "Let them ravish my body; you, Christ, must ravish my soul! [*hi rapiant artus, tu rape, Christe, animam*]" (*Perist*. 11.110).

The whole oeuvre of Prudentius thrills to the "splendid death" (*Cath*. 12.6) of such martyrs, and the splendor clearly depends on artificial embellishment: in addition to Seneca, Prudentius bases his accounts on subsequent depictions of the martyrs' ruin, above all the graphic iconography adorning their tombs, which his own poetry reduplicates through ekphrasis. That descriptive mode—Bruce Holsinger calls it "the most idolatrous of literary practices"[67]—allowed for particularly lavish illustration in medieval manuscripts, with the result that a tenth-century illumination could accompany Prudentius' description of a painting in which St. Cassian is stabbed by the styli of his enraged students (Figure 5.3). Pagan writing here is the same as bloodletting, but the blood is redeemed by the paint of an icon, then by medieval ink. An icon of Hippolytus similarly intervenes between the writing of Prudentius and his pagan source: "there is a picture of the outrage painted on the wall showing in many colors the sacrilege [*nefas*] in all its details ... where a hand that was skilled in portraying green bushes had also figured the red blood in vermillion" (*Perist*. 11.123–24, 29–30).[68] The painter converted gratuitous violence to art so that the violence might live on—in subsequent artworks if nowhere else—as a sacrilege delimiting God's grace.

Prior to Christianity, a common purpose of depicting Roman gore had been to commemorate a patron's extravagant munificence in providing worthy spectacles to the community.[69] It was the brilliance of early Christians to transfer to the martyr not only the aura of sanctity sometimes imputed by pagans to the arena's victims but also the prestige and authority normally reserved for the patron who had victimized them—with the result that the cult of the saints eventually provided an outlet, akin to the games, for the increasing wealth of the church: if it could not sponsor a circus to go with the communion bread, it could nonetheless shower abundance on the iconography of bloodshed: "Lavish building, splendid ceremonial, and even feasting at such a shrine washed clean the hard facts of accumulated wealth and patronage, as they were now practiced in real life, even by bishops, a short distance away within the walls of the city of the living."[70] The shrines of the saints baptized Roman *spectacula*, so to speak, making the pagan culture of violence available for Christian enjoyment. Trying to decide whether this is a story of continuity or discontinuity almost misses the point, which was to provide *both* a break from the pre-Christian world *and* a perpetual connection to it: as even Brown notes, Prudentius expressed his outlook "in language which is so faithful a reversal of the traditional worldview as to amount to a tacit recognition of its resilience."[71]

FIGURE 5.3: Death of St. Cassian in Prudentius' *Liber Peristephanon*. Bern, Burgerbibliothek, Cod. 264 (*c.* ninth century). Photo: Codices Electronici AG (www.e-codices.ch).

Case in point is the way his ekphrasis freezes the dispersal of Hippolytus' corpse *before* its miraculous reassembly, recalling the tragic fragmentation of his pagan predecessor, whose parts were scattered beyond full recovery.[72] The ultimate pay-off (and focus) for Prudentius is less the collection of Hippolytus' body parts than the subsumption of non-Christian elements into a Christian collective that looks deliberately jumbled, haphazard, and inchoate as a result of its extreme catholicity: "the love of religion masses Latins and strangers together in a mixed *cuneum*" (*Perist.* 11.190–1). That last word originally meant wedge but was also applied to the similarly shaped phalanx of military troops (*Psych.* 197), as well as the wedge-shaped section of Roman theaters and amphitheaters. Suetonius reports, for example, that Augustus Caesar forbid the "confused and disorderly way of watching" Roman *ludi* out of irritation that unequal social classes and genders—plus citizens and non-citizens alike—had grown accustomed to watching the games together without differentiation; so he assigned each group to a specific section or *cuneum* and banned women altogether from enjoying the gladiators.[73] The *cuneum* of Prudentius, by contrast, welcomes the unrestricted social mixing that had long been part of the games' transgressive appeal, made worse when Latin audiences began to follow the Greek protocol of forming "irresponsible seated assemblies" (rather than standing) in *permanent* theaters, which Romans were notoriously slow to adopt for fear of legitimating unregulated hordes.[74]

One reason Christianity spread as effectively as it did was its embrace of a counter-public that welcomed to some extent both women and the enslaved, as well as those whom God himself might eventually deem reprobate: hence Augustine's view, which Prudentius here radicalizes, of the church as a "mixed body."[75] What better occasion to assemble this new membership, which notoriously put the traditional body politic completely out of joint, than the feast of Hippolytus? On that day, writes Prudentius, "the majestic city disgorges her Romans in a stream; with equal ardor patricians and plebian host are jumbled together shoulder to shoulder, for the faith banishes distinctions of birth" (*Perist.* 11.199–202). In this case the faith has erased ordinary hierarchies through the ordinary Roman means of convening an audience before a tragic vivisection. Indeed the poem's end calls for future observations of the saint's feast day, when this *vita* itself might be sung as an integral part of the celebration. That "nod to oral delivery and performance," writes Cillian O'Hogan, stresses the importance of the martyr as "a source of civic communal memory,"[76] and yet what it memorializes is the extraordinary, spectacular violence of *pagan* Rome, in part through a "contrafactum of Seneca."[77]

IV. THE MEDIEVAL RENASCENCE OF TRAGEDY

Historians have traditionally had to wait for two tenth-century developments before referring to the liturgy as a bona fide form of theater: first is the emergence during the Easter rite of spoken dialogue between an angelic boy and three clerics acting as if they were the Marys visiting Christ's empty tomb. (In fact from this episode's earliest mention in the original or shorter ending of Mark, it was probably already involved in a performative setting and seems explicitly modeled on the *deus ex machina* of Greek tragedy.)[78] The second development—which has played a less central role in scholarly narratives even though it may have sprung from related liturgical reforms[79]—is the work of Hrotsvit of Gandersheim. Her drama avowedly follows a pagan model, often features pagan violence against Christians, and provides the earliest unambiguous example of a saint play. In time her sort of play would spread widely throughout the European vernaculars, paving the way for the early modern renascence of Senecan tragedy. As we'll see, the Renaissance proper appears in this case less like an unprecedented, modern revival of neglected classics than the belated flourish of an established medieval tradition.

According to Hrotsvit's own preface, her urge to write plays arose from a heartfelt anxiety over the persistence and allure of classical literature: "Many Catholics can be found—and we cannot fully exculpate ourselves of this crime—who for the eloquence of cultivated language prefer the vanity of pagan books to the usefulness of sacred scripture."[80] This tension between the high-brow, if empty, sophistication of idolatrous writing and the low-brow usefulness of scripture was by her day ancient but still invariably class-based: for Aristotle the search for "utility" was "entirely unsuited to men that are great-souled and free"[81] because the mortifying world of pure instrumentality was fit only for the ruled, not for their rulers. Scripture's humble style had been interpreted from the church fathers forward as a testimony to its radical revaluing of humility—the medium was the message—and yet long after the process of Christianization was all but complete, the European upper-crust still indulged in the guilty refinement of classical rhetoric. Hrotsvit herself was probably high-born and lived in a convent with close connections to the Ottonian court, which begins to explain her extraordinary education and the curious remark that "many" Catholics prefer the classics to scripture (most were of course unable to read either). The emperor's brother, Bruno, was known for his love of "unseemly jests and mimetic matter (scurrilia et mimica) that, in comedies and tragedies, are presented by various personages,"[82] and he had direct contact with Gandersheim: his niece was both Hrotsvit's abbess and one of her dedicatees. Although we cannot say which specific "tragedies" Bruno enjoyed, he would not be alone, even in the tenth century, if they were Seneca's.

Whether Hrotsvit or anyone in her immediate environment had access to his plays directly, they could read Prudentius, together with the flourishing hagiographical tradition he helped inspire, which nearly always had, in Walter Berschin's words, "a latent dramatic structure"[83] and which had penetrated deeply into the performance of the liturgy (the monastic office especially).[84] Hagiography at this point tended to present two kinds of saints: the "public" one, who had suffered death at the hands of pagans (or, sometimes, hostile Christians). The other, "hidden" kind of saint suffered mortification voluntarily, by his or her "own hand," through a life of ascetic or even masochistic and borderline suicidal abnegation.[85] Saints of the latter sort effectively internalized and extended into a world that had been otherwise Christianized the persecution of Christians by non-Christian powers; which is to say, they kept persecution alive even in its absence to strengthen their own moral fiber. They carried their adversaries within themselves and "trained" (the meaning of *ascesis*) for conflict as athletes of Christ in a lifelong, if solitary *agon*. Within a Latin context this struggle began to look less like *Olympiacis disciplinis* and more like gladiatorial combat, as though a hermit could become *damnatus ad bestias* in spirit and "settle the outcome of the battle merely by castigating the flesh and subjugating his own body."[86] The ancient glory of the Colosseum could thus be transferred to a monk's cell, which Peter Damian describes as "the divine battlefield, the arena of spiritual combat, the angels' amphitheater."[87]

Hrotsvit and her fellow nuns, locked in combat with their own bodies, routinely heard recited at mass the kindred struggle of saints persecuted for their faith and may have seen performed her own dramas, modeled on "Terence" (*Opera* 132.5). This remark—the only specific pagan that Hrotsvit names—has been a bit of a puzzle to theater history insofar as no one finds her drama especially Terentian. A reference in a contemporaneous manuscript to a play by Terence "which is called a tragedy"[88] opens the tantalizing possibility that his corpus in the Middle Ages could include generic elements we no longer associate with it, though there is at least one element in the Terence we know that speaks to Hrotsvit's adaptations: his career as a freedman and his rivalry with gladiatorial combat exemplify how the theater and amphitheater allowed even those damned to Rome's lowest substrate to earn, if not salvation, then at least a certain prestige otherwise beyond their ken—a context on which the stock *servus callidus* of Roman comedy, enslaved but superior in cunning, routinely capitalized (Figure 5.4). Hrotsvit's drama occasionally goes even further than anything in Terence so as to demonstrate the full ramifications of Christian redemption (literally: "buying back"): for example, Gallicanus, a pagan general under Constantine, promises upon conversion to "enrich my slaves—whom I have freed—and to relieve the poor" (*Opera* 156.4–5). That charitable deliverance parallels

FIGURE 5.4: Mask-wearing slave and prostitute from Terence's *Hecyra*. Latin 7899 (ninth century). Courtesy of the Bibliothèque Nationale de France.

Gallicanus' new-found liberation from the idolatrous chains of paganism; *all people* were formerly a "slave to sin" (Jn 8:34) but have now "been bought at a price" (1 Cor. 6:20); thus redeemed, they become "slaves of Christ [*servos Christi*]" (*Opera* 159.6). Gallicanus can be an agent of freedom, that is, only because he has "submitted [himself] completely to the will of God" (*Opera* 153.12–13).

The price of his freedom, such as it is, cannot be paid in money, however. On the contrary the foundation of all hagiographical writing concerned with saints who die by violence is that Christian redemption must be purchased with pain,[89] and the pain, for that reason, frequently erupts into bliss: "the more bitterly I am tortured," says Irena, "the more gloriously am I exalted" (*Opera* 173.8–9). Such expressions abound in Hrotsvit, as they will abound in subsequent hagiographical dramatizations of Roman torture, and they were easily assimilated to the stoic outlook. Now even the defeated, by becoming "a Christian," could become "a conqueror," as John (a chaplain to Constance) promises Gallicanus. When the empire reverts to paganism under Julian, Gallicanus is killed—a worldly calamity perhaps but for that very reason a *spiritual* triumph earning him "the martyr's crown" (*Opera* 158.1–2). Martyrdom allows even mere commoners to enjoy the immortal sanctification formerly restricted to deified emperors: after John, too, is executed—the protections of faith ultimately apply to the next world, not this—his "dead bones work astonishing miracles from the tomb as a testimony to their sanctity" (*Opera* 163.19–20).

A tragic death—or, in the case of the ascetic, a tragic *life*—serves in this way as the guarantor of Christianity's ultimate supremacy over paganism, since the suffering of martyrs and ascetics effectively proves both the strength of their faith and the authenticity of its object. The strength was needed for the same reason the authenticity had to be demonstrated: Christianity appeared to non-Christians as an obvious absurdity, lacking any historical pedigree or moral ballast; it was, in the words of Hrotsvit's pagan accusers, simply "the most recent superstition" (*Opera* 165.10–11). One of the more marked peculiarities of medieval drama overall is how often it revives and reiterates such accusations—how often, that is, it impersonates disbelief—in order to stage a belief impervious to doubt. Through the same paradoxical logic Hrotsvit's martyr plays return obsessively to historical moments of Christian downfall in order to demonstrate how the church vanquished other religions, which curiously take on all the attributes of medieval Christianity: for example, the Christian allegation that pagans "venerate a slave as if he were a lord" and that they purchase their idols "at an artificial price" (*Opera* 166.10–14) turns out to displace onto Christ's enemies a commonplace truth about the medieval trade in relics: such lifeless bones as John's—same as the slavish idols they had overcome and whose place they regularly took so as to Christianize former temples—could throughout the Middle Ages also be had for a price. Ancient slavery may have been displaced by medieval feudalism, but human bodies could still be traded on the market, so long as the bodies were dead and belonged to the blessed *servos Christi*, in which case they became, through a telling pun, *servandae reliquiae*—relics to be *saved* (*Opera* 265.2).

EPILOGUE: THE SENECAN RENAISSANCE IN ENGLAND

By the high Middle Ages, Christian theater may have frequently become indistinguishable from a theater of cruelty,[90] but this is not to say that the cruelty was more pronounced than the theatricality. The *passiones* that we have today—whether centering on Christ or the saints—tend to stress their contrafactual nature if for no other reason than that the various miracles invariably accompanying sacred anguish could, by definition, never seem real: whenever the impossible *appears* to happen there is no way to determine if the event is mere illusion (trickery, even) or divine intervention.[91] Hence the ancient alignment of tragedy with myth and lies, as distinct from history: "tragedy's classification as a fictional type of narrative arose in part from its treatment of supernatural subjects, in which gods and oracles assumed pivotal roles . . . It is, of course, the prominence of the gods in tragic drama that leads to the use of the *deus ex machina*, which was as notorious for its lack of credibility in antiquity as it is today."[92] The fictitiousness of medieval drama and the theatricality of medieval ritual—to say nothing of their indebtedness to paganism—routinely scandalized Christian authorities, and yet century after century of attempted reform had limited success, for the same reason that the early church had not been able (and did not really want) to eradicate totally pre-Christian idolatry. Even Protestants found it expedient to reoccupy the sacred modes they themselves had evacuated and to redirect that forbidden power to new ends.

Nowhere was the repurposing of Catholicism by Protestants more evident than in the theater. When the medieval English martyr play died with the Reformation,[93] the so-called Renaissance theater revived in its place the very form of tragedy from which the medieval martyr play had partly evolved. Early modern playwrights turned to Seneca, that is, in order to *restore* the blood tragedy they had lost to the Reformation: the buffetings and scourgings, the crucifixions and assorted passions that had formerly been ubiquitous. Take for example Thomas Kyd's *The Spanish Tragedy*. This extremely popular, deeply Senecan play has traditionally been used to illustrate what happens when the commercial stage draws inspiration from ancient models rather than the sacred drama that was by then largely out of favor. Filled with blood and classical allusion, it not only points the way to the drama of the future, we're often told, but stages the centrality of non-Christian texts to the modern, disenchanted wasteland that will drive Hieronymo mad againe. And yet more often than not Kyd's paganism works as a familiar code for *Catholicism*: his Spain is governed in equal measure by the old pantheon and by the old religion of England, sometimes simultaneously. Hieronimo walks on stage at one point "with a book in his hand" (3.13.1S.D.) quoting several phrases verbatim from Seneca's plays, plus one less perfect parallel whose real source is clearly the Bible: "Vindicta mihi" (3.13.1)—revenge is mine!

Saith the Lord, saith Nero, saith Hieronimo.[94] The latter's hope—and the hope of subsequent avengers from Hamlet to Vindice—is that private revenge might align with, and receive aid from, a higher revelation. As he implores the "sacred heavens" not to let the murder of his son "unrevealed and unrevenged pass" (3.2.5, 9), "a letter falleth" from out of nowhere, according to a stage direction, written in "red ink" (3.2.24–5S.D.) and revealing in no uncertain terms exactly whom his revenge should target. After some initial doubts about its authenticity, he decides to trick the murderers into playing the victims in a drama so that he and his conspirators can play the murderers "for real." I have to use scare quotes here because of course the "real" murder in the play-within-the-play(-within-yet-another-play, if you count the otherworldly frame story) is as fake as anything else. In other words, we can only say that these deaths "resemble the Roman custom from Nero's day described by Heywood in his *Apology for Actors* (1612), according to which criminals sentenced to capital punishment were chosen to act in tragedies in which they could be killed during the performance"[95] if we stress that the resemblance is not, in fact, the thing it resembles any more than representations of the crucifixion during the Middle Ages were actual crucifixions. The entirety of Christian liturgy and drama is predicated on the difference—a literally *saving* difference—between death and its depiction.

The person who wrote the additions to the 1602 quarto of *The Spanish Tragedy* understood perfectly well that the model for secular tragedy was the contrafactuality of sacred tragedy—and, for what it's worth, that person may well have been Shakespeare.[96] The earlier quarto is somewhat vague about the hanging of Horatio's body, whether "in the arbour" (2.4.53S.D.) or in a "bower"—or as Hieronimo has it, "on a tree" (4.4.111) (see Figure 5.5). The recollection of the rood-tree is the one adopted—and strengthened—by the 1602 additions when Hieronimo longs to see the death of his son rendered artistically, even iconographically, as though aesthetic reduplication might somehow work to salve his loss: "O stretch thine art, and let [the murderers'] beards be of Judas his own color" (3.12A.132–3). The painter's challenge, according to Hieronimo, is to match a depiction of Christ's betrayal without depicting Christ's betrayal. When Hieronimo further insists on a painting that can both move and speak, what he effectively demands is a *performance* of his son's death that might rival the biblical drama on which Shakespeare's generation had been raised. If only the painter could manage such a thing, Hieronimo exclaims, "there you may show a passion, there you may show a passion" (3.12A.151).

Elsewhere on stage you no longer could. Pagan literature had come to stand in for the iconic death of God, just as Hieronimo immediately shifts from talk of showing a passion to its Senecan counterpart: "Draw me like old Priam of Troy" (3.12A.152–3). The shift was relatively seamless because the passion and Roman tragedy already had a genetic relation: "the horrors of the 'Senecan' plays of the Elizabethan period," writes G.K.

FIGURE 5.5: Thomas Kyd, *The Spanish Tragedy* (London, 1633). Woodcut from title page showing the hanging of Horatio. Courtesy of The Huntington Library, San Marino California.

Hunter, "are often very close to those in the medieval plays concerned with the lives (and deaths) of the saints"[97]—to say nothing of their proximity to the expiatory death of Christ, performed yearly in the cycles. Secular Renaissance playwrights who turned to Seneca with the hope of recovering a lost Christian relevance were in fact not far removed from Tertullian, the father especially beloved of early modern antitheatricalists, when he listed the afflicted heroes of pagan literature as a positive parallel for the suffering of the martyrs and in the course of the list managed to name some of the figures who would populate the London stage once the saints disappeared: Dido, Cleopatra, or a nameless Athenian courtier who, like Hieronimo, "bit off her tongue and spat it in the tyrant's face, that he might be convinced of the uselessness of his torments."[98] And yet because early drama studies has been organized for so long around an alleged divide between the Middle Ages and the Renaissance, we have largely failed to see how much the Renaissance restoration of classical theater owes specifically to the medieval sanctification of pagan violence, without which the return to antiquity would not have been nearly as rich in artistry—and artificiality.

CHAPTER SIX

Politics of City and Nation

HANNAH SKODA

An Aristotelian sense of the origins and purpose of politics was pervasive in the Middle Ages; Aristotle's comments on tragedy were not (the *Poetics* was rather little read before the fifteenth century).[1] This essay, then, is not about political tragedy as a genre, nor does it trace a linear account of connections and definitions.[2] Instead, I suggest that there was a predominant way of thinking about politics in the Middle Ages as an immanent tragic mode.[3] This mode encompassed shattered expectations and the fall of the mighty: it is defined not by formal qualities but by the interweaving of motifs of fortune and excess, across philosophical tracts, history writing, epic poetry, political theory, lyric poetry, satire, and Arthurian legend, to reveal a rich tapestry of responses to political downfall.[4] Isidore of Seville defined tragedy as "lofty, sorrowful poetic songs about the crimes of wicked ancient kings."[5] Chaucer famously had his monk describe tragedy as "a certeyn storie,/ As olde books maken us memorie,/ Of hym that stood in greet prosperitee,/ And is yfallen out of heigh degree/ Into myserie, and endeth wrecchedly."[6]

Whilst a recognizable philology emerges ("misery," "misfortune," "fall," "sorrow"), the essay argues that this political tragic mode was one beset by tensions: was tragedy caused by blind misfortune, or by moral failings? What was the relation between the fall of individuals and the communities over whom they ruled? What binds these questions together is the very question of history and narrative itself. Could narrating tragedy serve a function of moral exemplarity and essentially stand above time? Or was tragedy simply part of the essentially incomprehensible circularity of human suffering relieved only by the prospect of the end of time?

Political tragedy is not just about the misfortunes of kings, queens, councilors, or aristocrats. For Aristotle, politics is about a community of citizens, and should attempt to ensure the well-being and happiness of that community through legislation: "every community is established with a view to some good; for everyone always acts in order to obtain that which they think good. But, if all communities aim at some good, the state or political community, which is the highest of all, and which embraces all the rest, aims at good in a greater degree than any other, and at the highest good."[7] Political tragedy obtains when the well-being and happiness of the community is compromised, and the nature of politics is subverted when authorities cease to act in the interests of the wider community. The tragic mode colored a series of political critiques which centered on the tension between the individual and the collectivity. It was a tension cut across by a further pull between a Boethian sense of innocent victimhood, versus an Aristotelian framework of moral fault.

These tensions so cut to the quick of the political project that they evoke a set of reflections on the nature of history itself. If the recounting of tragedy inevitably involves the work of history, is this history as rhetorical exemplar, or as senseless postlapsarian fall? Tragic events might be deemed to carry didactic moral weight and permit the linear progression of humankind, but there was also a sense of the inexplicability of endless tragic cyclical temporalities.[8] Fundamentally, then, two kinds of tragic thought emerged out of these tensions: in one, misery could be construed as a kind of foundation sacrifice,[9] appalling but ultimately constructive if only through its exemplary function; in another, the misery simply engendered ongoing and monotonous destruction.

This essay takes a tour of politically engaged texts, exploring their use of these motifs and the tensions they evoked and sustained. The texts discussed here provide a somewhat idiosyncratic selection, some more obvious than others. I visualize this as a rich tapestry of responses to political life. And whilst we can trace shifting responses to the fraught relationship between chance and the moral, the individual and the collective, the historical and the exemplary, this is not an exercise in teleology. Rather, we shall follow the shuttle as these motifs are woven to reveal political responses, critiques, and laments, and the vivid patterns of emotional responses which emerge.

BOETHIUS' *CONSOLATION OF PHILOSOPHY* AND OTTO OF FREISING'S *CHRONICLE*

In many ways, Boethius' *Consolation of Philosophy* serves as a kind of urtext for the political tragic mode. Boethius provides an emblematic medieval response to political misfortune which resonated across the Middle Ages.[10] Writing in the early sixth century, Anicius Manlius Severinus Boethius was a Roman senator who suffered a spectacular fall from grace during the rule of the Ostrogothic King Theoderic the Great. Boethius suffered a long imprisonment, culminating in his execution in 524 on charges of trying to overthrow Theoderic. During his time in prison, Boethius wrote his most influential text, framing it as a narrative of the comfort offered to him in his darkest days by the appearance of Lady Philosophy.[11] The text is written alternately in verse and prose, and was wildly popular across the Middle Ages, surviving in a large number of manuscripts, and woven across a dizzying array of later texts. Boethius presents a set of reflections on the workings of fortune, visualized both as an allegorical figure with a stony heart, and as a wheel whose turning is both unpredictable and relentless. The image of the wheel of Fortune was central to the medieval tragic mode, and Boethius' depiction was seminal. It is an immensely powerful and terrifying picture of rapid rise and equally crushing descent.[12] The wheel's presence across the iconography of the Middle Ages is well attested,[13] and as an image of the uncontrollable fall of the mighty, it evokes, more than any other emotion, tragic despair. When Fortune appears to Boethius, she asks him rhetorically, "what does *the cry of tragedians* [*clamor tragoediarum*] mourn if not Fortune's overthrowing of happy kingdoms with indiscriminate blows?" (Book II, prose II. 16) In the face of understandable self-pity, Boethius learns to respond with stoic fortitude, and the personified Philosophy restores all that is most noble about him. The influence of classical stoicism is plain in the text, as is Boethius' Aristotelian framework, although Boethius accepts neither at face value.[14]

The text appears to chart a fairly straightforward journey from despair to acceptance and elevation above the vicissitudes of this life. Boethius does not accept that his own behavior could have caused the distress in which he finds himself. He wholeheartedly lays the blame at the foot of the heartless Fortune. However, the text further explores the relationship between Fortune and Divine Providence, and ultimately establishes an Augustinian understanding of providence underwriting with a greater plan than even the most inexplicably cruel workings of chance.[15] In a sense, this is the dialectic of despair and hope: despair at the power of chance, hope in the workings of God, and moral responsibility in the choice between the two. Despite Fortune, there is room for ethical choices in how one responds to tragedy.

There is a biblical figure somewhat akin to Boethius in the apparent senselessness of the trials and tribulations to which he was subjected. This is Job.[16] A virtuous man, on whom poverty, disease, and death have rained down, Job is an enormously problematic biblical figure, but one who enables the thinking through of apparently inexplicable suffering. Put bluntly, how can a good God allow such undeserved misery? Gregory the Great's *Moralia in Job* was composed in 578, not much later than the writings of Boethius, and was widely copied throughout the Middle Ages: Gregory was following in a line of commentators from Ambrose of Milan to John Chrysostom.[17] Gregory's treatment of Job offsets the apparent senselessness of Job's suffering against the need for moral responsibility. Job's rebellious phase, wherein he laments the injustice of his situation, is chastised, and we are reminded of the ultimately unknowable plan of God. When viewed through this lens, Boethius' exploration of the balance of Fortune and Divine Providence is set in relief.[18] And moral responsibility is shown, by Gregory, to lie in one's response to misfortune—this is Job's lesson, won at unimaginable personal cost.[19] Indeed, Gregory's particular focus was upon the moral battle that one must fight: in contrast to the Stoic position of patient acceptance of suffering, Gregory suggested that suffering provided an opportunity for spiritual soldiery.[20] It emerges then, that despite the undeserved nature of Boethius' fall from grace, a moral framework and ethical prerogatives and choices survive.

If Job, via Gregory, becomes emblematic for all medieval Christians facing daily suffering, Boethius' use of allegorical figures also shifts it discursively towards the exemplum. That exemplary quality would seem to indicate this is a moral tale which stands above time in its lessons of how to respond philosophically to suffering. And in many ways, this element of the tragic mode is Boethius' most enduring legacy: even nowadays, we talk of "philosophical" responses to misfortune. It was an element which directly and crucially influenced historiography. Otto of Freising, the twelfth-century chronicler, for example, constructs his history as a series of exempla of suffering, and explicitly states in the prologue of his *Chronicle* that "the discerning reader will be able to find not so much histories as pitiful tragedies [*tragediae*]."[21] He approves Boethius' message of active acceptance of the "tragedies of the disasters of humankind [*mortalium calamitatum tragediae*]" in the work's dedication: "the greatest solace in life is to be found in handling and thoroughly learning all the teachings of philosophy."[22]

On the other hand, Boethius, unlike Job, had an immediate political context. The narrative is created through personal experience, and through the deliberate slippage between the historical Boethius and his literary incarnation, or, put differently, between Boethius as author and Boethius as character. In its inextricable intertwining with historical circumstance, the narrative arc is complicated and disrupted, and any sense of moral closure is profoundly problematized. Medieval readers knew, as we know, that Boethius' personal acceptance of his lot is but a small flicker of resolution in a landscape otherwise beset for many centuries to come by what often seemed senseless historical conflict and injustice. The exemplary and the historical intertwined to create an intensely personal story which resonated across the medieval centuries in the tragic mode of political thinking. The tensions evoked by Boethius tugged at the strands of political critique across discourses and genres: political tragedy engaged both with a sense of moral exemplarity, and with a far more dispiriting gesture towards historical cycles of misery.

THE *SONG OF ROLAND*

Boethius' portrayal of Divine Providence provides a moral-theological framework for thinking through the presence of misery in the world across a range of genres. This informed and complicated popular epics such as the *Song of Roland*.

The *Song of Roland* is a text in tragic mode.[23] The proud and mighty rearguard of the army of Charlemagne is destroyed by the wicked pagans through the treachery of Roland's stepfather Ganelon: this is the Battle of Roncevaux in 778, although the text appears to date in its surviving form to between 1040 and 1115.[24] Roland became a figure emblematic of a certain kind of chivalric heroism—even if the ethical system of chivalry evolved rather later than Roland's first appearances—but the story also became a prototypical tragedy, with Ganelon cited as a metonymic figure of the traitor who engenders tragedy in Chaucer's *Monk's Tale*.[25] The tragic mode is evoked most simply by the motif of the fall of the mighty—Roland is the nephew of Charlemagne, he is handsome, brave, and admired. His death is prolonged, excessively painful and gory, and his fall spectacular.

The *Roland*'s drawing upon Boethius is not always obvious, but there are moments at which the threads seem to be interwoven. Roland himself is enmeshed in a discussion of fortune, as a hero whose splendid prospects are tragically destroyed by his ill-luck in having a stepfather writhing with senseless hatred and envy. In this sense, Roland is destroyed by chance and by the evil of others. Charlemagne's response to his nephew's death is couched in terms of the overturning of order (l. 2890). But fortune here is integrated into an ethical-religious framework, whereby Roland's death is the work both of his Saracen enemies and of his ill-willing stepfather Ganelon.

The role of ill-luck is complicated by the key line: "Your courage brought ill fortune" (l. 1731). Roland's companion-in-arms, Olivier, urges him to summon back the main army by blowing on his horn: Roland repeatedly refuses. It is the choices made by Roland himself which give fortune (via the treachery of Ganelon) its purchase on his death. Indeed, it is around the same time that William of Conches wrote his riposte to Boethius' view of blind fortune, asserting that tragedy is the depiction of the moral failings of the protagonists.[26] The plot offers some narrative resolution. Charlemagne returns with the main army to avenge the death of Roland, the pagans under King Marsilion are brutally defeated, and the survivors forced to convert to Christianity (*pace* canon law),[27] Ganelon is eventually tortured and put to death for his betrayal of his stepson. But any apparent closure achieved through this brutal revenge is offset by an unanswerable question which lay at the heart of much political critique throughout the Middle Ages.[28] "Roland is courageous (*proz*) and Olivier is wise (*sage*)" (l. 1093). In one sense then, Roland's extreme courage verges on hubris and folly, as witnessed by his refusal to summon back the army by blowing on his horn: this pride brings about his downfall, as well as that of the twenty thousand men for whom he was effectively responsible. But Roland is the great chivalric hero, and he remains so throughout the text. Superficially, Olivier's caution would seem to speak in his favor, but there is a flatness in his pleas. As an audience, we are caught up in Roland's charisma: we admire Olivier, but we are not encouraged to take his side unilaterally against Roland. The latter speaks powerfully through the assonant stanzas (known as laisses), his claims of glory and integrity sustained by the insistent bluntness of his voice. And yet, the very repetitiveness of his refusal and the static nature of his obstinacy in the face of Oliver's urgings frustrate the listeners whose sense of the rhythm and pace of the poem is thus stilted. We might assume medieval audiences to feel similarly torn by the clash of rationalities, of charisma and wisdom, of epic heroics and yet narrative circularity which these heroics entail. This is no catharsis.

The text as we have it is a written form of an array of oral performances. We must imagine minstrels singing or declaiming the poem, helped by the various musical elements built into the text: the repeated motifs, the assonant lines, the rhythmic use of caesurae, the use of successive stanzas offering different cinematic perspectives on the action.[29] This is a text whose assonant form and intense musicality appeal emotionally in ways which can move beyond the meaning of words. We experience pity, fear, awe, and misery, sometimes simultaneously. But the knot of emotions is never really disentangled, and we are left with a critical moral dilemma.

There is a fraught political context for all of this. France in the late eleventh century was in the midst of what might loosely be termed the "Feudal Revolution":[30] it was an increasingly fragmented polity with high levels of violence. Indeed, this was a situation which persisted late into the Middle Ages.[31] But the *Roland* is no straightforward critique of this. Brutal violence may have brought political tragedy on a dispiritingly regular basis, but it was not rejected out of hand. The song is not set up as a contest between wisdom and bravery (*sagesse* and *proece*): the problem is the impossibility of disentangling the roles of these qualities in the kind of heroism sustained by brutal cultures of violence and political fragmentation. It is this entanglement which lies at the heart of the tragedy of the epic. And in the political context of the production of the song, this invoked a further, highly pertinent, question: what was the relationship between personal tragedy, the choices which lead to it, and the political community? Twenty thousand men perish alongside Roland: his concern is for his personal integrity ("He is poor of heart who balks at danger," l. 1107), Oliver's concern is for the community for which they are responsible ("Franks are dead because of your whim," l. 1726). The tension was not just between wisdom and courage, but between personal ethics and the well-being of the community.

JOHN OF SALISBURY AND GILES OF ROME

Perhaps the most striking and influential ways of conceptualizing community was via a corporeal analogy. The most substantial working out of the metaphor of the body politic was by John of Salisbury, the author of the *Policraticus* (*c.* 1159):[32] "The excellence of the head [the political leader] must always flourish because the health of the whole body depends upon it."[33] John was attuned to what he described as the "tragedia" of the human condition,[34] so the corporeal metaphor provided ways to conceptualize the relationship between individual and collective tragedy. John of Salisbury was particularly interested in the figure of the tyrant as responsible for the downfall and disintegration of communities: "the tyrant is, therefore, one who oppresses the people by violent domination, just as the prince is one who rules by the laws."[35] The first tyrant was, he claims, Nimrod, the Old Testament king whose excessive pride led him to attempt to erect a tower which would reach up into the heavens.[36] Nimrod is driven ever onwards by boundless ambition, unrestrained by the boundaries of law. According to John, Nimrod's tragedy is that of a king struck down by an angry God (after all, "all tyrants reach a miserable end"[37])—but it is also one of the tragedy of the community which Nimrod was supposed to lead. Indeed, his tyranny is exercised through the laboring of his people who construct the ridiculous tower. And John does not hesitate to take a step further and explore the implication that the community itself must be held responsible for "this affliction" of tyranny in the first place.[38]

The relationship between the tragedy of community and that of their leader gained even more traction over the course of the thirteenth century, with explicit discussions about the nature of the common good. If the subject of politics is essentially the relationship between individuals and their communities, the latter taken to be something more than just the sum of its parts, then discussions of the common good addressed the goals of those communities, the ways in which they might be assured, and the ways in which they might be catastrophically destroyed.[39] This provided a fresh articulation of the effects of tragedy on communities, as something more than a collection of individuals. If the tragic mode until this point had left unresolved the relationship between personal miseries, and the effects on the political community, discussions of the common good provided a new lens.

Giles of Rome's *De Regimine Principum* was a mirror for a prince, an emerging genre that explicitly addresses the relationship between the individual and the collectivity.[40] As a set of reflections on how to be a good prince, the text explores the ways in which the actions and experiences of that prince as an individual impact upon, and should indeed be shaped by, the interests of the political community as a whole. The sins of the prince, could rapidly become the misery of the community. It is an explicitly didactic text, written between 1277 and 1280, apparently in response to a request from King Philip III of France. Giles draws on Aristotelian rhetoric to discuss the goal of political power and how it might be achieved. He did not explicitly articulate a vision of the tragic, but it is nevertheless implied here, as the model of the good prince is set beside the tyrant, under whose rule the whole political community suffers.[41]

Matthew Kempshall argues that Giles places Aristotelian rhetoric center stage in both the constitution and the delivery of the common good.[42] Giles critically engaged with the idea that the manipulation of emotions through language and performance might shape responses to politics. The wicked prince, then, is he who ignores the laws by which he should be bound, and who acts and speaks in self-interest, rather than in the interests of the common good and the community whose well-being his role should be to assure. The relationship between the wicked personal traits of that ruler, and the "misery" of the community as a whole is more fully articulated. It is the role of rhetoric—both for princes, and for writers like Giles—in assuring, or, misdirected, in destroying, the interests of the commons which opens up the relationship between personal and political tragedy.[43]

This political ("deliberative") rhetoric was about general principles, rather than specific actions. This kind of rhetoric was crucial in the relationship or breakdown between ruler and common good. But it was also the rhetoric in which Giles himself was interested as a purveyor of political advice, and as a potential writer in the tragic mode. In this sense, the implications for the tragic mode cut to the heart of the relationship between tragedy as moral exemplum, and as historical contingency. Giles weighed in against the narration of particular historical events, as lacking the wider applicability required by deliberative rhetoric, and in doing so, he radically reconfigured the ways in which didactic texts might function.[44] In other words, the narration of individual tragedies were deemed to serve no moral function. The use of deliberative rhetoric in the interests of the political community was a push-back against the idea that historical tragedies might indeed serve as moral exempla, with obvious implications for medieval historiography, as well as for the tragic mode more generally. Giles, along with other Aristotelians of the fourteenth-century schools, railed against what Peter of Abano termed "the laborious and pointless piling up of examples."[45] By this token, the recounting of tragic historical episodes was deemed to be contrary to the goal of rhetoric, and permitted no lessons to be drawn: tragedy was rooted in time, and limited in its capacity to educate.

DANTE'S *COMMEDIA*

But this shift in emphasis did not entirely undermine the moral function of tragedy. Its didactic purpose continued to be held in tension with a sense of the rootedness of misery in contingent human histories. The seminal figure of Dante Alighieri in the early fourteenth century looms over all such discussions. Dante was a highly politically engaged writer, composing the *Commedia* in the shadow of exile from violence and factionalism in Florence. His own personal tragedy is interwoven with a sense of the tragedy of Florence, and indeed the tragedy of all humanity. The temporality of the narrative vignettes presented by Dante, character, as he makes his way first through Hell, is juxtaposed with the eschatological setting of the text as a whole. The sins embodied so gruesomely in the *Inferno* evoke a series of political tragedies which are both characteristic of a postlapsarian world and can bear no resolution, and whose presentation might serve as a moral exemplum to the reader: the characters encountered by Dante in the text frequently exhort him to take heed of their troubles and carry the message back to Florence. This tragic mode then is both rooted in time, and stands beyond it.

Just as the tragic here is set in an obviously postlapsarian context, the sinners in *Inferno* paying the price for humanity's first sin, so political distress is here also depicted as the inevitable consequence of an angry Mars. Given the entire conceit of the *Commedia* as a journey through Hell, Purgatory, and eventually Heaven, one might expect that Dante would privilege the role of pride and moral responsibility in the causes of political tragedy. But he presents, in fact, a more complex interweaving of those tensions: the planets are aligned so that misery will ensue. We encounter once again the irresolvable tension between the moral responsibility of humanity for its own downfall, and a sense that this was always bound to happen. It is perhaps in this sense that the role of Boethius' *Consolation of Philosophy* functions most strikingly as an effective intertext to the politically tragic mode of the *Commedia* as a whole.[46] One can see the figure of Lady Philosophy in Dante's love, Beatrice; and Boethius himself appears as a martyr in heaven in *Paradiso* X (ll. 124–9). If tragedy is at once a matter of Divine Providence, and owing to humankind's own moral failings, Beatrice offers a way to transcend these vicissitudes.

John of Salisbury's tyrant Nimrod reappears at the center of Dante's Hell in the early fourteenth century. His positioning at the very bottom of the *Inferno* gives him a foundational role in the tragedy of the entire human community. The fall of the tower of Babel was accompanied by the breakdown of language: crushed, dispirited, or destroyed, the humans who had attempted to reach the heavens found themselves unable to communicate with one another. In *Inferno* XXXI, he is unable to utter anything meaningful, but disrupts the linguistic flow with his futile expletive: "Raphèl may amèch zabi almi" (l. 67).[47] The collapse of his tower is the collapse of human communities, left undone by the disintegration of language as a fundamental social glue. For Boccaccio, fifty years later, Nimrod signified both the effects of excessive pride on the political community, and its futility in the face of the relentless passage of time.[48]

In *Inferno* X, Dante character encounters the shade of a contemporary embodiment of pride: the great nobleman, Farinata. Farinata recognizes Dante's Tuscan dialect, and epitomizes the political tragedy of the city: the nobleman had led the Ghibelline party in Florence against the rising power of the Guelfs. His sin is one of heresy, the ultimate sin of division: he and his wife had been posthumously convicted and their bones scattered. But Farinata's tragedy is rooted in pride. He looks at Dante character "disdainfully" (l. 41), and asks him about his ancestors. Dante's response is met with an utterly unrepentant account of how he, Farinata, scattered them, accompanied by the marvelously understated movement of his eyebrows (l. 45). Farinata's tragedy is that of a great man brought as low as can be, and it is emotionally elevated by his uncompromising arrogance.

In *Inferno* VII, the Dante character had asked his guide, Virgil, to tell him about "this fortune whom you speak of / Who is she, who holds the riches of the world in her arms?" (ll. 68–9). Virgil replies with a description of a Boethian figure of fortune, "who in due course transfers the empty wealth/ From one people to another, and from one family to another" (ll. 79–80). If the workings of fortune are unknowable, we should nevertheless, like Boethius, learn to accept them for fortune has been instituted by "He whose wisdom transcends everything" (l. 72). The struggle against the throes and whims of these movements of fortune bears its own moral weight: it is a refusal to accept Divine Providence. Farinata's pride in *Inferno* X represents something graver than the continuation of his earthly arrogance. If we struggle against the dictates of fortune, Virgil tells Dante, we become "those who should give her praise / [yet] wrongfully blame and slander her" (VII: ll. 92–3).

But if Divine Providence appears to provide a framework for understanding the fall of figures such as Farinata, it is held in tension not only with his own arrogance, but also with the figure of Mars, glowering over contemporary Florence. To Farinata's question about the continued violence against his kindred, Dante character describes the "torment and great slaughter" as sacrifices to Mars (X: ll. 85–7). Mars is again invoked in *Paradiso* XVI, when Dante character encounters his great-great-grandfather, Cacciaguida, and hears his famous lament for Florence, now beset by division, greed, and violence. It is a lengthy passage shot through with nostalgic longing for what Dante poet considers to be the good old days.[49] A lost nobility of blood is intertwined with the decline and disintegration of the common good of the city. Cacciaguida evokes the murder of the young nobleman Buondelmonte, the moment at "when were born your sorrows [fleto] / ... / And put an end to your life of happiness [lietro]." The tragedy is presented here as one of concentric circles: it is that of those immediately involved, that of their families, that of Florence, and that of subsequent generations. And the murder was committed beneath "that dreadful stone / Which guards the bridge" (ll. 145–6): the statue of Mars, god of war. This becomes, then, tragedy arbitrarily inflicted by cruel gods, standing in for Divine Providence. The tension extends to the temporality of Cacciaguida's speech. He evokes a sense of exemplarity through his moralistic and nostalgic longing for a past age, and effectively critiques the present Florentine tragedy as "mal de la cittade" (l. 68, also ll. 149–50), not least by a series of counterfactual "would that"s or "what if"s (e.g., ll. 52, 58). But there is also a sense of terminal decline and uncontrollable misery with the setting of his speech in the poem within the celestial sphere of Mars, and the whims of "la Fortuna" (l. 84): in this perspective, no morals can be drawn, and there is no rhetoric of exemplarity.

Cacciaguida's narrative most effectively intertwines personal tragedy with that of the city of Florence. But the community could be wider still, and the personal tragedy all the more intimate. Piero delle Vigne is encountered by Dante character amongst the suicides in *Inferno* XIII. He was a counselor to Frederick II, who rose up from low rank only to come crashing down. He was imprisoned and eventually killed himself. The passage might be set in dialogue with Boethius' *Consolation of Philosophy*. Here we have a Boethian-like figure, whose political success mirrored Boethius' own senatorial position, and whose seemingly inexplicable fall was followed by imprisonment of a particularly cruel kind. Piero delle Vigne in fact wrote his own *Consolation of Philosophy*, but he remained unconsoled (ll. 70–2). Piero's own elaborate speech in the *Commedia* reminds Dante character and the wider circle of readers that Piero was himself a great counselor and rhetorician (l. 58–9): his was a position as an individual at the heart of a political community; his tragedy is the tragedy of the community as a whole. The encounter is followed by one with an anonymous Florentine suicide who tells Dante character that "I made a gibbet for myself from my own house" (l. 151). The very silence regarding his name reveals that his suicide is somehow also that of a political body, and the evocation of his house renders his personal downfall that of the city. Once again, his short and painful speech to Dante evokes Mars, watching with impassive face the war and tragedy rending the city. The relationship between individual and collective tragedy is now indissociable.

The *Commedia* is underpinned by Dante's own sense of personal tragedy: in many ways, his own exile from Florence is emblematic of a wider project to connect individual loss with the destruction of the city he loved, and with the disintegration and fragmentation of the Christian community more widely.

LE ROMAN DE FAUVEL

If Dante's *Commedia* is anything but funny,[50] satires similarly entangled the personal and contingent, and the moral and exemplary, often through self-consciously excessive allegory. The defeat of the Black Guelphs in 1301 was a catastrophic moment for Dante himself, and a central figure in this defeat was deemed to be Charles of Valois, named in *Purgatorio* VII as the man whose invasion of Italy caused such tragedy. Various pieces of circumstantial evidence link him to the production of a satirical text known as the *Roman de Fauvel* by Gervais du Bus, a brutal up-ending of a mirror for a prince.[51]

Charles, the younger brother of Philip IV of France, is a somewhat shadowy figure at the heart of many of the tragic political events of the early fourteenth century. France in the early fourteenth century was contending with a contest with the papacy over the relationship between spiritual and temporal power, an unpopular king, the debasement of the coinage, war with England, rising taxes, and the fall of the Templars.[52] Much was explained via the trope of evil counselors, and this was interwoven with the motif of the Wheel of Fortune in the *Roman de Fauvel*. Fauvel is a horse. His name is an acronym, and stands for *flaterie, avarice, vilanie, variété, envie,* and *lascheté*. The conceit of the poem is that all the king's counselors, all the churchmen of the land, and even the pope, cannot resist fawning over this horse who is plied with gifts, stroked, and flattered.

Fauvel is a text which invites exasperated laughter of the uncomfortable kind. It resonates with Adam de la Halle's almost contemporaneous *Jeu de la Feuillée*: the latter is a kind of satirical review which explores the fragility of the ever speedier pace of urban and commercial life. Adam de la Halle positions figures from contemporary Arras on a vast wheel of Fortune turned in surreal fashion by a desperately over-hyped Fée Morgane.[53] It is partly the intertextuality of these texts which sharpens the laughter they elicit. The *Jeu de la Feuillée* has a charivari-like quality to it,[54] mocking those who are down and policing social boundaries through cruel and noisy laughter. It forms part of a quite different emotional register for the tragic mode: this is still about horror and bewilderment at the fall of the mighty, but tears are subsumed in mockery and acrid giggles. The *Roman de Fauvel* also famously contains a charivari scene, which may in the surviving manuscript indeed be the earliest pictorial depiction of a charivari. In it, we see Fauvel serenaded by a group of peasants dressed in outlandish costumes, often half-man, half-beast, banging wildly on diverse instruments in an ugly cacophony.[55] The excessive ambition, flattery, and self-service which the text sets up as the tragedy of the political community, are met with bruising mockery.

Charles of Valois had a particularly loathing for the royal counselor Enguerrand de Marigny, a figure who stood in popular opinion as the epitome of self-serving and divisive political machinations. It is highly likely that the *Roman de Fauvel* was intended as a thinly veiled attack on Marigny. Like Piero delle Vigne, Marigny rose from relatively humble origins to assume a position as the king's most trusted adviser: Philip IV granted him the position of grand chamberlain, and he was hated by many of the older aristocratic families at court who felt their position and approach to be usurped. After Philip's death in 1314, Marigny was arrested by Louis X, spurred on by Charles of Valois, now the uncle of the king.[56] Charges of corruption were unprovable, but Charles came up with further charges of sorcery which resulted in Marigny's ignominious hanging on April 30, 1315. The afterlife of the *Roman de Fauvel* then, saw its target suffer his own tragedy on the wheel of an unmoved Fortuna. But the attack on this figure in the *Roman* itself presented the tragedy as that of the king, of France, and of Christendom. All were brought low by deceit, ambition, and avarice: "He [Fauvel] leads everyone a dance / The better to interfere and to corrupt / He spins and spins them around again / He devotes all his ability and effort to this / So that today, every creature / Is turned contrary to what God / Intended him for" (ll. 492–8). The political purpose of the tragic mode—the probable targeting of Marigny himself—was possible precisely because of a far clearer articulation in the text of the relationship between the individual and the community.

The *Fauvel* might provoke troubled and angry laughter against Marigny, but he is never named and the reliance of a series of types in the text renders the sense of tragedy all the more capacious. In other words, the *Roman de Fauvel* works through allegory. The political disaster of contemporary France is allegorized, so that the individual tragedy at its heart assumes a universal dimension as the sins embodied by Fauvel the horse resonate across time and space. Marigny's master, Philip IV, is referred to on multiple occasions in Dante's *Commedia*, but also never by name. He is the "mal di Francia." Dante holds in tension the personal tragedy of a king deemed to be a wicked tyrant, with the collective tragedy of a scourge so recognizable it needs no name. This relationship between allegory and individual may evoke the collective implications of political tragedy, but it also complicates the sense of tragedy as exemplary: universality and historical specificity are interwoven.

Philip IV's great crime was to divide that which should be united. This is, of course, a theme running through Dante's political thought, and most clearly embodied in the theory of universal monarchy of his *Monarchia*.[57] Dante's intra-textual guide, Virgil, is emblematic of the tragedy of the fall of Troy and the hope which eventually sprung from it. But the other great classical tragedy which forms a diptych for Dante with the *Aeneid* was Lucan's *Pharsalia*, an account of the civil wars between Julius Caesar and Pompey.[58] If Virgil presents a new city emerging out of the ashes of Troy's tragic destruction, the *Pharsalia* is the blood-bath into which that new Roman empire so rapidly sank. It is a text whose tragedy is evoked through repulsive scenes of horrific violence, all the result of political division and the privileging of personal interest above that of the common good. Dante follows Lucan in attributing the fundamental cause of political tragedy to division.

LYDGATE'S *SERPENT OF DIVISION* AND THOMAS MALORY'S *MORTE DARTHUR*

Lucan then provides yet another weft in the medieval tragic mode, notably coloring John Lydgate's *Serpent of Division*. If Dante's use of Lucan is complex and sophisticated,[59] Lydgate's references to Lucan in his *Serpent of Division* seem more basic, name-checking rather than fully integrating him intertextually into his writing. It is clear that Lucan had, by this stage in 1422, become a cultural reference point.

Lydgate (1370–1451) was an impressively prolific writer, actively engaged in royal service in producing vernacular accounts of the fall of Troy, the siege of Thebes, saints' legends, and the massive *Fall of Princes*.[60] The tragic mode in all of these texts is clearly prominent, notably because of their models. By 1422, classical definitions of tragedy were well-known, and generic expectations more clearly delineated: in his *Fall of Princes*, Lydgate, following Laurent Premierfait, defined tragedy as "Touchyng the vices off flesshli fantasies / . . . / And ech thynge punshe that was to God odible" (II.3071–3). Many scholars have traced the connections between the Senecan tragedies and Boethius, and these later texts in tragic vein.[61] Genealogies might stretch from Dante to Boccaccio, via the latter's *Esposizioni* on Dante's *Inferno*,[62] Boccaccio's *De Casibus* on the fall of great men,[63] to Chaucer who wrote his *Monk's Tale*, a catalog of tragic heroism, after a visit to Italy,[64] to Gower and Lydgate. But this is not the aim of this essay, and the tapestry is more complex than such a linear account might suggest.

The *Serpent of Division* was written in 1422, the year of the death of Henry V. After the glory years of military conquest in France and the apparently astounding coup that was the Treaty of Troyes in 1420, granting Henry the regency and the inheritance of the kingdom of France, he died suddenly leaving an infant son, and a very unclear will.[65] Inevitably, despite the very able work of his brother, the Duke of Bedford, quarreling and factionalism ensued. The *Serpent of Division* is quite explicitly set in tragic mode by an opening reference to Chaucer's *Monk's Tale*, the source of a fresh definition of tragedy.[66] The motifs of fortune and overweening pride are prominent: "fals convitise brought Inne pride and vayne ambicion." Fortune's wheel is as cruel and as relentless as ever: "ladye Dame Fortune the blynde and the perverse goddes with hir gery and unware violence sparith nother Emperour nor kygne to plonge him down sodeynely frome heist prikke of hir unstable whele."[67] But the text does more than just recycle these motifs. It is perhaps the injection of a more explicitly classical vein of tragedy, but also the ever-clearer articulation of the relationship between individual and collective tragedy which lends a particular poignancy. The sustained references to Lucan place the relationship between individual and community at the very heart of the text: "lyche as Lucan rehersith in his poeticall boke that the denyenge of this worship to Julius was chefe grownde and occasion of all the werre that began in Rome." Indeed, in the explicit, this is clear: "And for teschewe stryf and dissencion, / Within yowreself beth not contrarious, / Remembring ay in yowre discreccion / Of Pompey and Cesar Iulius."[68]

It is a text often dismissed as rather crude, failing to resolve the relationship between fortune and moral responsibility.[69] But this is surely the point. One of the central threads running through the tragic mode over the course of the Middle Ages, from Boethius onwards, had always been the impossibility of grasping how one's own ethical accountability might be reconciled with the workings of fate: and indeed, how Divine Providence might frame that tension. Indeed, Boccaccio's introduction to his accounts of tragic falls of great men, the *De Casibus*, makes precisely this point:[70] it was one picked up upon by Lydgate in his own *Fall of Princes*.[71] This complexity takes the *Serpent of Division* beyond a straightforward political critique into a different sphere altogether. It is a far more complex and problematic text: after all, Henry was dead anyway, so who could be the single target?

Tensions in the text remain deliberately unresolved, time itself is left knotted. Is history an exemplar, or will this happen again? Is this a narrative or a myth? One reading might see the political division and tragedy in the text as a kind of foundation sacrifice on an Augustinian model,[72] a point also made in the *Monk's Tale*. But the *Serpent* swiftly follows Lucan in showing this misery, *pace* Virgil, to be unending and cyclical.

This last question is, in a sense, thematized in *Le Morte Darthur*,[73] the late medieval retelling of the Arthurian legends by the absurdly talented and violently criminous Thomas Malory. Generically, the text is a far cry from the classically-learned and politically-loaded texts of Lydgate, but Arthurian legends too have a tragic mode. The final episode of the text describes the end of Arthur himself: "For I will into the vale of Avilion to heal me of my grievous wound; and if thou hear never more of me, pray for my soul" (516). In a Lucanian vein, it is division and treachery which finally dissolves the round table, that ultimate symbol of chivalric and political community and governance. Mordred's treachery lies at the heart of the final battle, "the traitor that all this woe hath wrought" (512). Fortune makes an implicit appearance here in Arthur's final dream, wherein "he sat upon a chaflet in a chair, and the chair was fast to a wheel, and thereupon sat King Arthur in the richest cloth of gold that might be made . . . And suddenly the King thought that the wheel turned upside down, and he fell among the serpents, and every beast took him by a limb" (510). But there is a very real tension between the moral responsibilities of the characters, and the wider framework in which they are caught: the episode features an emblematic reminder of Tristan's love potion (477), which, like the magic throughout the text, served to complicate personal responsibility with the intrusion of forces beyond human control.[74] It is a highly emotive episode, evoking pity, anger, and distress. The length, beauty, and intricate characterizations of the Arthurian figures over several centuries render this downfall all the more distressing.

But the very elevation of the subject matter leaves the readers wondering about the role of narrative and causation. Is this a mythological and moral story standing above and beyond the time of a postlapsarian world, rhetorically appealing with a generalized message of political community? Or is it a narrative of endless cyclical violence? Malory's own enigmatic presence behind the text, the brigand and gentleman, reminds us of a political context in which this tension between moral exemplum transcending time and relentless historical violence must have seemed particularly poignant.

CONCLUSION

The medieval political tragic mode was a richly textured tapestry of motifs. It told the stories of the fall of the powerful, and the disintegration of the communities over which they were supposed to rule; its resonant imagery was that of the Wheel of Fortune, and the theme of obstinate pride. Political tragedy was expressed across a range of genres: its tone and its themes were addressed in medieval historiography, epic, lyric poetry, political theory, satire, and romance. It was complicated by a series of tensions, never resolved, always problematic. Was tragedy induced by the moral failings of protagonists, or the workings of blind fortune? Was it about individuals, or the communities over whom they ruled, a tension at the very heart of politics? Could its re-tellings serve an exemplary purpose, providing moral guidance and cutting across time, or were tragedies wrapped up in the relentless accumulation of pain and human suffering, rooted in time and unable in any way to transcend it? In other words could it be rhetorical, or was it merely narrative?

Implicit across all these questions is the purpose of political tragedy. It could be construed as didactic, providing moral guidance on behavior to avoid, and how to accept one's fate. It could be pointedly critical of particular rulers and regimes. But the reality of the tensions at the heart of the tragic mode meant that none of these purposes were served unambivalently. Ultimately readers, viewers, audiences were left with the most profoundly troubling sense that all the misery might mean nothing more than the probability of further suffering.

CHAPTER SEVEN

Society and Family

THERESA COLETTI

This essay pursues an encounter between late-medieval English biblical drama and some historical, literary, and critical traditions accompanying the discussion of tragedy as a dramatic genre in the West. It focuses on Middle English dramas representing the Massacre of the Innocents, whose six surviving witnesses—the most for any biblical subject in the corpus of that drama—span fifteenth- and early sixteenth-century traditions of late-medieval community performance. Adapting the event recounted only in the gospel of Matthew 2:1–18, the plays dramatize King Herod's attempt to thwart Hebrew prophecies of a new king's birth by ordering the killing of all male children under the age of two, among whom he believes the promised young king to be numbered. All of the English plays dealing with this disturbing subject radically juxtapose maternal care for children, and anguish about their slaughter, with violent acts of masculine sovereignty within hierarchical political worlds, producing spectacles of bodily dismemberment, mourning, and justice. And because they focus on the domestic sphere's invasion by realms of official power, these plays allow us to see how medieval tragedies of society and family figure in a larger cultural history of theater.

MEDIEVAL TRAGEDY: THINKING THE POSSIBILITIES

More than half a century ago, V.A. Kolve famously asserted that "medieval drama owes nothing to the tragedy and comedy of either Greece or Rome; it was a fresh beginning, unrooted in any formal tradition of theater."[1] Among his many important contributions, Kolve explained how vernacular biblical drama's capacious aesthetic—especially its propensity for "religious laughter"—exploited the comedic potential in episodes of scriptural history that had usually been understood as deeply serious, even potentially tragic. In this view, medieval drama undermined both the generic expectations of classical antiquity and those of the early modern playhouse. Yet, despite his study's freshness, Kolve's ready dismissal of medieval biblical theater's possible kinship with its dramatic forebears participated in a familiar literary and historical narrative of tragedy's demise during the medieval millennium (c. 500–1500).

Recent developments in medieval drama scholarship, however, have established that medieval intellectuals and artists exhibited curiosity about, if also misunderstandings of, the substance and form of ancient tragic drama, and did much to develop and sustain awareness of its traditions.[2] Groundbreaking work by Carol Symes, for example, points to medieval patristic authorities' lively, nuanced awareness of ancient dramatic forms and to continuous traditions whereby medieval exegetes, scholars, scribes—and players— appropriated and renewed classical theatrical texts and practices. Symes' work has also mapped the intellectual currents that, in the modern era, helped to fashion the narrative of tragedy's disappearance from medieval cultures, while also emphasizing the crucial role that the exigencies of textual transmission and reception have played in the shaping of that story.[3] Whereas traditional scholarship on tragedy fundamentally sidelined medieval performative and textual traditions, new evidence invites a reassessment of tragedy's medieval possibilities.

This volume's project of reclaiming tragedy's role in the history of medieval theater and performance joins a larger critical conversation that has recently focused on "rethinking tragedy" more generally.[4] Any drama or performance scholar coming to this conversation from the perspective of a discrete historical period should be encouraged, if also a bit daunted, by the ways that ideas and discourses of tragedy have preoccupied some of modernity's most influential theorists and their influential interpreters.[5] These modern interventions, indeed, have even extended the narrative of tragedy's disappearance into the eighteenth century, by arguing that tragedy could only be reinvented under the auspices of the Enlightenment, when ultimate authority was transferred from divine to human agency. According to this narrative, tragedy was then further refined under the aegis of Kantian aesthetics and romantic idealism, thereby grounding this recent theoretical trend in that weighty intellectual and philosophical heritage.[6] But as critics of this trend have convincingly shown, the tragedy of fifth-century BCE Athens was subject to reinvention from the moment of its first appearance. Hugh Grady observes that the tragedies of ancient Athens were already anachronistic, deriving their auspices from religious rituals that predated them. Aristotle's *Poetics* further re-contextualized these civic dramas by ignoring their ritual dimensions and recasting them as "rhetoric," thereby preparing the path that made a literary phenomenon out of complex cultural performances.[7]

Thus a key moment in tragedy's serial reinvention involves its construction, by Enlightenment thinkers, as both "a literary genre with philosophical implications that investigated profound issues of the meaning of life, the nature of humanity, and the interactions of freedom and necessity" and "an utterly secular discourse, a humanist and aesthetic alternative to religious beliefs."[8] As Blair Hoxby has shown, this discourse, especially that of its romantic practitioners, idealizes the (generally male) tragic subject's singular selfhood as well as tragedy itself as an authorial, textual art form.[9] Although Hoxby's critique focuses on the critical misrecognition of early modern tragedy by those under the spell of these Enlightenment formulations, his long view also exposes the misrecognitions that have helped to make medieval tragedy another "world we have lost." As Rita Felski has noted, this "philosophical appropriation of tragedy may ... entirely overlook its theatrical, performative, and embodied dimensions" and further reveals how the intellectual and political projects of modernity have rendered medieval tragic drama and its meanings invisible.[10]

These recent interventions present us with new opportunities to conceptualize medieval tragic drama and new tools for recognizing it. They even have a bearing on the way we understand the "original" tragedies of ancient Athens, whose reception has been almost indelibly colored by Aristotle's reading of them in his *Poetics*. Aristotle, who did not "live in the fifth century and ... was not Athenian," was hardly well positioned to absorb or understand the extent to which the dramatic tragedies of fifth-century Athens were "cultural artifacts embedded in the society that generated them."[11] As Simon Goldhill has argued, Aristotle's idea of tragedy silences its "civic frame," in the process also dissipating tragedy's connections to Athenian democratic modes of social organization and their consequent link to the communal voices represented by tragedy's chorus.[12] What Aristotle offered in place of these crucial contexts—a focus on the individual rather than the collective, concern for the formal shape of tragedy's dramatic action and the nature of its verbal idiom—would become key topics in the modern Western tradition's subsequent interpretation of tragic drama. By erasing Athenian tragedy's social framework, Aristotle also dislocated that drama from the religious and ritual contexts that motivated it. The "largest gathering of citizens in the calendar," the festival of Dionysus at which tragedies were performed, was "a festival of the *polis*," as much "a stage for political celebration and display" as it was for drama.[13] Athens, by enacting "its political and ritual life in public tragic performances," notes Page duBois, "made itself into a theater" of "political reflection and political education through its worship of Dionysus."[14]

Recapturing this convergence of dramatic performance, politics, civic life, and religious celebration is also crucial to understanding the social and religious contexts and festive environments of medieval English biblical theater. Occasions for these performances were consistently (if not universally) tied to religious observances in specific cities and towns, in which local institutions, such as parishes and guilds, were central to the co-construction of these communities' political lives and religious cultures.[15] The shared resonances I invoke here by no means collapse differences across cultures and continents, especially ones separated by two millennia. Rather, I propose that recognizing parallel sites and occasions of ancient and medieval dramatic forms can be heuristically useful to an investigation of tragedy within the social conditions of medieval performance.[16]

Moreover, as we move from occasions and sites of performance to the matters performed, ancient Athenian tragedy's points of contact with medieval English dramas accumulate. Although the six Middle English plays about the Massacre of the Innocents differ significantly in tone, plot, and constructions of character, their dramatic renderings of Matthew's account collectively display features aligned with the tragic dramas of antiquity. Medieval biblical drama and Athenian tragedy both take a mythic past as their subject matter—scriptural story and ancient heroic times, respectively.[17] "Thickly plotted," as Felski states, with "internecine strife," ancient tragedies unfold conflicts "centered in the family and the *polis* rather than the individual," conflicts of desire and sexuality, to be sure, but also ones entailing generational rivalries, "gender inequality [and] mother-child relations," concerns that also dominate the English Innocents plays.[18] Recent work by Helene Foley and Jean Howard demonstrates how the social roles performed by female characters in Greek tragedy also fit the gendered scenarios of the Massacre plays. Foley and Howard locate ancient tragedy in a "political system [that] marginalized women to the domestic and religious spheres"; they observe the ways in which female characters in these dramas find their voices "outside the house," where they assertively and visibly "take action" and speak eloquently about "the subjects of political life and justice." Calling attention to the increased prominence of "female" choruses in fifth-century Attic drama, they highlight the political and social significance of female lament as a mode of speaking that traverses public and private, even as the intervention of such gendered voices is complicated by the reality of an Athenian theater "created and enacted by men primarily for a male audience."[19] Edith Hall's attention to the imbrication of ancient tragic drama in social class and her notice that "dead babies . . . have been . . . intimately bound up" with the history of tragedy further invite us to locate medieval Massacre of the Innocents plays in a long tradition of dramatized infant slaughter.[20] And it may be the case that the conflicted aesthetic of the Middle English Innocents plays, careening as they do between high seriousness and performative modes that some might label as slapstick, finds an ancient tragic counterpart in the cross-dressed theater of Euripides' *Bacchae*, to which

Page duBois attributes "an unnerving, unfamiliar, untranslatable, and disturbing quality." DuBois' observation that ancient tragedy deserves "a more heterogeneous, unstable, polymorphous kind of reading," one attentive to that drama's disruptive forces, offers another context for approaching medieval English performances of the Massacre of the Innocents through a tragic lens.[21]

Pursuing this call for a recognition of ancient tragedy's continuous reinvigoration in Western culture thus proves useful for investigating the tragic potential of medieval dramas. In bringing to light what modern philosophical and interpretive traditions have occluded, recent scholarship foregrounds ancient tragedy's deep investment in the power struggles and fractured relationships within and between societies and families, themes that are writ large in English dramas of the Massacre of the Innocents. With their depictions of dynastic and familial conflict; dramatic images of murder, mourning, female protest and lament; and feminine-gendered challenges to the masculine political realm, medieval English dramas on this subject unwittingly—and provocatively—mirror the preoccupations of ancient tragic drama. Whatever medieval thinkers, writers, and playwrights may or may not have known about antique drama, it is clear, however counterintuitively, that the tragic dramas of classical antiquity can help us to think about these medieval Massacre plays in new and different ways.

MIXED MESSAGES

Although the prospects for conceptualizing the tragic dimensions of medieval biblical drama have received little attention overall, the tragic potentialities of the Massacre of the Innocents as both an episode in scriptural history and a popular subject for medieval performance have not gone unnoticed. Alluding to the mingling of comedy and tragedy in the Chester *Massacre*, Katharine Goodland identifies the dramatic agency of maternal mourning as the voice "that bestows tragic significance upon the biblical story."[22] So too, Jane Tolmie speaks to the ways in which "comic strands . . . mitigate horrific violence" in the Chester play's unruly juxtaposition of comedy and tragedy.[23] In calling out the comic moments that punctuate these spectacles of horror, though, such critical assessments speak to the difficulty of ascribing purely tragic valences to this dramatic corpus, whether those of plot (human infants are gratuitously murdered by a brutal tyrant) or affect (mothers mourn for their lost children and themselves). Tolmie's characterization of the aesthetic and formal challenges of the Massacre plays is apt: "High and low, serious and unserious, sacred and secular, painful and pleasurable—these plays on the darkest of subjects shift modes with a speed that can seem dizzying to the modern reader."[24]

Across verbal, visual, and performative media, the robust medieval traditions of representing Herod further complicate the effort to ascribe tragic modalities to the Middle English Massacre plays. Within the corpus of Middle English Innocents plays, David Staines posits two traditions for representing these plays' central and enduringly memorable character, Herod: the comic braggart and the tragic hero.[25] Addressing these contradictions, Robert Weimann was perhaps the first interpreter of medieval biblical performance to examine the Herod figure as a dense symbolic site as well as a dramatic character. Weimann linked Herod's role to festive customs of status inversion and mock ceremonial that, from the eleventh century at least, characterized European observances of the Feast of the Innocents during the Christmas season. In such celebrations, lower clergy and choristers in monastic and cathedral churches created Herod as a lord of misrule.[26] When these festive Herods migrate to the liturgical performances of Christmastide, they retain the transgressive character that was "ever lurking on the outskirts of the liturgy of the twelve days of the ... season." A famous Epiphany play from Padua, *Representatio Herodis in nocte Epyphanie*, depicts Herod punctuating the ceremony's liturgical singing by throwing his wooden staff at the chorus while his ministers, *cum magno furore*, beat fellow celebrants with inflated bladders.[27]

For Weimann, these festive customs constitute the "genetic background" of medieval English drama's exaggerated, bombastic Herod figure, an epitome of feudal tyranny who endowed Christmastide rites of inversion and misrule with social meanings and political commentary.[28] Weimann's most influential contribution to reading medieval English dramatic Herods was to emphasize the figure's self-conscious, deliberate performance of his role, whose popularity is attested by medieval and early modern memories of the character inscribed in Chaucer's *Miller's Tale*, Shakespeare's *Hamlet*, and the fifteenth-century Paston Letters.[29] The profound theatricality of these Middle English Herods has likewise inspired important commentary on the verbal and visual signs that constitute it.[30] These readings foreground the hyperbole inflecting all aspects of the dramatic Herod as well as the figure's narcissism; obsession with personal appearance; grounding in the material world; associations with bodily dismemberment and disaggregation; and hybrid linguistic discourse. Paramount in these analyses is attention to the medieval dramatic Herod who represents "essential qualities of theater itself," realized in "Herodic theatricality," "Herodian language," and a Herodian "style of performance."[31] The Towneley manuscript's *Magnus Herodis* exemplifies this recognized tradition of the over-the-top tyrant. Its Nuncius (Herald) takes more than one hundred lines to warm up the dramatic audience, feeding expectations of what they are about to experience: "Here he commys now, I cry, / That lord I of spake!"[32]

Weimann locates "the unique force and dramatic effect" of the Herod role in "the tension and interaction of the horrible and the comic."[33] The fundamental ambivalence that defines Herodian performativity, its co-construction of horror and amusement, monstrous and ludicrous, also structures contemporary (late medieval) understandings of the Massacre of the Innocents, which were embedded in the long traditions of scriptural commentary and liturgical and festive performance that provide one backdrop for medieval vernacular representations of this episode. As a subject for scriptural commentary and impetus for liturgical feast and festive play, the Massacre of the Innocents was inherently conflicted and unsettling, simultaneously an occasion for mourning and celebration, lament and rejoicing. Far from signaling a departure from exegetical and representational conventions, the competing emotional registers and dramatic idioms of the Middle English Massacre plays, when viewed from this perspective, can be seen as an inevitable outgrowth and heir of these traditions.

Medieval exegetes took pains to incorporate the sorrow and suffering of Matthew 2 into a broader Christian message that recuperated that suffering in eschatological terms. Peter Abelard (1079–1142) and Bernard of Clairvaux (1090–1153) sought to justify that suffering in relation to its fundamentally joyous and triumphal transformation in the Nativity of Jesus.[34] Augustine of Hippo (354–430), in a series of sermons for the Innocents feast, underscores that the very innocence of the young victims of Matthew 2 ensured that they are "'born happily into [eternal] life.'"[35] As Christian heroes, virgin martyrs, and types of Christ, the slaughtered Innocents were "assimilated to the basic paradigm of the Christian myth and viewed from what was believed to be the divine perspective," their murder "regarded as a victory over the forces of evil."[36] The most famous of the Herod and Innocents plays in the liturgical dramatic repertoire, the *Ordo ad interfectionem puerorum* from the Fleury playbook (Orléans, Bibliothèque municiaple, MS 201), typifies this joyful inflection of the dark and painful record of Matthew's gospel. It opens with a procession of singing Innocents, already transported to eschatological glory as followers of the Lamb (Revelation 14:1–5)—before their deaths have been contemplated, much less executed. So when Herod orders the infants' slaughter, the Innocents have already assumed hermeneutic control of the action, announcing their salvation through Christ.[37] And yet in performance, the triumphal joy of the Innocents is not always the main emotional current. Emphasizing the dual character of the feast, Susan Boynton highlights the affective dissonances of the liturgies celebrating it, noting that the manuscript record points to the omission, at key moments, of the "glorias," "alleluias," and other expressions of praise that would normally accompany a Christmas feast.[38] Despite an exegetical tradition that called for rejoicing over salvation rather than mourning for loss, the Old Testament heroine Rachel, who often represents the mothers in liturgical performances, is not always comforted, her grief not always "explain[ed] away."[39] Such tokens of resistance underscore the "antithesis and oxymoron that were central to the commentary tradition" and celebration of the Innocents' feast.[40] The Middle English Innocents plays also witness these conflicted understandings of the biblical event. Realizing this hermeneutic duality in demotic images and idioms, they reinforce the notion that the Massacre of the Innocents as occasion for vernacular performance could only be ambivalent in action and affect.

MEDIEVAL TRAGEDY: A CASE STUDY

What kind of tragedy is possible in such exegetical, aesthetic, textual, and social circumstances? To whom might such tragedy belong? The Innocents themselves are likely, though inarticulate, tragic subjects; their mothers and caregivers must voice a shared suffering in the laments that are a signature aspect of the feminine tragic role. Herod's antics and evil would seem to remove him from consideration; but specters of tragedy nonetheless circle around him. As Rebecca Bushnell argues, something about the very idea of the tyrant invites association with tragic theater because the tyrant himself "is identified with the tragic actor."[41] From a different perspective, the medieval English dramatic Herod comports with the tragic *de casibus* portrait of the "fallen" great man brought down by his misdeeds.[42] Three of the six Middle English Innocents plays conclude with Herod's death, portrayed as the fulfillment of divine and human justice. In the N-Town compilation, while the king mistakenly rejoices in the purported outcome of the massacre ("He [Jesus] is ded, I haue no dowte"), Mors (Death) gleefully appears to slay him for "his wykkyd werkynge."[43] The Digby Herod remains an antic if remorseful character through his rapid demise, apparently brought on by the uproar of the Innocents' mothers: "'A vengeaunce take Kyng Herode, for he hath our children sloon!'"[44] In the Chester Massacre, Herod goes down just as quickly, overtaken by visions of "feindes swarmes" as his body rots.[45] Like the Innocents whose murder Herod orders, representations of his own death are subject to the ambivalent logic that attended medieval understandings of events described in Matthew 2, as the vernacular biblical drama translates the exegetical interplay of sorrow and joy into spectacles of horror and amusement.

I have shown that the English Massacre plays, through their social contexts and religious occasions, as well as their plots and protagonists, invite consideration through a lens unexpectedly provided by ancient Greek tragic drama. However much the widely recognized, hybrid aesthetic of this medieval biblical theater appears to unsettle such considerations, I suggest that the tragic potentiality of these dramas emerges from within and through their staging of competing registers of action, affect, and language. This oxymoronic aesthetic makes its most convincing and detailed case for tragic understanding in the Chester cycle's Massacre of the Innocents, wherein an aggressive and ostensibly comedic banter facilitates exchanges that have tragic repercussions for the future of society and family.

Among the extant Middle English treatments of the biblical subject, only the Chester Massacre includes a key episode from medieval apocryphal stories of Herod's life: a tale that told how, in ordering the slaughter of young male children with the intent of eliminating the infant king, he also inadvertently caused the death of his own son, who "had been given to a woman in Bethlehem for nursing and was slain with the other children." Works such as the *Legenda aurea* of Jacobus de Varagine (*c*. 1230–98), and the ancient and medieval histories from which it drew, understood this incident as Herod's divine punishment for the Massacre.[46] But in a larger sense, this unanticipated outcome marks the ironic fulfillment of a life devoted to violent deeds, as recorded most influentially by Josephus (37/38–*c*. 100 CE), who in *The Jewish War* and *Jewish Antiquities* portrays Herod as a tyrant who readily and repeatedly kills members of his own family to further his political and dynastic ambitions.[47]

In the Chester play, this storied incident from the life of Herod inspires a subplot in which the identity of Herod's son is kept hidden from his father's homicidal soldiers by the woman in whose keeping he had been placed. I have argued elsewhere that the inclusion of this episode brings the genealogical preoccupations that dominated Herod's medieval story to bear on the generational struggles and social and political conflicts endemic to the governing structures of late-medieval communities.[48] In marking the convergence of Herod's public and private, social and familial roles, the subplot that spins off from this legendary moment also exposes the fragility of the most basic categories of social and familial identity, their vulnerability to unreliable readings and falsification, and hence their openness to tragic interpretations. Josephus and the historians writing in his wake regularly point out the utter failure, within Herod's continual dynastic struggles, of his domestic life and family arrangements. Translating the Latin universal history of Ranulf Higden (*c*. 1280–1364), John Trevisa (fl. 1342–1402) declared Herod to be "most ungracious in homeliche thinges" ["*In rebus quidem domesticis infelicissimus*"].[49] The Chester Innocents play overwrites this Herodian portrait of individual misfortune with a broader narrative of its collective implications.

The Massacre of the Innocents is a story about the destruction of a new generation by the older one that should be its guardian. Because this story gestures toward the reproduction of society in and through the bodies of the young, it points toward a community's potential for life and death. The biblical account also involves rivalry over issues of legitimate rule through the sacrifice of male infants. This deed identifies gendered spheres of action and meaning: masculine power and violence control the political realm and Rachel mourns for her children.[50] The Chester Goldsmiths' Massacre play represents this scripturally-sanctioned divide between the women who protect the Innocents and the Herodian soldiers who would kill them through mutually-inflicted verbal and physical assaults that risk making a farce of the impending scene of infant slaughter. The women respond to the soldiers' violent overtures with aggressively sexual language, such as this retort from *Prima mulier*: "Whom callest thou 'queane,' scabde biche? / Thy dame, thy daystard, was never syche?" (ll. 297–8); or this from *Secunda mulier*: "Saye, rotten hunter with thy gode, / stytton stallon, styck-tode" (ll. 313–14).[51] In the midst of this profusion of abusive epithets there is a startling exchange between *Secunda mulier* and the soldier who is about to murder the child in her care. The soldier taunts: "Dame, shewe thou me thy child there; / hee must hopp uppon my speare. / And hit any pintell beare, / I must teach him a playe." To the soldier's threat that he will kill the child if it has a pintell (penis), *Secunda mulier* retorts: "Naye, freake, thou shalt fayle: / my child shall thou not assayle. / Hit hath two hooles under the tayle; kysse and thou may assaye" (ll. 361–8). Withholding the fact that the infant in her care is Herod's own son, the woman aims to secure the child's safety by intimating that it is female, having "two hooles under the tayle." But masculine brute force quickly puts an end to hermeneutic and gender confusion, as the stage direction makes clear: "*Tunc Secundus Miles transfodiet secundum puerum*" ["Then the second soldier shall pierce the second male child"], after l. 376.

Although the editors of the Chester Cycle for the Early English Text Society withhold commentary on the raucous idiom through which the Goldsmiths' play enacts the central scene of child murder, recent scholarship has attended to the proclivity for abusive language exhibited by all the English Innocents plays, none more provocative than the instances examined here. This work has demonstrated how such gender-inflected language and the violence accompanying it, for example, comport with instances of slanderous discourse in medieval society; draw attention to the making of sexual and gender identities through performance; and expose the vulnerabilities of official power in action.[52] In sullying the soldiers' honor and excoriating them as both sexual aggressors and emasculated beasts, the Chester *mulieres* also contribute to the reflexive critique of masculinity that all the English Innocents plays pursue to some degree. In so doing, they support Christina Fitzgerald's claim that the biblical dramas performed by guilds in towns such as Chester—and the towns themselves—constituted virtual theaters of masculinity, performative sites in which late-medieval gender ideologies were creatively tested against the social and cultural realities that authorized them.[53]

This dramatic scene provides the most explicit instance of the gender marking that characterizes all extant versions of the Slaughter of the Innocents in early English drama. As such, the scene mobilizes gender-inflected obscenity and violence to probe the unknowability of the bodily signs that were foundational to social and familial life in medieval communities. When Chester's *Secunda mulier* substitutes female for male, she undermines the ostensibly natural act of discerning sexual difference, exposing its intersections with power and knowledge. What seems to be—indeed is—a crass and bawdy joke sets in motion the play's efforts to "assay" the uncertainties that confound assumptions about social and familial identities, especially as these inform the major categories of difference that structure civil and domestic order. At stake in the challenge of distinguishing a pintell from an ambiguous hole are discoveries with potentially tragic consequences.

In the Chester Massacre, the solution to the problem of identifying the "tender male babes" (as the Innocents are called in the Late Banns for the cycle) seems, at first, to ratify sexual difference as a natural category: if "hit any pintell beare," the infant must be male. The effort by Herod's soldiers to make this identification thus recognizes what Chaucer's Wife of Bath, in a different context, deemed one of the principal purposes of "oure bothe thynges smale," namely "to knowe a femele from a male."[54] The *mulier* who responds to this challenge appears to validate the soldier's mode of knowing: she issues the counter command that *Secundus miles* verify that her child has "two hooles under the tayle." These gestures are but feints in a dramatic plot that graphically interrogates corporeal signs of gender and status, a plot that makes Herod's destructive command an occasion for testing the impact of gendered knowledge on the social order. The play translates Herod's troublesome decree into the more concrete problem of discerning the signs that identify an infant as male. This problem is rendered dramatically plausible by the medieval custom of infant swaddling, which, because it rendered all infants visually similar, ironically underscores the play's preoccupation with—and confusion about—the socially constructed signs by which gender identity and difference are recognized. Herod's command to his soldiers acknowledges this very problem of discernment even as it ties enactment of the proper assessment to performances of violent masculinity: "Goe slaye that shrewe; lett yt be seene / and you be men of mayne. / Preeves manfully what they binne, / that non aweye from you fleene" (ll. 139–41). The soldiers echo the challenge of determining sexual difference a little later in the play when *Primus miles* confronts the mothers: "Dame, abyde, and lett mee see / a knave-child if that yt bee" (ll. 305–6).⁵⁵

The Chester Massacre play compounds the problem of reading material signs of gender and social identity by situating these issues within the larger framework of incarnational mystery. The play's epistemological preoccupations build upon vernacular drama's fretful encounter with that mystery: if man is created in God's image and God takes human form, by what signs will the deity be known to and recognized by humanity?⁵⁶ Such questions mark the inscrutability of the divine realm and, at the same time, expose what the play world increasingly represents as a similarly inscrutable world of human signs. Chester's Herod anxiously acknowledges this central dilemma when he wonders how to identify the child king who, he fears, poses a challenge to his rule: "Because I knowe not which is hee, / all for his sake shalbe slayne" (ll. 39–40).⁵⁷ Admitting such unknowability, Herod can only resort to an absolutist approach: "all knave-children" (119) will be his victims.⁵⁸

Although biblical history may have dictated the infants' deaths, the dramatic interaction of soldier and *mulier* slows down that inevitability, inventing acts of misrecognition and the interpretive possibilities that they create. This moment underscores how gender is signified as both a set of body parts and of social attributes. *Secunda mulier*'s substitution of female for male ironically turns the absence of the phallus, the conventional sign of social and symbolic power, into a pragmatically positive, i.e., lifesaving, attribute: two "hooles" should signal exemption from the soldier's eager spear. As a verbal performance, *Secunda mulier*'s substitution of female for male also enacts a symbolic castration because her words metaphorically dismember the infant in her care. Overturning the play's self-conscious performance of masculine social and sexual power, the woman's gesture also resonates across the Slaughter's many political contexts. The "medieval biology lesson" in which the woman engages thus ends up, as E. Jane Burns states in a related context, having "more to do with the male body politic than with female body parts."⁵⁹ Because the child at issue happens to be the king's son, *Secunda mulier*'s speech strikes a symbolic wound upon the masculine, hierarchical body politic that was microcosmically figured in the play world itself, as well as ritualized and celebrated in urban dramas such as the Chester plays.

The dissolution of community and social order adumbrated in the encounter of mother and soldier is tragically contradictory because the violence figured in that symbolic castration is actualized in the king's self-inflicted wound: the soldier's murder of Herod's son ironically fulfills Herod's command. The significance of that wound resonates simultaneously on the level of the society and family. For the body politic, the very reproduction of the social order is jeopardized because the king now has no heir. The symbolic castration and actual death of Herod's son offer the spectacle of masculine power undermining itself by undermining its own continuation. It calls to mind the "waynis and waggyns" of dead "man-chyldur" paraded before Herod's eyes in another Massacre play, the Coventry Shearmen and Tailors' pageant, as well as the social disarray at the end of the Digby *Killing of the Children*, where "alle the children be dede, / and alle the men out of the cuntre be goon."⁶⁰ This wounding of the social body is replicated in the fracturing of familial and domestic relationships in the domestic, feminine sphere. Here, Herod's son serves as a critical token of the inevitable intersection of the communal and the individual, the public and the private. As the king's son he is implicated in all the public authority and power his father can claim; as a helpless infant consigned to female care, he is under the control of women.

By putting Herod's infant son in the care of a woman who, at first, tries to pass him off as female and, second, fights robustly against his attacker, the play demonstrates that the continuity of authority in the realm of high politics and maintenance of social order itself are vulnerable to gendered interventions and the power of women's knowledge and agency. Only when the soldier impales *Secunda mulier*'s child on his spear does the woman reveal the babe's true identity, telling the soldiers that they will be hanged for their deed and promising to report to the king how his son was killed right before her eyes (l. 386): "Loe, lord, looke and see / the child that thou tooke mee. / Men of thy owne contrey / have slayne yt—here the bine" (ll. 393–6).[61] Herod's response both condemns and queries her behavior: "Fye, hoore, fye! God give the pyne! / Why didest thou not say that child was myne?" (ll. 397–8). Rather than answer the question, the woman instead asserts that the soldiers should have recognized the legible markers of the son's royal identity: "For in gould harnesse hee was dight, / paynted wonders gaye" (ll. 403–4). Herod repeats the woman's point about his son's dress: "Hee was right sycker in silke araye, / in gould and pyrrie [bejeweled] that was so gaye. / They might well knowe by this daye / he was a kinges sonne" (ll. 409–12). Reversing the conventional conceit of denigrating feminine garrulousness, Herod chides the woman for *not* speaking: "Whye weare thy wyttes soe farre awaye? / Could thow not speake? Could thou not praye / and say yt was my sonne?" (ll. 414–16).

Her answer to the question, "What, didn't you tell them he was my son?" should properly be "No, I told them he was a girl." In the face of the spear poised for penetration, her silence on the matter of the infant's social rank and status thus foregrounds the gender substitution she has employed, ostensibly as a saving tactic. She has not attempted to rescue Herod's son by identifying the attire that should have been recognized as sign of the male-dominated status hierarchies that it represents. Rather, she has chosen to make the king's son female, thus inadvertently (or not) bringing about his death. Her prevarication asks whether the claims for male status implicit in identifying the king's son could have—or should have—superseded the claims for the second female "hool." In the end, *Secunda mulier*'s recourse to gender rather than status difference reverses both gender and status hierarchies, substituting female for male, not-king's son for king's son. It makes the high low; it brings the king's son down to her feminine level. These substitutions introduce major disorder within and among the overlapping material, bodily, and symbolic categories of social difference that the play represents. *Secunda mulier* pits one set of unstable cultural signs against another, the gay "gould harnesse" of the king's son against pintells and holes, only to discover their failure as adequate markers of social categories: the king's son is unambiguously signified by neither. Herod's assertion that the soldiers "might well knowe" his son by his array belies his own earlier uncertainty about identifying the Christ child. In the end it proves impossible to tell any low-born "swayne" from a royal child.

As a faulty signifier, the golden apparel of the king's son also points to the status anxiety that characterized the larger urban social context of the Innocents plays. As Derek Neal observes, late-medieval masculinity was very much a matter of physical display realized in attire.[62] The mis-interpreted apparel of Herod's son invokes late-medieval sumptuary laws that stipulated how social identity and status should be signified. The special identifying signs that Herod expected to make this son distinctive—"Hee was right sycker in silke araye, / In gould and pyrrie that was so gaye"—accord with late fifteenth-century English laws which declared that only the king, queen, king's mother, children, brother and sisters may wear "cloth of gold, silk, or color purple."[63] Yet, as recent scholarship has shown, such laws were notoriously ineffectual; even if the play's royal child were swaddled in gold and silk, a contemporary viewer might well have mistaken him for a wealthy merchant's son.[64] The ostensible purpose of sumptuary legislation, to make hierarchy legible, is thus put to the test in the Chester Massacre play and found wanting, just as actual sumptuary rulings, as Claire Sponsler notes, could bring only discursive rather than material order to "shifting, flexible, and overlapping social groups" for whom status had come to be based on the acquirable signs of furnishings, clothing, or civic offices.[65]

"Alas, what the divell is this to meane?" (l. 417) Herod asks, as he attempts to understand how his son could have been slaughtered among the Innocents and as he faces his own death in the very same stanza. By dramatizing the failure of conventional signs of gender and social identity to secure the social order, the Chester play underscores the fragile architecture of differences upon which urban authority and masculine public power rested. Despite Herod's best efforts to enforce categories of age, gender, and status as he understands them, his order of succession is breached and his lineage destroyed. Women, by virtue of their association with child-bearing and child-rearing, encroach upon the male sphere, demeaning masculine privilege by feminizing it while also appropriating verbal and physical signs of masculine power. Sartorial tokens of acquired status fail to establish rank, resulting in a loss to the family and the body politic. The older generation asserts superiority over the young only to commit generational genocide, and the reproduction of society and the symbolic order is by no means assured. As if the instabilities that the Chester Massacre unleashes for the dramatic audience were not enough, Jane Tolmie reminds us that the unsettling of all of these social and temporal categories occurs through the medium of a cross-dressed, transvestite theater. Displaying the fluidity of social identities that can be made up on the spot and then destroyed or reconstructed, this performative context enacts the "category crisis" that informs the Chester Massacre's dramatic narrative by bringing forward the "terror of inbetween-ness" of the third sex of cross-dressed male body."[66]

The Chester play's breathtaking interweaving of the semiotic and the social seems to offer tragic prospects for the survival of society and family, and for the ambitions and desires of individuals within them. The play's disruption of normative social categories by this series of substitutions displays the contradictory hermeneutic of the Massacre of the Innocents and the subversive potential of medieval theater: the high can be brought low and the low made high. But in the end, the Chester Slaughter works to rein in the anxieties unleashed by its very pushing at the boundaries of semiotic, and a concomitant, social chaos. It localizes the horror of its action by giving Herod the fate that biblical history and medieval legend frequently accorded him: his body rots, and demons carry him off to hell as he makes a rare admission of fault ("I have donne so much woo," l. 426) and bequeaths his soul to Satan. In the play's dramatic logic, Herod's physical and spiritual demise represents the work of an unambiguous divine judgment that for the moment appeases all the uncertainty generated by the circulation of so many fungible categories. The play's epistemological dilemmas, including Herod's own, attain closure, if not resolution, as matters of personal morality, thereby averting the tragic possibilities—for society and family—that its interrogation of the signs of social identity sets in motion.

By asserting that the Chester Slaughter of the Innocents takes this turn, I do not mean to privilege an ethical reading of the play's dramatic action, especially one in which the struggles of Herod, his soldiers, and the *mulieres* constitute an elaborate foil for the central biblical plot of Christ's deliverance. From the perspective of Christian narrative, we might say—and many readers of medieval biblical drama have taken this route—that the play's disorder, its flirtation with the tragic prospect of social disintegration, is ultimately recuperated in the stable, concordant image of the holy family with which it concludes: an angel announces to Joseph and Mary that their enemy is dead and they are free to take the child Jesus to Judea. In this view, tragedy proves irreconcilable with Christian teleology and the arc of biblical narrative. Elsewhere in the infancy story, for example, the Chester cycle demonstrates the proper reading of signs by those whom divinity inspires: the shepherds and Magi have no trouble at all discerning the "verye tokeninge" of a child in a star that properly signifies the heavenly king's son.[67] But the deliverance of Joseph, Mary, and their infant son is a necessary though insufficient explanatory component of a dramatic narrative that repeatedly frames uncertainties about the foundations of social identity as more fundamental problems of human knowledge and discernment. From an opening play, in which Lucifer mistakenly thinks he can appropriate the identifying signs of the Godhead, to a penultimate drama of the arch-deceiver Antichrist, to a Last Judgment in which damned souls protest that they did not recognize Christ in "the least" of those "that on yearth [Earth] suffered pyne," the Chester cycle is uniquely preoccupied with the problem of knowing divinity.[68] This feature of the Chester plays, including its drama of the Slaughter of the Innocents, may draw upon the aspect of Christian narrative that elaborated the inherent theatricality of a performative god who, as John Parker argues, costumed himself as a human being, a disguised dissembler.[69]

Aristotle might have appreciated the accidental resonances of ancient tragedy that inflect the Chester Massacre's rendering of biblical history and legend. Herod's efforts to evade the prophecy of a new king, to stop an inevitable future, recall the dilemmas of ancient tragic protagonists, as does the play's crucial focus on acts of misrecognition. The sudden reversal of Herod's fortunes upon the horrifying recognition of the consequences of his own acts further speaks to the fundamentals of Aristotelian tragic action.[70] And there is more than a bit of the *deus ex machina* in the angel who suddenly appears to warn Joseph and Mary to flee into Egypt (ll. 257–64). But these are not the terms through which I want to view the tragic prospects of the Chester Massacre of the Innocents.[71] Rather, I suggest that problems of knowledge, discernment, the proper (or improper) reading of signs—and the potential for interpretive failures that these elicit—might help us to think about larger questions that medieval biblical drama engaged on the cusp of the Reformation. To the extent that a dramatic cycle as historically belated as Chester is aware of its own uncertain and potentially blasphemous aspiration to represent the sacred (and I think it is deeply aware of such matters), it enacts the very dilemmas of recognition and misrecognition of divinity that so often burden the cycle's biblical actors.[72] In this context, the Massacre's disclosure of the inscrutability of material signs that sustain the order of society and family might help us to think about the many ways that these essential components of human community are vulnerable to actions and interpretations that transport them into the realm of tragedy.

MEDIEVAL TRAGEDY AND TIME

In pursuing the tragic potentialities of medieval biblical drama, I have been careful to juxtapose that drama's provocative points of contact with ancient tragedy, rather than to imply that medieval playwrights were aware of or influenced by classical dramatic traditions—even though the work of Carol Symes suggests that both of these may have been possible. But in light of the tentative conclusions I have proposed regarding the contributions that English Massacre of the Innocents plays might make to reflections on medieval tragedies of society and family, I want to return to Symes' investigation of specific appearances, in the *Patrologia Latina* database, of the word "tragedy" (or *tragoedia* or *tragedia*) and its grammatical variants.[73] Of the five categories into which Symes organizes her data, one (accounting for a notable eighteen percent of the total) comprises "tragedy as denoting a disruptive event in the history of a community or a way of reporting past events."[74] In these data, the word "tragedy" is employed, especially by historians, "as a powerful lens through which to view and interpret certain critical moments in the past." "Most often," Symes notes, "an event or series of events is associated with tragedy only when it results in the dissolution—the public dissolution—of a community through civil unrest." "However little they actually knew about Athenian tragedy," Symes continues, the historians who used the term "understood that it . . . was supposed to come about through some breach of family bonds or some violation of the social contract."[75] These uses of the term "tragedy" in the patristic lexicon strengthen the possible connections of biblical story to the long and fraught medieval reception of ancient tragedy and, I think, adumbrate the potential for tragic vision in the Middle English Innocents plays.

Like their ancient tragic counterparts, medieval dramas devoted to the Massacre communicate, through spectacle, the violent narratives that attend anxieties about the future of societies and families in specific historical communities. In their implicit traversing of times and cultures, the English Innocents plays precociously signal the polychronicity that Rebecca Bushnell has recently identified as a signature of conceptual and material realizations of tragedy itself.[76] Appealing to the "urgency of tragedy now," Foley and Howard, in their introduction to the 2014 *PMLA* issue devoted to that subject, seek to recuperate for contemporary readers, performers, and audiences the affordances of tragedy's long historical legacy. Positing that, for now, ideas of tragedy's historical and cultural influence are less important than its concrete connections to thinking and performative media over time, they identify present possibilities for reclaiming the spare biblical event of Matthew's gospel for other interpretations.[77]

Recent performances of the Middle English Massacre of the Innocents plays have tacitly picked up this charge, struggling with the issue of capturing these dramas' labile temporalities and perhaps a justifiable imperative to interpret the biblical event in terms of vulnerable populations around the globe.[78] No longer the province of history alone, the medieval Herod's murderous rages, fueled by gender trouble and other semiotically inflected histrionics, migrate from the province of theater and performance to provide cultural and historical context for current demonstrations of fragile masculinities dangerously acting out their insecurities on vulnerable, young human bodies. If the Middle English Massacre of the Innocents plays are to be part of Western tragedy's continual reinvention, that will be, in part, because their violent spectacles of societal and familial tragedy unfortunately have enduring life.

CHAPTER EIGHT

Gender and Sexuality

KAREN SULLIVAN

Long after classical tragedies had ceased to be performed in Western Europe, the notion of tragedy survived in the memory of late antique and medieval clerics. In the seventh century, the encyclopedist Isidore of Seville wrote, "Comedians proclaim the deeds of private people, tragedians public matters and the histories of kings."[1] In the twelfth century, the Cistercian monk Aelred of Rievaulx built upon Isidore's influential definition of this genre when he cited an abbot in conversation with one of his novices. "In tragedies and in vain songs," the abbot observes, "someone of loveable handsomeness, marvelous courage, and gracious manner is depicted as injured or oppressed,"[2] in a way that emotionally affects an audience. The novice admits that he himself has been distressed by such stories: "I remember being moved by fictions in the vernacular that treat a certain Arthur . . ., sometimes to the point of shedding tears."[3] In their discussion of tragedies, these two clerical authors were thinking, not of classical Greek and Roman drama, to which they and their contemporaries had no access, but of narratives of their own time which forefront rulers and other prominent men, like King Arthur,[4] and which recount the suffering and death of these personages. As public figures, these tragic heroes are concerned with the outer, political world, and their downfall acquires a grandeur insofar as it impacts, not just themselves and their families, but the states they govern. While these clerical authors do not use Aristotle's language of pity and terror, Aelred in particular expects the audience of tragedy to respond emotionally to these tragic heroes' destruction, even to the point of weeping. Though tragedy did not survive the classical period in the dramatic form that we identify with it, it did linger on as a great and sorrowful storyline.[5]

It is not to be taken for granted that the conception of tragedy in late antiquity and the Middle Ages would exclude women, yet the effect of it was to do so. In ancient Athens, women had been confined to their own quarters in upper-class households and thus secluded from public life, yet they had nonetheless figured prominently in the tragedies of their city, from Aeschylus' *Oresteia*, to Sophocles' *Antigone*, to Euripides' *Iphigenia in Aulis*.[6] Aristotle had asserted that the characters in tragedy should be "good" (*spoudaios*),[7] in the sense of serious, excellent, and important, and he had acknowledged that "even a woman can be good, . . . although an inferior thing."[8] Tragic characters had to be capable of actions of a certain magnitude, as people of "high station and good fortune, like Oedipus, Thyestes, and the famous men of such families as these";[9] but, as he saw it, there was no reason why the wife, sister, or daughter of a powerful man should not be capable of such deeds. In early modern Europe as well, women were featured in tragedies such as Gian Giorgio Trissino's *Sophonisba* (1515) or Jean Racine's *Phèdre* (1677). Yet in the centuries between the classical period and the Renaissance, when authors spoke of the characters in tragedy, they either deemed women people who had nothing to do with public life, or they condemned them as people who *should* have nothing to do with public life. When they considered those few women in tragic works who play public roles, such as Clytemnestra, Medea, and Helen of Troy, they criticized them for having ventured outside their proper domain and for having unleashed chaos around them in so doing. Saint Jerome declares in 393, "Whatever swells in tragedies, whatever subverts houses, cities, and kingdoms, concerns the contentions of wives and concubines."[10] Bishop Marbod of Rennes, writing after 1096, refers to "the prostitute born of Leda over whom a ten-year world war was fought, and others whose lives tragedians are accustomed to recite to the people."[11] As these clerics conceive of them, women are not tragic heroines, but, rather, the source of disorder in their societies, to which the tragic hero will be obliged to respond. When the classical view of female propriety was reinforced by a Christian view of female holiness, it became all the more imperative for women to remain sequestered from public life and, by extension, from tragedy.

Yet though women were sidelined from late antique and medieval notions of tragedy, I would like to suggest here that the position they occupied became all the more central to discussions of drama and to drama itself.[12] While the public life with which men were occupied defined tragedy, the private life to which women were consigned now assumed a public importance. In late antiquity, the Church Fathers criticize those women who venture into the theater, where they exhibit their charms to spectators, and they represent all women as actresses who, whether onstage or off, exult in such performances. At the same time, they suggest that women can transform their exhibitionist tendencies in a way that will encourage virtue rather than vice in those who see them. In the Early and High Middle Ages, the first two women playwrights in Western history urge members of their sex to remain secluded from public view, but they represent this cloistered life as preferable for Christians in general, whether male or female. Even as women were being relegated to the private sphere, that sphere was becoming seen as the primary locus of spiritual transformation. While tragedy mourns the downfall of men in public life, suffering and death, whether of men or of women, was no longer seen as something necessarily to be avoided. In the Late Middle Ages, a mystery play about Joan of Arc—the woman whose public career, with its meteoric rise and equally rapid fall, might seem most to fit the medieval definition of tragedy—represents this heroine, not as physically defeated, but as spiritually triumphant at her end. Writings from the century in which Joan lived depict her passion as redeeming the sinful France she came to save and, hence, not as something to lament. Even in the modern world, convent drama, which continued to be written into the twentieth century, praises women who conceal themselves from public view and who suffer and die for a good cause, as the martyrs suffered and died. In the transvaluation of values brought about by Christianity, an individual's retirement from public life and experience of misfortune, commonly bewailed in classical tragedy, is now celebrated in a new, Christian drama.

If Christian dramatic writings are of interest in a study of tragedy, it is, not because the women in these works are tragic heroines, but on the contrary, because they serve as a foil to the tragic heroines elsewhere in literature. As much as modern Western feminists may want women to play public roles in the world, this literature prizes women who play private roles, cloistered in homes and convents. As much as we may value the outer world of action, these texts valorize the inner life of contemplation. As much as we may regard suffering and death as experiences to be avoided, these texts regard them as experiences to be honored, if willingly undergone for a good purpose. By turning on their head the values of tragedy, these Christian works portray women as exemplifying a new, recognizably feminine kind of heroism.

THE CHURCH FATHERS

Around 524, when the philosopher Boethius was awaiting execution for treason in Pavia, he relates in *The Consolation of Philosophy* that the Muses visited him in his prison, soothing him in this time of sorrow as they once delighted him in happier moments. While they are dictating to him the elegiac verses he is writing down, Lady Philosophy arrives, her robe torn by thinkers who have ripped from it scraps of cloth. "Who," she demands angrily, "has allowed these theatrical harlots [*scenicas meretriculas*] to approach this sick man? These women are they who, with the infertile thorns of emotion, destroy the fertile crop of reason and accustom the minds of men to disease instead of setting them free."[13] Sweet as the Muses' gifts may be, she charges, that which they offer her pupil cannot heal him. During her subsequent conversation with Boethius, Lady Philosophy persuades him that, far from deploring the turning of Fortune's wheel, he should accept that such revolutions are to be expected in the human condition: "What does the cry of tragedies lament but Fortune's overthrow of happy kingdoms by an indiscriminate strike?"[14] A proper reading of tragedy, she indicates, would prompt rational recognition of the mutability of fortune instead of emotional lamentation about such changes. During the period when Boethius was writing, the Church Fathers—figures like Tertullian, Ambrose of Milan, Augustine of Hippo, Cyprian of Carthage, Clement of Alexandria, Jerome, and John Chrysostom—performed both of the moves that Lady Philosophy enacts in these passages. On one hand, they railed against theatrical performances, including tragedies, in large part because they saw them as seducing their unwary audiences, as the Muses attempt to seduce Boethius, by appealing to their emotion rather than to their reason, not least through the meretricious charms of their actresses.[15] On the other hand, they acknowledged a potential good in another, non-tragic kind of performance—that of martyrdom—where the emotional charge of the action would be subordinated to the rational doctrine of Christianity. Gendered as feminine, theater in late antiquity was seen as dangerous in the same way that women were seen as dangerous, but it was also viewed as capable of redemption, just as women were viewed as capable of being redeemed.

For the Church Fathers, women are essentially theatrical, like actresses on a stage. A young girl attends to the appearance of her face, her hair, and her body. As she enters into womanhood, Tertullian writes, she undergoes a change not unlike that which Adam and Eve underwent when they awakened to their nakedness. He says of young girls overall that, as soon as "they have understood themselves to be women, they are drawn out of being virgins, laying aside what they were."[16] For Tertullian, as the young girl becomes aware of her femininity in a new way, the danger is not so much that she becomes interested in men but, rather, that she becomes interested in her own beauty. Like an actress preparing for her debut onstage, she spends hours gazing at a mirror, applying cosmetics, and experimenting with different hairstyles. Excessive in her attention to her toilette, the young girl is excessive in her attention to her attire. She carefully selects the clothing, the shoes, and the accessories that will most become her. In doing so, Cyprian writes, she forgets that "she has no struggle greater than that against the flesh and no contest more relentless than that of vanquishing and dominating the body."[17] Once the young girl has adorned herself to her satisfaction, she ventures out in public, flaunting her beauty to all and basking in the admiration she receives from strangers. It is thus, Jerome complains, that such young girls "proceed ostentatiously [*notabiliter*] through the public and, with furtive glances of the eyes, draw flocks of youths after themselves."[18] Though such young girls technically remain virgins, they have become women, not insofar as they take pleasure in others' bodies, but insofar as they take pleasure in their own bodies as displayed to others. Their eroticism resides not so much in lust, which would make them want to have sex with men, as in pride, which makes them want to be admired for their beauty. Though Christians are supposed to be humble, these women are repeatedly said "to exalt [*exaltavi*] in their beauty, "to glory" [*gloriari*] in their looks, and to become "elated" [*elatae*] by the attention they receive. As women make themselves attractive and exhibit their attractions to others for their approval, they become like harlots or, even more damning, like actresses. Chrysostom contrasts the love of wisdom, the repentance, and the continual prayer of pious women with the elaborate clothing, jewelry, and seductive airs of actresses and singers: "This is the ornament of the Church, not that of the theaters [*houtos tēs Ekklēsias ho kosmos, ekeinos tōn theatrōn*]."[19] In their love of performing for a crowd, all women, it seems, resemble their sisters on the stage.

As women are for the Church Fathers essentially theatrical, actresses are essentially women. In his fifth-century account of the life of Pelagia, "the first among the actresses of Antioch,"[20] Jacob the Deacon recounts how this young woman one day paraded through the city on a donkey, with bare head and shoulders, gorgeous clothes clinging to her body, and an entourage of elaborately-dressed male and female slaves. At that time, a synod of ecclesiastics was meeting in the city. While the other bishops averted their eyes as Pelagia passed by, Nonnus, the bishop of Edessa, gazed outright at her. He declared, "Think, beloved ones. How many hours did this woman spend in her chamber, washing, arraying, and adorning herself with every care and *with the intention of being a spectacle* [*intentione ad spectaculum*], so that there might be nothing lacking in her bodily beauty and ornament?"[21] At the same time, however, he reproached himself and his fellows for not taking equal care to adorn themselves in order to please God. In the fifth century, when the hermit Pambos came forth from his desert retreat to Alexandria, Socrates Scholasticus tells us, he beheld an actress and began to weep. He explained to his companions that "two causes have affected me: one is the destruction of this woman; the other is that I exert myself less to please my God than she does to please obscene characters."[22] In her ability to attract the attention of onlookers, the actress epitomizes women's interest in the body as opposed to the soul; the material as opposed to the spiritual; and the self, as opposed to the other.[23] With actresses understood as women who display themselves to others, the theater is understood as the place where people go to look at such women. Chrysostom complains that Christian men attend less to preachers of God than they do to "the harlot women in satanic theaters [*tais pornais gunaiksin en tois satanikois theatrois*]."[24] He protests that they abandon Christ in the manger, "so that [they] may see women on the stage."[25] Not only the actresses themselves, but the skits they perform, with their themes of fornication and adultery, train their audiences in wantonness. If all women seek to be seen, admired, and desired by spectators, then actresses, who present themselves professionally for such a purpose, succeed in this unfortunate ambition more than any other women.

Even as the Church Fathers condemned women as essentially theatrical, however, they praised virgins—that is, true virgins—as essentially reclusive. Instead of spending her time before a mirror, beautifying her face, the true virgin spends her time at her books or at prayer, improving her mind. Of the Virgin Mary, whose life serves as a model for all true virgins, Ambrose writes that she "was a virgin not only in body but also in mind, ... in heart humble, in words grave, in spirit prudent, in speech sparing, in learning studious, ... so that the very appearance of her body might be the image of her mind, the figure of probity."[26] This true virgin does not often venture out into public places but, rather, remains in her private room. If she does go outdoors to attend church services or to visit a martyr's shrine, she proceeds veiled, with her eyes cast down. She does not look at others, nor does she wish others to look at her. Instead of directing her attention outward, in observation, she directs it inward, in contemplation. Instead of delighting in the desire of earthly lovers, she delights in the grace of a celestial Spouse. In the Song of Songs, the Bridegroom (typically interpreted as God) says of his bride (typically interpreted as the soul or the Church), that "a garden enclosed is my sister, my spouse; a spring shut up, a fountain sealed."[27] It was because the Virgin Mary was enclosed in her room, it was said, that the angel came to her. It is because other virgins are enclosed in their rooms that God likewise comes to them. Jerome advises one of his female correspondents, "Jesus is jealous. He does not choose that your face should be seen by others."[28] With an echo of the parable of the foolish and wise virgins,[29] he recommends that, even though foolish virgins may wander about, others remain "indoors with the Bridegroom, because if you close the door and, . . . pray to your father in secret, he will come and knock."[30] In shutting themselves off from the world, virgins are thought to open themselves up to God.

Yet the Church Fathers also suggest that, in their reclusiveness, virgins too can become actresses. It is precisely because the virgin does not seek to attract men that she succeeds in doing so. Ambrose writes of a virgin in Antioch who avoided being seen in public: "The more she avoided men's eyes, the more she inflamed them. For beauty which is heard of but not seen is more desired."[31] Jerome writes similarly of the holy Paula, that "she hid herself, and yet she was not hidden. Fleeing glory, she earned glory, for glory follows virtue as its shadow, and, deserting those who strive for it, it strives for those who despise it."[32] In accounts of the lives of the martyrs, so popular from the earliest years of the Church, young Christian women were dragged out of their homes, brought to theaters or amphitheaters, and stripped of their clothes before all. In the *Acts of Paul and Thecla* from the second century, for example, the virgin Thecla is thrown naked into an arena with wild beasts, but a cloud of fire surrounds her so that she cannot be seen. Ambrose reports that the lions themselves turned their eyes to the ground out of modesty, "fearing that any person or beast should see the virgin naked."[33] In *The Passion of Saints Perpetua and Felicity* from the early third century, the young married woman Perpetua is exposed in an amphitheater and gored by a savage cow. Yet we are told that once "she had sat upright, her robe being rent at the side, she drew it over to cover her thigh, mindful rather of modesty than of pain."[34] Exposed to all in the amphitheater, these young women preserve their modesty, either through God's intervention or through their own efforts, and these external acts manifest their internal virtue. In this context, martyrdom itself becomes a performance and the martyrs actresses. As Cyprian writes of a virgin who takes pride in her physical appearance, "if she is to glory in the flesh, then surely let her do so when she is tortured in confession of the name [of Christ]."[35] Referring to the fire, the sword, and the beasts that stand to bring about such a virgin's death, he affirms that these are "the precious jewelry of the flesh, these are the superior ornaments of the body."[36] If it is an eroticism peculiar to women to glory in the flesh, as Cyprian suggests, then this eroticism will be turned to good account should women use their bodies, not to exult in themselves, but to exult in God. Forced out into the world, virgins and other holy women perform like other women, but in a heroic way, displaying, through their fortitude under suffering, that their faith is one worth dying for.

The identification of the stage as a place where women display their beauty for the appreciation of men remains a constant in criticism of the theater. In the sixth century, Procopius describes Theodora, the powerful wife of the emperor Justinian and a former actress, as a specialist in the lowest level of comedy: "She had an especially quick and biting wit and soon became a star feature of the show."[37] Theodora's performances were as bawdy as they were comical, he writes, including acts where she lifted her skirt and exposed herself onstage and even employed trained geese to explore her body. After having attracted the interest of men through her performances, she reportedly arranged trysts with them, either for pay or for pleasure. Given such behaviors among actresses, Isidore of Seville concludes that "a theater is the same as a brothel [*prostibulam*], because, after the games are over, harlots 'prostrate themselves' [*prostrari*] there."[38] It was in large part because the theater was so associated with the activities of lewd women that it was shut down throughout the Roman Empire. Yet, in a religion where the woman caught in adultery becomes Mary Magdalene, the Roman centurion who pierces Christ with his spear becomes the Blessed Longinus, and the persecutor Saul becomes the Apostle Paul, an actress can also become a saint. According to Jacob the Deacon, Pelagia heard Nonnus preach and was moved to repent of her sinful lifestyle, to receive baptism, and to retreat to a cell on the Mount of Olives. Having once been seen by all, she now ensured that she would be seen by none. Having once expended her energy on her appearance, she now expended it on her devotions. But as the actress-as-harlot was cast offstage with the closing of the ancient theaters, the actress-as-penitent was waiting in the wings to reenter, in a new Christian guise, in medieval drama.

HROTSVITHA AND HILDEGARD

In the Early and High Middle Ages, two women play instrumental roles in reviving dramatic writings, but they do so by turning decisively against tragedy. In the tenth century, Hrotsvitha of Gandersheim, a canoness in Lower Saxony, became not only the first woman playwright but the first playwright since late antiquity and the first Christian playwright, with six plays to her credit, including *The Fall and Repentance of Mary* (*Abraham*) and *The Conversion of the Harlot Thaïs* (*Paphnutius*). In the twelfth century, Hildegard of Bingen, a Benedictine abbess in the Rhineland and the author of numerous works of visionary theology, music, science, and medicine, composed *The Play of the Virtues* (*Ordo Virtutum*), a precursor to the morality plays that would come to flourish in the fifteenth and sixteenth centuries. Unlike the Church Fathers, Hrotsvitha and Hildegard see value in dramatic works, not only writing them but recruiting canonesses and nuns from their communities to read and perhaps even to perform in them. While their patristic predecessors had associated women with the flesh and with the letter of the text—negatively, as for harlots, or positively, as for virgin martyrs—these playwrights associate them with the spirit and with allegory. And, while these clerics had identified theater with poetry and its pernicious appeal to the emotions, these women now link it with philosophy and its salutary appeal to reason. At the same time, like the Church Fathers, Hrotsvitha and Hildegard depict women as exposing themselves to sin if they venture out into the world, to be seen and desired by men, and as protecting themselves from danger if they remain enclosed and hidden from sight. While tragedians had traditionally represented the turn away from public life as a source of sorrow, they depict this conversion as a cause for celebration.

In her plays, Hrotsvitha depicts women as at risk once they venture out into the world and as safe once they return to their cells. In *Abraham*, for example, Mary has been raised by her uncle, the hermit Abraham, in a cell next to his, hidden from the sight of men, but, at the age of eighteen, she is persuaded by a monk who was supposed to instruct her to break free of this enclosure and to unite with him in love. In despair at the loss of her virginity, she flees her hermitage and becomes a harlot. When Abraham tracks down his wayward niece in the inn where she is working, he presents himself as a potential client. He explains to the innkeeper that he has heard of Mary's beauty and that he "arrived for no reason than to see her."[39] After the innkeeper has taken Abraham's money, he calls out, "Come forth, come forth, Mary. Show your beauty to our newcomer."[40] In *Paphnutius*, the young woman Thaïs is already a harlot by the time the play begins and is therefore already accessible to the gaze of men. When the hermit Paphnutius seeks her out, he too pretends to seek her services. He informs her that he has traveled far "to speak with you and to contemplate your face,"[41] to which she replies, "I do not withdraw my aspect, nor do I deny my conversation."[42] Like the young women in the Church Fathers' accounts, Mary and Thaïs come to live in the world, where they expose themselves to the sight, the admiration, and the lust of strangers. In order to repent of their sins, these young women must, like Pelagia, withdraw from the world into hidden rooms. Abraham brings Mary back to her cell, bidding her, "Enter into the interior cell, lest the ancient serpent find another opportunity for deceiving you."[43] Paphnutius brings Thaïs to a cell he has constructed for her in a convent, with no entry or exit, but only a small window through which food can be introduced. "Withdraw yourself," he commands, "to a secret place [*secretum locum*], in which . . . you may lament the enormity of your crimes."[44] Having sinned by exposing themselves to men, these women atone for their sins by allowing themselves to be seen by God alone.

Interestingly enough, however, Hrotsvitha suggests that it is a kind of theater in general that will lure errant women back to their cells, once they have left them, and will perhaps persuade other women not to leave these cells, if they have ever been tempted to depart. If women are to exchange virtue for vice, she indicates, it is because they are deceived by a kind of actor, who seems to be good when he is, in fact, wicked. When Abraham explains Mary's seduction to a friend, he faults "the illicit affection of a certain imposter [*simulatoris*], who, coming in a monastic habit, frequented her in deceptive visits."[45] If this man was an imposter, it is, not just because he was a seducer in the guise of a monk, but because he was the Devil himself in the guise of a man. Mary confirms the identity of her seducer as "He who cast down the first men."[46] Yet, if women are to exchange vice for virtue, Hrotsvitha establishes, it is because they are happily tricked by another kind of actor, who seems to be wicked when he is, in fact, good. In order to gain access to Mary, Abraham approaches her "in the appearance of a lover,"[47] with the costume of a soldier and a hat to cover his tonsure. Once at the inn, he eats meat, drinks wine, and makes merry, all in contravention of his eremitical rule. As he puts it himself, "I, an old hermit, have become a lascivious table-companion."[48] In a similar manner, Paphnutius approaches Thaïs "in the appearance of a lover."[49] He banters with the harlot's lovers, and he arranges to meet with her in a hidden room for the purpose of an illicit encounter. The Devil, appearing in the guise of a monk, intends to bring about the young women's downfall, but Abraham and Paphnutius, appearing in the guise of lechers, intend to bring about their salvation. The harlot's secret chamber in which they would contribute to the young woman's sinfulness becomes the penitent's secret cell in which they bring about her redemption. Not only do Abraham and Paphnutius play the actor, but Hrotsvitha herself becomes a kind of actress. In the Preface to her dramatic works, she acknowledges that she has composed in the manner of Terence, a pagan playwright noteworthy both for the elegance of his style and for the depravity of his plots. Yet, if she has imitated Terence, she insists, it was only so that, "in the very same form of composition through which the shameless acts of lascivious women were depicted, the laudable chastity of sacred virgins may be celebrated."[50] Like the hermits who assume the guise of wanton men because they seek to rescue wanton women, the canoness depicts "the detestable madness of illicit lovers and their wickedly sweet conversations"[51] because she seeks to rescue those who might have taken pleasure in such folly. As Ephraim reassures Abraham, "He who knows the secrets of our hearts and understands with what intention a thing is done does not disapprove when one of us descends, for a time, from the rigor of our strict way of life and fits in with those who are weaker, by which he may more effectively recall a soul that has erred."[52] If these characters and their author adopt, at times, wicked personae, like actors in classical drama, it is only in order to achieve a virtuous purpose.

In *Ordo virtutum*, Hildegard also represents a female figure as at risk once she ventures out into the world and as safe once she returns to her proper place. While Hrotsvitha's plays might have merely been read aloud, Hildegard's works are often thought to have been performed in Hildegard's church, perhaps, as Peter Dronke argues, for the consecration of her newly-founded convent at Rupertsberg in May 1152,[53] or perhaps, as Pamela Sheingorn proposes, for the consecration of virgins entering the convent.[54] During the performance, the Devil (presumably played by Volmar, Hildegard's secretary), who would have been standing outside the church sanctuary, shouts his words to the seventeen Virtues (presumably played by Hildegard's nuns), who would have been standing inside the sanctuary, on a raised dais.[55] He tells Chastity, "Your belly is devoid of the beautiful form that woman receives from man: in this you transgress the command that God enjoined in the sweet act of love."[56] God ordered that women should join with men in sexual unions and conceive children, he points out, echoing the biblical injunction to be fruitful and multiply, yet, he asserts, Chastity scorns this command. The Soul (in the Latin, the feminine *Anima*) (perhaps played by Hildegard's closest companion, Richardis von Stade) is at first located with the Virtues in the sanctuary, but she is swayed by the Devil's arguments. Under his influence, she quits the sanctuary and wanders off, perhaps out of the church itself. Later, the Soul regrets what she has done and wishes to return the sanctuary. She tells the Virtues, "How delectable is your home, and so, what woe is mine that I fled from you!"[57] In her defiled state, she does not dare to enter this sacred space again, but the Virtues encourage her to do so: "You who escaped, come, come to us, and God will take you back."[58] Like the young women in the Church Fathers' accounts and like Mary and Thaïs in Hrotsvitha's plays, the Soul goes to live in the world and succumbs to sins of the flesh; yet, like a wayward nun returning to her convent, she too regains the sanctuary with her sisters.

The female figure is at risk in Hildegard's play because she stands to be deceived by someone who pretends to be different from what he is, but she is rescued because she is capable of seeing through his disguise. Once again, the Devil is a kind of actor. His argument seems reasonable, grounded as it is in the scriptural account of Creation, yet, as the Soul points out, he is a "trickster [*illusor*]"[59] who speaks only to deceive. Though the Devil claims that the Virtues do not enjoy "the sweet act of love," they do, in fact, partake in such intercourse. Chastity reminds Virginity that she "burns sweetly in the embraces of the King, when the Sun shines through you."[60] As consorts of the King of Kings, the Virtues take delight in their Beloved, but, she suggests, they do so in such a way that they are unharmed by his embrace; they thus resemble, she indicates, a window left intact by the ray that shines through it. Though the Devil claims that the Virtues do not bear "the beautiful form that woman receives from man," they have, in fact, given birth. Chastity points out that, "In a virgin form, I nurtured a sweet miracle when the Son of God came into the world."[61] The Devil declares that the processes of coition and reproduction can only be understood in physical terms, which are defined by the law of Nature, but the Virtues insist that they can also be understood in metaphysical terms, which, miraculously, can break those laws. While Hrotsvitha suggests that a deception—like that of a good man who plays the part of a lover or that of a Christian playwright who imitates the forms of classical drama—can bring someone to the truth, Hildegard maintains that only the exposure of deception as deception can lead to such a revelation. Humility informs the Devil, "My comrades and I know very well that you are the dragon of old."[62] While the Devil, with his false, literal interpretation of Scripture, sought to limit the soul to the flesh, the Virtues, with their true, figurative interpretation of this text, argue that the virgin can transcend the body. The beauty of *Ordo virtutum* lies, not in the physical drama, where characters assume disguises and banter about carnal assignations, but in a kind of metaphysical drama, where characters strip the disguise from their deceivers and solemnly praise, not carnal, but spiritual unions.

In their accounts of young women who, having gone astray in the world, only to return to their cloisters, Hrotsvitha and Hildegard recuperate the theater for Christianity, though in a way that distances it from tragedy. Like the Church Fathers, they represent harlots or wanton women who abandon themselves to sin. Unlike their patristic predecessors, however, they depict these women, not as alluring in their sinfulness, but as penitent. While Hrotsvitha follows her source texts in portraying Mary and Thaïs from the perspective of the hermits who counsel them, both she and Hildegard partake in a medieval Christian discourse which treats the female and not the male as the universal category. In accordance with the Latin of the Bible, they conceive of the "soul" [*anima*] as feminine, in its union with the masculine Christ, and the self, by extension, as female. When the fallen woman turns from sin to sanctity, her conversion is understood as emblematic of the conversion of all human beings, who are capable of such a transformation. Hrotsvitha acknowledges her debt to Boethius, who, she says, inspired her to "rip small patches from Philosophy's robe and weave them into this little work of mine."[63] She too rejects "the cry of tragedies" which he saw as setting itself against the workings of God's Providence in the world. At the same time, however, she honors the Muses, whom Boethius had rejected, when she revives drama for a Christian world. For both Hrotsvitha and Hildegard, theater is not a harlot, enervating its audience by pandering to their emotions, including those cultivated by tragedy, but, rather, a branch of philosophy, fortifying them by appealing to their reason.

JOAN OF ARC

In the Late Middle Ages, no woman playwright offers us dramatic productions as Hrotsvitha and Hildegard had once done, but a woman does nonetheless emerge whose remarkable life story will provide material for the plots of plays—including tragedies—for centuries to come. On June 8, 1429, during the Hundred Years' War, the French armies, led largely by Joan of Arc, succeeded in relieving the city of Orleans from the siege the English had set before it many months before. Through the end of the fifteenth century, the burghers commemorated the anniversary of that event every year, ringing church bells, marching in processions, and performing "mysteries" in memory of that happy occasion. The anonymous *Mystery of the Siege of Orleans* (1450s) reflects the dramas that would have been enacted at that time. Feminist critics who have addressed the mystery plays of the Late Middle Ages have commended what they have seen as the unruly women of these works. Natalie Zemon Davis, in her well-known essay "Women on Top," celebrates the wives of the Corpus Christi cycles, such as Mrs. Noah, Dame Procula, and Gyll, as disorderly beings ruled, not by their upper bodies, or reason, but by their lower bodies, or passions. In carnival festivities, the Feast of Fools, and popular revolts, Davis recalls, men would dress in women's clothes and, in doing so, give themselves license to act in accordance with this stereotype.[64] Though she recognizes that the notion of the unruly woman was often used to justify the subjection of women, she argues it could also be used "to widen behavioral options for women ... and ... to sanctify riot and political disobedience for both men and women, in a society that allowed lower orders few formal means of protest."[65] In their studies of the mystery plays, Theresa Coletti and Katie Normington, following Davis, read these unruly women as "figurations of female disorder"[66] and, hence, as challengers of the social structures that confine their sex as a whole. Yet if one considers Joan of Arc—the late medieval woman who, as much as any woman in history, overturned gender categories—one sees that it was her opponents who depicted her as an unruly woman, like these wives, while it was her supporters who portrayed her as a vessel of God's grace, like the Virgin Mary. Even as modern feminists associate feminism with an affirmation of the fleshly, the imminent, and the self-actualizing, medieval women and men, it is clear, associated the defense of women with the spiritual, the transcendent, and the self-sacrificing, in a way that, with the passage of centuries, would come to be interpreted as the tragic.

In the *Mystery of the Siege of Orleans*, the English soldiers who fight against Joan perceive her as an unruly woman. She is a peasant girl who has become a captain-at-arms. Richard Guestin, bailly of Evreux and captain of Beaugency, asks her, "Are you not ashamed, hussy, to arm yourself against us? Do you want to become a duke, a count, or a baron?"[67] She is a daughter who has become an independent agent in society. John Talbot, the first Earl of Shrewsbury and marshal of France, jeers that she abandoned her parents, "like a madwoman running about in order to satisfy [her] will."[68] As Joan has rebelled against social and parental authority in the private sphere, she has caused France to rebel against English authority in the public sphere. Witnessing Joan's success in bringing about French victories at Orleans, Patay, and Jargeau, Guestin reflects, "Since this cursed Maid came into France and into this country, it has been in rebellion against us."[69] If such a figure of disorder has triumphed over their men, the English leaders reason, it can only have been with diabolic assistance. William Neville, Lord Falconbridge, concludes, "It is the devil who has brought her."[70] Because Joan is a figure of private and public disorder, allied with the Enemy, these men feel that it will not be enough to defeat her, to take her prisoner, or even to kill her in battle, as they do with other French officers. Instead, they announce repeatedly, they are determined to execute her in a public spectacle, in order to demonstrate her wickedness to one and all and thus to counteract the effect she has had in rallying her countrymen. William Pole, the Count of Suffolk, declares, "I will have you die in great suffering, because it is necessary that your misfortune be shown."[71] As the English envision it, Joan's execution will be a performance establishing, by the very fact that they have been able to seize her and put her to death, that she has no lasting power and that the order she once upset is now restored.

As this mystery reflects, the English of the fifteenth and sixteenth centuries did indeed condemn Joan for her unruliness. She was, in their eyes, a woman who acted like a man. Edward Hall speaks in his *Chronicle* (1548–50) of "a mayd of the age of XX yeres, and in mans apparell, named Ione, ... of suche boldnesse, that she would course horsses and ride theim to water, and do thynges, that other yong maidens, bothe abhorred and wer ashamed to do."[72] He makes clear that it is not only unusual, but undesirable, for a young woman to take up such masculine activities. Among the qualities essential for a good woman, he cites "shamefastenesse, which the Romain Ladies so kept, that seldome or never thei wer seen openly talkying with a man" and "womanly behavor, advoydying the occasion of evill iudgement, and causes of slaundre."⁷³ A decent woman, he insists, shrinks from consorting with men, yet Joan kept company with the roughest members of this sex. A decent woman, he continues, comports herself in such a way that she preempts any rumors from developing about her, yet Joan wore men's clothes, "geuyng occasion to all men to iudge, and speake evill of her, and her doynges."⁷⁴ A woman who acts as a man, Joan is, again, a peasant girl who acts as a captain-at-arms. Hall sees it as disgraceful that the French should have depended for their victories in battle, not upon their king or barons, but upon "a shepherdes daughter, a chamberlein in an hostrie, and a beggers brat."⁷⁵ Finally, Joan is, once more, a sorceress who acts as a holy prophetess. During the time of her military leadership of the Hundred Years' War, English soldiers were said to refuse to cross the Channel to fight out of fear of the Maid, and those who were already there were said to desert the armies for the same reason. John of Lancaster, Duke of Bedford and regent for the king in his minority, refers in a letter of 1434 to "a disciple and lyme of the Feende, called the Pucelle, that used fals enchauntements and sorcerie"⁷⁶ in a way that caused the number of English recruits to plummet and the hearts of those still fighting to quail. By transgressing the boundaries between men and women, noblemen and peasants, seers and witches, Joan inspired in the English a horror that seemed to their leaders to justify her death at the stake.

Yet even as the English soldiers in the *Mystery of the Siege of Orleans* perceive Joan as having overturned socio-religious norms, the French citizens in this play see her as having strengthened them. While the English view Joan as an unruly woman, the French see her as a prude (*preude*), that is, as a valiant woman, outstanding in her prowess (*proësse*).⁷⁷ (It would only be in the seventeenth century, especially through Molière's plays, that the word "prude" would acquire its current, negative connotation.) Despite what the mystery acknowledges to be her humble origins, her countrymen address her as "Lady Joan" (*Dame Jehanne*),⁷⁸ "Lady Joan, noble princess,"⁷⁹ and "very noble and very powerful lady."⁸⁰ Joan is a lady, as they see it, not because she is of high birth, but because she is of high authority. And she is of high authority on account of her virtue and the force of arms that, through God's grace, she acquired through that virtue. Davis imagines the French people to have been prepared to accept Joan as a leader because of the precedent of the disorderly woman in the cultural consciousness, yet it was the example of orderly women, like the Virgin, Judith, and Deborah—all honored in the Christian tradition—that commentators of this time regularly cited to authorize her.⁸¹ Just as the English in this mystery seek to put Joan to death, in a spectacle that will demonstrate her infamy to all, the French seek to celebrate her, in a spectacle that will recall the greatness of her deeds. It is Joan herself who first calls for an annual commemoration of the relief of the siege. She bids the burghers several times, even in the last lines of this work, to "Keep memory of this day,"⁸² to have processions, and to praise God and the Virgin, through whose intercession the city was preserved. As the play envisions it, the burghers' commemoration of Joan's relief of the siege—a ceremony to which the play itself presumably contributed—will be a performance establishing that she had lasting power and that the order she restored has survived.

Again, as the play reflects, the French of this time period honored Joan for her restoration of socio-religious norms, though not in a way from which she herself would profit. Shortly after Charles VII's coronation at Reims, the woman of letters Christine de Pizan asks presciently in her *Ditty of Joan of Arc* (1429), "And you, blessed Maid, must you be forgotten, seeing as God honored you so much that you have untied the rope which held France tightly bound? Could one praise you enough when you have bestowed peace upon this land humiliated by war?"[83] Even at this high point of Joan's career, when she has just enabled her dauphin to be recognized as a legitimate sovereign and definitively turned the tide of the Hundred Years' War to France's advantage, Christine suggests that she may end up being overlooked and insufficiently rewarded for these victories. In a similar manner, the poet-thief François Villon asks in his celebrated "Ballad of Ladies from Yesteryear" (1461), "Where is . . . Joan, the good woman from Lorraine, whom the English burned at Rouen?"[84] By contrasting the "goodness" of Joan, whose condemnation for heresy had recently been annulled, and the fate she had suffered at the hands of this foreign people, Villon also evokes the injustice the Maid had experienced. In a more scholarly vein, the historian Thomas Basin proposes in his *History of King Charles VII* (1471–84) that, after God had sent Joan to the French in order to help them in their campaign against the English, he had taken her away from them in order to chastise them for their ingratitude and their bad morals in general. He writes, "We admit that God permitted that she be taken by the enemies and conducted to her death because of the faults of the king and the people of France."[85] With these words, Basin suggests that Joan was treated so badly, not because of any failings on her part, but because of the failings of the ruler and the city for which she had fought so valiantly. The mournful tone of the contemporaneous French writings about Joan, though not yet tragic, anticipates the direction in which her story would develop in future centuries.

By the time of Friedrich Schiller's *The Maid of Orleans: A Romantic Tragedy* (1801), Joan had become a full-fledged tragic heroine. It may seem that the Maid of this play resembles her prototypes in late antique and medieval literature when she attempts to remain faithful to her vow of chastity. Courted by two of the French army commanders, she replies, "Like bodiless spirits, which are not subjected to worldly ways, I align myself with no sex, and this armor covers no heart."[86] Yet as vehement as her language of chastity is here, it is also false. On the stage, she is clearly not a "bodiless spirit," but someone very much with a body (and often, in performances, an attractive one at that). By insisting that she does not have a body, a sex, or a heart, she seems to be in denial about her essential nature as a young woman. It is no surprise therefore, when, later in the play, as Joan is preparing to kill the young English officer Lionel and removes his helmet for this purpose, she undergoes a transformation. She asks herself, "Do I bear the image of a man in my pure bosom? This heart, filled with the glory of Heaven, may it beat with a worldly love?"[87] She wonders, "Am I to be punished because I am human? Is pity a sin?"[88] However admirable Joan may be for Schiller for striving to preserve her fierce chastity, she becomes all the more appealing to him for giving in to a tender compassion for a man. Now that she has broken her vow, in her feelings, if not in her actions, she believes herself to be unworthy of her mission. Accused of witchcraft, she cannot bring herself to defend herself, and she is put to death as a result. She gives up her life, not out of love of her God or her country, as earlier versions of her story would have it, but out of misgivings for her love for an English soldier. While the tension between the sinful and the salutary aspects of women's theatricality are resolved through this return to the tragic, it is only by having the heroine become a private individual, whose sufferings reflect nothing more than her tormented psyche.

THÉRÈSE DE LISIEUX

Even as, in cities, towns, and courts, theater came to forefront beautiful, often tragic actresses for public admiration, behind the walls of the cloister, it preserved the legacy of convent drama, with its alternate vision of female heroism. In France, Italy, Spain, and the

Spanish colonies in the New World, nuns produced plays for major feast days, in part for the choir sisters' spiritual benefit; in part for their pupils' religious education; and in part for the entertainment of lay spectators, who were occasionally invited to attend.[89] Because these plays were intended primarily for the nuns themselves, their manuscripts seldom survived, especially after the suppression of the monasteries in the eighteenth and nineteenth centuries. Among the plays that have been preserved are those of Thérèse de Lisieux, a middle-class Norman girl who, at the age of fifteen, joined her sisters Marie, Pauline, and (eventually) Céline at the Carmelite convent in Lisieux. As a nun, Thérèse wrote, directed, and starred in a series of plays, including two about Joan of Arc, *The Mission of Joan of Arc* (January 21, 1894) and *Joan of Arc Accomplishing Her Mission* (January 21, 1895). We have virtually no information about what miracle and mystery plays meant to women (or men) of the Middle Ages, yet the same is not true for Thérèse's productions. When one puts the text of these plays together with her abundant other writings, as well as with the records and photographs from the convent, one sees how a woman, even in the modern era, could internalize patristic warnings about venturing into public and flaunting her beauty, yet also transform these seemingly misogynistic teachings into something positive. Though non-Catholic feminist scholars have displayed almost no interest in Thérèse's writings, the influence of her spirituality upon women of her faith, especially in the early and mid-twentieth century, would be difficult to exaggerate. In this late representation of the medieval genre of convent drama, women characters, portrayed by a woman dramatist, speak and act in public, but in a way that dismantles the opposition between the heroine in the world and the nun in her cloister. Once again, the seclusion from the male gaze and the patient endurance of suffering that were admired in women in earlier centuries are celebrated, in contrast to the values of tragedy.

As dissimilar as Joan and Thérèse might seem to be, Thérèse suggests in her plays that the captain-at-arms longed to behave like the contemplative nun. At home in her village, in *The Mission of Joan of Arc*, Joan has no interest in making herself more beautiful in the manner of young girls. Her friend Germaine admires a garland Joan is weaving for the Chapel of Our Lady, but she remarks, "I have never seen you braid a single crown for yourself."[90] She reproaches her for not being "adorned"[91] for the village festival that is about to start. Instead of exposing herself to the sight of all, Joan wishes to hide herself from their view. When she learns from her voices that she must take up arms and go to the aid of France, she bursts into tears and covers her face with her hands. Though she accepts that it is the will of God that she depart, she resolves, "When my mission is finished, I will have only one desire: to hide myself in order to let God alone have the glory of the triumph."[92] After she brings the dauphin to Reims to be crowned, she throws herself at his feet and begs his permission to return to her village, which he refuses. If Joan entered into the public sphere, Thérèse shows, it was, not because she wished to do so, but because she was assigned this task by her voices and then by her king, In a similar manner, Thérèse indicates in her autobiography *The History of a Soul* that, from early on, she herself had felt uneasiness with women's beauty and the effect that beauty can have when it is exposed to the world. When she was at boarding school, she overheard one visitor praise her hair and another refer to her as a beautiful young girl. These comments had pleased her, showing her, as she puts it, "how I was filled with self-love."[93] Now, addressing her autobiography to her sister Pauline, the Mother Superior of their convent, she expresses thanks that she and Marie had never directed compliments to her and had thus taught her not to give importance to those she did receive. She states, "You took such care, my dear Mother, not to allow me to come into contact with anything that could tarnish my innocence, and above all, not to let me hear any word capable of letting vanity slip into my heart."[94] By entering the convent, where she will not be seen, Thérèse avoids the self-consciousness about her beauty and the pleasure in collecting admirers that the Church Fathers had attributed to women. From early on, she writes, "I felt that Carmel was the *desert* where God wished me to go and hide myself."[95] Both Joan and she wished to conceal themselves from the gaze of others, Thérèse suggests.

As Joan longs to behave like a nun, Thérèse makes clear, she longs to behave like a heroine. She recalls in her autobiography, "When reading accounts of the patriotic deeds of French heroines, especially those of the *Venerable* JOAN OF ARC, I had a great desire to imitate them, and I felt within myself the same ardor with which they were animated, the same Celestial inspiration."[96] Enclosed in her convent, Thérèse remained deeply concerned with events in the world. She prayed for the conversion of Henri Pranzini, who had been condemned to be executed for a triple murder, and rejoiced to learn that he had kissed a crucifix as he had mounted the scaffold. She corresponded with Carmelite missionaries in Indochina and would have joined them had she been in sufficient health to do so. In July 1894, as she lay dying of tuberculosis at the age of twenty-four, Thérèse wrote, "I feel above all that my mission is about to begin, my mission of having God loved as I love him, of giving my little way to souls."[97] The fact that she is apart from the world, whether in her convent or in heaven, does not mean that she has no effect upon it. On the contrary, she indicates, her very separation from other people allows her to touch them all the more. In *Joan of Arc Accomplishing Her Mission*, Joan also makes clear that her primary mission is, not to liberate France, but to save the souls of the French. At the end of her life, she announces, like Thérèse, "I want to fight for Jesus . . . to earn souls for him without number."[98] Whether by praying in her cloister or by fighting on the battlefield, Thérèse and Joan were united, as the young nun saw it, in their common goal of bringing their countrymen to God. In recognition of the affinity between these two young women, when Thérèse was canonized in 1925, it was as "a new Joan of Arc" and, eventually, as the second patroness of France, equal to her heroine.

In the end, the Christian literary tradition of late antiquity, the Middle Ages, and its aftermath presents an alternate vision of human agency than that considered elsewhere in this volume. In classical, Renaissance, and neo-classical tragedy, the arena for human activity is the public world, where men have customarily occupied the dominant role. While women have often figured importantly in tragic works, they have done so in a context where a man—an Agamemnon, a Creon, a Theseus, an Othello, a Macbeth—has occupied the seat of official power. In contrast, in the Christian dramatic tradition, the arena for human activity is the private world, where women possess equal if not superior status. An emperor may throw Thecla or Perpetua to wild beasts in an amphitheater, a seducer or the Seducer may tempt, for a time, Mary, Thaïs, or the Soul into the sins of the world, and the English may condemn Joan to the stake, but it is these women who ultimately triumph over their oppressors by choosing virtue over vice. However unjust their suffering and death, one feels, not sorrow for their downfall, but, rather, vindication at their victory. Insofar as these Christian playwrights deviated from the script of tragedy, they knew exactly what they were doing.

NOTES

Introduction

1. J. Anouilh, *Antigone*, trans. Lewis Galantière (New York and London: Methuen Drama, 1960), 34.
2. *The Jackass Conjecture*, trans. J. Enders, in *"Holy Deadlock" and Further Ribaldries: Twelve Medieval French Plays in Modern English*, The Middle Ages Series (Philadelphia: University of Pennsylvania Press, 2017), 163. All translations from the French are mine unless otherwise indicated. Whenever possible, I refer to primary sources in English translation only; and, in the interest of space, when I mention a source by title alone, please simply refer to the Bibliography.
3. Cited and analyzed by Hannah Skoda in *Medieval Violence: Physical Brutality in Northern France (1270–1330)* (Oxford: Oxford University Press, 2015): "Jehan de Sausuelle beat his pregnant wife, Alice, to death in 1332, but was finally acquitted when none of his friends or neighbours was prepared to provide any incriminating evidence" (220); and "in 1338 in Saint-Martin-des-Champs, Jehan le Saulnier engaged in excessive and noisy beating of his pregnant wife, and was reported by their neighbour, Perrin de la Chapelle" (219).
4. *The Chester Mystery Cycle: A New Edition with Modernised Spelling*, Medieval Texts and Studies, 9, ed. D. Mills (East Lansing, MI: Colleagues Press, 1992), 188; vv. 361–4; see T. Coletti, "'Ther Be but Women': Gender Conflict and Gender Identity in the Middle English Innocents Plays," *Medievalia* 18 (1995): 245–61.
5. On this oft-reproduced image, see G. Kipling, "Theatre as Subject and Object in Fouquet's 'Martyrdom of St. Apollonia,'" *Medieval English Theatre* 19 (1997): 26–80.
6. I review the primary and secondary sources for the "fun and games" of the Passion-play buffeting of Christ sources in *The Medieval Theater of Cruelty: Rhetoric, Memory, Violence* (Ithaca: Cornell University Press, 1999), 170–85.
7. Anonymous from the *Carmina Burana*, "Ich was ein chint so woltegan," in *Anthology of Ancient and Medieval Woman's Song*, ed. A.L. Klinck (New York and Basingstoke: Palgrave Macmillan, 2004), 96.
8. *Le Mistere de la Sainte Hostie*. Bibliothèque nationale, Réserve, Yf 2915, fol. 34v.
9. See, e.g., Tissier's edition of *Le Galant qui a fait le coup*, in *Recueil de farces (1450–1550)*, 13 vols. (Geneva: Droz, 1986–2000), 6: 309–66, v. 152; 159.
10. Philippe de Vigneulles on historical events of 1495; cited in my "Theater Makes History: Ritual Murder by Proxy in the *Mistere de la Sainte Hostie*," *Speculum* 79 (2004): 991–1016; at 1000–9.
11. Superb initiations include B. Hoxby, *What Was Tragedy? Theory and the Early Modern Canon* (Oxford: Oxford University Press, 2015); and R. Felski, "Introduction," in *Rethinking Tragedy*, ed. R. Felski (Baltimore: Johns Hopkins University Press, 2008), 1–25.
12. See A.M. Nagler, *A Source Book in Theatrical History* (1952; rpt. New York: Dover, 1959), 5.
13. Cited in Skoda, *Medieval Violence*, 213.
14. Archives d'Angers, BB 4 fol. 29; cited and discussed in J. Enders, *Death by Drama and Other Medieval Urban Legends* (Chicago: University of Chicago Press, 2002), 113; 270n.

15. I.A. Richards, *Principles of Literary Criticism* (London: Kegan Paul, 1924), 246; and, playing on Friedrich Nietzsche's *Birth of Tragedy*, George Steiner, *The Death of Tragedy* (New York: Knopf, 1961), 129.
16. The *Life of Saint Erkenwald* appears, e.g., in *The Complete Works of the Pearl Poet*, trans. Casey Finch, ed. Malcolm Andrew, Ronald Waldron, Clifford Peterson (Berkeley: University of California Press, 1993), 146–93, although its authorship has been called into question.
17. For the classic discussion of the trope as a likely origin of medieval drama, see, e.g., O.B. Hardison, Jr., *Christian Rite and Christian Drama in the Middle Ages: Essays in the Origin and Early History of Modern Drama* (Baltimore: Johns Hopkins University Press, 1965), esp. Essay V.
18. Here, of course, I paraphrase Luce Irigaray's *This Sex Which is Not One*.
19. See Kelly, *Ideas and Forms of Tragedy from Aristotle to the Middle Ages* (Cambridge: Cambridge University Press, 1993); and, e.g., Anthony Kubiak, *Stages of Terror: Terrorism, Ideology, and Coercion as Theatre History* (Bloomington: Indiana University Press, 1991), 48–71; R. Bushnell, "The Fall of Princes: Classical and Medieval Origins of English Renaissance Tragedy," in *A Companion to Tragedy*, ed. Rebecca Bushnell (Malden and Oxford: Blackwell, 2005), 289–306.
20. R. Lebègue, *La Tragédie religieuse en France: Les débuts (1514–1573)* (Paris: Champion, 1929).
21. See, e.g., F.H. Ristine, *English Tragicomedy: Its Origin and History* (New York: Columbia University Press, 1910); H.C. Lancaster, *The French Tragi-Comedy: Its Origin and Development from 1552 to 1628* (Baltimore: J.H. Furst, 1907); R. Henke, *Pastoral Transformations: Italian Tragicomedy and Shakespeare's Late Plays* (Newark: University of Delaware Press, 1997); and S. Mukherji and R. Lyne, eds, *Early Modern Tragicomedy* (Woodbridge: D. S. Brewer, 2007).
22. Kelly, *Ideas and Forms*, 37.
23. Sponsler's own work exemplifies such scope, as in *Ritual Imports: Performing Medieval Drama in America* (Ithaca: Cornell University Press, 2004); and, with co-editor X. Chen, in *East of West: Cross-Cultural Performance and the Staging of Difference* (New York and Basingstoke: Palgrave MacMillan, 2000). On the long Middle Ages, see my Introduction to *A Cultural History of Theatre*, vol. 2, *The Middle Ages*, ed. J. Enders (London and New York: Bloomsbury, 2017), 6–8.
24. See, e.g., H. White, *Metahistory: The Historical Imagination in Nineteenth-Century Europe* (Baltimore: Johns Hopkins University Press, 1973); J. Mali, *Mythistory: The Making of a Modern Historiography* (Chicago: University of Chicago Press, 2003).
25. Richards, *Principles*, 69.
26. R.J. Dorius, "Tragedy," in the *Princeton Encyclopedia of Poetry and Poetics*, enlarged edition, ed. Preminger (Princeton: Princeton University Press, 1974), 860–4; at 860.
27. See Plato, *Theaetetus* 149d, trans. Francis MacDonald Cornford (1957; rpt. Indianapolis: Bobbs-Merrill, 1977), 25.
28. T.S. Eliot, "Rhetoric and Poetic Drama," in *Selected Essays* (New York: Harcourt Brace, 1932), 26.
29. Aristotle was available in the writings of Averroës or Hermann the German. See, e.g., *Medieval Literary Theory and Criticism*, ed. Alastair Minnis and Ian Johnson with David Wallace, rev. edn. (Oxford: Clarendon Press, 1991), 277–313; and C. Symes, "Knowledge Transmission: Media and Memory," chap. 10 of *A Cultural History of Theatre*, vol. 2, ed. J. Enders, 203–7.

30. Lucian of Samosata, "The Dance," ed. and trans. A.M. Harmon, in vol. 5 of *Works*, Loeb Classical Library (1936; rpt. Cambridge, MA.: Harvard University Press, 1972), 68.
31. It took decades for there to appear English translations of *Isidori Hispalensis Episcopi, "Etymologiarum sive Originum," Libri XX*, 2 vols. ed. W.M. Lindsay, 2 vols. (1911; rpt. London: Oxford, 1962); bk. 18, chaps. 44–6. Now there are two: I cite from *The "Etymologies" of Isidore of Seville*, trans. Stephen A. Barney, W.J. Lewis, J.A. Beach, and Oliver Berghof (Cambridge: Cambridge University Press, 2006), 369; see also *Isidore of Seville's Etymologies: The Complete English Translation of Isidori Hispalensis Episcopi, "Etymologiarum sive Originum," Libri XX*, trans. Priscilla Throop, 2 vols. (Charlotte, Vt.: MedievalMS, 2005), unpaginated. On Isidore's book 18 as a veritable primer for performance studies, see J. Enders, *Rhetoric and the Origins of Medieval Drama*, Rhetoric and Society, 1 (Ithaca: Cornell University Press, 1992), 77–89.
32. Olson, "Interpretations," chap. 2 of *A Cultural History of Theatre*, vol. 2, ed. Enders, 137.
33. *Commentum in Boethii opuscula*, cited and translated by Kelly, *Ideas and Forms*, 52.
34. Bouchet, *Epistres (familières)*, cited in English translation in W. Tydeman, ed., *The Medieval European Stage, 500–1550*, Theatre in Europe: A Documentary History (Cambridge: Cambridge University Press, 2001), 333; my emphasis.
35. F. Faber, *Histoire du Théâtre en Belgique depuis son origine jusqu'à nos jours: d'après les documents inédits reposant aux Archives Générales du Royaume*, vol. 1 (Brussels: Olivier; Paris: Tresse, 1878), 15.
36. "Nos Moralités tiennent lieu entre nous de Tragédies et Comédies indifféremment," T. Sébillet, *Art Poétique françoys (1548)*, ed. Félix Gaiffe (Paris: Edouard Cornély, 1910), 165; discussed by A.E. Knight, *Aspects of Genre in Late Medieval French Drama* (Manchester: Manchester University Press, 1983), 10. See also I. Murakami, *Moral Play and Counterpublic: Transformations in Moral Drama, 1465–1599* (New York: Routledge, 2011), esp. on the slippage of genre at 137.
37. For Nicolas of Cusa, see, e.g., J. Hopkins, *A Concise Introduction to the Philosophy of Nicholas of Cusa* (Minneapolis: University of Minnesota Press, 1978), 8–9; and, on "consubstantiality," see Burke, *The Philosophy of Literary Form: Studies in Symbolic Action*, 3rd edn. (Berkeley: University of California Press, 1973), 107–9.
38. D.W. Robertson Jr., *A Preface to Chaucer: Studies in Medieval Perspectives* (Princeton: Princeton University Press, 1962), 11.
39. See D. Coppée, *La sanglante et pitoyable Tragédie de Nostre Sauveur et Rédempteur Iésus-Christ* (Liège: Leonard Streel, 1624), my emphasis; and L. Dupont, "Denis Coppée: Tradition religieuse, actualité politique et exotisme dans le théâtre à Liège au temps du baroque," *Revue Belge de philologie et d'histoire* 55 (1977): 802; both discussed in J. Enders, "The Theatrical Memory of Denis Coppée's *Sanglante et Pitoyable tragédie de nostre Sauveur et Rédempteur Jesu-Christ*," in *The Shape of Change: Essays on the Early Modern and La Fontaine in Honor of David Lee Rubin*, ed. Ann Birberick and Russell Ganim (Amsterdam: Rodopi, 2001), 1–21.
40. T.S. Eliot, "Rhetoric and Poetic Drama," 26; 35–6.
41. Lintilhac, *Histoire Générale du théâtre en France*, 5 vols. (Paris: Flammarion, 1904–11), 1: 57; also cited by Knight, *Aspects of Genre*, 9.
42. From a vast secondary literature, see, e.g., M. Bakhtin, *Rabelais and His World*, trans. Hélène Iswolsky (1965; Bloomington: Indiana University Press, 1984); M. Harris, *Sacred Folly: A New History of the Feast of Fools* (Ithaca: Cornell University Press, 2014); and B. Burningham, "Communities of Production," chap. 7 of *A Cultural History of Theatre*, vol. 2, ed. Enders, 131.

43. Ristine, *English Tragicomedy*, ix.
44. E. Lalou, "Le théâtre médiéval, le tragique et le comique: réflexions sur la définition des genres," 4; http://ceredi.labos.univ-rouen.fr/public/?le-theatre-medieval-le-tragique-et.html (accessed March 11, 2018); and Mazouer, *Le Théâtre médiéval* (Paris: SEDES, 1998), 18.
45. W. Russell, *Educating Rita*, ed. Suzy Graham-Adriani (London: Longman, 1991), act 1, sc. 6, 41.
46. Ibid.
47. See *Poetics* 1453a; and Vatican MS Lat. 5202; cited by Kelly, *Ideas and Forms*, 69, along with an extensive sampling of medieval thinkers in his chap. 4.
48. N. Frye, *Anatomy of Criticism, Anatomy of Criticism* (Princeton: Princeton University Press, 1957), 163–86.
49. *Extreme Husband Makeover*, in Enders, *Holy Deadlock*, 377–90; and on the staging challenges, 352–7.
50. W. Kerr, *Tragedy and Comedy* (New York: Simon & Schuster, 1967), 17.
51. Aristotle, *Poetics*, ed. and trans. W. Hamilton Fyfe, in *Aristotle, "The Poetics"; Longinus, "On the Sublime"; Demetrius, "On Style,"* 1–118, Loeb Classical Library (1927; rpt. Cambridge, MA: Harvard University Press, 1946), 1450b.
52. Olson, "Interpretations," 130.
53. Hoxby, *What Was Tragedy?*, 47–8; his emphasis.
54. Ibid, 345–55; and Richards, *Principles*, 247–8. In general, see also M. Bayless, *Parody in the Middle Ages: The Latin Tradition* (Ann Arbor: University of Michigan Press, 1996); and R.D. Giles, *The Laughter of the Saints: Parodies of Holiness in Late Medieval and Renaissance Spain* (Toronto: University of Toronto Press, 2009).
55. Paul Zumthor's *mouvance* involves the instability of meaning inherent in multiple oral and written versions of a medieval "text," *Essai de poétique médiévale* (Paris: Seuil, 1972), 65–72.
56. Kerr, *Tragedy and Comedy*, 17; my emphasis for "stand silent"; other emphasis, his.
57. Richards, *Principles*, 246; cited above.
58. Again, see the Bibliography for all sources cited in this paragraph. For those less familiar with pan-European medieval drama, an excellent place to start is "Medieval European Drama in Translation," created and maintained by Stephen Wright at http://english.cua.edu/faculty/drama/index.cfm (accessed March 16, 2018). On the Filipino reenactment, both the original news story and accompanying video are available online. See, e.g., "Catholic Devotees Nailed to Crosses on Good Friday in Philippines," Associated Press, March 30, 2018; and https://www.usatoday.com/videos/news/world/2018/03/30/catholic-devotees-nailed-crosses-good-friday-philippines/33419445/ (both accessed August 4, 2018).
59. On this urban legend and its underlying realities, see my *Death by Drama*, 169–81.
60. See, e.g., D. Bevington, *Medieval Drama* (Boston: Houghton Mifflin, 1975), 9; Hardison, *Christian Rite*, 39–40; and D. Dox's insightful discussion in *The Idea of the Theater in Latin Christian Thought: Augustine to the Fourteenth Century* (Ann Arbor: University of Michigan Press, 2007), 74–85.
61. Richards, *Principles*, 245–6.
62. Richards, *Principles*, 245–6; Richards' emphasis on *catharsis;* other emphasis mine.
63. Ibid., 245–6. This is consistent with one of Hoxby's five foundational premises: "*The passions are dramatic units of crucial significance in early modern tragedy*" (*What Was Tragedy?*, 48–51).
64. Richards, *Principles*, 246; my emphasis.
65. D. Stone, *French Humanist Tragedy: A Reassessment* (Manchester: Manchester University Press, 1974), 49–50.

66. R. Bushnell, *Tragic Time in Drama, Film, and Videogames: The Future in an Instant* (London: Palgrave Macmillan, 2016), 3; and the extensive philosophical engagement of her chaps. 1 and 2.
67. On Eco, see Symes, "Knowledge Transmission," 206–7; and, for York, *Records of Early English Drama: York*, ed. Alexandra F. Johnston and Margaret Rogerson, 2 vols. (Toronto: University of Toronto Press, 1979), 1: 47–8; 2: 732.
68. *A Parisian Journal, 1405–1449*, trans. Janet Shirley (Oxford: Clarendon,1960), 78.
69. Vives cited by É. Roy, *Le Mystère de la Passion en France du XIVe au XVIe siècle: Étude sur les sources et le classement des mystères de la Passion* (Dijon and Paris: Damidot Frères and Champion, 1904), 315; my emphasis.
70. Cited in translation in my *Death by Drama*, 114–15.
71. N.Z. Davis, *Fiction in the Archives: Pardon Tales and Their Tellers in Sixteenth-Century France* (Stanford, CA: Stanford University Press, 1987), 114; my emphasis.
72. *Monk-ey Business*, in *"The Farce of the Fart" and Other Ribaldries: Twelve Medieval French Plays in Modern English*, ed. and trans. J. Enders, The Middle Ages Series (Philadelphia: University of Pennsylvania Press, 2011), 290.
73. Davis, *Fiction in the Archives*, 114.
74. Augustine of Hippo, *Confessions*, ed. and trans. William Watts, 2 vols., Loeb Classical Library (1912; rpt. Cambridge, MA: Harvard University Press, 1950–51), 1: bk. 3, chap. 2; for the Latin, see http://faculty.georgetown.edu/jod/latinconf/3.html (accessed March 24, 2018).
75. See my *Medieval Theater of Cruelty*, 146–50.
76. Richards, *Principles*, 245–6.
77. Plato, *Laws*, 2 vols., ed. and trans. R.G. Bury, Loeb Classical Library (1926; rpt. Cambridge: Harvard University Press, 1942), 1: 817B, also cited in K. Eden, *Poetic and Legal Fiction in the Aristotelian Tradition* (Princeton: Princeton University Press, 1986), 29–30.
78. See Plato, *Laws*, 1: 663b-c; 636d; 700a-701b; and, on *mousike*, esp. B.W. Holsinger, *Music, Body, and Desire in Medieval Culture: Hildegard of Bingen to Chaucer* (Stanford, CA.: Stanford University Press, 2001), chap. 3. I review the relevance of the Platonic theatrocracy to medieval drama in "The Music of the Medieval Body in Pain," *Fifteenth-Century Studies* 27 (2002): 93–112.
79. Plato, *Laws*, 1: 659d-660; 800; my emphasis.
80. Ibid., 700c-701.
81. See esp., K. Ashley, "Social Functions," chap. 2 of *A Cultural History of Theatre*, vol. 2, ed. J. Enders, 45–7; and *A Tretise of Miraclis Pleyinge*, ed. Clifford Davidson (Kalamazoo, MI: Medieval Institute Publications, 1993).
82. See J. Goebel, Jr. *Felony and Misdemeanor: A Study in the History of Criminal Law* (Philadelphia: University of Pennsylvania Press, 1976), 50: 170–1; and, on the repeated imposition of silence at the theater, see my *Death by Drama*, 111–14.
83. Cited in L. Petit de Julleville, *Les Mystères*, 2 vols., (Paris: Léopold Cerf, 1880; rpt. Geneva: Slatkine, 1968), 1: 44; 50.
84. J. Le Goff, *Medieval Civilization, 400–1500*, trans. Julia Barrow (Oxford: Blackwell, 1988), 360–1.
85. Antonia Pulci, *The Play of Saint Theodora*, in *Florentine Drama for Convent and Festival: Seven Sacred Plays*, ed. James Wyatt Cook and Barbara Collier Cook, trans. James Wyatt Cook (Chicago: University of Chicago Press, 1996), 187–216; at 187–93.
86. I discuss multiple such accidents in my *Murder by Accident: Medieval Theater, Modern Media, Critical Intentions* (Chicago: University of Chicago Press, 2009), chap. 6.

87. I make this argument in "Comically Incorrect," *ROMARD* [*Research Opportunities in Medieval and Renaissance Drama*] 51 (2012): 75–82; at 77.
88. Cited and discussed in my *Death by Drama*, 55–9.
89. M. Lawson, "Farce Is Everywhere on Stage—but Why?" *Guardian*, June 10, 2012. http://www.theguardian.com/stage/2012/jun/10/farce-is-everywhere-why (accessed December 1, 2015).
90. See Bushnell's full discussion in *Tragic Time*, 2–20.

Chapter One

1. See e.g., H.A. Kelly, *Ideas and Forms of Tragedy from Aristotle to the Middle Ages* (Cambridge: Cambridge University Press, 1993); R. Garland, *Surviving Greek Tragedy* (London: Duckworth, 2004).
2. Rome, Biblioteca Vaticana cod. Palatinus graec. 287; and Florence, Biblioteca Laurenciana conventi soppressi 172 (the same manuscript containing *Helen*, pictured in Figure 1.1). See A. Turyn, *The Byzantine Manuscript Tradition of the Tragedies of Euripides* (Urbana: University of Illinois Press, 1957), 258–67; C. Symes, "Ancient Drama in the Medieval World," in *A Handbook to the Reception of Greek Drama*, ed. Betine van Zyl Smit (Hoboken, NJ: Wiley-Blackwell, 2016).
3. D.L. Page, *Actors' Interpolations in Greek Tragedy, Studied with Special Reference to Euripides' Iphigeneia in Aulis* (Oxford: Clarendon Press, 1934), 1–10. W.J. Slater, "Problems in Interpreting Scholia on Greek Texts," in *Roman Theatre and Society: E. Togo Salmon Papers I*, ed. W.J. Slater (Ann Arbor: University of Michigan Press, 1996), 37–61 at 38; Carol Symes, "The Medieval Archive and the History of Theatre: Assessing the Written and Unwritten Evidence for Premodern Performance," *Theatre Survey* 52 (2011): 1–30.
4. E.A. Havelock, "The Oral Composition of Greek Drama," *Quaderni Urbanati di Cultura Classica* n.s. 6 [35] (1980): 61–113, repr. in *The Literate Revolution in Greece and Its Cultural Consequences* (Princeton: Princeton University Press, 1982), 261–313; R. Thomas, *Oral Tradition and Written Record in Classical Athens* (Cambridge: Cambridge University Press, 1989), 49; D.F. Melia, "Orality and Aristotle's Aesthetics," in *New Directions in Oral Theory*, ed. Mark C. Amodio (Tempe: Arizona Center for Medieval and Renaissance Studies, 2005), 91–124.
5. E.G. Wilson, *Greek Papyri* (Princeton: Princeton University Press, 1968), 123; P.J. Wilson, "Tragic Rhetoric: The Use of Tragedy and the Tragic in the Fourth Century," in *Tragedy and the Tragic: Greek Theatre and Beyond*, ed. Michael S. Silk (Oxford: Oxford University Press, 1996), 310–31 at 316.
6. G. Zuntz, *An Inquiry into the Transmission of the Plays of Euripides* (Cambridge: Cambridge University Press, 1965), 250–3; T. Falkner, "Scholars versus Actors" "Scholars versus Actors: Text and Performance in the Greek Scholia," in *Greek and Roman Actors: Aspects of an Ancient Profession*, ed. Pat Easterling and Edith Hall (Cambridge: Cambridge University Press, 2002), 342–61; M. Fantuzzi and R. Hunter, *Tradition and Innovation in Hellenistic Poetry* (Cambridge: Cambridge University Press, 2004), 432–44.
7. J. Hanink, "The Classical Tragedians, from Athenian Idols to Wandering Poets," in *Beyond the Fifth Century: Interactions with Greek Tragedy from the Fourth Century* BCE *to the Middle Ages*, ed. Ingo Gildenhard and Martin Revermann (Berlin: De Gruyter, 2010), 39–67; P. Ceccarelli, "Changing Contexts: Tragedy in the Civic and Cultural Life of Hellensitic City-States," in *Beyond the Fifth Century*, ed. Gildenhard and Revermann, 99–150; M. Revermann, "Situating the Gaze of the Recipient(s): Theatre-Related Vase

Paintings and Their Contexts of Reception," in *Beyond the Fifth Century*, ed. Gildenhard and Revermann, 69–97; K. Bosher, ed., *Theatre Outside Athens: Drama in Greek Sicily and Italy* (Cambridge: Cambridge University Press, 2012); C. Dearden, "Whose Line Is It Anyway? West Greek Comedy in Its Context," in *Theatre Outside Athens*, ed. Bosher, 272–88; O. Taplin, *Pots and Plays*, and "How Was Athenian Tragedy Played in the Greek West?" in *Theatre Outside Athens*, ed. Bosher, 226–50; L. Todisco, "Myth and Tragedy: Red-Figure Pottery and Verbal Communication in Central and Northern Apulia in the Later Fourth-Century BC," trans. Thomas Simpson in *Theatre Outside Athens*, ed. Bosher, 251–71.

8. W.D. Lebek, "Moneymaking and the Roman Stage," in *Roman Theatre and Society*, ed. Slater, 29–48 ; P.G. McC. Brown, "Actors and Actor-Managers at Rome in the Time of Plautus and Terence," in *Greek and Roman* Actors, ed. Easterling and Hall, 225–37; I. Gildenhard, "Buskins and SQPR: Roman Receptions of Greek Tragedy," in *Beyond the Fifth Century*, ed. Gildenhard and Revermann, 153–85.
9. J. Bidez and F. Cumont, eds, *Imp.Caesaris Flavii Claudii Iuliani epistulae, leges, poemata, fragmenta varia* (Paris: Société d'édition "Les belles lettres", 1922), 172–3 (Ep. 89).
10. A.J. Boyle, *Tragic Seneca: An Essay in the Theatrical Tradition* (London and New York: Routledge, 1997); A. Zanobi, "Seneca and Pantomime," in *Beyond the Fifth Century*, ed. Ingo Gildenhard and Revermann, 269–88; E. Hall, "The Singing Actors of Antiquity," in *Greek and Roman Actors*, ed. Easterling and Hall, 3–38.
11. Symes, "Ancient Drama in the Medieval World." Negative attitudes toward theatrical activity are usually an excellent index of its prosperity: see J. Barish, *The Antitheatrical Prejudice* (Berkeley and Los Angeles: University of California Press, 1981).
12. T.D. Barnes, "Christians and the Theatre," in *Roman Theatre and Society*, ed. Slater, 161–80 at 161–4.
13. E.C. Bourbouhakis, "Rhetoric and Performance," in *The Byzantine World*, ed. Paul Stephenson (London and New York: Routledge, 2010), 175–87 at 182.
14. Hall, "Singing Actors," 37. See also J.L. Lightfoot, "Nothing to Do with the *Technītai* of Dionysius?" in *Greek and Roman Actors*, ed. Easterling and Hall, 209–24.
15. M.L. West, *Ancient Greek Music* (Oxford: Oxford University Press, 1992); A.W. White, "The Artifice of Eternity: A Study of Liturgical and Theatrical Practices in Byzantium," unpublished Ph.D. Dissertation (College Park: University of Maryland, 2006).
16. A. Kaldellis, *Hellenism in Byzantium: The Transformation of Greek Identity and the Reception of the Classical Tradition* (Cambridge: Cambridge University Press, 2007), 146–66.
17. Ibid., 140.
18. D. Dox, *The Idea of the Theatre. The Idea of the Theater in Latin Christian Thought: Augustine to the Fourteenth Century* (Ann Arbor: University of Michigan Press, 2004).
19. I offer a more comprehensive analysis of this evidence in C. Symes, "The Tragedy of the Middle Ages," in *Beyond the Fifth Century*, ed. Gildenhard and Revermann, 335–69.
20. Jerome, *Adversus Jovinianum*, I.48, in *Patrologia Latina*, ed. J.-P. Migne et al. (Paris, 1844–64), vol. 23: 278. Hereinafter this series is cited as *PL* [vol: page].
21. C. Symes, "Knowledge Transmission: Media and Memory," in *A Cultural History of Theatre in the Middle Ages*, ed. Jody Enders (London: Bloomsbury Publishing, 2017), 199–211.
22. E.g. Marbod of Rennes, *De apto genero scribendi* ("*De meretrice*"), in *PL* 170:1699.
23. *PL* 199:752 (John of Salisbury); 207:243 (Peter of the Blois).
24. Augustine of Hippo, *Confessions* III.2, in *PL* 32:893; see Dox, *Idea of the Theatre*, 12–29.
25. *PL* 41:53,55.
26. *PL* 32:937, 959, 1013.

27. Augustine, *De sermone Domini in monte libros duos* II:2–5, in *PL* 34:1271. "CUM ERGO FACIS ELEMOSYNAM, *inquit,* NOLI TUBA CANERE ANTE TE, SICVT HYPOCRITAE FACIVNT IN SINAGOGIS ET IN VICIS, VT GLORIFICENTVR AB HOMINIBVS. *Noli, inquit, sic uelle innotescere ut hypocritae. Manifestum est autem hypocritas non quod oculis praetendunt hominum id etiam corde gestare. Sunt enim hypocritae simulatores tamquam pronuntiatores personarum alienarum sicut in theatricis fabulis. Non enim qui agit partes Agamemnonis in tragoedia uerbi gratia sive alicuius alterius ad historiam uel fabulam quae agitur pertinentis uere ipse est, sed simulat eum et hypocrita dicitur.*" I have also consulted the edition of A. Mutzenbecher in *Corpus Christianorum Series Latina*, 35 (Turnhout: Brepols, 1967): 95–6.
28. Rabanus Maurus, *Commentarium in Matthaeum* II.6, in *PL* 107:815.
29. *PL* 69:643.
30. *PL* 69:1056.
31. Ambrose of Milan, commentary on Psalm 38, in *PL* 14:1039. "*Denique etiam in saecularibus scriptis alii erant qui scribebant, alii qui in scena, vel cantica, vel comoedias, vel tragoedias, canere consueverant.*"
32. Bede, *De arte metrica* (cap. 25), in *PL* 90:174. "*Dramaticum est, vel activum, in quo personae loquentes introducuntur, sine poetae interlocutione, ut se habent tragoediae et fabulae. Drama enim, Latine fabula dicitur.* . . . *Quo apud nos genere Cantica canticorum scripta sunt, ubi vox alternans Christi et Ecclesiae, tametsi non hoc interloquente scriptore, manifeste reperitur.*"
33. Rabanus Maurus, *Excerptio de Arte grammatica Prisciani*, in *PL* 111:668. "*Igitur comoedia a tragoedia differt, quod in tragoedia introducuntur heroes, duces, reges; in comoedia, humiles atque privatae: in illa luctus, exsilia, caedes; in hac amores, virginum raptus.*"
34. Gregory of Tours, *Historia* VI.46, in *PL* 71:412.
35. Aldhelm of Sherborne, *De laudibus virginitatis*, in *PL* 89:135.
36. Hugh of Fouilloy, in *PL* 177:78: "*qui deliciis hujus saeculi, et pompis et theatralibus voluptatibus delectantur, tragoediis et comoediis dissoluti.*"
37. *PL* 106:989, 994, 996, 999, 1001, 1032, 1045, 1131.
38. Paschasius Radbertus, *Expositio in Matthaeo. Libri XII*, in *PL* 120:515: "*in pretium tragoediae suae.*" I have also consulted the edition of B. Paulus in *Corpus Christianorum Series Latina*, 56 (Turnhout: Brepols, 1984), II:734 (VII:1399–1400).
39. Peter Chrysologus, *De D. Joanne Baptista et Herode* (Sermon 173), in *PL* 52:653: "tragoediam nefandam caneret"; Sermon 127, in *PL* 52:552.
40. Rupert of Deutz, *Commentariorum in Genesim* VIII.33, in *PL* 167:520. "*Haec de sensu litterali. Ceterum in typum Domini salvatoris illa feminae tragoedia synagogae vesania est . . . Nam Dominus noster, cum a Iudaeis frateribus suis comprehens et tota nocte irrisiones et opprobria passus fuisset, subsecuta luce ante praesidum adductus et cum testibus falsis accusatus est. Discendum igitur quid in Christo synagoga concupierit, quid non adeptem se esse dolens Christum praesidi suo tradiderit.*" I have also consulted the edition of H. Haack in *Corpus Christianorum, Continuatio Mediaevalis*, 21–24 (Turnhout: Brepols, 1971), I:521.
41. J. Van Engen, *Rupert of Deutz* (Berkeley and Los Angeles: University of California Press, 1983), 3.
42. Rupert of Deutz, *De operibus Spiritus Sancti*, in *PL* 167:1446.
43. *PL* 169:1062: "*tragoedias illorum temporum*"; cf. 169:1447.
44. *PL* 55:876, 878: "totam Manichaicam tragoediam; 55:1144: "*lugubrem hanc tragoediam.*"
45. Council of Carthage, in *PL* 3:1027.
46. Hincmar of Reims, in *PL* 126:428, 455, 498; cf. Flodoard of Reims, quoting Hincmar, in *PL* 135:208.

47. Cassiodorus, in *PL* 68:941, 1104.
48. *PL* 69:521: "*quod totius tragoediam reatus exsuperet*"; cf. *PL* 69:451, 600.
49. Anastasius the Librarian, *Historia de vitis pontificum Romanorum*, in *PL* 128:114, 219, 243, 306, 328, 398, 665; cf. *Passio S. Demetrii martyris*, in *PL* 129:772.
50. Paul the Deacon, *De gestis Langobardorum*, in *PL* 95:498, 501, 547, 562; Guibert of Nogent, *De vita sua*, in *PL* 156:907, 931; cf. *PL* 162:1169.
51. William of Malmesbury, *Gesta regum Anglorum*, in *PL* 179:1372: "*mane totius tragoediae actum expressit*." For other uses, see *PL* 179:1432, 1446.
52. Cosmas of Prague, *Chroncion Bohemorum*, in *PL* 168:211: "*explicuisse tragediam*."
53. Sigibert of Gembloux, *Miraculi S. Wicberti*, in *PL* 160:689. "[M]*ultae et magnae adversitates occurrerunt nobis. . . . Quam tragediam quia satis cantata est in mundi theatro hic referre supersedeo, cum proprium locum desideret ejus plena relatio.*"
54. Orderic Vitalis, *Historia ecclesiastica*, in *PL* 188:554 (cf. 188:576). "*Ecce subtiliter investigavi et veraciter enucleavi quae in lapsu ducis praeostendit dispositio Dei. Non fictilem tragoediam venundo, non loquaci comoedia cachinnantibus parasitis faveo, sed studiosis lectoribus varios eventus veraciter intimo.*"
55. Bourbouhakis, "Rhetoric and Performance," 184. Long dismissed as "merely" rhetorical exercises, these *tours-de-force* are now the object of significant re-assessment: see, e.g., Kaldellis, *Hellenism in Byznantium*; S. Papaioannou, "Letter-Writing," in *The Byzantine World*, ed. Stephenson, 188–99; A.W. White, "Adventures in Recording Technology : The Drama-as-Performance in the Greek East," in *Beyond the Fifth Century*, ed. Gildenhard and Martin Revermann, 371–96.
56. R. Janko, *Aristotle on Comedy: Towards a Reconstruction of* Poetics II (Berkeley and Los Angeles: University of California Press, 1984), 2–20. See also W. Watson, *The Lost Second Book of Aristotle's Poetics* (Chicago: University of Chicago Press, 2012.
57. *Tractatus Coislinianus*, ed. Janko in *Aristotle on Comedy*, 22 and 24 (my translation).
58. N. Vakonakis, *Das griechische Drama auf dem Weg nach Byzanz: der euripideische cento Christos Paschon* (Tübingen: Narr Verlag, 2011), offers no substantive new analysis.
59. P. Marciniak, *Greek Drama in Byzantine Times* (Katowic: Wydawnictwo Uniwersytetu Śląskiego, 2004); C. Livanos, "Trends and Developments in the Byzantine Poetic Tradition," in *The Byzantine World*, ed. Stephenson, 200–10.
60. See, e.g., the edition of J.G. Brambs, *Christus patiens: Tragoedia christiana, quae inscribit solet Χριστὸς πάσχων Gregorio Nazianzeno falso attributa* (Leipzig: B.G. Teubner, 1885), 25.
61. The key clause in the Vulgate is: "*es eis quasi carmen musicum quod suavi dulcique sono canitur et audient verba tua et non facient ea.*"
62. Jerome, in *PL* 25:322. "*Istiusmodi mihi videntur eorum similes, qui theatralibus luduntur carminibus: et vel tragoedos audiunt, vel comoedos, et ibi cum voluptate palpantur. . . . Tales sunt usque hodie multi in Ecclesiis, qui aiunt: Venite audiamus illum et illum, mira eloquentia praedicationis suae verba volventem: plaususque commovent, et vociferantur, et jactant manus, et quae operibus neglexerant.*"
63. The manuscript is Foligno, Biblioteca communale, MS C. 85, 87. It consists of 87 haphazardly gathered paper folios and booklets, measuring about 222 × 75 mm. For these excerpts (in my translations), see Y. Kimura, "The *Bildungsroman* of an Anonymous Francsican Preacher in Late Medieval Italy (Biblioteca Communale di Foligno, MS C. 85," *Medieval Sermon Studies* 58 (2014): 47–64.
64. On Shakespeare as a fundamentally *medieval* dramatist, see e.g., C. Perry and J. Watkins, eds, *Shakespeare and the Middle Ages* (Oxford: Oxford University Press, 2009); H. Cooper, *Shakespeare and the Medieval World* (London: Arden Shakespeare, 2010).

65. Cassiodorus, in *PL* 70:289: "*Nunquid tale est scenicas audire tragoedias, quale est in choris Ecclesiae salutiferas cognoscere psalmodias?*"
66. Agobard of Lyons, *Liber de correctione antiphonarii*, in *PL* 104:334 (cf. 26:528). "*Audiant haec adolescentuli, audiant hi quibus psallendi in Ecclesia officium est, Deo non voce, sed corde cantandum; nec in tragoedorum modum guttur et fauces dulci medicamine colliniendae* [sic: *colliniendas*] *sunt, ut in Ecclesia theatrales moduli audiantur et cantica; sed in timore, in opere, in scientia Scripturarum.*"
67. Gratian, *Concordia discordantia canonum* (Distinctio XCII), in *PL* 187:429. "*Ab officio autem cantandi et psallendi diaconi inveniuntur exempti, ne, dum vocis modulationi student, altaris ministeria negligant.*"
68. Sicard of Cremona, *Summa de officiis ecclesiasticis (De institutione et habitu personarum eccclesiasticarum)*, in *PL* 213:57: "*comoedi, tragoedi, historiographi.*"
69. Honorius, *Gemma animae* I.83, in *PL* 172:570. "*Sciendum quod hi qui tragoedias in theatris recitabant, actus pugnantium gestibus populo repraesentabant. Sic tragicus noster pugnam Christi populo Christiano in theatro Ecclesiae gestibus suis repraesentat, eique victoriam redemptionis suae inculcat. Itaque cum presbyter* Orate *dicit, Christum pro nobis in agonia positum exprimit, cum apostolos orare monuit. Per secretum silentium, significat Christum velut agnum sine voce ad victimam ductum. Per manuum expansionem, designat Christi in cruce extensionem. Per cantum praefationis, exprimit clamorem Christi in cruce pendentis. . . . Per pacem, et communicationem designat pacem datam post Christi resurrectionem et gaudii communicationem. Confecto sacramento, pax et communio populo a sacerdote datur, quia accusatore nostro ab agonotheta nostro per duellum prostrato, pax a judice populo denuntiatur, ad convivium invitatur. Deinde ad propria redire cum gaudio per* Ite missa est *imperatur. Qui gratias Deo jubilat et gaudens domum remeat.*"
70. Dox, *Idea of the Theatre*, 75–6. See also T. Bestul, *Texts of the Passion: Latin Devotional Literature and Medieval Society* (Philadelphia: University of Pennsylvania Press, 1996), 1–68.
71. Sicard of Cremona, in *PL* 213:145.
72. C. Symes, *A Common Stage: Theatre and Public Life in Medieval Arras* (Ithaca: Cornell University Press, 2007), 168–74.
73. Ruotger of Cologne, *Vita Brunonis*, in *PL* 134:946–7. "*Scurrilia et mimica, quae in comoediis et tragoediis a personis variis edita quidam concrepantes risu se infinito concutiunt, ipse semper serio lectitabat: materiam pro minimo, auctoritatem in verborum compositionibus pro maximo reputabat.*"
74. C. Symes, "The Performance and Preservation of Medieval Latin Comedy," *European Medieval Drama* 7 (2003): 29–50.
75. Peter the Venerable (Epistolae IX), in *PL* 189:78. "*Quid inani studio cum comoedis recitas, cum tragoedis deploras, cum metricis ludis, cum poetis fallis, cum philosophis falleris?*"
76. Peter of Blois, in *PL* 207:291.
77. John of Salisbury, in *PL* 207:234: "*in scribendis comoediis et tragoediis.*"
78. Peter of Blois, *Liber de confessione sacramentali*, in *PL* 207:1088–9. "*Saepe in tragoediis et aliis carminibus poetarum, in joculatorum cantilenis describitur aliquis vir prudens, decorus, fortis, amabilis et per omnia gratiosus. Recitantur etiam pressurae vel injuriae eidem crudeliter irrogatae, sicut de Arturo et Gangano et Tristanno, fabulosa quaedam referunt histriones, quorum auditu concutiuntur ad compassionem audientium corda, et usque ad lacrymas compunguntur. Qui ergo de fabulae recitatione ad misericordiam commoveris, si de Domino aliquid pium legi audias, quod extorqueat tibi lacrymas, nunquid propter hoc de Dei dilectione potes dictare sententiam? Qui compateris Deo, compateris et Arturo.*"
79. Ælred of Rievaulx, *Speculum caritatis* II.17, in *PL* 195:565–6.

80. Paris, Bibliothèque nationale, fonds latin 14925, fol. 132; cf. lat. 3594, fol. 192; ed. [J.-] B. Hauréau, *Notices et extraits de quelques manuscrits latins de la Bibliothèque nationale*, 6 vols. (Paris: Klincksieck, 1889–94), vol. 3, 317. "*Cum voce joculatoris, in plateis sedentis, quomodo illi strenui milites antiqui, scilicet Rolandus et Oliverius, etc., in bello occubuere recitatur, populus circumstans pietate movetur et interdum lacrymatur; sed cum voce Ecclesiæ inclyta Christi bella, quomodo scilicet mortem moriendo devicit et de hoste superbo triumphavit quotidie fere commemoratur, qui sunt qui pietate moventur?*" See Symes, *A Common Stage*, 154–74.
81. Kelly, *Ideas and Forms of Tragedy*, xiii, 36, 111.

Chapter Two

1. T. Eagleton, *Sweet Violence: The Idea of the Tragic* (Malden: Blackwell Publishing, 2003), xvi.
2. *The Castle of Perseverance*, ed. David N. Klausner (Kalamazoo: Medieval Institute Publications, 2007). Online access: TEAMS Middle English Texts, http://d.lib.rochester.edu/teams/text/klausner-castle-of-perseverance
3. A. Johnston, "'At the Still Point of the Turning World': Augustinian Roots of Medieval Dramaturgy," *European Medieval Drama* 2 (1998): 3.
4. C. Davidson, "Space and Time in Medieval Drama: Meditations on Orientation in the Early Theater," in *Word, Picture, and Spectacle*, ed. Clifford Davidson, (Kalamazoo: Medieval Institute Publications, 1984), 39–50.
5. A. van Helden, *Measuring the Universe: Cosmic Dimensions from Aristarchus to Halley* (Chicago: University of Chicago Press, 1985), 34–7.
6. M. Davis, "As Above, So Below: Staging the Digby *Mary Magdalene*," *Theatre Notebook*, 70.2 (2016): 76.
7. A. Johnston, "Parish Playmaking before the Reformation," in *The Parish in Late Medieval England: Proceedings of the 2002 Harlaxton Symposium* (322–38), ed. C. Burgess and E. Duffy (Donington: Shaun Tyas, 2006), 326–7.
8. H. Lefebvre, *The Production of Space*, trans. D. Nicholson-Smith (Malden: Blackwell Publishing, 1991), 236.
9. C. Symes, "Ancient Drama in the Medieval World," in *A Handbook to the Reception of Greek Drama*, ed. B. van Zyl Smit (Malden: Wiley Blackwell, 2016), 97–130; and "The Tragedy of the Middle Ages," in *Beyond the Fifth Century: Interactions with Greek Tragedy from the Fourth Century BCE to the Middle Ages*, ed. I. Gildenhard and M. Revermann (New York: De Gruyter, 2011), 335–69.
10. *The Confessions of Saint Augustine*, Book III, trans. E. Pusey (New York: P. F. Collier, 1909), 34–5.
11. "Isidore's sources are not Aristotle's *Poetics* but writings by Eusebius, Augustine, Tertullian, and Diomedes that were current in his day." C. Stern, *The Medieval Theatre in Castile* (Binghamton: SUNY Press, 1996), 55.
12. Symes, "The Tragedy," 366.
13. Excavation of the Roman theater at Carthage in 1904 suggests that the city may have possessed a theater from the time of Emperor Augustus. K. Ros, "The Roman Theater at Carthage," *American Journal of Archaeology* 100, no. 3 (1996): 449–89.
14. "De Spectaculis XXIX," in *Apology and De Spectaculis*, trans. T.R. Glover (Cambridge: Harvard University Press, 1977), 297.
15. *Etymologiae, sive Origine*, 18.42–4, trans. H.A. Kelly, *Ideas and Forms of Tragedy from Aristotle to the Middle Ages* (Cambridge: Cambridge University Press, 1993), 41–3.

16. Kelly, *Ideas and Forms*, 41.
17. The remains of twenty-three Roman semicircular theaters have been located on the Iberian Peninsula and three more are known to have existed. F. Sear, *Roman Theatres: An Architectural Study* (Oxford: Oxford University Press, 2006), 101.
18. W. Tydeman, *The Theatre in the Middle Ages: Western European Stage Conditions, c. 800–1576* (Cambridge: Cambridge University Press, 1978), 134.
19. H. Rey-Flaud, *Le Cercle mágique* (Paris: Bibliothèque des Idées, 1973), 50.
20. R. Wittman, "Monuments and Space as Allegory: Town Planning Proposals in Eighteenth-Century Paris," in *Thinking Allegory Otherwise*, ed. B. Machosky (Stanford: Stanford University Press, 2004), 143.
21. P. Butterworth, *Staging Conventions in Medieval English Theatre* (Cambridge: Cambridge University Press, 2014), 44.
22. R.M.R. Porto, "Greek Tragedy in Medieval Art," in *The Encyclopedia of Greek Tragedy*, vol. II (627–36), ed. H.M. Roisman (West Sussex: Wiley-Blackwell, 2014): 628.
23. Ibid., 629.
24. Ibid., 635.
25. P. Brook, *The Empty Space* (New York: Touchstone Books, 1968), 42.
26. D. Dox, "Theatrical Space, Mutable Space, and the Space of Imagination: Three Readings of the Croxton *Play of the Sacrament*," in *Medieval Practices of Space*, ed. B. Hanawalt and M. Kobialka (Minneapolis: University of Minnesota Press, 2000), 168.
27. G. Bachelard, *The Poetics of Space*, trans. Maria Jolas (Boston: Beacon Press, 1994), 47.
28. C. Belsey, *The Subject of Tragedy: Identity and Difference in Renaissance Drama* (London: Methuen, 1985), 58.
29. J. Sebastian, "Introduction," in *Croxton Play of the Sacrament*, ed. J. Sebastian (Kalamazoo: Medieval Institute Publications, 2012). Online access: TEAMS Middle English Texts, http://d.lib.rochester.edu/teams/text/sebastian-croxton-play-of-the-sacrament-introduction. See also V. Scherb, *Staging Faith: East Anglian Drama in the Later Middle Ages* (Danvers, MA: Rosemont Publishing, 2001), 193–5.
30. *Everyman and its Dutch Original, Elckerlijc*, ed. C. Davidson, M. Walsh, T. Broos (Kalamazoo: Medieval Institute Publications, 2007). Online access: TEAMS Middle English Texts, http://d.lib.rochester.edu/teams/text/davidson-everyman
31. W. Benjamin, *The Origin of German Tragic Drama*, trans. John Osborne (London: NLB, 1977), 29; 175.
32. *Policraticus* quoted from *Frivolities of Courtiers and Footprints of Philosophers*, trans. J. Pike (Minneapolis: University of Minnesota Press, 1938), 172; 176.
33. R. Green, "Introduction," in *The Consolation of Philosophy*, trans. R. Green (Mineola: Dover Press, 1962), xiii.
34. M. Merback, *The Thief, the Cross and the Wheel: Pain and the Spectacle of Punishment in Medieval and Renaissance Europe* (London: Reaktion Books, Ltd., 1999), 170–2.
35. Eagleton, 37.
36. See J. Enders, *Death by Drama and other Medieval Urban Legends* (Chicago: University of Chicago Press, 2002).
37. R. Warning, *The Ambivalences of Medieval Religious Drama*, trans. S. Rendall (Stanford: Stanford University Press, 2001), 127.
38. Ibid., 179–81; 233–9.
39. See Carol Symes' essay in this volume. Also Symes, "The Tragedy," and Kelly, *Ideas and Forms*.
40. Warning, *The Ambivalences*, 147.

41. See essays by L. Blanchfield, C. Swift, and F. Thürlemannvin in E. Gertsman, *Crying in the Middle Ages: Tears of History* (New York: Routledge, 2012).
42. E. Carrero Santamaría, "Entre el Transepto, El Púlpito y el Coro. El Espacio Conmenmorativo de la Sibilia," in *La Sibila. Sonido. Imagen. Liturgia. Escena*, ed. M. Gómez Muntané and E. Carrero Santamaría (Madrid: Alpuerto, 2015), 248–55; 260.
43. "... se asentará en una silla que a de estar puesta en parte alta de manera que sojuzgue a todos y que todos la vean, delante de la qual estará un blandón o hacha ardiendo pendiente de un hilo de hierro con su joja de lata encima, de arte que parezca que se tiene en el aire." D. Sánchez de Badajoz, *Recopilación en metro* (Sevilla, 1554), *reproducida en facsímil por La Academia Española* (Madrid: Tipografía de Archivos, 1929): f. cxxxix[v].
44. Benjamin, *The Origin*, 217.
45. E. Gertsman, *The Dance of Death in the Middle Ages: Image, Text, Performance* (Turnhout: Brepols, 2010), 67.
46. C. Davidson, *Visualizing the Moral Life: Medieval Iconography and the Macro Morality Plays* (New York: AMS, 1989), 113.
47. Gertsman, *The Dance*, 159.
48. K. Kreitner, *The Church Music of Fifteenth-Century Spain* (Woodbridge, UK: The Boydell Press, 2004), 23.
49. From Latin, transcribed in Gómez I Muntané, M. Carmen. *El Llibre Vermell de Montserrat: Cantos y danzas s. XIV* (Barcelona: Libros de la Frontera,1990), 19.
50. Kreitner, *Church Music*, 23–6.
51. Gertsman, *The Dance*, 74.
52. M.M. Hamilton, *Beyond faith: Belief, Morality, and Memory in a Fifteenth-Century Judeo-Iberian Manuscript* (Leiden: Brill, 2014), 211–14.
53. Ibid., 245–6.
54. K. Meyer-Baer, *Music of the Spheres and the Dance of Death* (Princeton: Princeton University Press, 1970. Reprint. New York: DaCao Press, 1984), 311–12.
55. F. Rokem, "The Ludic Logic of Tragedy," *Performance Research* 21.4 (2016): 26.
56. Davidson, *Visualizing*, 51.
57. Ibid., 117.
58. B. Murdoch, "The Cornish Medieval Drama," in R. Beadle, ed. *The Cambridge Companion to Medieval English Theatre* (Cambridge: Cambridge University Press, 1994), 211–39.

Chapter Three

1. *The Riverside Chaucer*, ed. L.D. Benson (3rd edn, Boston: Houghton Mifflin, 1987).
2. For treatments of non-dramatic tragic genres in the Middle Ages, see, e.g., J. Simpson, *Reform and Cultural Revolution: The Oxford English Literary History Volume 2. 1350-1547* (Oxford: Oxford University Press, 2002), chapter 3, "The Tragic," 68–120; H.A. Kelly, *Chaucerian Tragedy* (Cambridge: D.S. Brewer, 1997).
3. See C. Symes, "Forms and Media," in this volume; "The Tragedy of the Middle Ages," in *Beyond the Fifth Century: Interactions with Greek Tragedy from the Fourth Century BCE to the Middle Ages*, ed. I. Gildenhard and M. Revermann (Berlin: De Gruyter, 2010), 335–69; and "Ancient Drama in the Medieval World," in *A Handbook to the Reception of Greek Drama*, ed. Betine van Zyl Smit (Hoboken: Wiley-Blackwell, 2016), 97–130.
4. Symes, "Tragedy of the Middle Ages," 338–9.
5. Symes, "Ancient Drama," 108–14.
6. Symes, "Ancient Drama," 117.

7. R. Hodge and G. Kress, *Social Semiotics* (Ithaca: Cornell University Press, 1988), 7.
8. A. Hiatt, "Genre without System," in *Middle English*, ed. P. Strohm, Oxford Twenty-First Century Approaches to Literature (Oxford: Oxford University Press, 2007), 278.
9. J. Orlemanski, "Genre," in *A Handbook of Middle English Studies*, ed. M. Turner (Chichester: Wiley-Blackwell, 2013), 211.
10. Hiatt, "Genre without System," 287.
11. For a more expansive theoretical approach to delimiting the boundaries of the communities that produced and consumed drama in this period, see K. Ashley, "Social Functions," in *A Cultural History of Theatre in the Middle Ages*, ed. J. Enders (London: Bloomsbury, 2017). Ashley's anthropological analysis draws on the work of Mary Douglas in attending to how medieval persons experienced performance in line with their participation in and allegiance to a variety of communities and subgroups within those communities. In her investigation of forms of social identification within groups with distinctive systems of meaning-making, Ashley's study encompasses a wider range of performances—including processions, entry ceremonies, urban festivals, "seasonal" drama during Advent and Lent, and guild-sponsored plays—than I consider here.
12. Symes, "Tragedy of the Middle Ages," 336.
13. The following sketch of Trevet's academic life follows the biographical summary provided in L. Nauta, "The Scholastic Context of the Boethius Commentary by Nicholas Trevet," in *Boethius in the Middle Ages: Latin and Vernacular Traditions of the* Consolatio Philosophiae, ed. M.J.F.M. Hoenen and L. Nauta (Leiden: Brill, 1997), 46–9. See also the foundational work of B. Smalley, *English Friars and Antiquity in the Fourteenth Century* (New York: Barnes and Noble, 1960), 58–65.
14. Nauta, "The Scholastic Context," 47; J. Fleming, "The Friars and Medieval English Literature," in *The Cambridge History of Medieval English Literature*, ed. D. Wallace (Cambridge: Cambridge University Press, 1999), 366.
15. Nauta, "The Scholastic Context," 41.
16. Smalley, *English Friars*, 59–60; B. Fitzgerald, *Inspiration and Authority in the Middle Ages: Prophets and Their Critics from Scholasticism to Humanism* (Oxford: Oxford University Press, 2017), 153. Smalley does not include the commentary on the *Eclogae*, which appears not to have been known to her. On the authorship of the Virgil commentary, see M.L. Lord, "Virgil's *Eclogues*, Nicholas Trevet, and the Harmony of the Spheres," *Medieval Studies* 54 (1992): 186–273. Trevet's commentaries on Seneca's plays have been published piecemeal by a group of mostly Italian scholars, beginning with E. Franceschini's edition of the commentary on *Thyestes* published in 1938. In order of publication (which is not Trevet's ordering of the plays; he begins with *Hercules furens*) they are: *Il commento di Nicola Trevet al* Tieste *di Seneca*, ed. E. Franceschini (Milan: Società editrice "Vita e Pensiero," 1938); *Nicolai Treveti Expositio Herculis furentis*, ed. V. Ussani, Jr. (Rome: Athenaeum, 1959); *Nicolai Treveti Expositio L. Annaei Senecae Agamemnonis*, ed. P. Meloni (Palermo: Palumbo, 1961); *Nicolai Treveti Expositio L. Annaei Senecae Herculis Oetaei*, ed. P. Meloni (Palermo: Palumbo, 1962); *Commento alle* Troades *di Seneca*, ed. M. Palma (Rome: Edizioni di storia e letteratura, 1977); *Nicholas Trevet und die* Octavia praetexta*: Editio princeps des mittelalterlichen Kommentars und Untersuchungen zum pseudo-senecanischen Drama*, ed. R. Junge (Paderborn: Schoeningh, 1999); *Commento alla* Phaedra *di Seneca*, ed. M. Chiabò (Bari: Edipuglia, 2004); *Commento alla* Medea *di Seneca*, ed. L. Roberti (Bari: Edipuglia, 2004); *Commento alle* Phoenissae *di Seneca*, ed. P. Mascoli (Bari: Edipuglia, 2007); *Commento all'*Oedipus *di Seneca*, ed. A. Lagioia (Bari: Edipuglia, 2008). Lucius Annaeus Seneca (Seneca the Younger) was conflated with his father, Marcus Annaeus Seneca (Seneca

the Elder), throughout the Middle Ages, and is no longer considered the author of *Octavia*; likewise his authorship of *Hercules Oetaeus* has been subject to much scholarly debate.

17. For the dating of the commentaries, see P. Busonero, "La *Mise-en-Page* nei Primi Testimoni del Commento Trevetano a Seneca," *Aevum* 75:2 (2001), 451–2. For the two Nicholases, see R.J. Dean, "Cultural Relations in the Middle Ages: Nicholas Trevet and Nicholas of Prato," *Studies in Philology* 45:4 (1948): 541–64.
18. Isidore, *Etymologiarum sive originum libri XX*, ed. W.M. Lindsay, vol. 2 (Oxford: Clarendon Press, 1911), 18.45; translated in Isidore of Seville, *Etymologies*, trans. S.A. Barney et al. (Cambridge: Cambridge University Press, 2006), 369.
19. D. Dox, *The Idea of the Theater in Latin Christian Thought: Augustine to the Fourteenth Century* (Ann Arbor: University of Michigan Press, 2004), 30.
20. Quoted in Kelly, *Chaucerian Tragedy*, 51 and discussed at length in 51–61.
21. *Riverside Chaucer*, 409–10.
22. Kelly, *Chaucerian Tragedy*, 260 identifies Shakespearean tragedy as Chaucerian in contradistinction to the more overtly Senecan plays that came into vogue during the reign of Elizabeth, a trend which Kelly finds "deleterious." For a brief but persuasive critique of Kelly's assumptions and findings, see Symes, "Tragedy of the Middle Ages," 365–6.
23. J. Lydgate, *Troy Book: Selections*, ed. R.R. Edwards, TEAMS Middle English Text Series (Kalamazoo: Medieval Institute Publications, 1998), II.852–9.
24. R.J. Dean, "The Earliest Known Commentary on Livy Is by Nicholas Trevet," *Medievalia et Humanistica* 3 (1945), 86–98.
25. For the letters, see Franceschini, *Commento di Nicola Trevet al Tieste di Seneca*, 1–4. This passage is discussed in Smalley, *English Friars*, 60, and V. Fabris, "Il Commento di Nicola Trevet all'*Hercules furens* di Seneca," *Aevum* 27:6 (1953): 499. The translation is my own.
26. Fabris, "Il commento di Nicola Trevet," 507. For Fabris, Trevet's brand of scholasticism is the benighted predecessor to the more intellectually rewarding humanism that followed.
27. Seneca, *Tragedies*, ed. J.G. Fitch, The Loeb Classical Library (Cambridge: Harvard University Press, 2002), lines 963–4. The translation is Fitch's.
28. *Commento alla Medea di Seneca*, 116. All translations of Trevet's commentaries are my own.
29. G.G. Wilson, "'Amonges othere wordes wyse': The Medieval Seneca and the *Canterbury Tales*," *Chaucer Review* 28 (1993): 135–45, 144, note 10.
30. Trevet, *Expositio Herculis furentis*, 4–5. See also H.A. Kelly, *Ideas and Forms of Tragedy from Aristotle to the Middle Ages* (Cambridge: Cambridge University Press, 1993), 132.
31. Trevet, *Expositio Herculis furentis*, 29–30.
32. R.H. Rouse and A.C. de la Mare, "New Light on the Circulation of the A-Text of Seneca's Tragedies," *Journal of the Warburg and Courtland Institutes*, 40 (1977), 283–6.
33. Kelly, *Chaucerian Tragedy*, 153; M. Papio, "On Seneca, Mussato, Trevet, and the Boethian 'Tragedies' of the *De casibus*," *Heliotropia* 10:2 (2013): 53.
34. The Greek word *hamartia*, famous as the protagonist's "tragic flaw" of Aristotle's *Poetics* but perhaps better construed as "mistake," coincidentally makes scores of appearances in the Septuagint and appears to have been a particular favorite of Paul in his letter to the Romans; it recurs with striking frequency in 5:12–13 of that letter, wherein Paul reflects on the legacy of Adam's sin: "Wherefore as by one man sin entered into this world, and by sin death; and so death passed upon all men, in whom all have sinned. For until the law sin was in the world; but sin was not imputed, when the law was not." The five instances of "sin" in these two verses from the Douay-Rheims version all translate *peccatum* and its derivatives, which are the Vulgate's way of rendering *hamartia* and its morphological variants in Greek.
35. Symes, "Tragedy of the Middle Ages," 353.

36. *PL* 204: 362; quoted in Symes, "Tragedy of the Middle Ages," 353; the translation is slightly emended from that of Symes. For Henry of Marcy, see B.P. McGuire, *Friendship and Community: The Monastic Experience, 350-1250* (1988; revised edn, Ithaca: Cornell University Press, 2010), 367.
37. B. Murdoch, *Adam's Grace: Fall and Redemption in Medieval Literature* (Cambridge: D.S. Brewer, 2000), 27–35, and in general B. Murdoch, *The Apocryphal Adam and Eve in Medieval Europe: Vernacular Translations and Adaptations of the* Vita Adae et Evae (Oxford: Oxford University Press, 2009).
38. Murdoch, *Adam's Grace*, 25.
39. For the English tradition, see Murdoch, *Apocryphal Adam and Eve*, 77–119.
40. For the inclusion of the story of Adam and Eve in the English versions of the *Legenda aurea*, see *Gilte Legende*, ed. R. Hamer with the assistance of V. Russell, vol. 3, Early English Text Society Original Series no. 339 (Oxford: Oxford University Press, 2007), 42–6.
41. *Gilte Legende*, ed. R. Hamer with the assistance of V. Russell, vol. 2, Early English Text Society no. 328 (Oxford: Oxford University Press, 2007), 996.
42. *Gilte Legende*, 2:996.
43. *Gilte Legende*, 2:996.
44. *Gilte Legende*, 2:996–7. The performance of penance is a common element in apocryphal lives of Adam and Eve, though in many of these it is Adam who first proposes penance as a way of regaining God's favor.
45. *Gilte Legende*, 2:997.
46. *Gilte Legende*, 2:997.
47. *Gilte Legende*, 2:997.
48. *Gilte Legende*, 2:998.
49. Although I focus on the versions from York and Chester exclusively in my analysis, the Expulsion features in all four of the large-scale English sequences of biblical drama as well as in the two versions of the only surviving fragment of a cycle from Norwich. Towneley's Creation play breaks off shortly after Lucifer's entrance onto this scene and prior to the actual temptation. The N-Town compilation is compact by comparison with other surviving English analogues, and N-Town's Adam never performs the kind of lament extant in the York and Chester counterparts.

    The Expulsion does feature prominently in the two surviving plays attributed to the Norwich Grocers. Both versions of the play in the forms that we have them date from after the Reformation's arrival in England and survive only in eighteenth-century transcriptions, hence my decision to omit them from consideration here.

    Three other plays with origins in the British Isles need to be mentioned as well. The depiction of Adam's lament in the two pageants from York and Chester share much with the parallel scene in the twelfth-century Anglo-Norman *Ordo representacionis Ade* or *Play of Adam*. Here the performance of Adam's grief begins conventionally enough with the recognition that his failure to appreciate properly the blessings of Paradise has compelled him to a life of penance and suffering and concludes with an all-too-familiar condemnation of Eve for her culpability in leading them to their present state. In between Adam pauses, if only briefly, to berate himself and to wonder aloud what he was thinking.

    He answers his own question by blaming Eve for robbing him of his good sense and reason. It is noteworthy that he attributes his sin to a loss of memory which will be remedied by the preservation of his crimes in the annals of history. Adam stops short of expounding this striking observation, but this extradiegetic intrusion, however brief, reminds the audience that Adam stands in for all humankind in this cautionary tale. In the Cornish *Origo mundi*, Adam laments his undoing in a brief and generally unremarkable passage that precedes a more interesting dialogue between God and Adam concerning how much workable land is sufficient to support a growing family. Finally, the Cornish *Gwreans an bys*, also called *The Creacion of the World*, in the surviving manuscript, offers a briskly narrated depiction of the Expulsion before turning its energies to an extended treatment of Adam and Eve's sons.

50. For succinct and accessible overviews of the York Corpus Christi Play, see R. Beadle, "The York Corpus Christi Play," in *The Cambridge Companion to Medieval English Theatre*, ed. R. Beadle and A. J. Fletcher (2nd edn, Cambridge: Cambridge University Press, 2008), 99–124; P. King, *The York Mystery Cycle and the Worship of the City*, Westfield Medieval Studies 1 (Cambridge: D.S. Brewer, 2006), 1–36.

51. Surviving records reveal that the scaffolds had become a site of contest between York's governing authorities and those who sought to profit from the plays' spectators by 1417, when the scaffolds came under the regulation of the city:

> Nevertheless, the mayor, the honourable men, and the whole said commons, by their unanimous consent and assent, order that all those who receive money for scaffolds which they may build in the aforesaid places before their doors on public property at the aforesaid sites from those sitting on them shall pay the third penny of the money so received to the chamberlains of the city to be applied to the use of the same commons. And if they have refused to pay or agree upon a third penny of this kind or other with the chamber decently, that then the play be transferred to other places at the will and disposition of the mayor holding office at the time and of the council of the Chamber of the city.

> [*Nichilominus maior probi homines & tota communitas predicta eorum vnanimi consensu & assensu ordinarunt omnes illi qui pro skafaldis quas ante eorum ostia super solum communitatis edificant in locis predictis de supersedentibus monetam recipiunt soluant tercium denarium monete sic recepte Camerarijs ciuitatis ad vsum communitatis eiusdem applicandum & si huiusmodi tercium denarium soluere vel alias cum camera honeste concordare recusauerint quod tunc ludus transferatur ad alia loca ad disposicionem et voluntatem maioris qui pro tempore fuerit & consilij camere ciutiatis nemine ordinacioni huiusmodi contradictene.*]

See *Records of Early English Drama: York*, ed. A.F. Johnston and M. Rogerson, 2 vols. (Toronto: University of Toronto Press, 1979), 1:29 and 2:713–14.

52. *The York Play: A Facsimile of British Library MS Additional 35290*, ed. R. Beadle and P. Meredith with R. Rastall, Medieval Drama Facsimiles 7 (Leeds: The University of Leeds School of English, 1983), xxi–xxiii.

53. N.R. Rice and M.A. Pappano, *The Civic Cycles: Artisan Drama and Identity in Premodern England* (Notre Dame: University of Notre Dame Press, 2015), 3.

54. All references to the York play appear parenthetically by line number and are keyed to *The York Plays: A Critical Edition of the York Corpus Christi Play as Recorded in British Library Additional MS 35290*, vol. 1, Early English Test Society Supplemental Series 23 (Oxford: Oxford University Press, 2009), 29–34.

55. The pattern is disrupted by the stanza at lines 105–110, but if one were to skip over that stanza the phrase "Allas þe while" in line 104 does have an echo in line 111, "Allas, for bale." It is possible, then, that the intervening stanza is a later interpolation. Indeed, Adam's resolve in lines 109–10 to attempt to discover what course of action might be best, is not in keeping with the despairing tone of the rest of the lament. I wish to thank Britt Mize for pointing out the consistency in the concatenation if lines 105–10 are ignored.

56. S. McNamer, "Feeling," in *Middle English*, ed. P. Strohm, Oxford Twenty-First Century Approaches to Literature (Oxford: Oxford University Press, 2007), 248.

57. McNamer, "Feeling," 248.
58. For a recent reevaluation of the circumstances of the demise of the performance of the Chester plays, see the essays collected in *The Chester Cycle in Context, 1555-1575: Religion, Drama, and the Impact of Change*, ed. J. Dell, D. Klausner, and H. Ostovich, Studies in Performance and Early Modern Drama (Farnham: Ashgate, 2012).
59. All references to the York play appear parenthetically by line number and are keyed to *The Chester Mystery Cycle*, ed. R.M. Lumiansky and D. Mills, vol. 1, Early English Text Society SS 3 (London: Oxford University Press, 1974), 13–41.

Chapter Four

This chapter's overall content, structure, and methodology are the products of the collaborative efforts of the two authors. However, each author was responsible for the specific sections. Antonio Donato developed and wrote sections one, three, and four; Erith Jaffe-Berg sections two and five. Both authors would like to offer their deep thanks to Carol Symes for all her careful guidance and editorial input throughout the process of working on and revising the chapter.

1. O.G. Brockett and H.J. Franklin, eds, *History of the Theatre* (Boston: Pearson Education, 2008); S. Greenblatt, *The Swerve: How the World Became Modern* (New York: W.W. Norton, 2011); and H.A. Kelly, *Ideas and Forms of Tragedy from Aristotle to the Middle Ages* (Cambridge: Cambridge University Press, 1993).
2. C. Symes, "The Tragedy of the Middle Ages," in *Beyond the Fifth Century: Interactions with Greek Tragedy from the Fourth Century BCE to the Middle Ages*, ed. I. Gildenhard and M. Revermann (Berlin: de Gruyter, 2010), 335–69 and C. Symes, "Ancient Drama in the Medieval World," in *A Handbook to the Reception of Greek Drama*, ed. B. Van Zyl Smit (Hoboken: Wiley-Blackwell, 2016), 97–130.
3. K. Ashley, "Social Functions," in *A Cultural History of Theatre in the Middle Ages*, ed. Jody Enders (London and New York: Bloomsbury, 2017), 39–58.
4. K. Ashley, "Social Functions," 39–58.
5. Kelly, *Ideas and Forms of Tragedy*, 27–35.
6. Symes, "The Tragedy of the Middle Ages," 340–2.
7. Plato, *Res Publica* (Oxford: Clarendon Press, 1965), 604b–606d.
8. Aristotle, *De Arte Poetica Liber* (Oxford: Clarendon Press, 1965), 1448b4-17.
9. Tertullian, *De Spectaculis*, Corpus Christianorum, Series Latina 1 (Turnhout: Brepols, 1954), XXVI.
10. Augustine, *Confessiones*, Corpus Christianorum, Series Latina 27 (Turnhout: Brepols, 1981), III.2.
11. Plato, *Res Publica*, 387b–389b, 605c–608b.
12. Augustine, *Confessiones*, I. 20–21.
13. Plato, *Res Publica*, 377d–383c; 389d–392c.
14. Augustine, *Confessiones*, III.2.3-4. See also Augustine, *De civitate Dei*, Corpus Christianorum, Series Latina (Turnhout: Brepols, 1955), 47–48. II.6.
15. Lactantius, *Institutiones Divinae*, Corpus Scriptorum Ecclesiasticorum Latinorum 19 (Vienna, 1890–8) VI.21.
16. Tertullian, *De Spectaculis*, XXIX.
17. Gorgias, *Helenae Encomium*, in *Die Fragmente der Vorsokratiker*, ed. H. Diels and W. Kranz (Dublin and Zurich: Weidmann, 1951–2), 14–15.
18. Plato, *Leges* (Oxford: Clarendon Press, 1922), VII, 817B-D.

19. For Proclus' rejection of tragedy see Proclus, *Procli Diadochi in Platonis rem publicam commentarii* (Amsterdam: Hakkert, 1965), 49.19–51.26.
20. Proclus, *In Platonis rem publicam commentarii*, 9.25, 50.5-10, 50.26-27, 51.10-11, 51.18-23.
21. Proclus, *In Platonis rem publicam commentarii*, 48.11-13.
22. Olympiodorus, *Life of Plato and On Plato First Alcibiades 1–9*, trans. M.J. Griffin (London: Bloomsbury, 2015), 2.55-86.
23. Olympiodorus, *Life of Plato*, 6–7, 45, 165; I. Hadot, *Arts libéraux et philosophie dans la pensée antique* (Paris: Vrin, 2005).
24. Iamblichus, *De Mysteriis Aegyptiorum* (Stuttgart: Teubner, 1975), I.11.
25. According to most scholars, Boethius wrote the *Consolation* while he was imprisoned and waiting to be executed by the Ostrogothic king of Italy, Theodoric. Although the character in the dialogue overlaps with the historical figure to a considerable extent, the two should not be conflated.
26. Boethius, *Consolatio*, in *Opuscula Sacra, De consolatione Philosophiae*, ed. C. Moreschini (Munich/Leipzig: K.G. Saur, 2000), I.1.8-11, II.1.8
27. Honorius Augustodunensis, *Gemma animae*, I.83, in *Patrologia Latina*, ed. J-P. Migne, Vol. 172 (Paris, 1854), 570.
28. P. Wilson, "Music," in *A Companion to Greek Tragedy*, ed. J. Gregory (Malden: Blackwell Pub., 2005), 183–93.
29. See Elias, *In Porphyrii Isagogen et Aristotelis Categorias* (Berlin: De Gruyter, 1975), 31.8-25, 64.32–65.9; Iamblichus, *De Vita Pythagorica* (Stuttgart: Teubner, 1975), 110, 114; Iamblichus, *De Mysteriis Aegyptiorum*, 3.9; Olympiodorus, *Olympiodori in Platonis Gorgiam commentaria* (Leipzig: Walter de Gruyter, 1970), 40.30–41.24.
30. On this topic, see D.J. O'Meara, "The Music of Philosophy in Late Antiquity," in *Philosophy and the Sciences in Antiquity*, ed. R.W. Sharples (Ashgate: Ashgate Publishing, 2005), 131–47; A. Sheppard, "Music Therapy in Neoplatonism," in *Philosophy and the Sciences in Antiquity*, 148–55.
31. Boethius, *De Musica* (Leipzig: Teubner, 1867), I.1-2.
32. B.H. Rosenwein, *Emotional Communities in the Early Middle Ages* (Ithaca: Cornell University Press, 2006).
33. O. Münz-Manor, "Liturgical Poetry in the Late Antique Near East: A Comparative Approach," in *Journal of Ancient Judaism* 1 (2010): 336–61, esp. 336-8; S. Bar-Asher, T. Novich, and C. Hayes, eds. *The Faces of Torah: Studies in the Texts and Contexts of Ancient Judaism in Honor of Steven Fraade. Journal of Ancient Judaism Supplements* V. 22. (Göttingen: Vandenhoeck & Ruprecht, 2017), 408; and M.D. Swartz and J. Yahalom, trans. and eds. *Avodah: Ancient Poems for Yom Kippur* (University Park, Pennsylvania: Penn State Library of Jewish Literature, 2013), 2.
34. C. Symes, "The Medieval Archive and the History of Theatre: Assessing the Written and Unwritten Evidence for Premodern Performance," *Theatre Survey* 52 (2011): 1–30, esp. 30.
35. Swartz and Yahlom, *Avodah* 1.
36. Swartz and Yahlom, *Avodah*, 1 and 10.
37. Swartz and Yahlom, *Avodah*, 1.
38. Symes, "The Tragedy of the Middle Ages," 344.
39. B. Holsinger, *Music, Body, and Desire in Medieval Culture: Hildegard of Bingen to Chaucer* (Palo Alto: Stanford University Press, 2001), 252.
40. Holsinger, *Music, Body and Desire*, 253.
41. Holsinger, *Music, Body and Desire*, 253.

42. S. Sticca, "Italy: Liturgy and Christocentric Spirituality," in *The Theatre of Medieval Europe: New Research in Early Drama*, ed. E. Simon (Cambridge: Cambridge University Press, 1991), 169–88, esp. 169.
43. Sticca, "Italy: Liturgy," 170–1 and 179.
44. A.J. Novikoff, *The Medieval Culture of Disputation: Pedagogy, Practice, and Performance* (Philadelphia: University of Pennsylvania Press, 2013), 148.
45. Novikoff, *The Medieval Culture of Disputation*, 151.
46. C. Symes, *A Common Stage: Theater and Public Life in Medieval Arras* (Ithaca: Cornell University Press, 2007); J. Saltzstein, "Cleric-Trouvères and the Jeux-Partis of Medieval Arras," *Viator* 43 (2012): 147–63.
47. In this section, we offer a brief overview of the role tragedy played in the Byzantine world during the Middle Ages. Our analysis relies on Symes' excellent synthetic treatment of this issue. See Symes, "Ancient Drama in the Medieval World," 114–17.
48. Kaldellis has persuasively argued that the Byzantines not only considered themselves Greeks and Christians as scholars have traditionally believed, they also regarded themselves to be the Romans of the eastern Empire. In the Byzantine world, these three identities did not merely coexist, but their integration was the distinctive feature of this culture. A. Kaldellis, *Hellenism in Byzantium: The Transformations of Greek Identity and the Reception of the Classical Tradition* (Cambridge: Cambridge University Press, 2008).
49. J. Tzetzes, *Commentarium in Aristophanis Ranas* (Groningen: Amsterdam, 1962), 22–4; M. Psellus, *The Essays on Euripides and George of Pisidia and on Heliodorus and Achilles Tatius*, ed. A.R. Dyck (Wien: Verlag der Österreichischen Akademie der Wissenschaften 1986), 66–7.
50. A. Tullier, *La Passion du Christ* (Paris: Ed. du Cerf, 1969), 3–4 and 124–5.
51. Symes offers a more in-depth analysis of the *Christos Paschon*'s debt to the *Bacchae* and the implication of this borrowing on its audience. Symes, "Ancient Drama in the Medieval World," 117.
52. Symes, "The Tragedy of the Middle Ages."
53. Boethius, *Consolatio*, II.12: "Quid tragoediarum clamor aliud deflet nisi indiscreto ictu fortunam felicia regna uertentem?"
54. Aristotle, *De Arte Poetica Liber*, 1451a 13-15.
55. Boethius, *Consolatio*, II.1.19; II.2.9.
56. Symes, "The Tragedy of the Middle Ages," 355–8.
57. H.R. Patch, *The Tradition of the Goddess Fortuna in Medieval Philosophy and Literature* (Cambridge: Harvard University Press, 1927), 179–203.
58. According to an ancient etymology, the literal meaning of the Greek term *tragoedia* is "goat (*tragos*) song (*oide*)." See Kelly, *Ideas and Forms*, 38.
59. William of Conches, *Glosae super Boetium*, in *Opera Omnia* 2, ed. L. Nauta, Corpus Christianorum Continuatio Mediaevalis 158 (Turnhout: Brepols, 1999), flo. 13 v.: "*tragedium est scriptum de magnis iniquitatibus a prosperitate incipiens et in adversitate desinens. . . . Et dicta est tragedia quia descriptores illius ad designandum fetorem viciorum que in ea sunt hirco emunerabantur.*"
60. Kelly, *Ideas and Forms*, 125–30.
61. Dedeck-Héry V. L., "Boethius' *De Consolatione* by Jean de Meun," *Medieval Studies* 14 (1952): 165–275, 189, lines 41–2.
62. G. Chaucer, *Monk's Tale*, in *The Canterbury Tales* (London: Penguin, 2005), 1991–8.

> I wol biwaille in manere of tragedie
> The harm of hem that stoode in heigh degree,

>   And fillen so that ther nas no remedie
>   To brynge hem out of hir adversitee.
>   For certein, whan that Fortune list to flee,
>   Ther may no man the cours of hire withholde.
>   Lat no man truste on blynd prosperitee;
>   Be war by thise ensamples trewe and olde.

63. Kelly, *Ideas and Forms*, 111–25.
64. Symes, "Ancient Drama in the Medieval World," 119–20.
65. Dante, *Il trattato de vulgari eloquentia*, (Firenze: Le Monnier, 1896), II.4-8.
66. Dante, *Divina Commedia: Inferno*, 20.113.
67. Dante, *De vulgari eloquentia*, II.5-8.
68. Peter of Blois, *Liber de Confessione Sacramentali*, in *Patrologia Latina*, ed. J-P. Migne, Vol. 207 (Paris, 1855), 1088–9.
69. T. Lerud, "Quick Image: Memory and the English Corpus Christi Drama," in *Moving Subjects: Processional Performances in the Middle Ages and Renaissance*, ed. K. Ashley and W. Hüsken (Amsterdam and Atlanta: Rodopoi, 2001).
70. Symes, *A Common Stage*, 8.
71. Ashley, "Social Functions," 39.
72. D. Dox, "Repertoires and Genres: Emotions at Play," in *A Cultural History of Theatre in the Middle Ages*, ed. J. Enders (London: Bloomsbury, 2017), 163–78, esp. 164.
73. C. Sponsler, "Circulation: A Peripatetic Theatre," in *A Cultural History of Theatre*, 105–21, esp. 108.
74. J. Enders, *The Medieval Theater of Cruelty: Rhetoric, Memory, Violence* (Ithaca: Cornell University Press, 1999), 118–30.
75. Dox, "Repertoires and Genres," 177.
76. Dox, "Repertoires and Genres," 167.
77. J. Bossy, "The Mass as Social Institution 1200–1700," *Past and Present* 100 (1983): 29–61, esp. 32; M. Rubin, *Corpus Christi: The Eucharist in late Medieval Culture* (Cambridge: Cambridge University Press, 1991).
78. V.A. Kolve, *The Play Called Corpus Christi* (Stanford: Stanford University Press, 1966), 175.
79. K. Normington, *Medieval English Drama: Performance and Spectatorship* (Cambridge, UK: Polity Press, 2009).
80. Enders, *The Medieval Theatre*, 99.
81. Enders, *The Medieval Theatre*, 118.
82. Normington, *Medieval English Drama*.
83. D. Bevington, *Medieval Drama* (Boston: Houghton Mifflin Company, 1975), esp. 229–30; see also Kolve, *The Play Called Corpus Christi*.
84. C. Davidson, "Sacred Blood and the Medieval Stage," in *History, Religion, and Violence: Cultural Contexts for Medieval and Renaissance Drama*, ed. C. Davidson (Aldershot: Ashgate, 2002), 180–204.
85. N. Shaughnessy, *Applying Performance: Live Art, Socially Engaged Theatre and Affective Practice* (New York: Palgrave Macmillan, 2012). 6.
86. Dox, "Repertoires and Genres," 164.
87. S. Beckwith, "Drama," in *The Cambridge Companion to Medieval English Literature 1100–1500*, ed. Larry Scanlon (Cambridge: Cambridge University Press, 2009), 84–5.
88. Beckwith, "Drama," 83 and Kolve, *The Play Called Corpus Christi*, 175.
89. Beckwith, "Drama," 84.

90. Beckwith, "Drama," 84.
91. R. Schechner, *Performance Studies: An Introduction.* 3rd edn. Rprnt (2002) (London and New York, Routledge, 2013), 2.
92. S. Kemal, *The Philosophical Poetics of Alfarabi, Avicenna and Averroës: The Aristotelian Reception* (London and NY: Routledge, 2012), 269; N. Shaughnessy, *Applying Performance*, 111.
93. On the tragic aspects of this play, see R.B. Davies, "Reading Ezekiel's Exagoge: Tragedy, Sacrificial Ritual, and the Midrashic Tradition," *Greek, Roman and Byzantine Studies* 48 (2018): 393–415; and E. Nahshon, *Jews and Theatre in an Intercultural Context* (Leiden: Brill, 2012).
94. N. Roth, "Ibn 'Akhnin – Biographical Details," in *Medieval Jewish Civilization: An Encyclopedia*, ed. N. Roth (New York and London: Routledge, 2003), 344–345, esp. 345.
95. M.R. Cohen, *Under Crescent and Cross: The Jews in the Middle Ages* (Princeton: Princeton University Press, 1994), esp. 186.
96. M. Maimonides, *The Guide of the Perplexed*, vol I, trans. S. Pines (Chicago: The University of Chicago Press, 1963), 35–6.
97. The poetry and writing of Ibn Gabirol and of Yehudah Halevi attest to this. See Halkin's translation of the poems. H. Halkin, trans., *The Selected Poems of Yehudah Halevi*, (Massachusetts: Nextbook Press, 2011).
98. G. Wickham, *The Medieval Theatre*, 3rd edition, (Cambridge: Press Syndicate of the University of Cambridge, 1987, first published in 1974), 101.
99. Wickham, *The Medieval Theatre*, 100–1.
100. D. Klausner, "Introduction," in *The Castle of Perseverance*. TEAMS Middle English Texts Series (2010). Online version accessed through d.lib.rochester.edu
101. Beckwith, "Drama," 91.
102. L. Guo, *The Performing Arts in Medieval Islam: Shadow Play and Popular Poetry in Ibn Dāniyāl's Mamluk Cairo* (Leiden and Boston: Brill, 2012),96. For the alternative possibility, Guo, *The Performing Arts*, 106–7 and S. Moreh, *Live Theatre and Dramatic Literature in the Medieval Arab World* (Edinburgh: Edinburgh University Press; New York: New York University Press, 1992), 124.
103. Lerud, "Quick Image," 213–38, esp. 214.
104. J. Marenbon, *Later Medieval Philosophy 1150–1350* (New York: Routledge, 1987), 128; J.I. Jenkins, *Knowledge and Faith in Thomas Aquinas* (Cambridge: Cambridge University Press, 1997), 192.
105. T. Lerud, *Memory, Images, and the English Corpus Christi Drama* (New York: Palgrave Macmillan, 2008), 46
106. Lerud, *Memory, Images*, 41.
107. Moreh, *Live Theatre*, 4 and 116.
108. Guo, *The Performing Arts*, and Moreh, 124.
109. Guo, *The Performing Arts*, 106.
110. Guo, *The Performing Arts*, 25.
111. See S. Mahfouz, and M. Carlson, eds and trans., *Theatre from Medieval Cairo: The Ibn Dāniyāl Trilogy* (New York: Martin E. Segal Theatre Center, 2013).
112. Guo, *The Performing Arts*, 73.

Chapter Five

1. F. Nietzsche, *The Birth of Tragedy out of the Spirit of Music*, trans. Shaun Whiteside (New York: Penguin, 1993), 22; paraphrasing Sophocles, *Oedipus at Colonus* 1224–5 by way of Plutarch, *Letter of Consolation to Apollonius* 115D and Pliny, *Natural History* 7.0.4–5.

2. T.S. Eliot, "Shakespeare and the Stoicism of Seneca," in *Selected Essays* (New York: Harcourt, Brace and Co., 1932), 107–120 at 110 and 112.
3. Eliot, *Selected Essays*, 110.
4. J. Parker, "Persona," in *Cultural Reformations: Medieval and Renaissance in Literary History*, ed. Brian Cummings and James Simpson (Oxford: Oxford University Press, 2010), 591–608.
5. K.M. Coleman, "Fatal Charades: Roman Executions Staged as Mythological Enactments," *Journal of Roman Studies* 80 (1990): 44–73; G. Clark, *Christianity and Roman Society* (Cambridge: Cambridge University Press, 2004), 39–47; T. Wiedemann, "Das Ende der römischen Gladiatorenspiele," *Nikephoros* 8 (1995): 145–59; idem, *Gladiators and Emperors* (London: Routledge, 1992), 147–60; C.A. Barton, "Savage Miracles: The Redemption of Lost Honor in Roman Society and the Sacrament of the Gladiator and the Martyr," *Representations* 45 (1994): 41–71; D. Potter, "Martyrdom and Spectacle," in *Theater and Society in the Classical World*, ed. Ruth Scodel (Ann Arbor: University of Michigan, 1993), 53–88.
6. K.E. Welch, *The Roman Amphitheatre: From its Origins to the Colosseum* (Cambridge: Cambridge University Press, 2007), 63.
7. *Natural History* 36.24 in *Pliny: Natural History*, trans. D.E. Eichholz, vol. 10 (Cambridge: Harvard University Press, 1962), 93.
8. C. Schultze, "Making a Spectacle of Oneself: Pliny on Curio's Theatre," in *Vita Vigilia Est: Essays in Honour of Barbara Levick*, ed. Edward Bispham et al. (London: Institute of Classical Studies, School of Advanced Studies, University of London, 2007), 127–46 at 135.
9. *Hecyra* 33–41 in *Terence*, ed. and trans. John Barsby, vol. 2 (Cambridge: Harvard University Press, 2001), 150–1.
10. Ibid.
11. Preserved by Athenaeus 14 (615e) in *Athenaeus: The Learned Banqueters*, ed. and trans. S. Douglas Olson, vol. 7 (Cambridge: Harvard University Press, 2011), 110–11.
12. *De spect.* 22 in *Tertullian: Apology, De Spectaculis; Minucius Felix*, trans. T.R. Glover and Gerald H. Rendall (Cambridge: Harvard University Press, 1931), 284–5 (modified).
13. K. Baus, *Der Kranz in Antike und Christentum: Eine religionsgeschichtliche Untersuchung mit besonderer Berücksichtigung Tertullians* (Bonn: Peter Hanstein, 1940).
14. *Ad martyras* 3.3–4 in Corpus Christianorum, Series Latina (Turnhout: Brepols, 1953-), 1:5 (hereafter CCSL); translation in The Ante-Nicene Fathers, 10 vols (Buffalo: The Christian Literature Publishing Company, 1887), 3:694 (modified; hereafter ANF).
15. *Ad martyras* 5.1–2 (CCSL 1:7; ANF 3:695 [modified]).
16. F. Nietzsche, *On the Genealogy of Morals and Ecce Homo*, trans. Walter Kaufmann (New York: Vintage, 1989), esp. 48–52 on Tertullian's *De spectaculis*.
17. Jerome, *Adversus Jovinianum* 1.49 in Patrologia cursus completus, Series Latina, 221 vols. (Paris, 1844–64), 23:280C (hereafter PL); translation in Nicene and Post-Nicene Fathers, Second Series, 14 vols (Grand Rapids: Eerdmans, 1978–9 [Reprint]), 6:385 (hereafter NPNF 2); Tertullian, *De anima* 20.1 (CCSL 2:811; ANF 3:200).
18. "Shakespeare and the Stoicism of Seneca," in *Selected Essays*, 112.
19. M.T. Griffin, *Seneca: A Philosopher in Politics* (Oxford: Oxford University Press, 1992), 67–171. Cf. G. Braden, *Renaissance Tragedy and the Senecan Tradition: Anger's Privilege* (New Haven: Yale University Press, 1985), 16–24.
20. M. Wistrand, "Violence and Entertainment in Seneca the Younger," *Eranos* 88 (1990): 31–46; P. Monaghan, "Bloody Roman Narratives: Gladiators, 'Fatal Charades' & Senecan Theatre," *Double Dialogues* 4 (Winter 2003), http://www.doubledialogues.com; Braden, *Renaissance Tragedy and the Senecan Tradition*, 25–7; B.L. Hijman Jr., "Drama in Seneca's Stoicism," *Transactions and Proceedings of the American Philological Society* 97 (1966): 237–51.

21. *De prov.* 4.1 in *Seneca: Moral Essays*, trans. John W. Basore, vol. 1 (Cambridge: Harvard University Press, 1928), 25.
22. *Ep.* 70.19 in *Seneca: Epistles*, trans. Richard M. Gummere, 3 vols. (Cambridge: Harvard University Press, 1917–25), 2:66–7. All further quotations are drawn from this edition.
23. Augustine, *De civ. dei* 14.9 in *The City of God Against the Pagans*, trans. Philip Levine, vol. 4 (Cambridge: Harvard University Press, 1966), 308–9.
24. Ps.-Seneca, *Epistolae Senecae ad Paulum et Pauli ad Senecam*, ed. and trans. Claude W. Barlow (Horn: for the American Academy in Rome by F. Berger, 1938), 7. A contested view nonetheless accepted by W. Trillitzsch, "Seneca tragicus—Nachleben und Beurteilung im lateinischen Mittelalter von der Spätantike bis zum Renaissancehumanismus," *Philologus: Zeitschrift für klassische Philologie* 122.1 (1978): 120–36 at 123; cf. L.A. Panizza, "Biography in Italy from the Middle Ages to the Renaissance: Seneca, Pagan or Christian?" *Nouvelles de la république des lettres* 2 (1984): 47–98.
25. W. Trillitzsch, *Seneca im Literarischen Urteil der Antike: Darstellung und Sammlung der Zeugnisse*, 2 vols. (Amsterdam: Adolf M. Hakkert, 1971), 1:196; cf. *Consolatio philosophiae* 1.3, 3.5.
26. J. Ker, *The Deaths of Seneca* (Oxford: Oxford University Press, 2009), 200–3, 276–7, 307–8.
27. G. Parisi, *La prima dimora di S. Paolo in Roma* (Torino: Casa Editrice Carteggio, 1959), 12; other citations in *Epistolae Senecae ad Paulum*, 7n.3.
28. Trillitzsch, "Seneca tragicus," 125 and those he cites in n.17; on the manuscript history as a whole, see O. Zwierlein, *Prolegomena zu einer kritischen Ausgabe der Tragödien Senecas* (Mainz: Akademie der Wissenschaften und der Literatur, 1983), 8–181.
29. C. Weyman, *Beiträge zur Geschichte der christlich-lateinischen Poesie* (Munich: M. Hueber, 1926), 254; Trillitzsch, "Seneca tragicus," 127.
30. Trillitzsch, "Seneca tragicus," 130.
31. A. Wessels, *Ästhetisierung und ästhetische Erfahrung von Gewalt: Eine Untersuchung zu Senecas Tragödien* (Heidelberg: Universitätsverlag Winter, 2014), 190.
32. All citations (by line number) are from *Seneca: Tragedies*, trans. John G. Fitch, vol. 8 (Cambridge: Harvard University Press, 2002), 174–271; here 1125, 1148, 1153, 1102 respectively.
33. *Vita Malchi* 10 (PL 23:60B; NPNF 2, 6:318). See the preceding chapter for the lines quoted directly from Seneca (PL 23:58C; NPNF 2, 6:318); cf. *Trojan Women* 510–2.
34. N. Guynn, "Translating Catharsis: Aristotle and Averroës, the Scholastics and the Basochiens," in *Rethinking Medieval Translation: Ethics, Politics, Theory*, ed. Emma Campbell and Robert Mills (Cambridge: D.S. Brewer, 2012), 84–106.
35. A.J. Boyle, *Seneca's Troades: Introduction, Text, Translation and Commentary* (Leeds: Francis Cairns, 1994), 141.
36. Wessels, *Ästhetisierung*, 193; cf. Wistrand, "Violence and Entertainment;" Monaghan, "Bloody Roman Narratives."
37. *Meditations* 11.6 in *Marcus Aurelius*, ed. and trans. C.R. Haines (Cambridge: Harvard University Press, 1930), 296–7 (modified). Cf. Liddell Scott s.v. ψυχαγωγέω.
38. Nietzsche, *Birth of Tragedy*, 20–1.
39. For a different interpretation of the grammar, see E. Fantham, *Seneca's Troades: A Literary Introduction with Text, Translation and Commentary* (Princeton: Princeton University Press, 1982), 216.
40. Nietzsche, *Genealogy of Morals*, 68.
41. E. Netzer, *The Architecture of Herod, the Great Builder* (Tübingen: Mohr Siebeck, 1996), 112–18; A. Segal, *Theatres in Roman Palestine and Provincia Arabia* (Leiden: Brill, 1995);

E.M. Smallwood, *The Jews under Roman Rule: from Pompey to Diocletian* (Leiden: Brill, 1976), 79–85.
42. Josephus, *Jewish Antiquities*, trans. Ralph Marcus, vol. 8 (Cambridge: Harvard University Press, 1963), 16.137–8 and 15.274; all further citations are from this edition.
43. D. Kyle, *Spectacles of Death in Ancient Rome* (London: Routledge, 1998), 51.
44. *Martial: Liber Spectaculorum*, ed. Kathleen M. Coleman (Oxford: Oxford University Press, 2006), 83 (epigram 9 [7]). See also Coleman, "Fatal Charades" and S. Bartsch, *Actors in the Audience: Theatricality and Doublespeak from Nero to Hadrian* (Cambridge: Harvard University Press, 1994), 50–62.
45. Hom. in paralyt. 12, quoted in Baus, *Kranz in Antike und Christentum*, 207.
46. J. Parker, *The Aesthetics of Antichrist: From Christian Drama to Christopher Marlowe* (Ithaca: Cornell University Press, 2007), 233.
47. J. Jay, *The Tragic in Mark: A Literary-Historical Interpretation* (Tübingen: Mohr Siebeck, 2014); J. Marcus, *Mark 1–8* (New York: Doubleday, 1999), 68–9; M. Hengel, *Studies in the Gospel of Mark* (Philadelphia: Fortress, 1985), 34–7; G.G. Bilezikian, *Liberated Gospel: A Comparison of the Gospel of Mark and Greek Tragedy* (Grand Rapids: Baker, 1977). Cf. J-A. A. Brant, *Dialogue and Drama: Elements of Greek Tragedy in the Fourth Gospel* (Peabody, MA: Hendrickson, 2004).
48. J. Enders, *Death by Drama and Other Medieval Urban Legends* (Chicago: University of Chicago Press, 2002), 185.
49. Clark, *Christianity and Roman Society*, 44.
50. R. Mills, *Suspended Animation: Pain, Pleasure and Punishment in Medieval Culture* (London: Reaktion Books, 2005), 14.
51. Towneley 21.498 in *The Towneley Plays*, ed. Martin Stevens and A.C. Cawley, 2 vols. (Oxford: Oxford University Press, 1994), 1:265; cf. Towneley 21.241–3.
52. S. Billington, *Mock Kings in Medieval Society and Renaissance Drama* (Oxford: Clarendon, 1991), 93; the same motif also appears in York 31.235–7, 342–70; 33.238, 294, 373–4, 387–8 in *The York Plays: A Critical Edition of the York Corpus Christi Play as Recorded in British Library Additional MS 35290*, ed. Richard Beadle, 2 vols. (Oxford: Oxford University Press, 2009); see esp. the editorial notes on 2:302.
53. N-Town 29.188 in *The N-Town Play: Cotton MS Vespasian D. 8*, ed. Stephen Spector, 2 vols. (Oxford: Oxford University Press, 1991), 1:303 (substituting Jews for scripture's soldiers).
54. P. Brown, *The Cult of the Saints: Its Rise and Function in Latin Christianity* (Chicago: University of Chicago Press, 1981), 6.
55. See M.F. Hansen, *The Eloquence of Appropriation: Prolegomena to an Understanding of Spolia in Early Christian Rome* (Rome: "L'Erma" di Bretschneider, 2003); for the church's dependence on pagan astrology to calculate the timing of its own feast days, see S.C. McCluskey, *Astronomies and Cultures in Early Medieval Europe* (Cambridge: Cambridge University Press, 1999) and N. Campion, *The Dawn of Astrology: A Cultural History of Western Astrology*, 2 vols. (London: Continuum, 2008), 1:245–56. For the relevance of pagan ritual to the development of Christian drama see E.K. Chambers, *The Mediaeval Stage*, 2 vols. (Oxford: Oxford University Press, 1903), esp. 1:95–6 and J. Parker, "Who's Afraid of Darwin? Revisiting Chambers and Hardison . . . and Nietzsche," *Journal of Medieval and Early Modern Studies* 40.1 (2010): 7–35, esp. 23–35.
56. *Cath.* 9.81 in *Prudentius*, trans. H.J. Thomson, 2 vols. (Cambridge: Harvard University Press, 1949), 1:80–1; all further citations from Prudentius are keyed to line numbers in this edition.

57. See M. Simon, *Hercule et le christianisme* (Paris: Belles Lettres, 1955); D.W. Robertson, Jr., *A Preface to Chaucer: Studies in Medieval Perspective* (Princeton: Princeton University Press, 1962), 141–2, 355, 378.
58. For other instances of the Harrowing borrowing from Seneca's version of Hercules' descent see *Cath.* 11.1/*Herc.* 279–83;*Cath.* 12.45–8/*Herc.* 47; more generally *Cath.* 1.69–70 and 12.161–4; discussed in G. O'Daly, *Days Linked by Song: Prudentius' Cathemerinon* (Oxford: Oxford University Press, 2012), 280–1, 334, 341. For the integration of Seneca's phrasing via Prudentius into the liturgy, see A.S. Walpole, *Early Latin Hymns* (Cambridge [Eng.]: The University Press, 1922), 123. Cf. Justo Fernandez Alonso, *La cura pastoral en la España romanovisigoda* (Rome: Iglesia Nacional Española, 1955), 374–83.
59. *Cath.* 12, stanzas 28–31; cf. *Medea* 1012–13. The parallels are further explored by J-L. Charlet, *La création poétique dans le Cathemerinon de Prudence* (Paris: Société d'édition "Les Belles lettres," 1982), 185–7.
60. M. Roberts, *Poetry and the Cult of the Martyrs: The Liber Peristephanon of Prudentius* (Ann Arbor: University of Michigan, 1993), 150–67; A-M. Palmer, *Prudentius and the Martyrs* (Oxford: Clarendon Press, 1989), esp. 188–93; P-A. Deproost, "Le martyre chez Prudence: sagesse et tragédie. La reception de Sénèque dans le Peristephanon Liber," *Philologus* 143 (1999): 161–80; G. Sixt, "Des Prudentius Abhängikeit von Seneca und Lucan," *Philologus: Zeitschrift für das classische Alterthum* 51, n. F. 5 (1892), 501–6.
61. W. Schubert, "Seneca the Dramatist," in *Brill's Companion to Seneca: Philosopher and Dramatist*, ed. Andreas Heil and Gregor Damschen (Leiden: Brill, 2013), 76.
62. W. Ludwig, "Die christliche Dichtung des Prudentius und die Transformation der klassischen Gattungen," in *Christianisme et formes littéraires de l'Antiquité tardive en Occident*, ed. Alan Cameron (Geneva: Fondation Hardt, 1977), 303–72 at 336; R. Henke, "Die Nutzung von Senecas (Ps.-Senecas) Tragödien im Romanus-Hymnus des Prudentius," *Würtzburger Jahrbücher für die Altertumswissenschaft* n. s. 11 (1985): 135–50.
63. P.L. Schmidt, "Rezeption und Überlieferung der Tragödien Senecas bis zum Ausgang des Mittelalters," in *Der Einfluss Senecas auf das Europäische Drama*, ed. Eckard Lefèvre (Darmstadt: Wissenschaftliche Buchgesellschaft, 1978), 12–73 at 55.
64. D. Cassius 43.22.3 in *Roman History*, trans. Earnest Cary, vol. 4 (Cambridge: Harvard University Press, 1914), 250–1; Welch, *Amphitheatre*, 41–2.
65. M. Lawrence, "The Phaedre Sarcophagus in San Clemente," in *In Memoriam Otto J. Brendel: Essays in Archaeology and the Humanities*, ed. Larissa Bonfante and Helga von Heintze (Mainz: Philipp Von Zabern, 1976), 173–8.
66. S. Brown, "Death as Decoration: Scenes from the Arena on Roman Domestic Mosaics," *Pornography and Representation in Greece and Rome*, ed. Amy Richlin (Oxford: Oxford University Press, 1992), 180–211.
67. B.W. Holsinger, "Lollard Ekphrasis: Situated Aesthetics and Literary History," *Journal of Medieval and Early Modern Studies* 31.5 (2005): 67–90 at 78.
68. See G. Bertonière, *The Cult Center of the Martyr Hippolytus on the Via Tiburtina* (Oxford: BAR International Series, 1985), esp. 33–43; C. Gnilka, *Prudentiana II: Exegetica* (Munich: K.G. Saur, 2001), 292–98.
69. K.M.D. Dunbabin, *The Mosaics of Roman North Africa* (Oxford: Clarendon Press, 1978), 85.
70. Brown, *Cult of the Saints*, 41.
71. Brown, *Cult of the Saints*, 2.
72. Cf. Malmud, *Poetics of Translation*, 84.
73. Suetonius, *De vita Caesarum* 2.44.1–2 in *Suetonius*, trans. J.C. Rolfe, vol. 1 (Cambridge: Harvard University Press, 1998), 220–1.

74. Cicero, *Pro Flacco* 16 (Fragmenta Scholiastae Bobiensis).
75. *En. in Ps.* 64.2 in PL 36:774; translation in Nicene and Post-Nicene Fathers, First Series, 14 vols. (Grand Rapids: Eerdmans, 1978–9 [Reprint]), 8:268. Cf. *De civ. Dei* 18.49.
76. C. O'Hogan, *Prudentius and the Landscapes of Late Antiquity* (Oxford: Oxford University Press, 2016), 87.
77. Schmidt, "Rezeption und Überlieferung," 55.
78. Cf. Jay, *Tragic in Mark*, 100–5, 198–204.
79. J.H. Forse, "Religious Drama and Ecclesiastical Reform in the Tenth Century," *Early Theatre* 5.1 (2002): 47–70.
80. *Hrotsvit: Opera Omnia*, ed. Walter Berschin (Munich: Saur, 2001), 132 (Book 2, pref., ll. 1–4). All further citations of Hrotsvit are keyed to this edition by page and line numbers.
81. Aristotle, *Politics* 8.3 (1338a) in *Politics*, trans. H. Rackham (Cambridge: Harvard University Press, 1944), 645.
82. Quoted in P. Dronke, *Women Writers of the Middle Ages: A Critical Study of Texts From Perpetua (D. 203) to Marguerite Porete (D. 1310)* (Cambridge: Cambridge University Press, 1987), 57.
83. W. Berschin, "Passio und Theater. Zur dramatischen Struktur einiger Vorlagen Hrotsvits von Gandersheim," in *The Theatre in the Middle Ages*, ed. Herman Braet, Johan Nowé, and Gilbert Tournoy (Leuven: Leuven University Press, 1985), 9.
84. T.J. Heffernan, "The Liturgy and the Literature of Saints' Lives," in *The Liturgy of the Medieval Church*, ed. Thomas J. Heffernan and E. Ann Matter (Kalamazoo: Medieval Institute, 2001), 73–108.
85. Gregory the Great, *Dialogi* 3.26.7 in *Dialogues*, ed. Adalbert de Vogüé, trans. Paul Antin, vol. 2 (Paris: Éditions du Cerf, 1979), 370.
86. J. Cassianus, *De institutis coenobiorum* 5.17.1 in *De institutis coenobiorum et de octo principalium vitiorum remediis libri XII*, ed. and trans. Jean-Claude Guy (Paris: Éditions du Cerf, 1965), 216.
87. P. Damian, *Opusculum undecimum, liber qui appelatur, Dominus Vobiscum. Ad Leonem Ermitam* 19 (PL 145:247D); trans. Patricia McNulty, *Selected Writings on the Spiritual Life* (London: Faber and Faber, 1959), 76. Cf. P. Damian, *Epistle* 27.2 and 27.10. Also S. Sticca, "The Hagiographical and Monastic Context of Hrotswitha's Plays," in *Hrotsvit of Gandersheim: Rara avis in Saxonia?*, ed. Katharina M. Wilson (Ann Arbor: Marc Publishing, 1987), 1–34.
88. H. Hagen, ed., *Anecdota helvetica quae ad grammaticam latinam spectant ex bibliothecis Turicensi Einsidlensi Bernensi* (Leipzig, 1870), 236. I am grateful to Carol Symes for this citation; for its full implications see her "The Tragedy of the Middle Ages," in *Beyond the Fifth Century: Interactions with Greek Tragedy from the Fourth Century BCE to the Middle Ages*, ed. Ingo Gildenhard and Martin Revermann (Berlin: de Gruyter, 2011), 335–69.
89. Parker, *Aesthetics of Antichrist*, 87–138.
90. See J. Enders, *The Medieval Theatre of Cruelty* (Ithaca: Cornell University Press, 1999).
91. See Parker, *Aesthetics of Antichrist*, 48–9, 61–86.
92. Jay, *Tragic in Mark*, 43.
93. See C. Davidson, "Violence and the Saint Play," *Studies in Philology* 98.3 (2001): 292–314.
94. Rom. 12:19; Deut. 32:35; *Octavia* 849.
95. Thomas Kyd, *The Spanish Tragedy*, ed. C. Calvo and J. Tronch (London: Bloomsbury Arden Shakespeare, 2013), 20.
96. Calvo and Tronch, eds., *Spanish Tragedy*, 319–28.
97. G.K. Hunter, *Dramatic Identities and Cultural Tradition: Studies in Shakespeare and His Contemporaries* (Liverpool: Liverpool University Press, 1978), 163n.6; c.f. J. Wasson, "The

Secular Saint Plays of the Elizabethan Era," in *The Saint Play in Medieval Europe*, ed. Clifford Davidson (Kalamazoo: Medieval Institute Publications, Western Michigan University Press, 1986), 241–60 and Wasson, "The Morality Play: Ancestor of Elizabethan Drama?" *Comparative Drama* 13 (1979): 210–21.

98. *Ad martyras* 4 (CCSL 1:6; ANF 3:695).

Chapter Six

1. H.A. Kelly, *Ideas and Forms of Tragedy from Aristotle to the Middle Ages*, Cambridge Studies in Medieval Literature; 18 (Cambridge: Cambridge University Press, 1993), 117.
2. My approach, then, is very different from that of Henry Ansgar Kelly. See also his *Chaucerian Tragedy*, Chaucer Studies, 24 (Woodbridge: D.S. Brewer, 2000). Z. Baranski, "'Tres Enim Sunt Manerie Dicendi . . .'. Some Observations on Medieval Literature, 'Genre', and Dante," in Baranski, *"Libri poetarum in quattuor species dividuntur": Essays on Dante and "Genre"* (Reading: University of Reading, 1995), 9–60. On definitions, see also Symes, this volume, and V.J. Scattergood, *Politics and Poetry in the Fifteenth Century, 1399–1485*, Blandford History Series, History and Literature (London: Blandford, 1971), particularly 138–41.
3. On the limitations of seeking a pre-defined tragic "genre" and the richness of medieval tragic writing, see C. Symes, "The Tragedy of the Middle Ages," in *Beyond the Fifth Century: Interactions with Greek Tragedy from the Fourth Century BCE to the Middle Ages*, ed. I. Gildenhard and M. Revermann (Berlin: De Gruyter, 2010), 335–69.
4. See H. Cooper, *Shakespeare and the Medieval World*, Arden Critical Companions (London: Bloomsbury, 2010), chapter 5.
5. Isidore of Seville, *Etymologiarum sive originum libri XX*. 2 vols. ed. W.M. Lindsay (Oxford: Clarendon, 1966), 8.7.5–6 and 18.45–46. See also A.J. Minnis, Brian Scott, and David Wallace, *Medieval Literary Theory and Criticism c.1100–c.1375: The Commentary-Tradition* (Oxford: Clarendon Press, 1988), 28.
6. *The Monk's Prologue*, 2770–4, in Geoffrey Chaucer, *Canterbury Tales*, ed. A. C. Cawley, (London: David Campbell, 1992), 433.
7. *Politics*, I.1.1252a1–7, in Aristotle, *The Complete Works of Aristotle: The Revised Oxford Translation*, ed. Jonathan Barnes, Bollingen Series; 71, 2 (Princeton; Guildford: Princeton University Press, 1984).
8. On the former view, see M.S. Kempshall, *Rhetoric and the Writing of History, 400–1500*, Historical Approaches (Manchester: Manchester University Press, 2011), especially chapter 5.
9. For foundation sacrifice see R. Girard, *Things Hidden since the Foundation of the World*, trans. Stephen Bann and Michael Metteer (London: Athlone Press, 1987); and Girard, *Sacrifice*, trans. Matthew Pattillo and David Dawson, Breakthroughs in Mimetic Theory (East Lansing: Michigan State University Press, 2011).
10. See H.R. Patch, *The Tradition of Boethius: A Study of His Importance in Medieval Culture* (New York: Oxford University Press, 1935); J. Norton-Smith, "Chaucer's Boethius and 'Fortune,'" *Reading Medieval Studies* 2 (1976): 63; A.J. Minnis, *Chaucer's Boece and the Medieval Tradition of Boethius*, Chaucer Studies, 18 (Cambridge: DS Brewer, 1993).
11. On *DCP*, see also Donato and Jaffe-Berg, this volume.
12. On Fortune's wheel, see also Swift, this volume.
13. There is a model for representing wheels of fortune in the famous *carnets* (notebooks) of Villard de Honnecourt (BNF, Manuscrits Français 19093, f. 21v). Other examples in BNF, Manuscrits Français 1581, f. 57r, in University of Glasgow Library, Sp Coll MS Hunter 371,

f. 1r; in the pavement of Siena's Cathedral, or in the tomb of Pedro I in Alcobaça. See also E. Meyer-Landrut, *Fortuna: die Göttin des Glücks im Wandel der Zeiten* (München; Berlin: Deutscher Kunstverlag, 1997).

14. On Stoicism and Aristotelianism in Boethius: M.D. Walz, "Stoicism as Anesthesia: Philosophy's 'Gentler Remedies' in Boethius's Consolation," *International Philosophical Quarterly* 51, no. 4 (2011): 501–19. On the general role of Aristotle in Boethius' works see S. Ebbesen, "The Aristotelian Commentator," in *The Cambridge Companion to Boethius*, ed. John Marenbon (Cambridge: Cambridge University Press, 2009), 34–55; J. Marenbon, *Boethius*, Great Medieval Thinkers (Oxford: Oxford University Press, 2003), particularly chapter 3.
15. See particularly Augustine, *City of God*, ed. M. Dods (London: Modern Library Edition, 2000), books 11 and 12.
16. A.W. Astell, *Job, Boethius, and Epic Truth* (Ithaca; London: Cornell University Press, 1994).
17. Pope Gregory I, *Moralia in Job*, ed. Marcus Adriaen, 3 vols., Corpus Christianorum. Series Latina; 143, 143A, 143B (Turnhout: Brepols, 1979); C-L. Seow, "History of Consequences: The Case of Gregory's Moralia in Iob," *Hebrew Bible and Ancient Israel* 1, no. 3 (2012): 370.
18. Marenbon, *Boethius*, 119.
19. Seow, "History of Consequences." Eg. *Moralia in Job*, III.x.17, 126; II.xvi.28, 77: cited in Astell, *Job, Boethius*, 81 and 84.
20. Seow, 371. *Moralia*, III.x.17, 126.
21. Otto of Friesling, *The Two Cities: A Chronicle of Universal History to the Year 1146 A.D.*, ed. Austin P. Evans, Charles Knapp, and Charles Christopher Mierow, ACLS Humanities E-Book (New York: Octagon Books, 1966), 94.
22. Otto of Friesling, *The Two Cities*, 90. On Nicholas Trevet's later comments on tragedy's potential morally to reform its viewers, see Sebastian, this volume. On Otto, see also B. Fitzgerald, *Impact and Authority in the Middle Ages: Prophets and their Critics* (Oxford University Press, 2017), 182–8.
23. See J. Enders, Introduction, this volume. Tony Hunt argues that the Song of Roland can indeed be read in terms of Aristotelian tragedy: "The Tragedy of Roland: An Aristotelian View," *Modern Languages Review* 74 (1979), 791–805. But Kelly argues precisely the opposite (*Ideas and Forms of Tragedy*, 6) on the basis of a lack of any clear "horizon of expectation" for a contemporaneous [?] tragic genre. This essay is about a tragic mode, and makes no claims to identify a specific tragic genre.
24. G.S. Burgess, ed., *The Song of Roland* (London: Penguin, 1990). A digitised version of the oldest manuscript is available at http://image.ox.ac.uk/show?collection=bodleian&manuscript=msdigby23b
25. *Monk's Tale*, 3184 (445), in Geoffrey Chaucer, *Canterbury Tales*. There are further references to Ganelon in *The Shipman's Tale*, 194 (366) and *The Nun's Priest Tale*, 4024 (469).
26. See Donato and Jaffe-Berg, this volume.
27. R.H. Helmholz, *The Spirit of Classical Canon Law*, The Spirit of the Laws (Athens; London: University of Georgia Press, 1996), 224–7.
28. M. Ailes, *The Song of Roland—on Absolutes and Relative Values*, Studies in Mediaeval Literature; v. 20 (Lewiston, NY: Edwin Mellen Press, 2002).
29. On the Poetics of the *Chanson de Roland*, see E. Vance, *Reading the Song of Roland*, Landmarks in Literature (Englewood Cliffs: Prentice-Hall, 1970); R. Pensom, *Literary Technique in the Chanson de Roland* (Geneve: Droz, 1982); R. Pensom, "Histoire et poésie dans la Chanson de Roland," *Romania* 113, no. 451 (1992): 373–82. On the ethics of the

song, see S. Kay, "Ethics and Heroics in the Song of Roland," *Neophilologus* 62, no. 4 (1978): 480–91; Ailes, *The Song of Roland*.
30. T.N. Bisson, "The 'Feudal Revolution,'" *Past and Present* 142, no. 1 (1994): 6–42; C. Wickham, *Framing the Early Middle Ages: Europe and the Mediterranean 400–800* (Oxford: Oxford University Press, 2005).
31. J. Firnhaber-Baker, *Violence and the State in Languedoc, 1250–1400* (New York: Cambridge University Press, 2014).
32. John of Salisbury, *Policraticus: Of the Frivolities of Courtiers and the Footprints of Philosophers*, ed. Cary J. Nederman, Cambridge Texts in the History of Political Thought (Cambridge: Cambridge University Press, 1990), Book 3, chapter 1.
33. *Policraticus*, Book 5, chapters 6 and 7.
34. *Policraticus*, Book 3, chapter 8.
35. *Policraticus*, Book 7, chapter 17.
36. *Policraticus*, Book 8, chapter 20.
37. *Policraticus*, Book 8, chapter 2.
38. "I will be easily persuaded that tyrants instead of princes would have been deserved by a people of stiff neck and wild heart and a people who always resisted the Holy Spirit and who had provoked not only Moses, the servant of the law, but God Himself, the Lord of the law, to anger by their gentile abominations": *Policraticus*, Book 8, chapter 20 (207). This is in the context of a discussion about tyrannicide.
39. Kempshall, *The Common Good*.
40. Giles of Rome, *De Regimine Principum* (Venice: Andrea Torresano and Giovanni Rosso, 1502). See also F. Lachaud and L. Scordia, eds, *Le prince au miroir de la littérature politique de l'Antiquité aux Lumières* (Mont-Saint-Aignan: Publications des universités de Rouen et du Havre, 2007), particularly Frédérique Lachaud, "Le Liber de principis instructione de Giraud de Barry"; Dominique Boutet, "Le prince au miroir de la littérature narrative (12e–13e siècles)"; and Matthew S. Kempshall, "The rhetoric of Giles of Rome's *De regimine principum*."
41. *DRP* I.i.3. Kempshall points out that Giles also explores the possibility that some tyrants acting in self-interest do not necessarily compromise the well-being of the whole community, but the common good is then only an accidental consequence of self-interest (Kempshall, *The Common Good*, 147).
42. Kempshall, *The Common Good*, 131–6.
43. J. Enders, *Rhetoric and the Origins of Medieval Drama*, Rhetoric & Society (Ithaca; London: Cornell University Press, 1992); J. Enders, *The Medieval Theater of Cruelty: Rhetoric, Memory, Violence* (Ithaca, NY: Cornell University Press, 1999); Kempshall, *Rhetoric*.
44. See Kempshall, *Rhetoric*, 476–8; R. Southern, "Aspects of the European Tradition of Historical Writing, I: The Classical Tradition from Einhard to Geoffrey of Monmouth," *Transactions of the Royal Historical Society*, 20 (1970), 177, cited in Kempshall, *Rhetoric*, 478.
45. N.G. Siraisi, "The *Expositio Problematum Aristotelis* of Peter of Abano," *Isis* 61 (1970): 321–39, cited in Kempshall, *Rhetoric*, 479.
46. V. Goddard, "Poetry and Philosophy in Boethius and Dante" (ProQuest Dissertations Publishing, 2011), http://search.proquest.com/docview/924638402/?pq-origsite=primo; L. Lombardo, "Boezio in Dante: La Consolatio Philosophiae 'Nello Scrittoio Del Poeta'" (Venice: Edizioni Ca'Foscari, 2010). Thesis available at http://dspace.unive.it/bitstream/handle/10579/940/Tesi_Lombardo_Luca.pdf?sequence=2

47. This expletive is untranslatable: Dante indicates the multiplicity and incomprehensibility of languages after the fall of the tower of Babel, by having Nimrod speaking nonsensical syllables drawn from a range of language groups.
48. G. Boccaccio, *De Casibus*, Book I, iii, "De Nembroth." See *Giovanni Boccaccio's De Casibus Virorum Illustrium*, in *Tutte le opere di Giovanni Boccaccio*, ed. V. Branca, 12 volumes (Milan: Arnoldo Mondadori editor, 1983), vol IX.
49. On this passage, see K. Olson, *Courtesy Lost: Dante, Boccaccio, and the Literature of History* (Toronto: University of Toronto Press, 2014), 33.
50. R. Hollander, "Tragedy in Dante's 'Comedy,'" *The Sewanee Review* 91, no. 2 (1983): 240–60; J. Steinberg, *Dante and the Limits of the Law* (Chicago: University of Chicago Press, 2013), 161.
51. A. Långfors, ed., *Le roman de Fauvel* (Paris; New York: Didot Johnson Reprint Corp, 1968). See also N.F. Regalado, "Fauvel, Livre De," in *Medieval France: An Encyclopedia*, ed. William W. Kibler (New York; London: Garland, 1995); E. Lalou, "Le Roman de Fauvel ou le miroir déformant," in *Le prince au miroir de la littérature politique de l'Antiquité aux Lumières*, ed. Frédérique Lachaud and Lydwine Scordia (Mont-Saint-Aignan: Publications des universités de Rouen et du Havre, 2007), 217–28.
52. See for example J.R. Strayer, *The Reign of Philip the Fair* (Princeton: Princeton University Press, 1980).
53. On the *Jeu* in Arras, see C. Symes, *A Common Stage: Theater and Public Life in Medieval Arras* (Ithaca : Cornell University Press, 2007), 193–209.
54. E. Vance, "'Le Jeu de La Feuillée' and the Poetics of Charivari," *Modern Language Notes* 100, no. 4 (1985): 815–28.
55. Paris, BNF, ms. fr. 146, fol.36v. See E. Dillon, *The Sense of Sound: Musical Meaning in France, 1260–1330*, New Cultural History of Music (New York: Oxford University Press, 2012), 107–28. On Charivari, see J-C. Schmitt and Jacques Le Goff, *Le Charivari: actes de la table ronde organisée à Paris, 25–27 avril 1977 par l'Ecole des hautes études en sciences sociales et le Centre national de la recherche scientifique*, Civilisations et sociétés; 67 (Paris: Mouton, 1981).
56. J. Favier, *Un conseiller de Philippe le Bel: Enguerran de Marigny* (Paris: Presses universitaires de France, 1963).
57. Dante Alighieri, *Dante's Monarchia*, ed. Richard Kay (Toronto: Pontifical Institute of Mediaeval Studies, 1998).
58. Lucan, *Pharsalia*, Masters of Latin Literature (Ithaca; London: Cornell University Press, 1993). On the reception of Lucan in Dante's work see E. Tarantino, "Fulvae Harenae: The Reception of an Intertextual Complex in Dante's Inferno," *Classical Receptions Journal* 4, no. 1 (2012): 90–126; E. Narducci, "Pompeo in Cielo (Pharsalia IX 1–24; 186–217), Un Verso Di Dante (Parad. XXII 135) e Il Senso Delle Allusioni a Lucano in Due Epigrammi Di Marziale (IX 34; XI 5)," *Museum Helveticum* 58 (2001).
59. H. Skoda, "Anger in Inferno and Purgatorio," in *Dante and the Seven Deadly Sins: Twelve Literary and Historical Essays*, ed. John C. Barnes and Daragh O'Connell (Dublin: Four Courts Press, 2017), 125–50.
60. On Lydgate and his production see C. Sponsler, *The Queen's Dumbshows: John Lydgate and the Making of Early Theater*, Middle Ages Series (Philadelphia: University of Pennsylvania Press, 2014).
61. M. Papio, "On Seneca, Mussato, Trevet, and the Boethian 'Tragedies' of the *De Casibus*," *Heliotropia* 10, no. 2 (2013): 47–63.

62. G. Boccaccio, *Boccaccio's Expositions on Dante's Comedy*, ed. Michael Papio, Lorenzo Da Ponte Italian Library (Toronto; Buffalo, NY: University of Toronto Press, 2009).
63. On Boccaccio's attitude to classical tragedy, see also J.C. Kriesel, "Boccaccio and the Early Modern Reception of Tragedy," *Renaissance Quarterly* 69, no. 2 (2016): 415–448.
64. G. Chaucer, *The Riverside Chaucer*, ed. Larry Dean Benson and F.N. Robinson, 3rd edition (Oxford: Oxford University Press, 2008), 241–53.
65. See in particular R.A. Griffiths, *The Reign of King Henry VI*, 2nd edn. (Stroud: Sutton Publishing, 2004); P. Strong and F. Strong, "The Last Will and Codicils of Henry V," *The English Historical Review* 96, no. 378 (1981): 79–102.
66. J. Lydgate, *The Serpent of Division*, ed. Henry Noble MacCracken (London; New Haven: Oxford University Press; Yale University Press, 1911), 65. Referencing *Monk's Tale*, De Julio Cesare: see Chaucer, *Canterbury Tales*, 454–55.
67. Lydgate, *The Serpent of Division*, 65.
68. Lydgate, 67.
69. See MacCracken's Introduction in J. Lydgate, *The Serpent of Division*, ed. Henry Noble MacCracken (London; New Haven: Oxford University Press; Yale University Press, 1911). This is helpfully recalibrated by M.B. Nolan, "The Art of History Writing: Lydgate's Serpent of Division," *Speculum: A Journal of Medieval Studies* 78, no. 1 (2003): 102–6.
70. G. Boccacio, *De Casibus*, Book I, *Prohemium*. See *Giovanni Boccaccio's De Casibus Virorum Illustrium*, in *Tutte le opere di Giovanni Boccaccio*, ed. V. Branca, 12 volumes (Milan: Arnoldo Mondadori editor, 1983), vol IX.
71. J. Lydgate, *The Fall of Princes*, Chadwyck-Healey Literature Collections. English Poetry Full-Text Database (Cambridge: Chadwyck-Healey, 1992) Prologue (1–13), particularly verses 50–238 (pages 2–7). (Accessed November 1, 2018.)
72. Augustine, *City of God*. See H. Skoda, "Differentiation or Destruction? The Effects of War on Human and Social Bodies in Dante's Commedia," in *War and Peace in Dante*, ed. J. Barnes and D. O'Connell (Dublin: Four Courts Press, 2015).
73. Once again, the designation of this text as tragedy has caused debate. See, for example, W. Matthews, *The Tragedy of Arthur: A Study of the Alliterative "Morte Arthure"* (Berkeley: University of California Press, 1960); K. Pratt, "Aristotle, Augustine or Boethius? *La Mort Le Roi Artu* as Tragedy," *Nottingham French Studies* 30, no. 2 (1991): 81–109; J. Frappier, *Étude sur La Mort Le Roi Artu: roman du XIIIe siècle, dernière partie du Lancelot en prose* (Geneva: Droz, 1961). In contrast, Kelly, *Ideas and Forms of Tragedy*, 8.
74. T. Malory, *Le Morte Darthur*, ed. P.J.C. Field, Arthurian Studies (Cambridge: D.S. Brewer, 2013).

Chapter Seven

1. V.A. Kolve, *The Play Called Corpus Christi* (Stanford CA: Stanford University Press, 1966), 8.
2. I understand that medieval thinkers used the terms "tragedy" and "tragic" to denote nearly as many different generic, textual, social, and embodied phenomena as we find in contemporary discourse.
3. C. Symes, "The Tragedy of the Middle Ages," in *Beyond the Fifth Century: Interactions with Greek Tragedy from the Fourth Century BCE to the Middle Ages*, ed. Ingo Gildenhard and Martin Revermann (Berlin: De Gruyter, 2011), 342–3; "Ancient Drama in the Medieval World," in *A Handbook to the Reception of Greek Drama*, ed. Betine van Zyul Smit (Wiley Blackwell, 2016), 97–130; and "Forms and Media" in this volume. Symes is responding to

H.A. Kelly, *Ideas and Forms of Tragedy from Aristotle to the Middle Ages* (Cambridge: Cambridge University Press, 1993).
4. Here I invoke R. Felski, ed. *Rethinking Tragedy* (Baltimore, MD: The Johns Hopkins University Press, 2008). Reclaiming tragedy for medieval theater specifically and the Middle Ages more generally is also an interest of D. Aers and S. Beckwith, "The Fortunes of Tragedy," *Journal of Medieval and Early Modern Studies* 49.1 (2019): 1–5.
5. For example, Kant, Schiller, Hegel, Nietzsche, Freud, Benjamin, and more recently George Steiner, Raymond Williams, and Terry Eagleton. See Felski, "Introduction," 1.
6. Felski, "Introduction"; S. Goldhill, "The Ends of Tragedy: Schelling, Hegel, and Oedipus," *PMLA* 129.4 (2014): 634–48, and "Generalizing about Tragedy," in Felski, *Rethinking Tragedy*, 45–65; H. Grady, "The Modernity of Western Tragedy: Genealogy of a Developing Anachronism," *PMLA* 129.4 (2014): 790–8; B. Hoxby, "What Was Tragedy: The World We Have Lost, 1550–1795," *Comparative Literature* 64 (2012): 1–32.
7. Grady, "Modernity," 791–3. See also H.P. Foley and J.E. Howard, "Introduction: The Urgency of Tragedy Now," *PMLA* 129.4 (2014): 620–2.
8. Grady, "Modernity," 794, here citing Terry Eagleton, *Sweet Violence: The Idea of the Tragic* (Oxford: Oxford University Press, 2003), 276.
9. Hoxby, "What Was Tragedy?"
10. Felski, "Introduction," 3.
11. C. Sourvinou-Inwood, "Greek Tragedy and Ritual," in *A Companion to Tragedy*, ed. Rebecca Bushnell (Malden, MA: Blackwell, 2005), 18, 7.
12. Goldhill, "Generalizing about Tragedy," 54–5; quotation at 54. See also Symes, "Tragedy of the Middle Ages," 337–9.
13. Goldhill, "Generalizing about Tragedy," 54. See also Sourvinou-Inwood, "Greek Tragedy."
14. P. duBois, "Toppling the Hero: Polyphony in the Tragic City," in Felski, *Rethinking Tragedy*, 127.
15. For a convenient summary, see A.F. Johnston, "An Introduction to Medieval English Theatre," in *The Cambridge Companion to Medieval English Theatre*, ed. Richard Beadle, 2nd edn. (Cambridge: Cambridge University Press, 2008), 8–12.
16. A word about these medieval sites is in order. Three of the six plays comprising the dramatic corpus examined here take their names from the medieval cities—York, Chester, and Coventry—where they originated. The Yorkshire-Lancashire compilation known as the Towneley manuscript preserves another northern example; two versions from unspecified East Anglian auspices appear in manuscript compilations from that region.
17. Sourvinou-Inwood, "Greek Tragedy," 7.
18. Felski, "Introduction," 5.
19. Foley and Howard, "The Urgency of Tragedy Now," 627–8, quotations at 627.
20. E. Hall, "To Fall from High or Low Estate? Tragedy and Social Class in Historical Perspective," *PMLA* 129.4 (2014): 776.
21. Page duBois, "Toppling the Hero," 128–9.
22. K. Goodland, "'Veniance, Lord, apon thaym fall': Maternal Mourning, Divine Justice, and Tragedy in the Corpus Christi Plays," *Medieval and Renaissance Drama in England* 18 (2005): 174.
23. J. Tolmie, "Spinning Women and Manly Soldiers: Grief and Game in the English Massacre Plays," in *Laments for the Lost in Medieval Literature*, ed. Jane Tolmie and M.J. Toswell (Turnhout, Belgium: Brepols, 2010), 288.
24. Tolmie, "Spinning Women," 286.
25. D. Staines, "To Out-Herod Herod," *Comparative Drama* 10.1 (1976): 29–53, quotation at 50.

26. R. Weimann, *Shakespeare and the Popular Tradition of the Theater* (Baltimore: Johns Hopkins University Press, 1978), 64–72; quotation at 66. See also M. Harris, *Sacred Folly: A New History of the Feast of Fools* (Ithaca, NY: Cornell University Press, 2011, especially 41–53; K. Ashley, "Social Functions," in *A Cultural History of Theatre in the Middle Ages*, ed. Jody Enders, Vol. 2 (London: Bloomsbury, 2017), 43–5; T. Coletti, "Re-reading the Story of Herod in the Middle English Innocents Plays," in *Telling Tales: Structure, Context, and Innovation in Traditional Narratives*, ed. Thomas Hahn and Alan Lupack (Cambridge: D.S. Brewer, 1997), 37–9, and "'Ther be but Women': Gender Conflict and Gender Identity in the Innocents Plays," in *Medieval and Early Renaissance Drama: Reconsiderations*, ed. Martin Stevens and Milla Riggio, for *Mediaevalia* 18 (1995 [for 1992]): 247–8 and sources cited therein.
27. For the text of the Padua ceremony, see K. Young, *Drama of the Medieval Church* (Oxford: Clarendon), 2: 99–10, quotation at 100.
28. On other social and historical appropriations of medieval performances related to the Massacre of the Innocents, see K. Ashley, "The Politics of Playing Herod in Beaune," *European Medieval Drama* 9 (2005): 153–66, and J. Marlin, "The Investiture Contest and the Rise of Herod Plays in the Twelfth Century," *Early Drama, Art, and Music Review* 23.1 (2009): 1–18.
29. See Coletti, "Re-reading the Story of Herod," 35, for details and references cited.
30. The following characterization is drawn from D. Williams, "Sympathy for the Devil," in *The French Fetish from Chaucer to Shakespeare* (Cambridge: Cambridge University Press, 2004), 50–86, 246–52; J.G. Harris, "'Look not big, nor stamp, nor stare': Acting up in *The Taming of the Shrew* and the Coventry Herod Plays," *Comparative Drama* 34.4 (2000–1): 365–98; and R. Bushnell, *Tragedies of Tyrants: Political Thought and Theater in the English Renaissance* (Ithaca, NY: Cornell University Press, 1990), 80–8.
31. See, respectively, Williams, "Sympathy for the Devil," 58 and 84; Bushnell, *Tragedies of Tyrants*, 86; and Harris, "Acting up," 366. It is oddly fitting that Herod the Great built the first theater in the Holy Land and apparently had a great penchant for spectacle; see Parker in this volume.
32. *The Towneley Plays*, ed. M. Stevens and A.C. Cawley, EETS, s.s. 13 and 14 (Oxford: Oxford University Press, 1994), 1: 186, lines 92–3.
33. Weimann distanced this Herod from low comedy and farce as well as from a "tragic" spirit identified in previous characterizations; *Shakespeare*, 68 and 274 n.45.
34. C. Clifford Flanigan, "Rachel and her Children: From Biblical Text to Music Drama," in *Metamorphosis and the Arts*, Proceedings of the Second Lilly Conference, ed. Breon Mitchell (Bloomington, IN: Comparative Literature Program, Indiana University, 1979), 43–4.
35. Quoted in J.M. Ziolkowski, "Laments for Lost Children: Latin Traditions," in *Laments for the Lost in Medieval Literature*, ed. Tolmie and Toswell, 95.
36. Flanigan, "Rachel and her Children," 40.
37. The text appears in Young, *Drama of the Medieval Church*, 2: 110–13. See also C. Clifford Flanigan, "The Fleury *Playbook*, Traditions of Medieval Latin Drama, and Modern Scholarship," in *The Fleury Playbook: Essays and Studies*, ed. Thomas P. Campbell and Clifford Davidson, Early Drama, Art, and Music Monograph Series, 7 (Kalamazoo, MI: Medieval Institute Publications, 1985), 1–25.
38. S. Boynton, "Performative Exegesis in the Fleury *Interfectio Puerorum*," *Viator* 29 (1998): 41. See also Boynton, "From the Lament of Rachel to the Lament of Mary: A Transformation in the History of Drama and Spirituality," in *Signs of Change: Transformations of Christian Traditions and their Representation in the Arts, 1000–2000*, ed. Nils Holger Petersen, Claus Clüver, and Nicolas Bell (Amsterdam: Rodopi, 2004), 319–40.

39. Boynton, "Performative Exegesis," 51.
40. Boynton, "Performative Exegesis," 60.
41. Bushnell, *Tragedies of Tyrants*, 7. Walter Benjamin invoked the medieval dramatic Herod's tyrannical identity as he theorized tragedy in the modern, i.e., Baroque, era; *The Origin of German Tragic Drama*, trans. John Osborne (London: Verso, 1998), 69–76.
42. Rebecca Bushnell, "The Fall of Princes: The Classical and Medieval Roots of English Renaissance Tragedy," in Bushnell, *A Companion to Tragedy*, 292–6.
43. *The N-Town Plays*, ed. Stephen Spector, EETS, s.s. 11 and 12 (Oxford: Oxford University Press, 1991) 1: 193–97, quotations at lines 230 and 180. In The N-Town Massacre (lines 246–84), Mors also makes Herod's demise a moral exemplum for "all men."
44. *Late Medieval Religious Plays of Bodleian MSS Digby 133 and E Museo 160*, ed. Donald C. Baker, John L. Murphy, and Louis B. Hall, EETS, o.s. 283 (Oxford: Oxford University Press, 1982) 108–9, line 361.
45. *The Chester Mystery Cycle*, ed. R. M. Lumiansky and David Mills, EETS, s.s. 3 and 9, 2 vols. (Oxford, 1974, 1986), 1:201, lines 419–25. The Massacre play appears in 1: 185–204. Subsequent line citations from these pages in vol. 1 appear in the text.
46. J. de Voragine, *The Golden Legend*, trans. William Granger Ryan, 2 vols. (Princeton: Princeton University Press, 1993), 1:58.
47. Josephus, *The Jewish War*, trans. H. St. J. Thackery. Loeb Classical Library (Cambridge, MA: Harvard University Press, 1961), I: 95–321. I have argued elsewhere that the larger narrative of Herod's dynastic and familial struggles provides the back story for the Herod figure in the English *Magi* and *Innocents* plays; see Coletti, "Re-reading the Story of Herod," 40–5; and "Genealogy, Sexuality, and Sacred Power: The Saint Anne Dedication of the Digby *Candlemas Day and the Killing of the Children of Israel*," *Journal of Medieval and Early Modern Studies* 29.1 (1999): 25–59. This story of Herod finds an early modern afterlife in a spate of English tragic dramas following Thomas Lodge's 1602 translation of Josephus' *The Antiquities of the Jews*: R. Boyle, Earl of Orrery, *Herod the Great: A Tragedy*, 1694, ESTC R21923; E. Cary, *The Tragedie Of Mariam*, 1613, ESTC S107482; G. Markham and W. Sampson, *The True Tragedy of Herod and Antipater: with the death of faire Marriam*, 1622. STC 17401; S. Pordage, *Herod and Mariamne: A Tragedy*, 1673, ESTC R19069.
48. Coletti, "Re-reading the Story of Herod," 52.
49. Ranulf R. Higden, *Polychronicon Ranulph Higden, Together with English Translations of John Trevisa and an Unknown Writer of the Fifteenth Century*, ed. C. Babington and Rev. J.R. Lumby, Rolls Series, 9 vols. (London: Longman and Co. and Trübner and Co., 1865–86), 4: 288–9.
50. See Clifford Flanigan, "Rachel and Her Children." Here I draw from my "Re-reading the Story of Herod," 38.
51. A rough translation: "Whom are you calling whore/scold, you filthy, poxy bitch? Wasn't your mother/wife one of the same?" (297–8). Here I emend Lumiansky and Mills to recover the "biche" that appears in four of the five cycle manuscripts. For the language of the second, obscure quotation, see Lumiansky and Mills, *Chester Mystery Cycle*, 2: 154, note for these lines.
52. The conclusions, respectively of D. Ryan, "Womanly Weaponry: Language and Power in the Chester *Slaughter of the Innocents*," *Studies in Philology* (2001): 76–92; Tolmie, "Spinning Women"; and N.N. Sidhu, *Indecent Exposure: Gender, Politics, and Obscene Comedy in Middle English Literature* (Philadelphia PA: University of Pennsylvania Press, 2016), 223–5. See also R. Sturges, *The Circulation of Power in Medieval Biblical Drama* (New York, NY: Palgrave Macmillan, 2015), 51–79, 162–73.

53. C. Fitzgerald, *The Drama of Masculinity and Medieval English Guild Culture* (New York, NY: Palgrave Macmillan, 2007). See also N.R. Rice and M.A. Pappano, *The Civic Cycles: Artisan Drama and Identity in Premodern England* (Notre Dame, IN: University of Notre Dame Press, 2015) and D. Neal, *The Masculine Self in Late Medieval England* (Chicago: University of Chicago Press, 2008).
54. G. Chaucer, *The Riverside Chaucer*, ed. Larry D. Benson (Boston: Houghton Mifflin, 1987), III: 121–2.
55. Among the six versions of the Massacre in late medieval biblical drama, only the Coventry Shearmen and Tailors' pageant shows Herod's soldiers inquiring about the sex of their prospective victims; *The Coventry Corpus Christi Plays*, ed. P.M. King and C. Davidson, Early Drama, Art and Music Monograph Series 27 (Kalamazoo, MI: Medieval Institute Publications, 2000), 107, lines 786–7.
56. The implications for performance of this idea are rich. For example, what is the status of the human actor who in the course of the play, enacts the role of God.
57. See also ll. 118–24 and 173–5. The York cycle's Massacre also foregrounds this problem; see *The York Plays*, ed. R. Beadle, EETS, s.s. 23 and 24, 2 vols. (Oxford: Oxford University Press, 2009 and 2014) 1: XXX, lines 184–6, 264–5.
58. Repeated at lines 123, 151, 175–6, 179, 340. See also lines 185–6, 211–16, 235–6.
59. E.J. Burns, E. "Knowing Women: Female Orifices in Old French Farce and Fabliau." *Exemplaria* 4.1 (1992): 86.
60. *Coventry Corpus Christi Plays*, 107–8, lines 828, 787; *Late Medieval Religious Plays*, 108, lines 358–9.
61. A similar twist of the plot occurs in Italian Baroque poet Giambattista Marino's graphic and violent *Lo Strage degli innocenti* (1632), which was translated into English as *The Slaughter of the Innocents by Herod*, London 1675, ESTC R12633. See also *The Massacre of the Innocents*, trans. Erik Butler (Cambridge, MA: Wakefield Press, 2015).
62. Neal, *The Masculine Self*, 166–75.
63. Cited in C. Sponsler, "Narrating the Social Order: Medieval Clothing Laws," CLIO, 21 (1992): 279.
64. L. Wilson, "Common Threads: A Reappraisal of Medieval Sumptuary Law," *The Medieval Globe* 2.2 (2016): article 7. http://scholarworks.wmich.edu/tmg/vol2/iss2/7
65. Sponsler, "Narrating the Social Order," 280; see also 282–3.
66. Tolmie, "Spinning Women," see 284, 294, 296. Tolmie's attention to the ways that the Massacre plays express anxieties about issues of "essential importance to the heterosexual family and the state" (294) resonate with this essay's interest in their tragic implications for society and family. On the breakdown of social order in the English Massacre plays, see also C. Sponsler, *Drama and Resistance: Bodies, Goods, and Theatricality in Late Medieval England* (Minneapolis, MN: University of Minnesota Press, 1997), 140–6.
67. *Chester Mystery Cycle*, 159, lines 79–80.
68. *Chester Mystery Cycle*, 461, lines 637–8.
69. J. Parker, *The Aesthetics of Antichrist: From Christian Drama to Christopher Marlowe* (Ithaca, NY: Cornell University Press, 2007), 52.
70. K. Eden, "Aristotle's *Poetics*: A Defense of Tragic Fiction," in Bushnell, *A Companion to Tragedy*.
71. D. Heinsius' *Herodus Infanticida* (1632) provides a tragic interpretation of Herod and the Massacre of the Innocents thoroughly informed by Aristotelian perspectives. See Russ Leo, "Herod and the Furies: Daniel Heinsius and the Representation of Affect in Tragedy," *Journal of Medieval and Early Modern Studies* 49.1 (2019): 137–67.

72. T. Coletti, "The Chester Cycle in Sixteenth-Century Religious Culture," *Journal of Medieval and Early Modern Studies* 37.3 (2007): 531–47.
73. Symes, "Tragedy of the Middle Ages," 342–3.
74. Symes, "Tragedy," 343.
75. Symes, "Tragedy," 356–7.
76. Rebecca Bushnell, "Tragedy and Temporality," *PMLA* 129.4 (2014): 783.
77. Foley and Howard, "The Urgency of Tragedy Now," 625–31.
78. Roland Reed, "The Slaughter of the Innocents," *Early Theatre* 3 (2000): 219–28. See also Sturges, *The Circulation of Power*, 78–9.

Chapter Eight

1. Isidore of Seville, *Etymologiae*, in *Patrologiae Cursus Completus, Series Latina*, (hereafter, PL), ed. J-P. Migne, 217 vols. (Paris: Apud Garnier, 1841–55), vol. 82, VIII, vii, 6. 6.
2. Aelred of Rievaulx, *Liber de speculo caritatis*, ed. C.H. Talbot, in *Opera omnia*, ed. A. Hoste and C.H. Talbot, Corpus Christianorum Continuatio Mediaevalis 1 (Turnhout: Brepols, 1971), vol. 1, II, xvii, 50, p. 90.
3. Ibid.
4. See M.V. Guerin, *The Fall of Kings and Princes: Structure and Destruction in Arthurian Tragedy* (Stanford: Stanford University Press, 1995), but also H.A. Kelly, "The Non-Tragedy of Arthur," in *Medieval English Religious and Ethical Literature: Essays in Honour of G. H. Russell*, ed. G. Kratzmann and J. Simpson (Cambridge: D.S. Brewer, 1986), 92–114.
5. See, for example, William of Conches, *Glose super Librum Boecii de consolacione*, II, prosa ii, Vatican MS lat. 5202 fol. 13v, quoted in H.A. Kelly, *Ideas and Forms of Tragedy from Aristotle to the Middle Ages* (Cambridge: Cambridge University Press, 1991), 70n6; N. Trevet, *Expositio super librum Boecii*, Vatican MS lat. 562 (14 c.), fol. 29, quoted in ibid., 70n6; and G. Chaucer, *Boece*, II, prosa 2, *The Riverside Chaucer*, ed. Larry D. Benson (Oxford: Oxford University Press, 2008), 409–10.
6. On the paradox of women's seclusion in Greek history and prominence in Greek tragedy, see H. Foley, *Female Acts in Greek Tragedy* (Princeton: Princeton University Press, 2001); N. Loraux, *Façons tragiques de tuer une femme* (Paris: Hachette, 1985); and R. Bushnell, *Tragedy: A Short Introduction* (Malden, MA: Blackwell, 2008), 95–101.
7. Aristotle, *Poetics*, 1448a. http://data.perseus.org/citations/urn:cts:greekLit:tlg. Translations of all foreign-language materials are my own.
8. Ibid., 1454a.
9. Ibid., 1453a
10. Jerome, *Adversus Jovinianum*, PL 25, I, 48, col. 280.
11. Marbod of Rennes, *Liber decem capitulorum*, ed. R. Leotta (Rome: Herder, 1984), III, 42–4. Marbod is presumably thinking of Ovid's *Tristia*, which refers to Helen as "an adulteress over whom there was a battle between her lover and her husband" (I, 371–2).
12. The vast majority of surveys of gender in medieval drama concentrate on late medieval English plays, even when their titles seem to promise a far wider scope. See especially K. Normington, *Gender and Medieval Drama* (Rochester, NY: D.S. Brewer, 2006) and T. Coletti, *Mary Magdalene and the Drama of Saints: Theater, Gender, and Religion in Late Medieval England* (Philadelphia: University of Pennsylvania Press, 2004) and "A Feminist Approach to the Corpus Christi Cycles," in *Approaches to Teaching Medieval English Drama*, ed. R.K. Emmerson (New York: Modern Language Association of America, 1990), 79–89. A few such studies address the French context, either partially, such as M.A. Pappano, "Sister

Acts: Conventual Performance and the *Visitatio Sepulchri* in England and France," in *Medieval Constructions in Gender and Identity: Essays in Honor of Joan M. Ferrante*, ed. T. Barolini (Tempe, AZ: Arizona Center for Medieval and Renaissance Studies, 2005), 43–67, or entirely, such as L. Muir, "Women on the Medieval Stage: The Evidence from France," *Medieval English Theatre* 7 (1985): 107–19.
13. Boethius, *Philosophiae consolatio*, ed. L. Bieler, Corpus Christianorum, Series Latina 94 (Turnhout: Brepols 1957; rpt., 1984), bk. I, prosa 1.
14. Ibid., bk. II, prosa 2.
15. See D. Dox, *The Idea of the Theatre in Latin Christian Thought: Augustine to the Fourteenth Century* (Ann Arbor: University of Michigan Press, 2004).
16. Tertullian, *De Virginibus Velandis*, ed. E. Dekkers, in *Opera*, Corpus Christianorum, Series Latina 1 (Turnhout: Brepols, 1954), vol. 2, 1207–26, at ch. 12, 1222.
17. Cyprian, *De habitu virginum*, PL, vol. 4, ch. 5, col. 445.
18. Jerome, *Epistola 22 ad Eustochium*, PL, vol. 22, ch. 13, col. 402.
19. John Chrysostom, *Commentarius in Epistolam ad Romanos*, in *Patrologiae Cursus Completus, Series Graeca* (hereafter, PL), Homily 30, ed. J-P. Migne, 161 vols. (Paris: Apud Garnier, 1857–66), vol. 60, col. 668.
20. Jacob the Deacon, *Vita Sanctae Pelagiae meretricis*, PL, vol. 74, ch. 2, col. 644. Though he does not name Pelagia, Chrysostom provided the basis for her life in his Homily 67 on the Gospel of St. Matthew.
21. Ibid., ch. 3, col. 645; my emphasis.
22. Socrates Scholasticus, *Historia ecclesiastica*, PG, vol. 67, bk. IV, col. 513.
23. See R.H. Bloch, *Medieval Misogyny and the Invention of Western Romantic Love* (Chicago: University of Chicago Press, 1991), 37–64.
24. John Chrysostom, *Commentarius in Sanctum Matthaeum Evangelistam*, PG, vol. 57, Homily 1, col. 22.
25. Ibid., Homily 7, col. 79.
26. Ambrose, *De Virginibus, ad Marcellinam sororem suam*, PL, vol. 16, bk. II, ch. 2.7, col. 209.
27. Song of Songs 4:12.
28. Jerome, *Epistola 22 ad Eustochium*, PL, vol. 22, ch. 25, col. 411.
29. Cf. Mt 25:1-13.
30. Ibid., ch. 26, cols. 411–12.
31. Ambrose, *De Virginibus*, PL, vol. 16, bk. II, ch. 4.22, col. 224.
32. Jerome, *Epistola 108 ad Eustochium*, PL, vol. 22, col. 880.
33. Ambrose, *De Virginibus*, PL, vol. 16, bk. II, ch. 3.20, col. 224.
34. *The Passion of Perpetua and Felicity*, ed. T. J. Heffernan (Oxford: Oxford University Press, 2012), ch. 20, 121–2.
35. Cyprian, *De Habitu virginum*, PL, vol. 4, col. 446.
36. Ibid.
37. Prokopios, *The Secret History with Related Texts*, ed. and trans. A. Kaldellis (Indianapolis: Hackett Publishing Co., 2010), 41.
38. Isidore of Seville, *Etymologiae*, PL, vol. 82, bk. XVIII, ch. 42, col. 357.
39. Hrotsvit, *Abraham*, in *Hrotsvithae Opera*, ed. H. Homeyer (Munich: Verlag Ferdinand Schöningh, 1970), 298–320, at 313.
40. Ibid.
41. Hrotsvit, *Pafnutius*, in *Hrotsvithae Opera*, ed. Homeyer, 321–49.
42. Ibid., 337.
43. Hrotsvitha, *Abraham*, 319.

44. Hrotsvitha, *Pafnutius*, 339.
45. Ibid.
46. Ibid.
47. Ibid., 312.
48. Ibid., 316.
49. Hrotsvitha, *Pafnutius*, 345.
50. Hrotsvitha, *Praefatio*, 233.
51. Ibid.
52. Hrotsvitha, *Abraham*, 311.
53. P. Dronke, "*Ordo Virtutum*: *The Play of the Virtues*, by Hildegard of Bingen," in *Nine Medieval Latin Plays*, ed. and trans. P. Dronke (Cambridge: Cambridge University Press, 1994), 147–57.
54. P. Sheingorn, "The Virtues of Hildegard's *Ordo Virtutum*, It *Was* a Woman's World," in *The "Ordo Virtutum" of Hildegard of Bingen: Critical Studies*, ed. A.E. Davidson (Kalamazoo, MI: Medieval Institute Publications, 1992), 43–62.
55. I am following Dronke's reading of the casting here.
56. Hildegard of Bingen, *Ordo Virtutum*, in *Nine Medieval Latin Plays*, ed. and trans. Dronke, 160–81, at vv. 235–7.
57. Ibid., vv. 479–80.
58. Ibid., v. 165.
59. Ibid., v. 213.
60. Ibid., vv. 105–6.
61. Ibid., vv. 231–4.
62. Ibid., vv. 63–6.
63. Hrotsvit, *Epistola eiusdem ad quosdam sapientes huius libri fautores*, in *Hrotsvithae Opera*, ed. Homeyer, 235–6, at 236.
64. See N.Z. Davis, "Women on Top," in *Society and Culture in Early Modern France* (Stanford: Stanford University Press, 1975), 124–52.
65. Ibid., 131.
66. T. Coletti, "A Feminist Approach to the Corpus Christi Cycles," in *Approaches to Teaching Medieval English Drama*, ed. R.K. Emmerson (New York: Modern Language Association of America, 1990), 81.
67. *Le Mistere du siege d'Orleans*, ed. V.L. Hamblin (Genève: Librairie Droz, 2002), v. 11.941–4.
68. Ibid., vv. 12.043–4.
69. Ibid., vv. 18.149–59.
70. Ibid., v. 12.444.
71. Ibid., vv.12.051–2.
72. E. Hall, *The Union of the Two Noble and Illustre Families of Lancaster and York. commonly known as Hall's Chronicle, Containing the History of England During the Reign of Henry IV and the Succeeding Monarchs to the End of the Reign of Henry VIII* (London: J. Johnson, 1809; rpt., 1965), 148.
73. Ibid., 159.
74. Ibid.
75. Ibid., 157.
76. "Fragment d'une lettre du duc de Bedford," in *Procès de condamnation et de réhabilitation de Jeanne d'Arc, dite la Pucelle*, ed. J. Quicherat, 5 vols. (Paris: Jules Renouard, 1847), vol. 4, pp. 136–7.
77. *Le Mistere du siege d'Orleans*, ed. Hamblin, v. 17.520 and v. 14.698.

78. Ibid., v. 9.711.
79. Ibid., v. 15.209.
80. Ibid., v. 14.109.
81. See D. Fraioli, "Why Joan of Arc Never Became an Amazon," in *Fresh Verdicts on Joan of Arc*, ed. B. Wheeler and C.T. Wood (New York: Garland Publications, 1996), 189–204.
82. *Le Mistere du siege d'Orleans*, ed. Hamblin, vv. 14.376–81.
83. C. de Pisan, *Ditié de Jehanne d'Arc*, ed. A.J. Kennedy and K. Varty (Oxford: Society for the Study of Mediaeval Languages and Literature, 1977), XXI, 161–8.
84. F. Villon, *Le Testament*, in *Oeuvres poétiques*, ed. A. Mary (Paris: Garnier-Flammarion, 1965), 45–137, at XLI, p. 59.
85. T. Basin, *Histoire de Charles VII*, ed. C. Samaran, 2 vols. (Paris: Société d'Edition 'Les Belles Lettres,' 1933), vol. 1, ch. 16, pp. 164–6.
86. F. Schiller, *Die Jungfrau von Orleans*, in *Sämtliche Werke*, 5 vols. (Munich: Carl Hanser Verlag, 1981), vol. 2, 687–812, at II, 7, 1609–11.
87. Ibid., IV, I, 2542–5.
88. Ibid., IV, I, 2567–8.
89. See E.B. Weaver, *Convent Theatre in Early Modern Italy: Spiritual Fun and Learning for Women* (Cambridge: Cambridge University Press, 2002).
90. T. de Lisieux, *La Mission de Jeanne d'Arc*, in *Théâtre au Carmel: recréations pieuses*, ed. G. Gaucher (Paris: CERF, 1985), 57–83, at 61.
91. Ibid.
92. Ibid., 76.
93. Sainte Thérèse de l'Enfant-Jésus et de la Sainte-Face, *Histoire d'une âme: Manuscrits autobiographiques* (Editions du Cerf et Desclée De Brouwer, 1972), 102.
94. Ibid., 60.
95. Ibid., 70.
96. Ibid., 84.
97. Ibid., 302.
98. Thérèse, *Jeanne d'Arc accomplissant sa Mission*, in *Théâtre au Carmel: recréations pieuses*, ed. G. Gaucher (Paris: CERF, 1985), at 134.

BIBLIOGRAPHY

Aelred of Rievaulx. "Liber de speculo caritatis." Edited by C.H. Talbot. In *Corpus Christianorum Continuatio Mediaevalis*, volume 1, *Opera omnia*, edited by A. Hoste and C.H. Talbot. Turnhout: Brepols, 1971.
Aers, David, and Sarah Beckwith. "The Fortunes of Tragedy." *Journal of Medieval and Early Modern Studies* 49.1 (2019): 1–5.
Ailes, Marianne. *The Song of Roland – on Absolutes and Relative Values*. Lewiston, NY: Edwin Mellen Press, 2002.
Ali, Samer M. *Arabic Literary Salons in the Islamic Middle Ages: Poetry, Public Performance, and the Presentation of the Past*. Notre Dame, IN: University of Notre Dame Press, 2010.
Alonso, Justo Fernandez. *La cura pastoral en la España romaovisigoda*. Rome: Iglesia Nacional Española, 1955.
Anouilh, Jean. *Antigone*. Translated by Lewis Galantière. New York and London: Methuen Drama, 1960.
Ante-Nicene Fathers. 10 vols. Reprint, Grand Rapids: Eerdmans, 1950–3.
Aristotle. *The "Art" of Rhetoric*. Edited and translated John Henry Freese. 1926. Reprint, Cambridge, MA: Harvard University Press, 1975.
Aristotle. *The Complete Works of Aristotle*. Edited and translated by Jonathan Barnes. Princeton: Princeton University Press, 1984.
Aristotle. *De Arte Poetica Liber*. Oxford: Clarendon Press, 1965.
Aristotle. *De poetica liber Graece et Latine*. Edited by T.C. Harles. Leipzig: Siegfried Lebrecht Crusius, 1780.
Aristotle. *Poetics*. Edited and translated by W. Hamilton Fyfe. In *Aristotle, "The Poetics"; Longinus, "On the Sublime"; Demetrius, "On Style,"* 1–118. 1927. Reprint, Cambridge, MA: Harvard University Press, 1946.
Aristotle. *The Poetics of Aristotle: Translated from Greek into English and From Arabic into Latin*. Edited and translated by D.S. Margoliouth. London: Hodder and Stoughton, 1911.
Aristotle. *Politics*. Translated by H. Rackham. Cambridge, MA: Harvard University Press, 1944.
Ashley, Kathleen. "Social Functions." In *A Cultural History of Theatre in the Middle Ages*, edited by Jody Enders, 39–58, 218–21. London and New York: Bloomsbury, 2017.
Ashley, Kathleen. "The Politics of Playing Herod in Beaune." *European Medieval Drama* 9 (2005): 153–66.
Astell, Ann W. *Job, Boethius, and Epic Truth*. Ithaca; London: Cornell University Press, 1994.
Athenaeus. *Athenaeus: The Learned Banqueters*, vol. 7. Edited and translated by S. Douglas Olson. Cambridge: Harvard University Press, 2011.
Augustine. *The City of God Against the Pagans*, vol. 4. Translated by Philip Levine. Cambridge: Harvard University Press, 1966.
Augustine. *City of God*. Edited by M. Dods. London, Modern Library Edition, 2000.
Augustine. *The Confessions*. Translated by E. Pusey. New York: P.F. Collier, 1909.
Augustine. *Confessions*. Edited and translated by William Watts. 2 vols. 1912. Reprint, Cambridge, MA: Harvard University Press, 1950–1.

Augustine. *Confessiones, Corpus Christianorum Series Latina*, 27. Turnhout: Brepols, 1981.

Augustine. *De sermone Domini in monte libros duos. Corpus Christianorum Series Latina*, 35, edited by Almut Mutzenbecher. Turnhout: Brepols, 1967.

Augustine. *De civitate Dei. Corpus Christianorum Series Latina* 47–8. Turnhout: Brepols, 1955.

Augustodunensis, Honorius. *Gemma animae*. In *Patrologia Latina*, edited by Jacques-Paul Migne, vol. 172. Paris, 1854.

Aurelius, Marcus. *Meditations*. In *Marcus Aurelius*, edited and translated by C.R. Haines. Cambridge: Harvard University Press, 1930.

Bachelard, Gaston. *The Poetics of Space*. Translated by Maria Jolas. Boston: Beacon Press, 1994.

Baker, Donald C., John L. Murphey, and Louis B. Hall, eds. *Late Medieval Religious Plays of Bodleian MSS Digby 133 and E Museo 160*. EETS, o.s. 283. Oxford: Oxford University Press, 1982.

Bakhtin, Mikhail. *Rabelais and his World*. Translated by Hélène Iswolsky. 1965. Reprint, Bloomington: Indiana University Press, 1984.

Baranski, Zygmunt. *"Libri poetarum in quattuor species dividuntur": Essays on Dante and "Genre."* Reading: University of Reading, 1995.

Baranski, Zygmunt. "'Tres Enim Sunt Manerie Dicendi . . .'. Some Observations on Medieval Literature, 'Genre', and Dante." *The Italianist* 15 (1995): 9.

Bar-Asher, Siegal, Tzvi Novich Michal, and Christine Hayes, eds. *Journal of Ancient Judaism Supplements*, vol. 22, *The Faces of Torah: Studies in the Texts and Contexts of Ancient Judaism in Honor of Steven Fraade*. Göttingen: Vandenhoeck & Ruprecht, 2017.

Barker, Francis. *The Culture of Violence: Essays on Tragedy and History*. Chicago: University of Chicago Press, 1994.

Barnes, Timothy D. "Christians and the Theater." In *Roman Theatre and Society: E. Togo Salmon Papers I*, edited by W.J. Slater, 161–80. Ann Arbor: University of Michigan Press, 1996. Reprinted in *Beyond the Fifth Century: Interactions with Greek Tragedy from the Fourth Century BCE to the Middle Ages*, edited by Ingo Gildenhard and Martin Revermann, 315–34. Berlin: DeGruter, 2010.

Barton, Carlin A. "Savage Miracles: The Redemption of Lost Honor in Roman Society and the Sacrament of the Gladiator and the Martyr." *Representations* 45 (1994): 41–71.

Barish, Jonas. *The Antitheatrical Prejudice*. Berkeley and Los Angeles: University of California Press, 1981.

Bartsch, Shadi. *Actors in the Audience: Theatricality and Doublespeak from Nero to Hadrian*. Cambridge: Harvard University Press, 1994.

Basin, Thomas. *Histoire de Charles VII*. Edited by C. Samaran. 2 vols. Paris: Société d'Edition Les Belles Lettres, 1933.

Baus, Karl. *Der Kranz in Antike und Christentum: Eine religionsgeschichtliche Untersuchung mit besonderer Berücksichtung Tertullians*. Bonn: Peter Hanstein, 1940.

Bayless, Martha. *Parody in the Middle Ages: The Latin Tradition*. Ann Arbor: University of Michigan Press, 1996.

Beadle, Richard, ed. *Early English Text Society Supplemental Series*, vol. 23–4, *The York Plays: A Critical Edition of the York Corpus Christi Play as Recorded in British Library Additional MS 35290*. 2 vols. Oxford: Oxford University Press, 2009–13.

Beadle, Richard, and Alan J. Fletcher, eds. *The Cambridge Companion to Medieval English Theatre*, 2nd edn. Cambridge: Cambridge University Press, 2008.

Beadle, Richard, Peter Meredith, and Richard Rastall, eds. *Medieval Drama Facsimiles*, vol. 7, *The York Play: A Facsimile of British Library MS Additional 35290*. Leeds: The University of Leeds School of English, 1983.

Beckwith, Sarah. *Christ's Body*. London and New York: Routledge, 1994.
Beckwith, Sarah. "Drama." In *The Cambridge Companion to Medieval English Literature 1100–1500*, edited by Larry Scanlon, 83–94. Cambridge: Cambridge University Press, 2009.
Beckwith, Sarah. *Signifying God: Social Relation and Symbolic Act in the York Corpus Christi Plays*. Chicago: University of Chicago Press, 2001.
Belcari, Feo. "Abraham and Isaac." In *Three Florentine Sacre Rappresentazioni: Texts and Translations*, translated by Michael O'Connell, 1–35. Tempe, AZ: Arizona Center for Medieval and Renaissance Studies, 2011.
Belsey, Catherine. *The Subject of Tragedy: Identity and Difference in Renaissance Drama*. London: Methuen, 1985.
Benjamin, Walter. *The Origin of German Tragic Drama*. Translated by John Osborne. London: NLB, 1977; London: Verso, 1998.
Berschin, Walter. "Passio und Theater. Zur dramatischen Struktur einiger Vorlagen Hrotsvits von Gandersheim." In *The Theatre in the Middle Ages*, edited by Herman Braet, Johan Nowé, and Gilbert Tournoy. Leuven: Leuven University Press, 1985.
Bertonière, Gabriel. *The Cult Center of the Martyr Hippolytus on the Via Tiburtina*. Oxford: BAR International Series, 1985.
Bestul, Thomas H. *Texts of the Passion: Latin Devotional Texts and Medieval Society*. Philadelphia, University of Pennsylvania Press, 1996.
Bevington, David, ed. *Medieval Drama*. Boston: Houghton Mifflin, 1975.
Bidez, Joseph and Franz Cumont, eds. *Imp.Caesaris Flavii Claudii Iuliani epistulae, leges, poemata, fragmenta varia*. Paris: Société d'édition Les belles lettres, 1922.
Bilezikian, Gilbert G. *Liberated Gospel: A Comparison of the Gospel of Mark and Greek Tragedy*. Grand Rapids: Baker, 1977.
Billington, Sandra. *Mock Kings in Medieval Society and Renaissance Drama*. Oxford: Clarendon, 1991.
Bisson, T.N. "The 'Feudal Revolution.'" *Past and Present* 142 (1994): 6–42.
Bloch, R.H. *Medieval Misogyny and the Invention of Western Romantic Love*. Chicago: University of Chicago Press, 1991.
Boccaccio, Giovanni. *Boccaccio's Expositions on Dante's Comedy*. Edited by Michael Papio. Lorenzo Da Ponte Italian Library. Toronto: University of Toronto Press, 2009.
Boccaccio, Giovanni. *De Casibus*, Book I. In *Giovanni Boccaccio's De Casibus Virorum Illustrium. Tutte le opere di Giovanni Boccaccio*, edited by V. Branca, 12 volumes. Milan: Arnoldo Mondadori editor, 1983, vol IX.
Boccaccio, Giovanni. *The Fates of Illustrious Men*. Translated by Louis Brewer Hall. New York: F. Ungar Pub. Co., 1965.
Bloemendal, Jan, and Nigel Smith. "Introduction." In *Politics and Aesthetics in European Baroque and Classicist Tragedy*, edited by Bloemendal and Smith, 1–39. Leiden: Brill, 2017.
Boethius. *Corpus Christianorum Series Latina*, vol. 94, *Philosophiae consolatio*. Edited by L. Bieler. 1957. Reprint, Turnhout: Brepols, 1984.
Boethius. *De Musica*. Leipzig: Teubner, 1867.
Boethius. *Opuscula Sacra, De consolatione Philosophiae*. Edited by Claudio Moreschini. Munich/Leipzig: K.G. Saur, 2000.
Bosher, Kathryn, ed. *Theatre Outside Athens: Drama in Greek Sicily and Italy*. Cambridge: Cambridge University Press, 2012.
Bossy, John. "The Mass as Social Institution 1200–1700." *Past and Present* 100 (1983): 29–61.
Boucquey, Thierry, trans. *Six Medieval French Farces*. Lewiston, NY: Edwin Mellen, 1999.

Bourbouhakis, Emmanuel C. "Rhetoric and Performance." In *The Byzantine World*, edited by Paul Stephenson, 175–87. London and New York: Routledge, 2010.

Boyle, A.J. *Seneca's Troades: Introduction, Text, Translation and Commentary*. Leeds: Francis Cairns, 1994.

Boyle, A.J. *Tragic Seneca: An Essay in the Theatrical Tradition*. London and New York: Routledge, 1997.

Boyle, Roger, Earl of Orrery. *Herod the Great: A Tragedy*. London: 1694.

Boynton, Susan. "From the Lament of Rachel to the Lament of Mary: A Transformation in the History of Drama and Spirituality." In *Signs of Change: Transformations of Christian Traditions and their Representation in the Arts, 1000–2000*, edited by Nils Holger Petersen, Claus Clüver, and Nicolas Bell, 319–40. Amsterdam: Rodopi, 2004.

Boynton, Susan. "Performative Exegesis in the Fleury *Interfectio Puerorum*." *Viator* 29 (1998): 39–64.

Braden, Gordon. *Renaissance Tragedy and the Senecan Tradition: Anger's Privilege*. New Haven: Yale University Press, 1985.

Brant, Jo-Ann A. *Dialogue and Drama: Elements of Greek Tragedy in the Fourth Gospel*. Peabody, MA: Hendrickson, 2004.

Brault, Gerard J., ed. *La Chanson de Roland: An Analytical Edition*. 2 vols. University Park, PA: Pennsylvania State University Press, 1978.

Brockett, Oscar G. and Hildy J. Franklin. *History of the Theatre*. Boston: Pearson Education, 2008.

Brook, Peter. *The Empty Space*. New York: Touchstone Books, 1968.

Brouchoud, Claudius. *Les Origines du Théâtre de Lyon: Mystères, Farces et Tragédies, Troupes Ambulantes-Molière; avec fac-simile, notes et documents, par C. Brouchoud*. Lyon: N. Scheuring, 1865.

Brown, Peter G. McC. "Actors and Actor-Managers at Rome in the Time of Plautus and Terence." In *Greek and Roman Actors: Aspects of an Ancient Profession*, edited by Pat Easterling and Edith Hall, 225–37. Cambridge: Cambridge University Press, 2002.

Brown, Peter. *The Cult of the Saints: Its Rise and Function in Latin Christianity*. Chicago: University of Chicago Press, 1981.

Brown, Shelby. "Death as Decoration: Scenes from the Arena on Roman Domestic Mosaics." In *Pornography and Representation in Greece and Rome*, edited by Amy Richlin, 180–211. Oxford: Oxford University Press, 1992.

Burke, Kenneth. *The Philosophy of Literary Form: Studies in Symbolic Action*, 3rd edn. Berkeley: University of California Press, 1973.

Burgess, Glyn S., ed. and trans. *The Song of Roland*. London: Penguin, 1990.

Burningham, Bruce R. "Communities of Production." In *A Cultural History of Theatre*, edited by Christopher B. Balme and Tracy C. Davis, vol. 2, *A Cultural History of Theatre in the Middle Ages*, edited by Jody Enders, 145–61. London: Bloomsbury, 2017.

Burningham, Bruce R. *Radical Theatricality: Jongleuresque Performance on the Early Spanish Stage*. West Lafayette, IN: Purdue University Press, 2007.

Burns, E. Jane. "Knowing Women: Female Orifices in Old French Farce and Fabliau." *Exemplaria* 4.1 (1992): 81–104.

Bushnell, Rebecca. *A Companion to Tragedy*. Malden, MA and Oxford, UK: Blackwell, 2005.

Bushnell, Rebecca. *Tragedy: A Short Introduction*. Malden, MA and Oxford, UK: Blackwell, 2008.

Bushnell, Rebecca. *Tragic Time in Drama, Film, and Videogames*. London: Palgrave Macmillan, 2016.

Bushnell, Rebecca. "The Fall of Princes: Classical and Medieval Roots of English Renaissance Tragedy." In *A Companion to Tragedy*, edited by Rebecca Bushnell, 289–306. Oxford: Blackwell, 2005.

Bushnell, Rebecca. *Tragedies of Tyrants: Political Thought and Theater in the English Renaissance*. Ithaca, NY: Cornell University Press, 1990.

Bushnell, Rebecca. "Tragedy and Temporality." *PMLA* 129.4 (2014): 783–9.

Busonero, Paola. "La *Mise-en-Page* nei Primi Testimoni del Commento Trevetano a Seneca." *Aevum* 75 (2001): 449–76.

Butler, Sara M. "Abortion: Medieval Style? Assaults on Pregnant Women in Later Medieval England." *Women's Studies* 40 (2011): 778–99.

Butterworth, Phillip. *Staging Conventions in Medieval English Theatre*. Cambridge: Cambridge University Press, 2014.

Campion, Nicholas. *The Dawn of Astrology: A Cultural History of Western Astrology*. 2 vols. London: Continuum, 2008.

Carlson, Marvin. *Theories of the Theatre: A Historical and Critical Survey, from the Greeks to the Present. Expanded Edition*. 1984. Reprint, Ithaca: Cornell University, 1993.

Carrero Santamaría, Eduardo. "Entre el Transepto, El Púlpito y el Coro. El Espacio Conmenmorativo de la Sibilia." In *La Sibila. Sonido. Imagen. Liturgia. Escena*, edited by Maricarmen Gómez Muntané and Eduardo Carrero Santamaría, 207–60. Madrid: Alpuerto, 2015.

Cartier, Norman. "La Sagesse de Roland." *Aquila* 1(1968): 33–63.

Cary, Elizabeth. *The Tragedie Of Mariam*. London: 1613.

Cassianus, John. *De institutis coenobiorum et de octo principalium vitiorum remediis libri XII*. Edited and translated by Jean-Claude Guy. Paris: Éditions du Cerf, 1965.

Cassius Dio. *Roman History*, vol. 4. Translated by Earnest Cary. Cambridge: Harvard University Press, 1914.

"Catholic Devotees Nailed to Crosses on Good Friday in Philippines." Associated Press, March 30, 2018: http://www.foxnews.com/world/2018/03/30/catholic-devotees-nailed-to-crosses-on-good-friday-in-philippines.html; and https://www.usatoday.com/videos/news/world/2018/03/30/catholic-devotees-nailed-crosses-good-friday-philippines/33419445/ (both accessed August 2, 2018).

Ceccarelli, Paola. "Changing Contexts: Tragedy in the Civic and Cultural Life of Hellenistic City-States." In *Beyond the Fifth Century: Interactions with Greek Tragedy from the Fourth Century BCE to the Middle Ages*, edited by Ingo Gildenhard and Martin Revermann, 99–150. Berlin: De Gruyter, 2010.

Chambers, E.K. *The Mediaeval Stage*. 2 vols. Oxford: Oxford University Press, 1903.

Charlet, Jean-Louis. *La création poétique dans le cathemerinon de prudence*. Paris: Société d'édition "Les Belles Lettres," 1982.

Chaucer, Geoffrey. *The Canterbury Tales*. London: Penguin, 2005.

Chaucer, Geoffrey. *Canterbury Tales*. Edited by A.C. Cawley. London: David Campbell, 1992.

Chaucer, Geoffrey. *The Riverside Chaucer*. Edited by Larry D. Benson. Boston: Houghton Mifflin, 1987.

Chaucer, Geoffrey. *The Riverside Chaucer*. Edited by Larry Dean Benson and F.N. Robinson. 3rd edition. Oxford: Oxford University Press, 2008.

Chiabò, Maria, ed. *Commento alla Phaedra di Seneca*. Bari: Edipuglia, 2004.

Cicero. *Ad C. Herennium*. Edited and translated by Harry Caplan. 1954. Reprint, Cambridge: Harvard University Press, 1977.

Clark, Gillian. *Christianity and Roman Society*. Cambridge: Cambridge University Press, 2004.

Classen, Albrecht and Marilyn Sandidge. *Death in the Middle Ages and Early Modern Time: The Material and Spiritual Conditions of the Culture of Death*. Berlin and Boston: Walter De Gruyter, 2016.

Clopper, Lawrence M. *Drama, Play, and Game: English Festive Culture in the Medieval and Early Modern Period*. Chicago: University of Chicago Press, 2001.

Cohen, Gustave. *Etudes d'histoire du théâtre en France au Moyen-âge et à la Renaissance*, 7th edn. Paris: Gallimard, 1956.

Cohen, Gustave, ed. *Le Livre de conduite du Régisseur et Le Compte des dépenses pour le Mystère de la Passion joué à Mons en 1501*. Paris: Champion, 1925.

Cohen, Gustave, ed. *Recueil de Farces françaises inédites du XVe siècle*. Cambridge, MA: Mediaeval Academy of America, 1949.

Cohen, Mark R. *Under Crescent and Cross: The Jews in the Middle Ages*. Princeton: Princeton University Press, 1994.

Coleman, Kathleen M. "Fatal Charades: Roman Executions Staged as Mythological Enactments." *Journal of Roman Studies* 80 (1990): 44–73.

Coletti, Theresa. "A Feminist Approach to the Corpus Christi Cycles." In *Approaches to Teaching Medieval English Drama*, ed. R.K. Emmerson. New York: Modern Language Association of America, 1990.

Coletti, Theresa. "Genealogy, Sexuality, and Sacred Power: The Saint Anne Dedication of the Digby *Candlemas Day and the Killing of the Children of Israel*." *Journal of Medieval and Early Modern Studies* 29.1 (1999): 25–59.

Coletti, Theresa. *Mary Magdalene and the Drama of Saints: Theater, Gender, and Religion in Late Medieval England*. Philadelphia: University of Pennsylvania Press, 2004.

Coletti, Theresa. "Re-reading the Story of Herod in the Middle English Innocents Plays." In *Telling Tales: Structure, Context, and Innovation in Traditional Narratives*, edited by Thomas Hahn and Alan Lupack, 35–59. Cambridge: D.S. Brewer, 1997.

Coletti, Theresa. "The Chester Cycle in Sixteenth-Century Religious Culture." *Journal of Medieval and Early Modern Studies* 37.3 (2007): 531–47.

Coletti, Theresa. "'Ther Be but Women': Gender Conflict and Gender Identity in the Middle English Innocents Plays." *Medievalia* 18 (1995): 245–61.

The Complete Works of the Pearl Poet (Pearl Poet). Translated by Casey Finch, and edited by Malcolm Andrew, Ronald Waldron, and Clifford Peterson, 146–93. Berkeley: University of California Press, 1993.

Cooper, Helen. *Shakespeare and the Medieval World*. London: Arden Shakespeare, 2010.

Coppée, Denis. *La sanglante et pitoyable Tragédie de Nostre Sauveur et Rédempteur Iésus-Christ. Poëme mélangé de devotes meditations, figures, complaintes de la glorieuse Vierge, de la Magdalene, et de Sainct Pierre. Avec quinze sonnets en mémoire des quinze effusions de nôtre Sauveur*. Liège: Leonard Streel, 1624.

Corneille, Pierre. *Polyeucte*. http://www.gutenberg.org/files/2543/2543-h/2543-h.htm

Craig, Hardin. *English Religious Drama of the Middle Ages*. 1955. Reprint, Oxford: Clarendon, 1967.

Christos paschon. Edited as *Christus patiens: Tragoedia christiana, quae inscribit solet Χριστὸς πάσχων Gregorio Nazianzeno falso attributa*, by Johann Georg Brambs. Leipzig: B.G. Teubner, 1885.

Damian, Peter. *Opusculum Undecimum, Liber Qui Appelatur, Dominus Vobiscum. Ad Leonem Ermitam*. In *Patrologia Latina*, 145:231–52.

Damian, Peter. *Selected Writings on the Spiritual Life*. Translated by Patricia McNulty. London: Faber and Faber, 1959.

Dante (Alighieri). *Dante's Monarchia*. Edited by Richard Kay. Toronto: Pontifical Institute of Mediaeval Studies, 1998.

Dante (Alighieri). *Il trattato de vulgari eloquentia*. Firenze: Le Monnier, 1896.

Dante (Alighieri). *La Commedia secondo l'antica vulgata*. Edited by Giorgio Petrocchi. Firenze: Le Lettere, 1994.

D'Aubigné, Agrippa. *Les Tragiques*. Edited by Jacques Bailbé. Paris: Garnier-Flammarion, 1968.

Davidson, Clifford. "Sacred Blood and the Medieval Stage." In *History, Religion, and Violence: Cultural Contexts for Medieval and Renaissance Drama*, edited by Clifford Davidson, 180–204. Aldershot: Ashgate, 2002.

Davidson, Clifford. "Space and Time in Medieval Drama: Meditations on Orientation in the Early Theater." In *Word, Picture, and Spectacle*, edited by Clifford Davidson, 39–93. Kalamazoo, MI: Medieval Institute Publications, 1984.

Davidson, Clifford. "Violence and the Saint Play." *Studies in Philology* 98 (2001): 292–314.

Davidson, Clifford. *Visualizing the Moral Life: Medieval Iconography and the Macro Morality Plays*. New York: AMS Press, 1989.

Davies, Rachel Bryant. "Reading Ezekiel's Exagoge: Tragedy, Sacrificial Ritual, and the Midrashic Tradition." In *Greek, Roman and Byzantine Studies* 48 (2008): 393–415.

Davis, Matthew Evan. "As Above, So Below: Staging the Digby *Mary Magdalene*." *Theatre Notebook* 70 (2016): 74–108.

Davis, Natalie Zemon. *Fiction in the Archives: Pardon Tales and Their Tellers in Sixteenth-Century France*. Palo Alto: Stanford University Press, 1987.

Davis, Natalie Zemon. *Society and Culture in Early Modern France*. Palo Alto: Stanford University Press, 1975.

D'Avray, D.L. *Rationalities in History: A Weberian Essay in Comparison*. Cambridge: Cambridge University Press, 2010.

Dean, Ruth J. "Cultural Relations in the Middle Ages: Nicholas Trevet and Nicholas of Prato." *Studies in Philology* 45 (1948): 541–64.

Dean, Ruth J. "The Earliest Known Commentary on Livy is by Nicholas Trevet." *Medievalia et Humanistica* 3 (1945): 86–98.

Dearden, Chris. "Whose Line Is It Anyway? West Greek Comedy in Its Context." In *Theatre Outside Athens: Drama in Greek Sicily and Italy*, edited by Kathryn Bosher, 272–88. Cambridge: Cambridge University Press, 2012.

The Death of Pilate. In *Everyman and Medieval Miracle Plays*, edited by A.C. Cawley, 235–63. New York: Dutton, 1959.

Dedeck-Héry, Vanceslas Louis. "Boethius' *De Consolatione* by Jean de Meun." *Mediaeval Studies* 14 (1952): 165–275.

de Lisieux, Thérèse. *La Mission de Jeanne d'Arc*. In *Théâtre au Carmel: recréations pieuses*, edited by G. Gaucher. Paris: CERF, 1985.

Dell, Ruth J., David Klausner, and Helen Ostovich, eds. *The Chester Cycle in Context, 1555–1575: Religion, Drama, and the Impact of Change*. Farnham: Ashgate, 2012.

de Pisan, Christine. *Ditié de Jehanne d'Arc*. Edited by A.J. Kennedy and K. Varty. Oxford: Society for the Study of Mediaeval Languages and Literature, 1977.

Deproost, Paul-Augustin. "Le martyre Prudence: sagesse et tragédie. La reception de Sénèque dans le Peristephanon Liber." *Philologus* 143 (1999): 161–80.

de Rothschild, James, ed. "Abraham and Isaac." In *Le Mistére du Viel Testament*, Vol. 2, 28–79. 1878. Reprint, New York and London: Johnson Reprints, 1966.

Dillon, Emma. *The Sense of Sound: Musical Meaning in France, 1260–1330*. New York: Oxford University Press, 2012.

Dillon, Matthew. "Tragic Laughter." *The Classical World*, 84.5 (1991): 345–55.

Dollimore, Jonathan. *Radical Tragedy: Religion, Ideology, and Power in the Drama of Shakespeare and his Contemporaries*. Brighton: Harvester, 1984.

Donavan, Richard B. *The Liturgical Drama in Medieval Spain*. Toronto: Pontifical Institute, 1958.

Dorius, R.J. "Tragedy." In *Princeton Encyclopedia of Poetry and Poetics*, edited by Alex Preminger, 860–64. Enlarged edn. Princeton: Princeton University Press, 1974.

Dox, Donnalee. *The Idea of the Theater in Latin Christian Thought: Augustine to the Fourteenth Century*. Ann Arbor: University of Michigan Press, 2004.

Dox, Donnalee. "Repertoires and Genres: Emotions at Play." In *A Cultural History of Theatre*, edited by Christopher B. Balme and Tracy C. Davis, vol. 2, *A Cultural History of Theatre in the Middle Ages*, edited by Jody Enders, 163–78. London: Bloomsbury, 2017.

Dox, Donnalee. "Theatrical Space, Mutable Space, and the Space of Imagination: Three Readings of the Croxton *Play of the Sacrament*." In *Medieval Practices of Space*, edited by Barbara A. Hanawalt and Michal Kobialka, 167–98. Minneapolis: University of Minnesota Press, 2000.

Dronke, Peter, ed. and trans. *Nine Medieval Latin Plays*. Cambridge: Cambridge University Press, 1994.

Dronke, Peter. *Women Writers of the Middle Ages: A Critical Study of Texts from Perpetua. D. 203. to Marguerite Porete. D. 1310*. Cambridge: Cambridge University Press, 1987.

Dunbabin, Katherine M.D. *The Mosaics of Roman North Africa*. Oxford: Clarendon Press, 1978.

duBois, Page. "Toppling the Hero: Polyphony in the Tragic City." In *Rethinking Tragedy* by Rita Felski, 127–47. Baltimore: Johns Hopkins University Press, 2008.

Dupont, A. "Homiletic Perspectives on Augustine's Sacrificial Theology. Exegetical Approaches o/Sacrificium in the Sermones Ad Populum." *Annali Di Storia Dell'Esegesi* 35, no. 1 (2018): 141–160.

Dupont, Léopold. "Denis Coppée: Tradition religieuse, actualité politique et exotisme dans le théâtre à Liège au temps du baroque." *Revue Belge de philologie et d'histoire* 55 (1977): 791–840.

Eagleton, Terry. *Sweet Violence: The Idea of the Tragic*. Oxford: Blackwell, 2003.

Ebbesen, Sten. "The Aristotelian Commentator." In *The Cambridge Companion to Boethius*, edited by John Marenbon, 34–55. Cambridge: Cambridge University Press, 2009.

Eco, Umberto. *The Name of the Rose*. Translated by William Weaver. New York: Harcourt Brace Jovanovich, 1983.

Eden, Kathy. "Aristotle's *Poetics*: A Defense of Tragic Fiction." In *A Companion to Tragedy*, edited by Rebecca Bushnell, 41–50. Oxford: Blackwell, 2005.

Eden, Kathy. *Poetic and Legal Fiction in the Aristotelian Tradition*. Princeton: Princeton University Press, 1986.

Eglal Doss-Quinby, Egal, Joan Tasker Grimbert, Wendy Pfeffer, and Elizabeth Aubrey, eds. and trans. *Songs of the Women Trouvères*. New Haven, CT and London: Yale University Press, 2001

Ehrstine, Glenn. *Theater, Culture, and Community in Reformation Bern, 1523–1555*. Leiden: Brill, 2002.

Elias. *In Porphyrii Isagogen et Aristotelis Categorias*. Berlin: De Gruyter, 1975.

Eliot, T.S. *Selected Essays*. New York: Harcourt, Brace and Co., 1932.

Eliot, T.S. "Shakespeare and the Stoicism of Seneca." In *Selected Essays*, 107–20. New York: Harcourt, Brace and Co., 1932.

Enders, Jody. "Comically Incorrect." *ROMARD* [*Research Opportunities in Medieval and Renaissance Drama*] 51 (2012): 75–82.

Enders, Jody, ed. *A Cultural History of Theatre in the Middle Ages*, vol. 2 of *The Cultural History of Theatre*, edited by Christopher B. Balme and Tracy C. Davis. London and New York: Bloomsbury, 2017.

Enders, Jody. *Death by Drama and Other Medieval Urban Legends*. Chicago: University of Chicago Press, 2002.

Enders, Jody, ed. and trans. *"The Farce of the Fart" and Other Ribaldries: Twelve Medieval French Plays in Modern English*. Philadelphia: University of Pennsylvania Press, 2011.

Enders, Jody. "Foul Play: Marital Rape and the Medieval Theater of Everyday Life." *Cahiers de recherches médiévales* 25 (2013): 145–64.

Enders, Jody, ed. and trans. *"Holy Deadlock" and Further Ribaldries: Twelve Medieval French Plays in Modern English*. Philadelphia: University of Pennsylvania Press, 2017.

Enders, Jody. *The Medieval Theater of Cruelty: Rhetoric, Memory, Violence*. Ithaca: Cornell University Press, 1999; rpt. 2002.

Enders, Jody. *Murder by Accident: Medieval Theater, Modern Media, Critical Intentions*. Chicago: University of Chicago Press, 2009.

Enders, Jody. "The Music of the Medieval Body in Pain." *Fifteenth-Century Studies* 27 (2002): 93–112.

Enders, Jody. "Of Protestantism, Performativity, and the Threat of Theater." *Medievalia* 22 (1999): 53–72.

Enders, Jody. *Rhetoric and the Origins of Medieval Drama*. Ithaca: Cornell University Press, 1992.

Enders, Jody. "The Spectacle of the Scaffolding: Rape and the Violent Foundations of Medieval Theatre Studies." *Theatre Journal* 56 (2004): 163–81.

Enders, Jody. "Theater Makes History: Ritual Murder by Proxy in the *Mistere de la Sainte Hostie*." *Speculum* 79 (2004): 991–1016.

Enders, Jody. "The Theatrical Memory of Denis Coppée's *Sanglante et Pitoyable tragédie de nostre Sauveur et Rédempteur Jesu-Christ*." In *The Shape of Change: Essays on the Early Modern and La Fontaine in Honor of David Lee Rubin*, edited by Ann Birberick and Russell Ganim, 1–21. Amsterdam: Rodopi, 2001.

Epstein, Steven A. *An Economic and Social History of Later Medieval Europe, 1000–1500*. Cambridge: Cambridge University Press, 2009.

Esmoreit. In *Medieval Dutch Drama: Four Secular Plays and Four Farces from the Van Hulthem Manuscript*, translated by Joanna Prins, 3–41. New York: Pegasus, 1999.

Evans, E.P. *The Criminal Prosecution and Capital Punishment of Animals: The Lost History of Europe's Animal Trials*. 1906. Reprint, London: Faber & Faber, 1988.

Everyman and its Dutch Original, Elckerlijc. Edited by Clifford Davidson, Martin Walsh, and Ton Broos. Kalamazoo, MI: Medieval Institute Publications, 2007.

Everyman and Other Miracle and Morality Plays. Edited by Candace Ward. New York: Dover Thrift Editions, 1995.

Faber, Frédéric. *Histoire du Théâtre en Belgique depuis son origine jusqu'à nos jours: d'après les documents inédits reposant aux Archives Générales du Royaume*, vol. 1. Brussels: Olivier; Paris: Tresse, 1878.

Fabris, Valentino. "Il Commento di Nicola Trevet all'*Hercules furens* di Seneca." *Aevum* 27 (1953): 498–509.

Falkner, Thomas. "Scholars versus Actors: Text and Performance in the Greek Scholia." In *Greek and Roman Actors: Aspects of an Ancient Profession*, edited by Pat Easterling and Edith Hall, 342–61. Cambridge and New York: Cambridge University Press, 2002.

Fantham, Elaine. *Seneca's Troades: A Literary Introduction with Text, Translation and Commentary*. Princeton: Princeton University Press, 1982.

Fantuzzi, Marco and Richard Hunter. *Muse e modelli: La poesia ellenistica da Alessandro Magno ad Augusto*. Revised and translated as *Tradition and Innovation in Hellenistic Poetry*. Cambridge: Cambridge University Press, 2004.

Favier, Jean. *Un conseiller de Philippe le Bel: Enguerran de Marigny*. Paris: Presses universitaires de France, 1963.

Felski, Rita. *Rethinking Tragedy*. Baltimore: Johns Hopkins University Press, 2008.

Fenn, Richard. *The Death of Herod: An Essay in the Sociology of Religion*. Cambridge: Cambridge University Press, 1992.

Fiero, Gloria K., Wendy Pfeffer, and Mathé Allain, eds. and trans. *Three Medieval Views of Women*. New Haven, CT: Yale University Press, 1989.

Filippini, Cristiana. "Functions of Pictorial Narratives and Liturgical Spaces: The Eleventh-Century Frescoes of the Titular Saint in the Basilica of San Clemente in Rome." In *Shaping Sacred Space and Institutional Identity in Romanesque Mural Painting: Essays in Honour of Otto Demus*, edited by Thomas E.A. Dale with John Mitchell, 122–38. London: Pindar, 2004.

Firnhaber-Baker, Justine. *Violence and the State in Languedoc, 1250–1400*. New York: Cambridge University Press, 2014.

Fitzgerald, Brian. *Impact and Authority in the Middle Ages: Prophets and their Critics*. Oxford University Press, 2017.

Fitzgerald, Brian. *Inspiration and Authority in the Middle Ages: Prophets and Their Critics from Scholasticism to Humanism*. Oxford: Oxford University Press, 2017.

Fitzgerald, Christina M. *The Drama of Masculinity and Medieval English Guild Culture*. New York: Palgrave Macmillan, 2007.

Flanigan, C. Clifford. "The Fleury *Playbook*, Traditions of Medieval Latin Drama, and Modern Scholarship." In *Early Drama, Art, and Music Monograph Series, 7, The Fleury Playbook: Essays and Studies*, edited by Thomas P. Campbell and Clifford Davidson, 1–25. Kalamazoo, MI: Medieval Institute Publications, 1985.

Flanigan, C. Clifford. "Rachel and Her Children: From Biblical Text to Medieval Music Drama." In *Metamorphosis and the Arts: Proceedings of the Second Lilly Conference*, edited by Breon Mitchell, 31–52. Bloomington, IN: Comparative Literature Program Indiana University, 1979.

Fleming, John. "The Friars and Medieval English Literature." In *The Cambridge History of Medieval English Literature*, edited by David Wallace, 349–75. Cambridge: Cambridge University Press, 1999.

Fletcher, Alan, and Wim Hüsken, eds. *Between Folk and Liturgy*. Amsterdam: Rodopi, 1997.

Foley, H. *Female Acts in Greek Tragedy*. Princeton: Princeton University Press, 2001.

Foley, Helene P. and Jean E. Howard. "Introduction: The Urgency of Tragedy Now." *PMLA* 129 (2014): 617–33.

Forse, James H. "Religious Drama and Ecclesiastical Reform in the Tenth Century." *Early Theatre* 5 (2002): 47–70.

Foucault, Michel. *Discipline and Punish: The Birth of the Prison*. Translated by Alan Sheridan. New York: Pantheon, 1977.

Foulet, Alfred. "Is Roland Guilty of desmesure?" *Romance Philology* 10 (1957): 145–48.

"Fragment d'une lettre du duc de Bedford." In *Procès de condamnation et de réhabilitation de Jeanne d'Arc, dite la Pucelle*, edited by J. Quicherat, 5 vols. (Paris: Jules Renouard, 1847)

Fraioli, D. "Why Joan of Arc Never Became an Amazon." In *Fresh Verdicts on Joan of Arc*, edited by B. Wheeler and C.T. Wood. New York: Garland Publications, 1996.

Franceschini, Ezio, ed. *Il commento di Nicola Trevet al* Tieste *di Seneca*. Milan: Società editrice "Vita e Pensiero," 1938.

Frappier, Jean. *Étude sur La mort le roi Artur: roman du XIIIe siècle, dernière partie du Lancelot en prose*. Geneva: Droz, 1961.

Frivolities of Courtiers and Footprints of Philosophers. Translated by J. Pike. Minneapolis: University of Minnesota Press, 1938.

Frye, Northrop. *Anatomy of Criticism*. Princeton: Princeton University Press, 1957.

Gardiner, Harold C. *Mysteries' End: An Investigation of the Last Days of the Medieval Religious Stage*. New Haven: Yale University Press, 1946.

Garland, Robert. *Surviving Greek Tragedy*. London: Duckworth, 2004.

Gaskin, Richard. *Tragedy and Redress in Western Literature: A Philosophical Perspective*. London: Routledge, 2018.

Gertsman, E. *Crying in the Middle Ages: Tears of History*. New York: Routledge, 2012.

Gertsman, E. *The Dance of Death in the Middle Ages: Image, Text, Performance*. Turnhout: Brepols, 2010.

Gildenhard, Ingo and Martin Revermann. *Beyond the Fifth Century: Interactions with Greek Tragedy from the Fourth Century B.C.E. to the Middle Ages*. Berlin and New York: de Gruyter, 2010.

Giles of Rome. *De Regimine Principum*. Venice: Andrea Torresano and Giovanni Rosso, 1502.

Giles, Ryan D. *The Laughter of the Saints: Parodies of Holiness in Late Medieval and Renaissance Spain*. Toronto: University of Toronto Press, 2009.

Girard, René. *Sacrifice*. Translated by Matthew Pattillo and David Dawson. East Lansing: Michigan State University Press, 2011.

Girard, René. *Things Hidden since the Foundation of the World*. London: Athlone Press, 1987.

Giuliano, Paula, ed. and trans. *Arnoul Gréban: The Mystery of the Passion: The Third Day*. Asheville, NC: Pegasus Press, 1996.

Gnilka, Christian. *Prudentiana II: Exegetica*. Munich: K.G. Saur, 2001.

Goddard, Victoria. "Poetry and Philosophy in Boethius and Dante." ProQuest Dissertations Publishing, 2011. http://search.proquest.com/docview/924638402/?pq-origsite=primo

Goebel, Julius Jr. *Felony and Misdemeanor: A Study in the History of Criminal Law*. Philadelphia: University of Pennsylvania Press, 1976.

Goldhill, Simon. "The Ends of Tragedy: Schelling, Hegel, and Oedipus." *PMLA* 129.4 (2014): 634–48.

Goldhill, Simon. "Generalizing about Tragedy." In *Rethinking Tragedy*, edited by Rita Felski, 45–65. Baltimore: Johns Hopkins University Press, 2008.

Gómez I. Muntané, M. Carmen. *El Llibre Vermell de Montserrat: Cantos y danzas s. XIV*. Barcelona: Libros de la Frontera, 1990.

Goodland, Katherine. *Female Mourning and Tragedy in Medieval and Renaissance English Drama: From* The Raising of Lazarus *to* King Lear. Aldershot, Hampshire, UK, and Burlington, VT: Ashgate, 2005.

Goodland, Katherine. "'Veniance, Lord, apon thaym fall': Maternal Mourning, Divine Justice, and Tragedy in the Corpus Christi Plays." *Medieval and Renaissance Drama in England* 18 (2005): 166–92.

Gorgias. *Helenae Encomium*. In *Die Fragmente der Vorsokratiker*, edited by Diels Hermann and Walther Kranz, 6th edn. Dublin and Zurich: Weidmann, 1951–2.

Grady, Hugh. "The Modernity of Western Tragedy: Genealogy of a Developing Anachronism." *PMLA* 129.4 (2014): 790–8.

Gréban, Arnoul. *Le Mystère de la Passion*. Edited by Omer Jodogne. 2 vols. Brussels: Académie Royale, 1965–83.
Green, R. "Introduction." In *The Consolation of Philosophy*. Translated by R. Green. Mineola: Dover Press, 1962.
Greenblatt, Stephen J. *Shakespearean Negotiations: The Circulation of Social Energy in Renaissance England*. Berkeley: University of California Press, 1988.
Greenblatt, Stephen J. *The Swerve: How the World Became Modern*. New York: W.W. Norton, 2011.
Gregory the Great. *Dialogi* 3.26.7 in *Dialogues*. Edited by Adalbert de Vogüé and translated by Paul Antin, vol. 2. Paris: Éditions du Cerf, 1979.
Gregory I, Pope. *Moralia in Job*. Edited by Marcus Adriaen. 3 vols. *Corpus Christianorum. Series Latina*; 143, 143A, 143B. Turnhout: Brepols, 1979.
Griffin, Miriam T. *Seneca: A Philosopher in Politics*. Oxford: Oxford University Press, 1992.
Griffiths, Ralph A. *The Reign of King Henry VI*. 2nd edn. Stroud: Sutton Publishing, 2004.
Gildenhard, Ingo. "Buskins and SPQR: Roman Receptions of Greek Tragedy." In *Beyond the Fifth Century: Interactions with Greek Tragedy from the Fourth Century BCE to the Middle Ages*, edited by Ingo Gildenhard and Revermann, 153–85. Berlin: De Gruyter, 2010.
Gildenhard, Ingo and Martin Revermann, eds. *Beyond the Fifth Century: Interactions with Greek Tragedy from the Fourth Century BCE to the Middle Ages*. Berlin: De Gruyter, 2010.
Guerin, M.V. *The Fall of Kings and Princes: Structure and Destruction in Arthurian Tragedy*. Stanford: Stanford University Press, 1995.
Gumbrecht, Hans Ulrich. *Production of Presence: What Meaning Cannot Convey*. Palo Alto: Stanford University Press, 2003.
Guo, Li. *The Performing Arts in Medieval Islam: Shadow Play and Popular Poetry in Ibn Dāniyāl's Mamluk Cairo*. Leiden: Brill, 2012.
Guynn, Noah D. *The Many Faces of Farce: Ethics, Politics, and Urban Culture in Late Medieval and Early Modern France*. University of Pennsylvania Press, forthcoming.
Guynn, Noah D. "Translating Catharsis: Aristotle and Averroës, the Scholastics and the Basochiens." In *Rethinking Medieval Translation: Ethics, Politics, Theory*, edited by Emma Campbell and Robert Mills, 84–106. Woodbridge, UK: Boydell & Brewer, 2012.
Hadot, Ilsetraut. *Arts libéraux et philosophie dans la pensée antique*. Paris: Vrin, 2005.
Hagen, H., ed. *Anecdota helvetica quae ad grammaticam latinam spectant ex bibliothecis 011;0 Turicensi Einsidlensi Bernensi*. Leipzig, 1870.
Haidu, Peter. *The Subject of Violence: The Song of Roland and the Birth of the State*. Bloomington: Indiana University Press, 1993.
Halevi, Yehudah. *The Selected Poems of Yehudah Halevi*. Translated and annotated by Hilel Halkin. Massachusetts: Nextbook Press, 2011.
Hall, Edith. *Inventing the Barbarian: Greek Self-Definition Through Tragedy*. Oxford: Oxford University Press, 1993.
Hall, Edith. "The Singing Actors of Antiquity." In *Greek and Roman Actors: Aspects of an Ancient Profession*, edited by Pat Easterling and Edith Hall, 3–38. Cambridge: Cambridge University Press, 2002.
Hall, Edith. "To Fall from High or Low Estate? Tragedy and Social Class in Historical Perspective." *PMLA* 129 (2014): 773–82.
Hall, Edward. *The Union of the Two Noble and Illustre Families of Lancaster and York*, commonly known as *Hall's Chronicle, Containing the History of England During the Reign of Henry IV and the Succeeding Monarchs to the End of the Reign of Henry VIII*. London: J. Johnson, 1809; rpt., 1965.

Halle, Adam de la. *Le Jeu de la feuillée*. Paris: Garnier-Flammarion, 2007.
Halliwell, Stephen. *Greek Laughter: A Study of Cultural Psychology from Homer to Early Christianity*. Cambridge: Cambridge University Press, 2008.
Hamer, Richard, with the assistance of Vida Russell, eds. *Gilte Legende*, Early English Text Society Original Series, vols. 327, 328, 339. Oxford: Oxford University Press, 2006–12.
Hamilton, M.M. *Beyond Faith: Belief, Morality, and Memory in a Fifteenth-Century Judeo-Iberian Manuscript*. Leiden: Brill, 2014.
Hanawalt, Barbara. "Whose Story Was This? Rape Narratives in Medieval English Courts." In *Of Good and Ill Repute: Gender and Social Control in Medieval England*, 124–41. New York: Oxford University Press, 1998.
Hansen, Maria Fabricus. *The Eloquence of Appropriation: Prolegomena to an Understanding of Spolia in Early Christian Rome*. Rome: "L'Erma" di Bretschneider, 2003.
Hanink, Johanna. "The Classical Tragedians, from Athenian Idols to Wandering Poets." In *Beyond the Fifth Century: Interactions with Greek Tragedy from the Fourth Century BCE to the Middle Ages*, edited by Ingo Gildenhard and Martin Revermann, 39–67. Berlin: De Gruyter, 2010.
Happé, Peter, and Elsa Streitman, eds. *Urban Theatre in the Low Countries, 1400–1625*. Turnhout: Brepols, 2006.
Hardison, O.B., Jr. *Christian Rite and Christian Drama in the Middle Ages: Essays in the Origin and Early History of Modern Drama*. Baltimore: Johns Hopkins University Press, 1965.
Harris, Jonathan Gil. "'Look not big, nor stamp, nor stare': Acting up in *The Taming of the Shrew* and the Coventry Herod Plays." *Comparative Drama* 34.4 (2000–1): 365–98.
Harris, Max. *Aztecs, Moors, and Christians: Festivals of Reconquest in Mexico and Spain*. Austin: University of Texas Press, 2000.
Harris, Max. *Carnival and other Christian Festivals: Folk Theology and Folk Performance*. Austin: University of Texas Press, 2003.
Harris, Max. *Sacred Folly: A New History of the Feast of Fools*. Ithaca: Cornell University Press, 2011 and 2014.
Harrowing of Hell (Perugia). Online resource at http://www-personal.usyd.edu.au/~nnew4107/Texts/Fourteenth-century_Umbria_files/LausSabbatiSancti.pdf (accessed March 19, 2018).
Harrowing of Hell (Ukraine). *About the Harrowing of Hell: A Seventeenth-century Ukrainian Play in Its European Context*. Edited and translated by Irena R. Makaryk. Ottawa: Dovehouse, 1989.
Hauréau, [Jean-]Barthélemy, ed. *Notices et extraits de quelques manuscrits latins de la Bibliothèque nationale*. 6 vols. Paris: Klincksieck, 1889–94.
Havelock, Eric A. "The Oral Composition of Greek Drama," *Quaderni Urbanati di Cultura Classica* vol. 6 1980): 61–113. Reprinted in *The Literate Revolution in Greece and Its Cultural Consequences*, 261–313. Princeton: Princeton University Press, 1982.
Heffernan, Thomas J. "The Liturgy and the Literature of Saints' Lives." In *The Liturgy of the Medieval Church*, edited by Thomas J. Heffernan and E. Ann Matter, 73–108. Kalamazoo: Medieval Institute, 2001.
Helmholz, R.H. *The Spirit of Classical Canon Law*. Athens; London: University of Georgia Press, 1996.
Hengel, Martin. *Studies in the Gospel of Mark*. Philadelphia: Fortress, 1985.
Henke, Rainer. "Die Nutzung von Senecas. Ps.—Senecas. Tragödien im Romanus-Hymnus des Prudentius." *Würtzburger Jahrbücher für die Altertumswissenschaft* 11(1985): 135–50.
Henke, Robert. *Pastoral Transformations: Italian Tragicomedy and Shakespeare's Late Plays*. Newark: University of Delaware Press, 1997.

Herington, John. *Poetry into Drama: Early Tragedy and the Greek Poetic Tradition.* Berkeley: University of California Press, 1985.

Hiatt, Alfred. "Genre without System." In *Middle English: Oxford Twenty-First Century Approaches to Literature*, edited by Paul Strohm, 277–94. Oxford: Oxford University Press, 2007.

Higden, Ranulf. *Polychronicon Ranulph Higden, Together with English Translations of John Trevisa and an Unknown Writer of the Fifteenth Century.* Edited by C. Babington and Rev. J.R. Lumby. Rolls Series. 9 vols. London: Longman and Co. and Trübner and Co., 1865–6.

Hijman Jr., B.L. "Drama in Seneca's Stoicism." *Transactions and Proceedings of the American Philological Society* 97 (1966): 237–51.

Hodge, Robert, and Gunther Kress. *Social Semiotics.* Ithaca: Cornell University Press, 1988.

Holsinger, Bruce Wood. "Analytical Survey 6: Medieval Literatures and Cultures of Performance." *New Medieval Literatures* 6 (2003): 271–311.

Holsinger, Bruce Wood. "Lollard Ekphrasis: Situated Aesthetics and Literary History." *Journal of Medieval and Early Modern Studies* 31(2005): 67–90.

Holsinger, Bruce Wood. *Music, Body, and Desire in Medieval Culture: Hildegard of Bingen to Chaucer.* Palo Alto: Stanford University Press, 2001.

Hollander, Robert. "Tragedy in Dante's 'Comedy.'" *The Sewanee Review* 91 (1983): 240–60.

Hopkins, Jasper. *A Concise Introduction to the Philosophy of Nicholas of Cusa.* Minneapolis: University of Minnesota Press, 1978.

Hoxby, Blair. *What Was Tragedy? Theory and the Early Modern Canon.* Oxford: Oxford University Press, 2015.

Hoxby, Blair. "What Was Tragedy: The World We Have Lost, 1550–1795." *Comparative Literature* 64 (2012): 1–32.

Hrotsvit of Gandersheim. *Hrotsvithae Opera.* Edited by H. Homeyer. Munich: Verlag Ferdinand Schöningh, 1970.

Hrotsvit of Gandersheim. *A Florilegium of Her Works.* Edited by Katharina Wilson. Woodbridge, Suffolk: D.S. Brewer, 1998.

Hrotsvit of Gandersheim. *The Plays of Hrotsvit of Gandersheim.* Translated by Katharina Wright Wilson. New York and London: Garland, 1989.

Hrotsvit of Gandersheim. *Hrotsvit: Opera Omnia.* Edited by Walter Berschin. Munich: Saur, 2001.

Hunt, Anthony. "The Tragedy of Roland: An Aristotelian View." *Modern Languages Review* 74 (1979): 791–805.

Hunter, G.K. *Dramatic Identities and Cultural Tradition: Studies in Shakespeare and His Contemporaries.* Liverpool: Liverpool University Press, 1978.

Iamblichus. *De Vita Pythagorica.* Stuttgart: Teubner, 1975

Iamblichus. *De Mysteriis Aegyptiorum.* Stuttgart: Teubner, 1975.

Iamblichus. *Les mystères d'Egypte.* Edited and translated by Edward des Places. Paris: Belles Lettres, 1989.

Ibn Dāniyāl. *Theatre from Medieval Cairo; The Ibn Dāniyāl Trilogy: The Shadow Spirit; The Amazing Preacher and the Stranger; The Love-Stricken One and the Lost One Who Inspires Passion.* Edited and translated by Safi Mahfouz and Marvin Carlson. New York: Martin E. Segal Theatre Publications, 2013.

Irigaray, Luce. *Ce sexe qui n'en est pas un.* Paris: Editions de Minuit, 1977. Published in translation as *This Sex Which is Not One.* Translated by Catherine Porter with Carolyn Burke. Ithaca: Cornell University Press 1985.

Isidore of Seville. *Etymologiarum sive originum libri XX*, edited by W.M. Lindsay. Oxford: Clarendon Press, 1911.

Isidore of Seville. *The "Etymologies" of Isidore of Seville*. Translated by Stephen A. Barney, W.J. Lewis, J.A. Beach, and Oliver Berghof. Cambridge: Cambridge University Press, 2006.

Isidore of Seville. *Isidore of Seville's Etymologies: The Complete English Translation of Isidori Hispalensis Episcopi, "Etymologiarum sive Originum," Libri XX*. Translated by Priscilla Throop. 2 vols. Charlotte, VT: Medieval MS, 2005.

Isidore of Seville. *Isidori Hispalensis Episcopi, "Etymologiarum sive Originum," Libri XX*. Edited by W.M. Lindsay. 2 vols. 1911. Reprint, London: Oxford, 1962.

Jacobelli, Maria Katarina. *Il Risus paschalis e il fondamento teologico del piacere sessuale*. Brescia: Queriniana, 1991.

Jacobus de Voragine. *The Golden Legend*. Translated by William Granger Ryan. 2 vols. Princeton: Princeton University Press, 1993.

Janko, Richard. *Aristotle on Comedy: Towards a Reconstruction of "Poetics II."* Berkeley: University of California Press, 1984.

Jay, Jeff. *The Tragic in Mark: A Literary-Historical Interpretation*. Tübingen: Mohr, Siebeck, 2014.

Jenkins, J.I. *Knowledge and Faith in Thomas Aquinas*. Cambridge: Cambridge University Press, 1997.

Jerome. *Adversus Jovinianum*. In *Patrologia Latina* 23:205–338. Translated by Nicene and Post-Nicene Fathers 2, 6:346–416.

Jerome. *Vita Malchi*. In *Patrologia Latina* 23:53–60. Translated by Nicene and Post-Nicene Fathers 2, 6:315–18.

John of Salisbury. *Policraticus: of the frivolities of courtiers and the footprints of philosophers*. Edited and translated by Cary J. Nederman. Cambridge University Press, 1990.

Johnston, Alexandra F. "An Introduction to Medieval English Theatre." In *The Cambridge Companion to Medieval English Theatre*, 2nd edn, edited by Richard Beadle, 1–25. Cambridge: Cambridge University Press, 2008.

Johnston, Alexandra F. "Parish Playmaking before the Reformation." In *The Parish in Late Medieval England: Proceedings of the 2002 Harlaxton Symposium*, edited by Clive Burgess and Eamon Duffy, 322–38. Donington: Shaun Tyas, 2006.

Johnston, Alexandra F. "At the Still Point of the Turning World: Augustinian Roots of Medieval Dramaturgy." *European Medieval Drama* 2 (1998): 1–19.

Johnston, Alexandra F., and Margaret Rogerson, eds. *Records of Early English Drama: York*. 2 vols. Toronto: University of Toronto Press, 1979.

Johnston, Alexandra F., and Wim Hüsken, eds. *"Ludus": Medieval and Early Renaissance Theatre and Drama*, vol. 2, *Civic Ritual and Drama*. Amsterdam and Atlanta: Rodopi, 1997.

Jones, Gwenan, ed. and trans. *A Study of Three Welsh Religious Plays*. Aberystwyth: Bala, 1939.

Josephus. *Jewish Antiquities*, vol. 8. Translated by Ralph Marcus. Cambridge: Harvard University Press, 1963.

Josephus. *The Jewish War*. Translated by H. St. J. Thackery. 3 vols. Cambridge, MA: Harvard University Press, 1961.

Journal d'un bourgeois de Paris 1405–1449. Edited by Alexandre Tuety. Paris, 1881. Published in translation as *A Parisian Journal, 1405–1449*. Translated by Janet Shirley. Oxford: Clarendon, 1960.

Junge, Rebekka, ed. *Nicholas Trevet und die* Octavia praetexta*: Editio princeps des mittelalterlichen Kommentars und Untersuchungen zum pseudo-senecanischen Drama*. Paderborn: Schoeningh, 1999.

Kaldellis, Anthony. *Hellenism in Byzantium: The Transformations of Greek Identity and the Reception of the Classical Tradition*. Cambridge: Cambridge University Press, 2008.

Kaplan, Joel H. "Reopening King Cambises' Vein." *Essays in Theatre* 5 (1987): 103–14.
Kay, Sarah. "Ethics and Heroics in the Song of Roland." *Neophilologus* 62 (1978): 480–91.
Kelly, Henry Ansgar. "Aristotle-Averroes-Alemannus on Tragedy: The Influence of the 'Poetics' on the Latin Middle Ages." *Viator* 10 (1979): 161–209.
Kelly, Henry Ansgar. *Chaucerian Tragedy*. Cambridge: D.S. Brewer, 1997.
Kelly, Henry Ansgar. *Ideas and Forms of Tragedy from Aristotle to the Middle Ages*. Cambridge: Cambridge University Press, 1993.
Kelly, Henry Ansgar. *Tragedy and Comedy from Dante to Pseudo-Dante*. Eugene, OR: Wipf and Stock, 1989.
Kelly, Henry Ansgar. "The Non-Tragedy of Arthur." In *Medieval English Religious and Ethical Literature: Essays in Honour of G. H. Russell*. Edited by G. Kratzmann and J. Simpson. Cambridge: D.S. Brewer, 1986.
Kemal, Salim. *The Philosophical Poetics of Alfarabi, Avicenna and Averroës: The Aristotelian Reception*. London: Routledge, 2012.
Kempshall, M.S. *Rhetoric and the Writing of History, 400–1500*. Manchester: Manchester University Press, 2011.
Kempshall, M.S. *The Common Good in Late Medieval Political Thought*. Oxford Scholarship Online. Oxford: Clarendon, 1999.
Kennedy, George A. *Classical Rhetoric and Its Christian and Secular Tradition from Ancient to Modern Times*. Chapel Hill: University of North Carolina Press, 1980.
Ker, James. *The Deaths of Seneca*. Oxford: Oxford University Press, 2009.
Kerr, Walter. *Tragedy and Comedy*. New York: Simon & Schuster, 1967.
Kibler, William. "Roland's Pride." *Symposium* 26 (1972): 147–60.
Kimura, Yoko. "The *Bildungsroman* of an Anonymous Franciscan Preacher in Late Medieval Italy (Biblioteca Communale di Foligno, MS C. 85)." *Medieval Sermon Studies* 58 (2014): 47–64.
King, Pamela M. *Westfield Medieval Studies*, vol. 1, *The York Mystery Cycle and the Worship of the City*. Cambridge: D.S. Brewer, 2006.
King, Pamela M., and Clifford Davidson, eds. *The Coventry Corpus Christi Plays*. Kalamazoo, MI: Medieval Institute Publications, 2000.
Kipling, Gordon. *Enter the King: Theatre, Liturgy, and Ritual in the Medieval Civic Triumph*. Oxford: Clarendon, 1998.
Kipling, Gordon. "Theatre as Subject and Object in Fouquet's 'Martyrdom of St. Apollonia.'" *Medieval English Theatre* 19 (1997): 26–80.
Klausner, David, ed. *The Castle of Perseverance*. Kalamazoo, MI: Medieval Institute Publications, 2007.
Klausner, David. "Introduction." *The Castle of Perseverance*. TEAMS Middle English Texts Series, 2010. Online version accessed through d.lib.rochester.edu
Klinck, Anne L. *Anthology of Ancient and Medieval Woman's Song*. New York: Palgrave Macmillan, 2004.
Knight, Alan E. *Aspects of Genre in Late Medieval French Drama*. Manchester: Manchester University Press, 1983.
Knight, Alan E., ed. *Le Sacrifice d'Abraham*. In *Les Mystères de la procession de Lille*, vol. 1: 183–206. Genève: Librairie Droz, 2001–11.
Knight, Alan E, ed. *Les Mystères de la Procession de Lille*. 5 vols. Genève: Librairie Droz, 2001–11.
Kobialka, Michal. *This Is My Body: Representational Practices in the Early Middle Ages*. Ann Arbor: University of Michigan Press, 1999.

Kokotsaki, Archontissa. "Passions of the Soul and the Humanistic Society in the Theories of Plutarch, Aristotle, the Stoics, Boethius." *Dialogue and Universalism* 25 (2015): 195–202.

Kolve, V.A. *The Play Called Corpus Christi*. Stanford: Stanford University Press, 1966.

Kooper, Erik, ed. *Medieval Dutch Literature in Its European Context*. Cambridge: Cambridge University Press, 1994.

Koopmans, Jelle, ed. *Le Recueil de Florence: 53 farces imprimées à Paris vers 1515*. Orléans: Paradigme, 2011.

Koopmans, Jelle. *Le Théâtre des exclus au Moyen Âge: Hérétiques, sorcières et marginaux*. Paris: Imago, 1997.

Kriesel, James C. "Boccaccio and the Early Modern Reception of Tragedy." *Renaissance Quarterly* 69 (2016): 415–48.

Kreitner, Kenneth. *The Church Music of Fifteenth-Century Spain*. Woodbridge, UK: The Boydell Press, 2004.

Kubiak, Anthony. *Stages of Terror: Terrorism, Ideology, and Coercion as Theatre History*. Bloomington: Indiana University Press, 1991.

Krueger, Arthur F. *Synthesis of Sacrifice According to Saint Augustine; a Study of the Sacramentality of Sacrifice*. Dissertationes Ad Lauream (St. Mary of the Lake Seminary); 19. Mundelein, IL: apud aedes Seminarii Sanctae Mariae ad Lacum, 1950.

Kyd, Thomas. *The Spanish Tragedy*. Edited by Clara Calvo and Jesús Tronch. London: Bloomsbury, 2013.

Kyle, Donald G. *Spectacles of Death in Ancient Rome*. London: Routledge, 1998.

Labute, Neil. *Bash: Latterday Plays*. New York: Faber and Faber, 1999.

Lachaud, Frédérique, and Lydwine Scordia, eds. *Le prince au miroir de la littérature politique de l'Antiquité aux Lumières*. Mont-Saint-Aignan: Publications des universités de Rouen et du Havre, 2007.

Lactantius. *Institutiones Divinae. Corpus Scriptorum Ecclesiasticorum Latinorum* 19. Vienna: 1890–8.

Lagioia, Alessandro, ed. *Commento all'Oedipus di Seneca*. Bari: Edipuglia, 2008.

Lalou, Elisabeth. "Le théâtre médiéval, le tragique et le comique: réflexions sur la définition des genres." In *Tragique et comique liés, dans le théâtre, de l'Antiquité à nos jours (du texte à la mise en scène)*. Acts of a colloquy organized at the University of Rouen, April 2012. Publication by Milagros Torres and Ariane Ferry with the collaboration of Sofía Moncó Taracena and Daniel Lecler. Accessed at http://ceredi.labos.univ-rouen.fr/public/?le-theatre-medieval-le-tragique-et.html

Lalou, Elisabeth. "Le Roman de Fauvel ou le miroir déformant." In *Le prince au miroir de la littérature politique de l'Antiquité aux Lumières*, edited by Frédérique Lachaud and Lydwine Scordia, 217–28. Mont-Saint-Aignan: Publications des universités de Rouen et du Havre, 2007.

Lancaster, Henry Carrington. *The French Tragi-Comedy: Its Origin and Development from 1552 to 1628*. Baltimore: J.H. Furst, 1907.

Lang, Uwe Michael. "Augustine's Conception of Sacrifice in City of God, Book X, and the Eucharistic Sacrifice." *Antiphon: A Journal for Liturgical Renewal* 19 (2015): 29–51.

Långfors, Arthur, ed. *Le roman de Fauvel*. Paris; New York: Didot Johnson Reprint Corp, 1968.

Lawrence, Marion. "The Phaedre Sarcophagus in San Clemente." In *In Memoriam Otto J. Brendel: Essays in Archaeology and the Humanities*. Edited by Larissa Bonfante and Helga von Heintze, 173–8. Mainz: Philipp Von Zabern, 1976.

Lawson, Mark. "Farce Is Everywhere on Stage—but Why?" *Guardian*, June 10, 2012. http://www.theguardian.com/stage/2012/jun/10/farce-is-everywhere-why (accessed December 1, 2015).

Lebègue, Raymond. *La Tragédie religieuse en France: Les débuts (1514–1573)*. Paris: Champion, 1929.

Le Goff, Jacques. *La Civilisation de l'Occident médiéval*. Paris: Arthaud, 1964. Published in English as *Medieval Civilization, 400–1500*. Translation by Julia Barrow. Oxford: Blackwell, 1988.

Lebek, W.D. "Moneymaking and the Roman Stage." In *Roman Theatre and Society: E. Togo Salmon Papers I*, edited by W.J. Slater, 29–48. Ann Arbor: University of Michigan Press, 1996.

Lefebvre, Henri. *The Production of Space*. Translated by Donald Nicholson-Smith. Oxford: Blackwell Publishing, 1991.

Leo, Russ. "Herod and the Furies: Daniel Heinsius and the Representation of Affect in Tragedy." *Journal of Medieval and Early Modern Studies* 49.1 (2019): 137–67.

Le Roux de Lincy, Antoine, and Francisque Michel, eds. *Recueil de farces, moralités et sermons joyeux, publiés d'après le manuscrit de la Bibliothèque royale*. 4 vols. 1837. Reprint, Geneva: Slatkine, 1977.

Lerud, Theodore. "Quick Image: Memory and the English Corpus Christi Drama." In *Moving Subjects: Processional Performances in the Middle Ages and Renaissance*, edited by Kathleen Ashley and Wim Hüsken, 213–38. Amsterdam: Rodopoi, 2001.

Lerud, Theodore. *Memory, Images, and the English Corpus Christi Drama*. New York: Palgrave Macmillan, 2008.

Levy, Shimon. *The Bible as Theatre*. Sussex: Sussex Academic Press, 2000.

Lewicka, Halina. Introduction to *Recueil du British Museum: Facsimilé des 64 pièces de l'original*. Geneva: Slatkine, 1970.

Liddell, Henry George. *A Lexicon Abridged from Liddell and Scott's Greek-English Lexicon*. Oxford: Clarendon Press, 1994.

Lightfoot, Jane L. "Nothing to Do with the *Technītai* of Dionysius?" In *Greek and Roman Actors: Aspects of an Ancient Profession*, edited by Pat Easterling and Edith Hall, 209–24. Cambridge: Cambridge University Press, 2002.

Lintilhac, Eugène de. *Histoire Générale du théâtre en France*. 5 vols. Paris: Flammarion, 1904–11.

Livanos, Christopher. "Trends and Developments in the Byzantine Poetic Tradition." In *The Byzantine World*, edited by Paul Stephenson, 200–10. London and New York: Routledge, 2010.

Lombardo, Luca. *Boezio in Dante: La "Consolatio Philosophiae" Nello Scrittoio Del Poeta*. Venice: Edizioni Ca'Foscari, 2010.

Loraux, N. *Façons tragiques de tuer une femme*. Paris: Hachette, 1985.

Lord, Mary Louise. "Virgil's *Eclogues*, Nicholas Trevet, and the Harmony of the Spheres." *Medieval Studies* 54 (1992): 186–273.

Lucan. *Pharsalia*. Ithaca; London: Cornell University Press, 1993.

Lucian of Samosata. "The Dance." In *Works*, vol. 5, edited and translated by A.M. Harmon. 1936. Reprint, Cambridge, MA: Harvard University Press, 1972.

Ludwig, Walther. "Die christliche Dichtung des Prudentius und die Transformation der klassischen Gattungen." In *Christianisme et formes littéraires de l'Antiquité tardive en Occident*. Edited by Alan Cameron, 303–72. Geneva: Fondation Hardt, 1977.

Lumiansky, R.M., and David Mills, eds. *The Chester Mystery Cycle*. 2 vols. London: Oxford University Press, 1974 and 1986.

Lydgate, John. *Troy Book: Selections*. Edited by R. R. Edwards. Kalamazoo: Medieval Institute Publications, 1998.

Lydgate, John. *The Fall of Princes*. Chadwyck-Healey Literature Collections. Cambridge: Chadwyck-Healey, 1992.

Lydgate, John. *The Serpent of Division*. Edited by Henry Noble MacCracken. London; New Haven: Oxford University Press; Yale University Press, 1911.

Mahfouz, Safi and Marvin Carlson, ed. and trans. *Theatre from Medieval Cairo: The Ibn Dāniyāl Trilogy*. New York: Martin E. Segal Theatre Center, 2013.

Maimonides, Moses. *The Guide of the Perplexed*, vol. 1. Translated by S. Pines. Chicago: University of Chicago Press, 1963.

Mali, Joseph. *Mythistory: The Making of a Modern Historiography*. Chicago: University of Chicago Press, 2003.

Malory, Thomas. *Le Morte Darthur*. Edited by P.J.C. Field. Cambridge: D.S. Brewer, 2013.

Marbod of Rennes. *Liber decem capitulorum*. Edited by R. Leotta. Rome: Herder, 1984.

Marciniak, Przemysław. *Greek Drama in Byzantine Times*. Katowic: Wydawnictwo Uniwersytetu Śląskiego, 2004.

Marcus, Joel. *Mark 1–8*. New York: Doubleday, 1999.

Marenbon, John. *Boethius*. Oxford: Oxford University Press, 2003.

Marenbon, John. *Later Medieval Philosophy 1150 – 1350*. 1987. Reprint, New York: Routledge, 1991.

Marie de France. *The Lais of Marie de France*. Translated by Robert Hanning and Joan Ferrante. 1978. Reprint, Durham, NC: Labyrinth Press, 1982.

Marino, Giambattista. *The Massacre of the Innocents*. Translated by Erik Butler. Cambridge, MA: Wakefield Press, 2015.

Marino, Giambattista. *The Slaughter of the Innocents by Herod*. (*Lo Strage degli innocenti*). Trans. T.R. London: 1675.

Markham, Gervase, and William Sampson. *The Tragedy of Herod and Antipater: With the Death of faire Marriam*. London: 1622.

Marlin, John. "The Investiture Contest and the Rise of Herod Plays in the Twelfth Century." *Early Drama, Art, and Music Review* 23.1 (2009): 1–18.

Marot, Clément. *Les Oeuvres de Clement Marot de Cahors en Quercy*. Edited by Georges Guiffrey. 5 vols. 1911. Reprint, Geneva: Slatkine, 1969.

Maruli'c, Marko. *East European Monographs*, vol. 302, *Judith*. Edited and translated by Henry R. Cooper. Boulder: East European Monographs, 1991.

Martial. *Martial: Liber Spectaculorum*. Edited by Kathleen M. Coleman. Oxford: Oxford University Press, 2006.

Mascoli, Patrizia. *Commento alle* Phoenissae *di Seneca*. Bari: Edipuglia, 2007.

Matthews, William. *The Tragedy of Arthur: A Study of the Alliterative "Morte Arthure."* Berkeley: University of California Press, 1960.

Mazouer, Charles. *Le Théâtre médiéval*. Paris: SEDES, 1998.

McCluskey, Stephen C. *Astronomies and Cultures in Early Medieval Europe*. Cambridge: Cambridge University Press, 1999.

McCracken, Peggy. *The Curse of Eve, The Wound of the Hero: Blood, Gender, and Medieval Literature*. Philadelphia: University of Pennsylvania Press, 2003.

McCracken, Peggy. *The Romance of Adultery: Queenship and Sexual Transgression in Old French Literature*. Philadelphia: University of Pennsylvania Press, 1998.

McGuire, Brian Patrick. *Friendship and Community: The Monastic Experience, 350–1250*. Rev. ed. 1988. Reprint, Ithaca: Cornell University Press, 2010.

McLuhan, Marshall, and Quentin Fiore. *The Medium is the Message*. New York: Random House, 1967.

McNamer, Sarah. "Feeling." In *Middle English*, edited by Paul Strohm, 241–57. Oxford: Oxford University Press, 2007.

Medieval Dutch Drama: Four Secular Plays and Four Farces from the Van Hulthem Manuscript. Translated by Johanna Prins. Asheville, NC: Pegasus, 1999.

Medieval German Drama: Four Plays in Translation. Translated by Stephen K. Wright. Fairview, NC: Pegasus, 2002.

Melia, Daniel F. "Orality and Aristotle's Aesthetics." In *New Directions in Oral Theory*, edited by Mark C. Amodio, 91–124. Tempe, AZ: Arizona Center for Medieval and Renaissance Studies, 2005.

Meloni, Pietro, ed. *Nicolai Treveti Expositio L. Annaei Senecae Agamemnonis.* Palermo: Palumbo, 1961.

Meloni, Pietro. *Nicolai Treveti Expositio L. Annaei Senecae Herculis Oetaei.* Palermo: Palumbo, 1962.

Menocal, María Rosa. *The Arabic Role in Medieval Literary History.* Philadelphia: University of Pennsylvania Press, 1987.

Merback, Mitchell. *The Thief, the Cross, and the Wheel: Pain and the Spectacle of Punishment in Medieval and Renaissance Europe.* Chicago: University of Chicago Press, 1998; London: Reaktion Books, Ltd., 2001.

Meyer, Michel. *Le Comique et le tragique: Penser le théâtre et son histoire.* Paris: Presses Universitaires de France, 2003.

Meyer-Baer, Kathi. *Music of the Spheres and the Dance of Death.* Princeton University Press, 1984.

Meyer-Landrut, Ehrengard. *Fortuna: die Göttin des Glücks im Wandel der Zeiten.* München; Berlin: Deutscher Kunstverlag, 1997.

Mills, David, ed. *The Chester Mystery Cycle: A New Edition with Modernised Spelling.* Medieval Texts and Studies, vol. 9. East Lansing, MI: Colleagues Press, 1992.

Mills, Robert. *Suspended Animation: Pain, Pleasure and Punishment in Medieval Culture.* London: Reaktion Books, 2005.

Minnis, A.J. *Chaucer's Boece and the Medieval Tradition of Boethius.* Chaucer Studies, 18. Cambridge: D.S. Brewer, 1993.

Minnis, A.J. and A.B. Scott with David Wallace, eds. *Medieval Literary Theory and Criticism c. 1100–1375: The Commentary-Tradition.* Rev. ed. 1988. Oxford: Clarendon, 1991.

Le Mistere de la Sainte Hostie. Bibliothèque nationale, Réserve, Yf 2915.

Le Mistere du siege d'Orleans. Edited by V.L. Hamblin. Genève: Librairie Droz, 2002.

Le Mistére du Viel Testament. Edited by James de Rothschild. 6 vols. 1878. Reprint, New York and London: Johnson Reprints, 1966.

Monaghan, Paul. "Bloody Roman Narratives: Gladiators, 'Fatal Charades' & Senecan Theatre." *Double Dialogues* 4 (Winter 2003). http://www.doubledialogues.com

Moreh, Shmuel. *Live Theatre and Dramatic Literature in the Medieval Arab World.* Edinburgh: Edinburgh University Press; New York: New York University Press, 1992.

Morgan, David. *The Embodied Eye: Religious Visual Culture and The Social Life of Feeling.* Berkeley: University of California Press, 2012.

The Muhlhausen Play of St. Catherine. In *Medieval German Drama*, translated by Stephen K. Wright, 123–58. Fairview, NC: Pegasus, 2002

Muir, Lynette R. *The Biblical Drama of Medieval Europe.* Cambridge: Cambridge University Press, 1995.

Muir, L. "Women on the Medieval Stage: The Evidence from France." *Medieval English Theatre* 7 (1985): 107–19.

Mukherji, Subha and Raphael Lyne, eds. *Early Modern Tragicomedy*. Woodbridge: D.S. Brewer, 2007.

Münz-Manor, Ophir. "Liturgical Poetry in the Late Antique Near East: A Comparative Approach." *Journal of Ancient Judaism* 1 (2010): 336–61.

Murakami, Ineke. *Moral Play and Counterpublic: Transformations in Moral Drama, 1465–1599*. New York: Routledge, 2011.

Murdoch, Brian. *Adam's Grace: Fall and Redemption in Medieval Literature*. Cambridge: D.S. Brewer, 2000.

Murdoch, Brian. *The Apocryphal Adam and Eve in Medieval Europe: Vernacular Translations and Adaptations of the* Vita Adae et Evae. Oxford: Oxford University Press, 2009.

Murdoch, Brian. "The Cornish Medieval Drama." In *The Cambridge Companion to Medieval English Theatre*, edited by Richard Beadle, 211–39. Cambridge: Cambridge University Press, 1994.

Murphy, James J. *A Synoptic History of Classical Rhetoric*. New York: Random House, 1972.

Murphy, James J. *Rhetoric in the Middle Ages: A History of Rhetorical Theory from Saint Augustine to the Renaissance*. 1974. Reprint, Berkeley: University of California Press, 1981.

Murray, Alexander. *Suicide in the Middle Ages*, vol. 1, *The Violent Against Themselves*. Oxford: Oxford University Press, 1998.

Mystère des Actes des Apôtres représenté à Bourges en avril 1536. Edited by Auguste-Théodore de Girardot. Paris: Librairie archéologique Victor Didron, 1854.

Les Mystères de la procession de Lille, vols. 1–4. Edited by Alan E. Knight. Geneva: Droz, 2001–7.

Nahshon, Edna. *Jews and Theatre in an Intercultural Context*. Leiden, Brill, 2012.

Narducci, Emanuele. "Pompeo in Cielo (Pharsalia IX 1–24; 186–217), Un Verso Di Dante (Parad. XXII 135) e Il Senso Delle Allusioni a Lucano in Due Epigrammi Di Marziale (IX 34; XI 5)." *Museum Helveticum* 58 (2001).

Nauta, Lodi. "The Scholastic Context of the Boethius Commentary by Nicholas Trevet." In *Boethius in the Middle Ages: Latin and Vernacular Traditions of the* Consolatio Philosophiae, edited by M.J.F.M. Hoenen and L. Nauta, 41–67. Leiden: Brill, 1997.

Neal, Derek. *The Masculine Self in Late Medieval England*. Chicago: University of Chicago Press, 2008.

Netzer, Ehud. *The Architecture of Herod, the Great Builder*. Tübingen: Mohr Siebeck, 1996.

Nicene and Post-Nicene Fathers. First Series. 14 vols. Reprint, Grand Rapids: Eerdmans, 1978–9; Second Series. 14 vols. Reprint, Grand Rapids, Eerdmans, 1983.

Nietzsche, Friedrich. *The Birth of Tragedy and the Genealogy of Morals*. Translated by Francis Golffing. Garden City, NY: Doubleday, 1956.

Nietzsche, Friedrich. *The Birth of Tragedy out of the Spirit of Music*. Translated by Shaun Whiteside. New York: Penguin, 1993.

Nietzsche, Friedrich. *On the Genealogy of Morals and Ecce Homo*. Translated by Walter Kaufmann. New York: Vintage, 1989.

Nagler, A.M. *A Source Book in Theatrical History*. 1952; rpt. New York: Dover, 1959.

Nirenberg, David. *Communities of Violence: Persecution of Minorities in the Middle Ages*. Princeton: Princeton University Press, 1996.

Noah's Flood. In *"Everyman" and Other Miracle and Morality Plays*, edited by Candace Ward, 1–11. New York: Dover, 1995.

Nolan, Maura B. "The Art of History Writing: Lydgate's Serpent of Division." *Speculum* 78 (2003): 99–127.

Normington, Katie. *Gender and Medieval Drama*. Woodbridge, Suffolk: D.S. Brewer, 2004.

Normington, Katie. *Medieval English Drama: Performance and Spectatorship*. Cambridge: Polity Press, 2009.

Norton-Smith, John. "Chaucer's Boethius and 'Fortune.'" *Reading Medieval Studies* 2 (1976): 63.

The N-Town Play: Cotton MS Vespasian D. 8. Edited by Stephen Spector. 2 vols. Oxford: Oxford University Press, 1991.

Novikoff, A.J. *The Medieval Culture of Disputation: Pedagogy, Practice, and Performance*. Philadelphia: University of Pennsylvania Press, 2013.

O'Daly, Gerard. *Days Linked by Song: Prudentius'* Cathemerinon. Oxford: Oxford University Press, 2012.

Ogden, Dunbar H. *The Staging of Drama in the Medieval Church*. Newark, DE: University of Delaware Press, 2002.

O'Hogan, Cillian. *Prudentius and the Landscapes of Late Antiquity*. Oxford: Oxford University Press, 2016.

Olson, Kristina. *Courtesy Lost: Dante, Boccaccio, and the Literature of History*. Toronto: University of Toronto Press, 2014.

Olson, Glending. "Interpretations." In *A Cultural History of Theatre in the Middle Ages*, edited by Jody Enders, vol. 2 of *The Cultural History of Theatre*, edited by Christopher B. Balme and Tracy C. Davis, 123–44. London and New York: Bloomsbury, 2017.

Olson, Glending. *Literature as Recreation in the Later Middle Ages*. Ithaca: Cornell University Press, 1982.

Olson, Glending. "The Medieval Fortunes of 'Theatrica.'" *Traditio* 4 (1986): 265–86.

Olson, Glending. "Plays as Play: A Medieval Ethical Theory of Performance and the Intellectual Context of the *Tretise of Miraclis Pleyinge*." *Viator* 26 (1995): 195–221.

Olympiodorus. *Olympiodori in Platonis Gorgiam commentaria*. Leipzig: Walter de Gruyter, 1970.

Olympiodorus. *Life of Plato and On Plato First Alcibiades 1–9*. Translated by Michael J. Griffin. London: Bloomsbury, 2015.

O'Meara, Dominic J. "The Music of Philosophy in Late Antiquity." In *Philosophy and the Sciences in Antiquity*, edited by Robert W. Sharples, 131–47. Farnham: Ashgate Publishing, 2005.

Orlemanski, Julie. "Genre." In *A Handbook of Middle English Studies*, edited by M. Turner, 207–21. Chichester: Wiley-Blackwell, 2013.

Otto of Friesling. *The Two Cities: A Chronicle of Universal History to the Year 1146 A.D*. Edited by Austin P. Evans, Charles Knapp, and Charles Christopher Mierow. ACLS Humanities E-Book. New York: Octagon Books, 1966.

Page, Denys L. *Actors' Interpolations in Greek Tragedy, Studied with Special Reference to Euripides'* Iphigeneia in Aulis. Oxford: Clarendon Press, 1934.

Palma, Marco, ed. *Commento alle* Troades *di Seneca*. Rome: Edizioni di storia e letteratura, 1977.

Palmer, Anne-Marie. *Prudentius and the Martyrs*. Oxford: Clarendon Press, 1989.

Panizza, Laetizia A. "Biography in Italy from the Middle Ages to the Renaissance: Seneca, Pagan or Christian?" *Nouvelles de la république des lettres* 2 (1984): 47–98.

Papaioannou, Stratis. "Letter-Writing." In *The Byzantine World*, edited by Paul Stephenson, 188–99. London and New York: Routledge, 2010.

Papio, Michael. "On Seneca, Mussato, Trevet, and the Boethian 'Tragedies' of the *De casibus*." *Heliotropia* 10(2013): 47–63.

Pappano, M.A. "Sister Acts: Conventual Performance and the *Visitatio Sepulchri* in England and France." In *Medieval Constructions in Gender and Identity: Essays in Honor of Joan M.*

Ferrante, edited by T. Barolini. Tempe, AZ: Arizona Center for Medieval and Renaissance Studies, 2005.

Parisi, Giovanni. *La prima dimora di S. Paolo in Roma*. Torino: Casa Editrice Carteggio, 1959.

Parker, John. *The Aesthetics of Antichrist: From Christian Drama to Christopher Marlowe*. Ithaca, NY: Cornell University Press, 2007.

Parker, John. "Persona." In *Cultural Reformations: Medieval and Renaissance in Literary History*, edited by Brian Cummings and James Simpson, 591–608. Oxford: Oxford University Press, 2010.

Parker, John. "Who's Afraid of Darwin? Revisiting Chambers and Hardison . . . and Nietzsche." *Journal of Medieval and Early Modern Studies* 40 (2010): 7–35.

Parsons, Ben, and Bas Jongenelen. *Comic Drama in the Low Countries, c. 1450–1560: A Critical Anthology*. Cambridge: D.S. Brewer, 2012.

Paschasius Radbertus. *Corpus Christianorum Series Latina, 56, Expositio in Matthaeo. Libri XII*. Edited by Beda Paulus. Turnhout: Brepols, 1984.

The Passion of Perpetua and Felicity. Edited by T.J. Heffernan. Oxford: Oxford University Press, 2012.

Patch, Howard Rollin. *The Tradition of Boethius: A Study of His Importance in Medieval Culture*. New York: Oxford University Press, 1935.

Patch, Howard Rollin. *The Tradition of the Goddess Fortuna in Medieval Philosophy and Literature*. Northampton: Smith College, 1922.

Patrologiae Cursus Completus, Series Graeca. Edited by J-P. Migne. 161 vols. Paris: Garnier, 1857–66.

Patrologia Cursus Completus, Series Latina. Edited by J-P. Migne. 221 vols. Paris, 1844–64.

Patrologia Latina Database. In *Patrologiae cursus completus: series Latina*, edited by Jacques-Paul Migne et al. Paris: 1879–90.

Perfetti, Lisa. *Women and Laughter in Medieval Comic Literature*. Ann Arbor: University of Michigan Press, 2003.

Perry, Curtis, and John Watkins, eds. *Shakespeare and the Middle Ages*. Oxford: Oxford University Press, 2009.

Pensom, Roger. "Histoire et poésie dans la *Chanson de Roland*." *Romania* 113 (1992): 373–382.

Pensom, Roger. *Literary Technique in the Chanson de Roland*. Geneva: Droz, 1982.

Peter of Blois. *Liber de Confessione Sacramentali*. In *Patrologia Latina*, edited by Jacques-Paul Migne, vol. 207. Paris: 1855.

Petit de Julleville, L. *Histoire du théâtre en France*, vol. 1, *Les Mystères*. 1880. Reprint, Geneva: Slatkine, 1968.

Plato. *Minos, Leges, Epinomis, Epistulae, Definitiones*. Oxford: Clarendon Press, 1922.

Plato. *Laws*. Edited and translated by R.G. Bury. 2 vols. 1926. Reprint, Cambridge: Harvard University Press, 1942.

Plato. *Res Publica*. Oxford: Clarendon Press, 1965.

Plato. *Theaetetus*. Translated by Francis MacDonald Cornford. 1957. Reprint, Indianapolis: Bobbs-Merrill, 1977.

Pliny, the Elder. *Pliny: Natural History*, vol. 10. Translated by D.E. Eichholz. Cambridge: Harvard University Press, 1962.

Poole, Adrian. *Tragedy: A Very Short Introduction*. Oxford: Oxford University Press, 2005.

Pordage, Samuel. *Herod and Mariamne: A Tragedy*. London: 1673.

Potter, David. "Martyrdom and Spectacle." In *Theater and Society in the Classical World*. Edited by Ruth Scodel, 53–88. Ann Arbor: University of Michigan, 1993.

Preminger, Alex, O.B. Hardison, Jr., and Kevin Kerrane, eds. *Classical and Medieval Literary Criticism: Translations and Interpretations*. New York: Ungar, 1974.

Pratt, Karen. "Aristotle, Augustine or Boethius? La Mort Le Roi Artur as Tragedy." *Nottingham French Studies* 30(1991): 81–109.

Proclus. *Procli Diadochi in Platonis rem publicam commentarii*, Amsterdam: Hakkert, 1965.

Prokopios. *The Secret History with Related Texts*. Edited and translated by A. Kaldellis. Indianapolis: Hackett Publishing Co., 2010.

Prudentius. *Cathemerinon*. In *Prudentius*, translated by H.J. Thomson. 2 vols. Cambridge: Cambridge University Press, 1949.

Prudentius. *Liber Peristephanon*. In *Prudentius*, translated by H.J. Thomson. 2 vols. Cambridge: Cambridge University Press, 1949.

Psellus, Michael. *The Essays on Euripides and George of Pisidia and on Heliodorus and Achilles Tatius*. Edited by Andrew R. Dyck and Herbert Huger. Wien: Verlag der Österreichischen Akademie der Wissenschaften, 1986.

Pulci, Antonia. *Florentine Drama for Convent and Festival: Seven Sacred Plays*. Edited by James Wyatt Cook and Barbara Collier Cook, translated by James Wyatt Cook. Chicago: University of Chicago Press, 1996.

Raphael, D.D. *The Paradox of Tragedy: The Marlon Powell Lectures*. Bloomington: Indiana University Press, 1960.

Rayner, Alice. *To Do, to Act, to Perform: Drama and the Phenomenology of Action*. Ann Arbor: University of Michigan Press, 1994.

Reed, Roland. "The Slaughter of the Innocents." *Early Theatre* 3 (2000): 219–28.

Regalado, Nancy F. "Fauvel, Livre De." In *Medieval France: An Encyclopedia*, edited by William W. Kibler. New York: Garland, 1995.

Revermann, Martin. *Comic Business: Theatricality, Comic Technique, and Performance Contexts of Aristophanic Comedy*. Oxford: Oxford University Press, 2006.

Revermann, Martin. "Situating the Gaze of the Recipient(s): Theatre-Related Vase Paintings and Their Contexts of Reception." In *Beyond the Fifth Century: Interactions with Greek Tragedy from the Fourth Century BCE to the Middle Ages*, edited by Ingo Gildenhard and Martin Revermann, 69–97. Berlin: De Gruyter, 2010.

Rey-Flaud, Henri. *Le Cercle magique: Essai sur le théâtre en rond à la fin du Moyen Age*. Paris: Bibliothèque des Idées, 1973.

Richards, I.A. *Principles of Literary Criticism*. London: Kegan Paul, 1924.

Rice, Nicole R., and Margaret Aziza Pappano. *The Civic Cycles: Artisan Drama and Identity in Premodern England*. Notre Dame: University of Notre Dame Press, 2015.

Ristine, Frank Humphrey. *English Tragicomedy: Its Origin and History*. New York: Columbia University Press, 1910.

Roberti, Luciana, ed. *Commento alla* Medea *di Seneca*. Bari: Edipuglia, 2004.

Roberts, Michael. *Poetry and the Cult of the Martyrs: The Liber Peristephanon of Prudentius*. Ann Arbor: University of Michigan, 1993.

Robertson, D.W., Jr. *A Preface to Chaucer: Studies in Medieval Perspectives*. Princeton: Princeton University Press, 1962.

Rodríguez Porto, Rosa María. "Greek Tragedy in Medieval Art." In *The Encyclopedia of Greek Tragedy*, edited by Hanna M. Roisman, 627–36. 2 vols. West Sussex: Wiley-Blackwell, 2014.

Rokem, Freddie. "The Ludic Logic of Tragedy." *Performance Research* 21 (2016): 26–33.

Ros, Karen E. "The Roman Theater at Carthage." *American Journal of Archaeology* 100 (1996): 449–89.

Rosenwein, Barbara H. *Emotional Communities in the Early Middle Ages*. Ithaca: Cornell University Press, 2006.

Roth, Norman. "Ibn 'Akhnin—Biographical Details." In *Medieval Jewish Civilization: An Encyclopedia*, edited by Norman Roth, 344–5. New York: Routledge, 2003.

Rouse, Richard, and Albinia de la Mare. "New Light on the Circulation of the A-Text of Seneca's Tragedies." *Journal of the Warburg and Courtland Institutes* 40 (1977): 283–90.

Roy, Émile. *Le Mystère de la Passion en France du XIVe au XVIe siècle: Etude sur les sources et le classement des mystères de la Passion*. Dijon and Paris: Damidot Frères and Champion, 1904.

Rubin, Miri. *Corpus Christi: The Eucharist in Late Medieval Culture*. Cambridge: Cambridge University Press, 1991.

Rubin, Miri. *Gentile Tales: The Narrative Assault on Late Medieval Jews*. New Haven, CT: Yale University Press, 1999.

Rupert of Deutz. *Corpus Christianorum Continuatio Medievalis*, 21, *De sancta trinitate et operibus eius I*. Edited by H. Haack. Turnhout: Brepols, 1971.

Russell, Willy. *Educating Rita*. Edited by Suzy Graham-Adriani. London: Longman, 1991.

Rutebeuf. *Le Miracle de Théophile*. In *Jeux et sapience du Moyen Âge*, edited by Albert Pauphilet, 135–58. Paris: Gallimard, 1951. Published in translation in *Medieval French Plays*, translated by Richard Axton and John Stevens. Oxford, UK: Basil Blackwell, 1971.

Ryan, Denise Ryan. "Womanly Weaponry: Language and Power in the Chester *Slaughter of the Innocents*." *Studies in Philology* 98 (2001): 76–92.

Sacks, Oliver. *Musicophilia: Tales of Music and the Brain*. London: Picador, 2007.

Sánchez de Badajoz, Diego. *Recopilación en metro*. Reproduced in facsimile for La Academia Española. 1554. Madrid: Tipografía de Archivos, 1929.

Saltzstein, Jennifer. "Cleric-Trouvères and the Jeux-Partis of Medieval Arras." *Viator* 43 (2012): 147–63.

Scarborough, Connie L. "Gallows Humor in the *Tragicomedia de Calisto y Melibea*." In *Death in the Middle Ages and Early Modern Time: The Material and Spiritual Conditions of the Culture of Death*, edited by Albrecht Classen and Marilyn Sandidge, 357–72. Berlin: Walter De Gruyter, 2016.

Scattergood, V.J. *Politics and Poetry in the Fifteenth Century, 1399–1485*. London: Blandford, 1971.

Schechner, Richard. *Performance Studies: An Introduction*, 3rd edn. 2002. Reprint, New York, Routledge, 2013.

Scherb, Victor. *Staging Faith: East Anglian Drama in the Later Middle Ages*. Danvers, MA: Rosemont Publishing, 2001.

Schiller, Friedrich. *Sämtliche Werke*, vol. 2, *Die Jungfrau von Orleans*, 687–812. 5 vols. Munich: Carl Hanser Verlag, 1981.

Schmidt, Dennis. *On Germans and Other Greeks: Tragedy and Ethical Life*. Bloomington: Indiana University Press, 2001.

Schmitt, Jean-Claude, and Jacques Le Goff. *Le Charivari: Actes de la table ronde organisée à Paris, 25–27 avril 1977 par l'Ecole des hautes études en sciences sociales et le Centre national de la recherche scientifique*. Civilisations et sociétés; 67. Paris: Mouton, 1981.

Schmidt, Peter Lebrecht. "Rezeption und Überlieferung der Tragödien Senecas bis zum Ausgang des Mittelalters." In *Der Einfluss Senecas auf das Europäische Drama*, edited by Eckard Lefèvre, 12–73. Darmstadt: Wissenschaftliche Buchgesellschaft, 1978.

Schubert, Werner. "Seneca the Dramatist." In *Brill's Companion to Seneca: Philosopher and Dramatist*, edited by Andreas Heil and Gregor Damschen, 73–96. Leiden: Brill, 2013.

Schultze, Clemence. "Making a Spectacle of Oneself: Pliny on Curio's Theatre." In *Vita Vigilia Est: Essays in Honor of Barbara Levick*, edited by Edward Bispham et al., 127–46. London: Institute of Classical Studies, School of Advanced Studies, University of London, 2007.

Sear, Frank. *Roman Theatres: An Architectural Study*. Oxford: Oxford University Press, 2006.

Seow, Choon-Leong. "History of Consequences: The Case of Gregory's Moralia in Job." *Hebrew Bible and Ancient Israel* 1 (2012): 368–387.

Sebastian, John. "Introduction." In *Croxton Play of the Sacrament*, edited by John Sebastian. Kalamazoo, MI: Medieval Institute Publications, 2012.

Sébillet, Thomas. *Art Poétique françoys (1548)*. Edited by Félix Gaiffe. Paris: Edouard Cornély, 1910.

The Second Shepherd's Play. In *"Everyman" and Other Miracle and Morality Plays*, edited by Candace Ward, 12–35. New York: Dover, 1995.

Segal, Arthur. *Theatres in Roman Palestine and Provincia Arabia*. Leiden: Brill, 1995.

Seneca. *De providentia* 4.1. In *Seneca: Moral Essays*. Translated by John W. Basore. Vol. 1. Cambridge: Harvard University Press, 1928.

Seneca. *Epistolae Senecae ad Paulum et Pauli ad Senecam*. Edited and translated by Claude W. Barlow. Horn: for the American Academy in Rome by F. Berger, 1938.

Seneca. *Epistles*. Translated by Richard M. Gummere. 3 vols. Cambridge: Harvard University Press, 1917–25.

Seneca. *Tragedies*. Edited and translated by J.G. Fitch. Cambridge: Harvard University Press, 2002.

Shaughnessy, Nicola. *Applying Performance: Live Art, Socially Engaged Theatre and Affective Practice*. New York: Palgrave Macmillan, 2012.

Sheppard, Ann. "Music Therapy in Neoplatonism." In *Philosophy and the Sciences in Antiquity*, edited by Robert W. Sharples, 148–55. Farnham: Ashgate Publishing, 2005.

Sheingorn, P. "The Virtues of Hildegard's *Ordo Virtutum*, It Was a Woman's World." In *The "Ordo Virtutum" of Hildegard of Bingen: Critical Studies*, ed. A.E. Davidson, 43–62. Kalamazoo, MI: Medieval Institute Publications, 1992.

Shergold, N.D. *A History of the Spanish Stage from Medieval Times until the End of the Seventeenth Century*. Oxford: Clarendon Press, 1967.

Sidhu, Nicole Nolan. *Indecent Exposure: Gender, Politics, and Obscene Comedy in Middle English Literature*. Philadelphia: University of Pennsylvania Press, 2016.

Simon, Eckehard, ed. *The Theatre of Medieval Europe: New Research in Early Drama*. Cambridge: Cambridge University Press, 1991.

Simon, Marcel. *Hercule et le christianisme*. Paris: Belles Lettres, 1955.

Simpson, James. *Reform and Cultural Revolution: The Oxford English Literary History*, vol. 2, 1350–1547. Oxford: Oxford University Press, 2002.

Sixt, G. "Des Prudentius Abhängikeit von Seneca und Lucan." *Philologus: Zeitschrift für das classische Alterthum* 51, no. 5 (1892): 501–06.

Skoda, Hannah. "Anger in Inferno and Purgatorio." In *Dante and the Seven Deadly Sins: Twelve Literary and Historical Essays*, edited by John C. Barnes and Daragh O'Connell, 125–50. Dublin: Four Courts Press, 2017.

Skoda, Hannah. "Differentiation or Destruction ? The Effects of War on Human and Social Bodies in Dante's *Commedia*." In *War and Peace in Dante*, edited by J. Barnes and D. O'Connell. Dublin: Four Courts Press, 2015.

Skoda, Hannah. *Medieval Violence: Physical Brutality in Northern France (1270–1330)*. Oxford: Oxford University Press, 2015.

Slater, William J. "Problems in Interpreting Scholia on Greek Texts." In *Roman Theatre and Society: E. Togo Salmon Papers I*, edited by W.J. Slater, 37–61. Ann Arbor: University of Michigan Press, 1996.

Slater, William J. ed. *Roman Theatre and Society: E. Togo Salmon Papers I*. Ann Arbor: University of Michigan Press, 1996.

Smalley, Beryl. *English Friars and Antiquity in the Fourteenth Century*. New York: Barnes and Noble, 1960.

Smallwood, E. Mary. *The Jews under Roman Rule: from Pompey to Diocletian*. Leiden: Brill, 1976.

Solga, Kim. "Rape's Metatheatrical Return: Rehearsing Sexual Violence Among the Early Moderns." *Theatre Journal* 58 (2006): 53–72.

[*Song of Roland.*] La Chanson de Roland: *An Analytical Edition*. Edited by Gerard J. Brault. 2 vols. University Park, PA: Pennsylvania State University Press, 1978.

Sourvinou-Inwood, Christiane. "Greek Tragedy and Ritual." In *A Companion to Tragedy*, edited by Rebecca Bushnell, 7–24. Malden, MA: Blackwell, 2005.

Southern, Richard. "Aspects of the European Tradition of Historical Writing, I: The Classical Tradition from Einhard to Geoffrey of Monmouth." *Transactions of the Royal Historical Society* 20 (1970): 173–96.

Sponsler, Claire. "Circulation: A Peripatetic Theatre." In *A Cultural History of Theatre*, edited by Christopher B. Balme and Tracy C. David, vol. 2, *A Cultural History of Theatre in the Middle Ages*, edited by Jody Enders, 105–21. London: Bloomsbury, 2017.

Sponsler, Claire. *Drama and Resistance: Bodies, Goods, and Theatricality in Late Medieval England*. Minneapolis: University of Minnesota Press, 1997.

Sponsler, Claire. "Narrating the Social Order: Medieval Clothing Laws." *CLIO* 21 (1992): 265–83.

Sponsler, Claire. *The Queen's Dumbshows: John Lydgate and the Making of Early Theater*. Philadelphia: University of Pennsylvania Press, 2014.

Sponsler, Claire. *Ritual Imports: Performing Medieval Drama in America*. Ithaca: Cornell University Press, 2004.

Sponsler, Claire, and Xiaomei Chen, eds. *East of West: Cross-Cultural Performance and the Staging of Difference*. New York and Basingstoke: Palgrave MacMillan, 2000.

Staines, David. "To Out-Herod Herod." *Comparative Drama* 10 (1976): 29–53.

States, Bert O. *The Pleasure of the Play*. Ithaca: Cornell University Press, 1994.

Steinberg, Justin. *Dante and the Limits of the Law*. Chicago: University of Chicago Press, 2013.

Steiner, George. *The Death of Tragedy*. New York: Knopf, 1961.

Stern, Charlotte. *The Medieval Theater in Castile*. Binghamton: SUNY Press, 1996.

Stern, Tiffany. *Documents of Performance in Early Modern England*. Cambridge: Cambridge University Press, 2009.

Stevens, John E. *Words and Music in the Middle Ages: Song, Narrative, Dance, and Drama, 1050–1350*. Cambridge: Cambridge University Press, 1986.

Stevens, Martin, and A.C. Cawley, eds. *The Towneley Plays*. 2 vols. Oxford: Oxford University Press, 1994.

Sticca, Sandro. "The Hagiographical and Monastic Context of Hrotswitha's Plays." In *Hrotsvit of Gandersheim: Rara avis in Saxonia?*, edited by Katharina Wilson, 1–34. Ann Arbor: Marc Publishing, 1987.

Sticca, Sandro. "Italy: Liturgy and Christocentric Spirituality." In *The Theatre of Medieval Europe: New Research in Early Drama*, edited by Eckehard Simon, 169–88. Cambridge: Cambridge University Press, 1991.

Stock, Brian. *Listening for the Text: On the Uses of the Past*. Baltimore: Johns Hopkins University Press, 1990.
Stone, Donald, ed. *Four Renaissance Tragedies*. Cambridge, MA: Harvard University Press, 1996.
Stone, Donald. *French Humanist Tragedy: A Reassessment*. Manchester: Manchester University Press, 1974.
Strayer, Joseph R. *The Reign of Philip the Fair*. Princeton: Princeton University Press, 1980.
Strong, Patrick, and Felicity Strong. "The Last Will and Codicils of Henry V." *The English Historical Review* 96 (1981): 79–102.
Sturges, Robert S. *The Circulation of Power in Medieval Biblical Drama*. NY: Palgrave Macmillan, 2015.
Struve, Tilman. *Die Entwicklung der organologischen Staatsauffassung im Mittelalter*. 1. Aufl. Monographien zur Geschichte des Mittelalters, Bd. 16. Stuttgart: Hiersemann, 1978.
Suetonius. *De vita Caesarum*. In *Suetonius*, vol. 1, translated by J.C. Rolfe. Cambridge, MA: Harvard University Press, 1998.
Swartz, Michael D., and Joseph Yahalom, trans. and ed. *Avodah: Ancient Poems for Yom Kippur*. University Park, PA: Penn State Library of Jewish Literature, 2013.
Symes, Carol. "Ancient Drama in the Medieval World." In *A Handbook to the Reception of Greek Drama*, edited by Betine van Zyl Smit, 97–130. Hoboken, NJ: Wiley-Blackwell, 2016.
Symes, Carol. *A Common Stage: Theater and Public Life in Medieval Arras*. Ithaca, NY: Cornell University Press, 2007.
Symes, Carol. "Knowledge Transmission: Media and Memory." In *A Cultural History of Theatre*, edited by Christopher B Balme and Tracy C. David, vol. 2, *A Cultural History of Theatre in the Middle Ages*, edited by Jody Enders, 199–211. London: Bloomsbury, 2017.
Symes, Carol. "The Medieval Archive and the History of Theatre: Assessing the Written and Unwritten Evidence for Premodern Performance." *Theatre Survey* 52 (2011): 1–30.
Symes, Carol. "The Performance and Preservation of Medieval Latin Comedy." *European Medieval Drama* 7 (2003): 29–50.
Symes, Carol, ed. *The Play of Adam (Ordo representacionis Ade)*. In *The Broadview Anthology of Medieval Drama*, edited by C.M. Fitzgerald and J.T. Sebastian, 23–67. Peterborough: Broadview Press, 2013.
Symes, Carol. "The Tragedy of the Middle Ages." In *Beyond the Fifth Century: Interactions with Greek Tragedy from the Fourth Century BCE to the Middle Ages*, edited by Ingo Gildenhard and Martin Revermann, 335–69. Berlin; New York: de Gruyter, 2010.
Tanon, L. *Histoire des Justices des anciennes églises et communautés monastiques de Paris*. Paris: Picard, 1883.
Taplin, Oliver. "How Was Athenian Tragedy Played in the Greek West?" In *Theatre Outside Athens: Drama in Greek Sicily and Italy*, edited by Kathryn Bosher, 226–50. Cambridge: Cambridge University Press, 2012.
Taplin, Oliver. *Pots and Plays: Interactions between Tragedy and Greek Vase-Painting of the Fourth Century B.C.* Los Angeles: J. Paul Getty Museum, 2007.
Tarantino, Elisabetta. "Fulvae Harenae: The Reception of an Intertextual Complex in Dante's Inferno." *Classical Receptions Journal* 4 (2012): 90–126.
Terence. *Hecyra*. In *Terence*, vol. 2, edited and translated by John Barsby. Cambridge: Harvard University Press, 2001.
Tertullian. *Ad martyras*. In *Corpus Christianorum* 1:1–8. Translated by Ante-Nicene Fathers 3: 693–96. Turnhout: Brepols, 1954.

Tertullian. *Apology and De spectaculis*. Translated by T.R. Glover. Cambridge: Harvard University Press, 1977.
Tertullian. *De anima*. In *Corpus Christianorum* 2:779–870. Translated by Ante-Nicene Fathers. 3:181–235. Turnhout: Brepols, 1973.
Tertullian. *De spectaculis*. In *Corpus Christianorum Series Latina*, 1. Turnhout: Brepols, 1954.
Tertullian. *De spectaculis*. In *Tertullian: Apology, De Spectaculis; Minucius Felix*, translated by T.R. Glover and Gerald H. Rendall. Cambridge: Harvard University Press, 1931.
Tertullian. *De Virginibus Velandis*. Ed. E. Dekkers. In *Opera*, Corpus Christianorum, Series Latina 1. Turnhout: Brepols, 1954.
Thérèse de l'Enfant-Jésus et de la Sainte-Face (Sainte). *Histoire d'une âme: Manuscrits autobiographiques*. Paris: Editions du Cerf et Desclée De Brouwer, 1972.
Thérèse de l'Enfant-Jésus et de la Sainte-Face (Sainte). *Jeanne d'Arc accomplissant sa Mission*. In *Théâtre au Carmel: recréations pieuses*, edited by G. Gaucher. Paris: CERF, 1985.
Thomas, A. "Le Théâtre à Paris et aux environs." *Romania* 21 (1892): 606–12.
Thomas, Rosalind. *Oral Tradition and Written Record in Classical Athens*. Cambridge: Cambridge University Press, 1989.
Tinkle, Theresa. "Saturn of the Several Faces: A Survey of the Medieval Mythographic Traditions." *Viator: Medieval and Renaissance Studies* 18 (1987): 289–307.
Tissier, André, trans. *Farces françaises de la fin du Moyen Âge*. 4 vols. Geneva: Droz, 1999.
Tissier, André, ed. *Recueil de farces (1450–1550)*. 13 vols. Geneva: Droz, 1986–2000.
Todisco, Luigi. "Myth and Tragedy: Red-Figure Pottery and Verbal Communication in Central and Northern Apulia in the Later Fourth-Century BC," translated by Thomas Simpson. In *Theatre Outside Athens: Drama in Greek Sicily and Italy*, edited by Kathryn Bosher, 251–71. Cambridge: Cambridge University Press, 2012.
Tolmie, Jane. "Spinning Women and Manly Soldiers: Grief and Game in the English Massacre Plays." In *Laments for the Lost in Medieval Literature*, edited by Jane Tolmie and M.J. Toswell, 283–98. Turnhout: Brepols, 2010.
Three Florentine Sacre Rappresentazioni: Texts and Translations. Trans. Michael O'Connell. Tempe, AZ: Arizona Center for Medieval and Renaissance Studies, 2011.
A Tretise of Miraclis Pleyinge. Edited by Clifford Davidson. Kalamazoo, MI: Medieval Institute Publications, 1993.
Trexler, Richard C. *Reliving Golgotha: The Passion Play of Iztapalapa*. Cambridge, MA: Harvard University Press, 2003.
Trible, Phyllis. *Texts of Terror: Literary-Feminist Readings of Biblical Narratives*. Philadelphia: Fortress Press, 1984.
Trillitzsch, Winfried. *Seneca im Literarischen Urteil der Antike: Darstellung und Sammlung der Zeugnisse*. 2 vols. Amsterdam: Adolf M. Hakkert, 1971.
Trillitzsch, Winifried. "Seneca tragicus—Nachleben und Beurteilung im lateinischen Mittelalter von der Spätantike bis zum Renaissancehumanismus." *Philologus: Zeitschrift für klassische Philologie* 122.1 (1978): 120–36
Tullier, André, ed. and trans. *La Passion du Christ*, Paris: Editions du Cerf, 1969.
Turyn, Alexander. *The Byzantine Manuscript Tradition of the Tragedies of Euripides*. Urbana: University of Illinois Press, 1957.
Tydeman, William, ed. *Theatre in Europe: A Documentary History*, vol. 7, *The Medieval European Stage, 500–1550*. Cambridge: Cambridge University Press, 2001.
Tydeman, William. *The Theatre in the Middle Ages: Western European Stage Conditions, c. 800–1576*. Cambridge: Cambridge University Press, 1978.

Tzetzes, Joannes. *Commentarium in Aristophanis Ranas*. Edited by W.J.W. Koster. Groningen: Amsterdam, 1962.

Ussani, Jr., Vicenzo, ed. *Nicolai Treveti Expositio Herculis furentis*. Rome: Athenaeum, 1959.

Vakonakis, Nikolaos. *Das griechische Drama auf dem Weg nach Byzanz: der euripideische cento Christos Paschon*. Tübingen: Narr Verlag, 2011.

Vance, Eugene. "'Le Jeu de La Feuillée' and the Poetics of Charivari." *Modern Language Notes* 100 (1985): 815–28.

Vance, Eugene. *Reading the Song of Roland*. Englewood Cliffs: Prentice-Hall, 1970.

Van Engen, John. *Rupert of Deutz*. Berkeley: University of California Press, 1983.

Van Helden, Albert. *Measuring the Universe: Cosmic Dimensions from Aristarchus to Halley*. Chicago: University of Chicago Press, 1985.

Vernant, Jean-Pierre. *The Origins of Greek Thought*. Ithaca: Cornell University Press, 1982.

Vernant, Jean-Pierre, and P. Vidal-Naquet. *Tragedy and Myth in Ancient Greece*. Translated by J. Lloyd. Brighton: Harvester Press, 1981.

[La Vie de Saint Alexis.] *The Language of the Eleventh-Century* Vie de Saint Alexis: *A Philological Commentary*. Edited and translated by Frede Jensen. Newark, DE: LinguaText, 2003.

de Vigneulles, Philippe. *La Chronique de Philippe de Vigneulles*. Edited by Charles Bruneau. 4 vols. Metz: Société d'histoire d'archéologie de la Lorraine, 1927–33.

de Vigneulles, Philippe. *Gedenkbuch des Metzer Bürgers Philippe von Vigneulles aus den Jahren 1471–1522*. Edited by Heinrich Michelant. 1852. Reprint, Amsterdam: Rodopi, 1968.

Villon, François. *Le Testament*. In *Oeuvres poétiques*. Edited by A. Mary. Paris: Garnier-Flammarion, 1965.

Viollet le Duc, E.L.N., ed. *Ancien Théâtre françois*. 10 vols. Paris: P. Jannet, 1854–57.

de Voragine, Jacobus. *The Golden Legend: Readings on the Saints*. 2 vols. Translated by William Granger Ryan. Princeton: Princeton University Press, 1993.

Wallace, Jennifer. *The Cambridge Introduction to Tragedy*. Cambridge: Cambridge University Press, 2007.

Walpole, A.S. *Early Latin Hymns*. Cambridge: The University Press, 1922.

Walz, Matthew D. "Stoicism as Anesthesia: Philosophy's 'Gentler Remedies' in Boethius's Consolation." *International Philosophical Quarterly* 51 (2011): 501–19.

Warning, Rainer. *The Ambivalences of Medieval Religious Drama*. Translated by Steven Rendall. 1974. Reprint, Palo Alto: Stanford University Press, 2001.

Warning, Rainer. "On the Alterity of Medieval Religious Drama." *NLH* 10 (1979): 265–92.

Wasson, John. "The Morality Play: Ancestor of Elizabethan Drama?" *Comparative Drama* 13 (1979): 210–21.

Wasson, John. "The Secular Saint Plays of the Elizabethan Era." In *The Saint Play in Medieval Europe*. Edited by Clifford Davidson, 241–60. Kalamazoo: Medieval Institute Publications, Western Michigan University Press, 1986.

Watson, Walter. *The Lost Second Book of Aristotle's Poetics*. Chicago: University of Chicago Press, 2012.

Weaver, Elissa B. *Convent Theatre in Early Modern Italy: Spiritual Fun and Learning for Women*. Cambridge: Cambridge University Press, 2002.

Weaver, Elissa B., ed. *Scenes from Italian Convent Life: An Anthology of Convent Theatrical Texts and Contexts*. Ravenna: Longo, 2009.

Weigert, Laura. *French Visual Culture and the Making of Medieval Theatre*. Cambridge: Cambridge University Press, 2015.

Welch, Katherine E. *The Roman Amphitheatre: From its Origins to the Colosseum*. Cambridge: Cambridge University Press 2007.

Wessels, Antje. *Ästhetisierung und ästhetische Erfahrung von Gewalt: Eine Untersuching zu Senecas Tragödien*. Heidelberg: Universitätsverlag Winter, 2014.

West, Martin L. *Ancient Greek Music*. Oxford: Oxford University Press, 1992.

Weyman, Carl. *Beiträge zur Geschichte der christlich-lateinischen Poesie*. Munich: M. Hueber, 1926.

White, Andrew Walker. "Adventures in Recording Technology: The Drama-as-Performance in the Greek East." In *Beyond the Fifth Century: Interactions with Greek Tragedy from the Fourth Century BCE to the Middle Ages*, edited by Ingo Gildenhard and Martin Revermann, 371–96. Berlin: De Gruyter, 2010.

White, Andrew Walker. "The Artifice of Eternity: A Study of Liturgical and Theatrical Practices in Byzantium." Unpublished Ph.D. Dissertation. College Park: University of Maryland, 2006.

White, Hayden. *Metahistory: The Historical Imagination in Nineteenth-Century Europe*. Baltimore: Johns Hopkins University Press, 1973.

Wickham, Chris. *Framing the Early Middle Ages: Europe and the Mediterranean 400–800*. Oxford: Oxford University Press, 2005.

Wickham, Glynne. *The Medieval Theatre*. 3rd edition. Cambridge: Press Syndicate of the University of Cambridge, 1987.

Wiedemann, Thomas. "Das Ende der römischen Gladiatorenspiele." *Nikephoros* 8 (1995): 145–59.

Wiedemann, Thomas. *Gladiators and Emperors*. London: Routledge, 1992.

Weimann, Robert. *Shakespeare and the Popular Tradition in the Theater*. Edited by Robert Schwartz. Baltimore: Johns Hopkins University Press, 1978.

William of Conches. *Corpus Christianorum Continuatio Mediaevalis 158, Opera omnia 2, Glosae super Boetium*. Edited by Lodi Nauta. Turnhout: Brepols, 1999.

Williams, Deanne. *The French Fetish from Chaucer to Shakespeare*. Cambridge: Cambridge University Press, 2004.

Wilson, Eric G. *Greek Papyri*. Princeton: Princeton University Press, 1968.

Wilson, Grace G. "'Amonges othere wordes wyse': The Medieval Seneca and the *Canterbury Tales*." *Chaucer Review* 28 (1993): 135–45.

Wilson, Laurel Ann. "Common Threads: A Reappraisal of Medieval European Sumptuary Law." *The Medieval Globe* 2, no. 2 (2016): article 7. http://scholarworks.wmich.edu/tmg/vol2/iss2/7

Wilson, Peter. "Music." In *A Companion to Greek Tragedy*, edited by Justina Gregory, 183–93. Malden: Blackwell, 2005.

Wilson, Peter J. "Tragic Rhetoric: The Use of Tragedy and the Tragic in the Fourth Century." In *Tragedy and the Tragic: Greek Theatre and Beyond*, edited by Michael S. Silk, 310–31. Oxford: Oxford University Press, 1996.

Winkler, John J., and Froma I. Zeitlin, eds. *Nothing to do with Dionysos? Athenian Drama in its Social Context*. 1990. Reprint, Princeton: Princeton University Press, 1992.

Wistrand, Magnus. "Violence and Entertainment in Seneca the Younger." *Eranos* 88 (1990): 31–46.

Wittman, Richard. "Monuments and Space as Allegory: Town Planning Proposals in Eighteenth-Century Paris." In *Thinking Allegory Otherwise*, edited by Brenda Machosky, 142–60. Palo Alto: Stanford University Press, 2010.

Woolf, Rosemary. *The English Mystery Plays*. 1972. Reprint, Berkeley: University of California Press, 1980.

The York Plays. Edited by Richard Beadle. London: Edward Arnold, 1982.

The York Plays: A Critical Edition of the York Corpus Christi Play as Recorded in British Library Additional MS 35290. Edited by Richard Beadle. 2 vols. Oxford: Oxford University Press, 2009 and 2014.

Young, Karl. *The Drama of the Medieval Church*. 2 vols. Oxford: Clarendon, 1933.

Zanobi, Alessandra. "Seneca and Pantomime." In *Beyond the Fifth Century: Interactions with Greek Tragedy from the Fourth Century BCE to the Middle Ages*, edited by Ingo Gildenhard and Martin Revermann, 269–88. Berlin: De Gruyter, 2010.

Ziolkowski, Jan M. "Laments for Lost Children: Latin Traditions." In *Laments for the Lost in Medieval Literature*, edited by Jane Tolmie and M.J. Toswell, 81–107. Turnhout: Brepols, 2010.

Zumthor, Paul. *Essai de poétique médiévale*. Paris: Seuil, 1972.

Zuntz, Günther. *An Inquiry into the Transmission of the Plays of Euripides*. Cambridge: Cambridge University Press, 1965.

Zwierlein, Otto. *Prolegomena zu einer kritischen Ausgabe der Tragödien Senecas*. Mainz: Akademie der Wissenschaften und der Literatur, 1983.

INDEX

Ab urbe condita (Livy) 51
Abelard, Peter 117
absence, theme of 34–5
absolute space 31
acting out 13
actors/actresses 2, 5–8, 11, 13, 17, 19–20, 25, 36–8, 41, 50, 60, 82, 87–8, 97, 118, 124, 130, 131–2, 133–4
Acts of the Apostles 84
Acts of Paul and Thecla 131
Ad martyras (Tertullian) 83, 98
Ad Mortem Festināmus ("We Hasten Towards Death") 42–3
Adam 51, 57–64, 156n.44, 156n.49, 157n.49
Adam de la Halle, *Jeu de la Feuillée* 36, 107–8
Ælred of Rievaulx 25, 127
Aeneid (Virgil) 67, 108
Aeschylus 2, 72
aesthetics 2, 4–6, 9, 11–13, 15, 97, 114–6, 118–9
    Kantian 114
    of violence 81, 84–7, 89, 91, 96–8
Æthelwold of Winchester 70
affect
    participatory performance and 78
    tragic 44
affective dissonance/stylistics 62
agency, human 140
Agobard of Lyons 24, 150n.66
Al Ghazālī 80
Al-Jurjānī 80
Aldhelm of Malmesbury, "In Praise of Virginity" 21
Alemannus, Hermannus 3, 57, 75
Alexandria, Neo-Platonic school of 68
Alfonso XI of Castile 33
Alighieri, Pietro 57
aljamiado 44
allegorical drama 31, 35
allegory, *Roman de Fauvel* and 108
ambition 103, 108, 119, 123
Ambrose of Milan 20, 130–1, 148n.31
amphitheaters 32–3, 82–6, 87
Anicius, Lucius 82

Anouilh, Jean 1, 3, 8
Antigone (Sophocles) 29
Apamea, Syria 68
Apollodorus, *Hecyra* 82
Apology for Actors (Heywood) 97
applause 18, 23
Aquinas, Thomas 76, 80
Arabic literature 8, 44, 75, 79, 80
    Arabic shadow plays 8, 79, 80
architecture
    Christian 88
    ritual 31
    Roman 32, 33
Aristophanes 22
    Frogs 72
Aristotle (*see also* catharsis)
    cause-and-effect dramaturgy 36
    focus on the individual 115
    philosophy and 66, 67
    Poetics 4–5, 6, 22, 68, 75, 76, 114
    politics and 93, 99, 104
    spectacle and 7
    tragedy and 15, 17
    women, tragedy and 127
Arras 38, 71
ars moriendi 34, 41, 43
art (visual)
    late medieval 40–1
    violence and 91
Arthur 25, 110, 127
artistry 3, 14–15, 20, 36, 80, 82, 90, 97–8
asceticism 25, 94, 95–6
Ashley, Kathleen 66, 76
assimilation, of classical stories/images/ideas 34
astronomers, medieval Christian and Muslim 28
Athanasios of Alexandria 18
Athens
    academies of 18
    Dionysia 17
    tragedy and 20, 21, 69, 127
    women and 127
athlete(s), of Christ 89–94
Attic drama 18, 115 (*see also* Greek drama)

audiences 1–2, 4–5, 8–9, 11–14, 17–18, 20–3, 25, 27–8, 31, 34–5, 38–40, 45, 47, 50–2, 54, 56, 60, 62–3, 72, 77–83, 85, 91, 93, 102–3, 111, 115, 117, 125, 127, 129–130, 135, 156
Augustine of Hippo
  the Apostle Paul and 84
  Confessions 12, 17, 67
  De civitate Dei 51
  the Innocents and 117
  tragedy and 19–20, 31, 49, 67
Augustus, Caesar 92–3
Aurelius, Marcus 85
authority 7, 13, 15, 17–19, 21–2, 52, 57, 60, 70, 75, 83, 91, 113–14, 120, 122–3, 136–137
  cultural and moral 17
avarice 35
Averroës 75, 78
Avodah *piyyut* 70

Bacchae (Euripides) 16–17, 72, 115–16
Bachelard, Gaston 34
"Ballad of Ladies from Yesteryear" (Villon) 138
Basil the Great 20
Basin, Thomas: *History of King Charles VII* 138
Beckwith, Sarah 78–9
Bede the Venerable 20, 28, 148n.32
Bedford, Duke of 109
Belcari, Feo 8
belief, medieval structures of 33
Belsey, Catherine 35
Benjamin, Walter 35, 40
Beowulf 8
Bernard of Clairvaux 117
Berschin, Walter 94
Beunans Meriasek 79
Bible
  Acts of the Apostles 84
  1 Corinthians 84–5
  Ezekiel 23
  Galatians 84
  Genesis 57, 59, 60–1
  Mark 86–7
  Matthew 19–20, 113, 117–18, 125
  New Testament 18
  Old Testament 8, 21, 103, 118
  Philippians 84
  Revelation 118
  scripture 24, 83, 93–4, 135
  Song of Songs 20, 131
  theatrical lamentation and 28
  Timothy 84
biblical drama 38, 63, 113, 115, 116, 118, 120, 124, 156n.49, 176n.55
Boccaccio, Giovanni
  De casibus virorum illustrium 36, 110
  De genealogia deorum gentilium 57
  Nimrod and 105
  Seneca and 57
Boethius, Anicius Manlius Severinus
  Boethian tragedies 74
  De consolatione philosophiae (*Consolation of Philosophy*) 36, 51, 52, 53, 69, 72–4, 75, 76, 100–2, 105, 129
  Hrotsvitha of Gandersheim and 135
  On Music 69
  tragedy and 5, 52, 73, 75
Book of Crowns (*Liber Peristephanon*) (Prudentius) 83, 88–90, 91–2
Bouchet, Jean 5
Boynton, Susan 118
Brook, Peter 34
Brown, Peter 88, 91
Bruno of Cologne 25, 94
Burana, Carmina 36
Burke, Kenneth 5–6, 9
Burns, E. Jane 121
Bushnell, Rebecca 10–11, 118, 125
Byzantine education 22–3, 71
Byzantium. *See* Roman Empire

Cacciaguida 106
Caesar. *See* Julius Caesar
canon law 24, 102
canon (promulgated) 24
canon(s) (literary) 12, 16–17, 24, 49
Canterbury Tales (Chaucer). *See The Miller's Tale*; *The Monk's Tale*
carnival 39, 88, 136
Carrero Santamaría, Eduardo 39
Carthage 19, 32, 151n.13
Cassian, Saint 91, 92
Cassiodorus 20–1, 23–4, 150n.65
Castile 39–40
Castle of Perseverance 28, 29, 31, 35
  stage plan 44–5, 79
Catalonia 39–40
catharsis 9–10, 12, 14, 22, 24, 69, 85
Cathemerinon (Prudentius) 88–9
Catherine, Saint 36
Catholic ritual 87

INDEX

Catholicism 87, 96, 97 (*see also* Roman [Catholic] Church)
Celestina 3
censorship 13
cento 23
champions 24
chant, Gregorian/Jewish/Mozarbic/Visigothic/agontheta 70
chaos, order and 6
charity 7
Charlemagne 24–5, 102
Charles of Valois 107, 108
Charles VII of France 137
Chastity (in *Ordo Virtutem*) 134
chastity, Joan of Arc and 138
Chaucer, Geoffrey
　Canterbury Tales. See The Miller's Tale; The Monk's Tale
　The Miller's Tale 117
　The Monk's Tale 36, 52, 74, 102, 103, 109, 160n.62
　tragedy and 49, 52, 99
　Troilus and Criseyde 52
Chester
　civic religious drama 60
　Drapers of Chester 63
　Goldsmiths' of Chester 119, 120, 121
Chester (mystery) cycle
　Massacre of the Innocents play 116, 118, 119–21, 123–4
　Play of Adam and Eve 60, 63, 156n.49
chivalry 102
chivalric romance 25–6, 110, 127
choral odes 18
choruses
　in church 24
　female 115
　tragic 12, 33, 56, 114, 117
Chrétien de Troyes 25
Christendom
　western and tragedy 16, 23, 26
　western, Roman theaters in 32
Christians/Christianity
　adversity faced by early 17–18, 86
　assimilation of pagan spectacles 88
　birth of from the spirit of tragedy 86–8
　Catholicism 87, 96, 97 (*see also* Roman [Catholic] Church)
　Christian drama 128
　Christian humility 81
　Christian poetry 20, 70
　Christian tragedy 34, 89
　Church Fathers 81, 129–32, 133
　cult of the martyrs 88
　early 18, 86
　Fortune's Wheel and Christian theology 36, 73–4
　Franciscans 23
　funerary rites 44
　Hellenism and 17–18, 22, 71–2
　human suffering and 76, 81, 83, 85–7
　institutionalization of 19
　music and 18, 70–1
　performance and 76
　persecution of 83, 90, 94
　Protestants, Protestantism 96
　rejection of classical culture 65, 93
　Roman (Catholic) Church 18, 21, 24, 25 (*see also* Catholicism; Franciscans)
　the Romans and 33, 49, 82–4, 90
　theater and 18, 135
　tragedy and 9, 10, 11, 21, 67, 68, 69, 76–7, 86–9
　women and 93, 128
Christine de Pizan, *Ditty of Joan of Arc* 137
Christmas 88–9, 116, 117, 118
Christos Paschon (Euripides) 23, 24, 72
Chronicle (Hall) 136–7
Chronicle (Otto of Freising) 101
Chronicle(s) 2, 21
Chrysostom, John 18, 101, 129, 130
Church Fathers 17–18, 129–32, 133
Church, tragedy and the 8, 26 (*see also* Christians/Christianity)
churches, of Catalonia and Castile 39
Le Cid 27
Cistercians 25, 127
civil unrest 21
class 6, 50, 71, 83, 92–3, 115, 127, 139 (*see also* elites)
classical literature 93–4
classicism 11
Clement V, Pope 78
clerics/clergy 18, 24, 25, 26, 71, 93, 116, 127, 128, 132
Cluny 25
Coletti, Theresa 136
comedy
　myth of Christian distaste for 25
　tragedy and 4, 5–8, 20, 27, 116
Commedia (Dante) 105–7
common good 12, 103–4
Communion 24, 77, 91 (*see also* Eucharist; Mass)

communities
    downfall and disintegration of 103–4
    inclusion and exclusion in 76, 92–3
    political 99
    producing and consuming drama 51, 154n.11
    relationship between individual and 109
confession 25, 38, 79
Confessions (Augustine of Hippo) 12, 17, 67
conflict, music and 71
confraternities, *see* guilds
Consolation of Philosophy (Boethius). *See De consolatione philosophiae*
Constantine 33
Constantinople
    fall of 17–18
    Trullan Synod of 22
consumption and production, of medieval drama 51
convent drama 92–6, 128, 138–9
conversion, forced 79
The Conversion of the Harlot Thaïs (Paphnutius) (Hrotsvitha) 132, 133, 135
Coppée, Denis 6
Corbie 21
Corinthians, First Epistle to the 84, 85
Corneille, Pierre 6, 27
Cornwall
    circular arena stages of 31, 79
    Gwreans an bys 157n.49
    open-air amphitheaters 33
    Ordinalia 31, 38, 46–7
    Origo mundi 156n.49
    St Meriasek 79
Corpus Christi cycles 80, 87–8, 135–6
Corpus Christi (Feast) 60, 77, 78
Counter (Catholic) Reformations 24
Coventry Shearmen and Tailors' pageant 121–2, 176n.55
craft guilds, York 60 (*see also* guilds)
Cronica Troyana 33
Croxton *Play of the Sacrament* 8, 34, 35
crucifix, religious symbolism of 36
Crucifixion
    of Jesus Christ 21, 24, 37–8, 86–7
    performances of 78, 86–7
cult of the saints 91
culture(s)
    cultural authority 17
    cultural identity 66, 72
    cultural knowledge 20
    of the Middle Ages 64

pagan. *See* pagan culture
    pre-Christian 52, 53–4
    rejection of classical culture 65
    Roman 49
    tragedy and comedy and 19
    tragedy as a cultural force 66, 68
cuneum 92–3
Curio, C. Scribonius 82
cycle dramas 78, 87–8
Cyprian 129, 131
Cyril of Jerusalem 86

Damian, Peter 94
dance 5, 21, 31, 32, 40, 42–3
Dance of Death (*Totentanz, danse macabre. Dança General de la Muerte*) 31, 40–1, 42, 44
    Castle of Perseverance and 45
Dante Alighieri 3, 26, 67, 70
    Commedia 105–7
    De vulgari eloquentia 75
    Inferno 75, 105–6, 171n.47
    Monarchia 108
Davidson, Clifford 40, 45
Davis, Natalie Zemon 11–12, 135–7
De arte metrica 20
De casibus virorum illustrium (Boccaccio) 36, 110
De civitate Dei (Augustine) 51
De consolatione philosophiae (*Consolation of Philosophy*) (Boethius) 36, 51, 52–3, 69, 72–6, 84, 100–2, 105, 129
De genealogia deorum gentilium (Boccaccio) 57
De regimine principum (Giles of Rome) 104
De spectaculis (Tertullian) 19, 32
De tragoediis (Honorius Augustodunensis) 9
Dean, Ruth J. 53
Death of Herod 40
Death of Tragedy (Steiner) 2
death, spectacle of 81
deception, revelation and 135
Denmark 23
despair 100
deus ex machina 21, 76, 96, 124
Devil 133, 134, 135
devotional drama 13, 16
dialectic 66, 101
"Dialogue on Dramatic Poetry" (Eliot) 6
didactic 16, 31, 35–6, 44, 52, 57, 100, 104–5, 111
Digby Plays 28, 118, 121–2, 175n.47
Dionysus 17, 85

INDEX

Dionysus, festival of (Dionysia) 23, 27, 115
discipline, audience 12–13
dislocation, crises of 27
Ditty of Joan of Arc (de Pizan) 137
Divine Providence 101–2, 105–6, 110
divinity, recognition of 124
domestic violence 1, 7
Donatus, Ælius 19
Dox, Donnalee 19, 34, 52, 76, 78
drama (*see also* theater)
    allegorical drama 31, 35
    ancient tragic 113
    Attic drama 115
    biblical drama 38, 63, 87–8, 113, 115–16, 118, 120, 124, 156n.49, 176n.55
    Christian 128
    civic religious 60
    convent drama 128, 138–9
    cycle dramas 78
    devotional drama 13, 16
    fictitiousness of medieval 96
    liturgical drama 3, 18, 38–9, 117
    medieval 31, 76
    medieval English drama (Middle English drama; medieval English biblical drama) 113, 115, 116, 117, 118, 123
    production and consumption of medieval 51, 154n.11
    sacramental drama 23
    sacred drama 96
    transvestite or cross-dressed theater in 123
    as a treasure-store of key Christian images 80
    vernacular drama 57, 113
Drapers' *Play of Adam and Eve* (Chester) 63
Dronke, Peter 94n.82, 134
duBois, Page 115–16
duel(s) 24
Dupont, Henri 6

Eagleton, Terry 27, 37
East Anglia
    Bury St. Edmunds 57
    circular arena stages of 31
    East Anglian morality plays/saint's plays 30–1, 44–5
    vernacular English play scripts 57
Easter 3, 93
Easter rite. See *Visitatio sepulchri*
Eccerino 3, 7
Eco, Umberto (*The Name of the Rose*) 11
Educating Rita (Russell) 6

education
    Byzantine education 71
    of emotions 66, 67, 68
    sentimental education 66
Egypt 15, 124
Eliot, T. S. 4, 6, 81, 83
elites
    clerical 26
    in the eastern Roman Empire 71
    Greek tragedy and 17
    Latin 19, 20, 83, 93–4
    protecting the manuscripts of tragedies 18
    women 17
emotion(s)
    education of 66, 67, 68
    music and 70
    production of 62
    purification of 69
    reconciliation of conflicting 9
    tragedy and 66, 67, 72, 78, 80, 127
Enders, Jody 27, 76, 77, 87
England
    audience discipline 13
    Cornwall 31, 33, 38, 46–7, 79, 156n.49, 157n.49
    East Anglia 30–1, 44–5, 57
    English literature 28
    English Mary plays 38
    English morality plays 32, 44–5
    London stage 13, 81, 98
    medieval English biblical theater 87–8, 113, 115–16, 117, 118
    medieval English martyr plays 96
    Middle English Innocents plays 115–18, 120, 125
    Old St. Paul's Cathedral 41
    the Senecan renaissance in 96–8
    vernacular drama 57
Enlightenment 114
entertainments, popular 15–16, 18, 40
Erkenwald, Saint 3
eroticism, women and 130–1
Esmoreit 8
Esne, Bishop of 5
ethical responses, to tragedy 101
ethopoiia 22
Etruscus 84
Etymologies (Isidore of Seville) 5, 31, 52
Eucharist (*see also* Communion; Mass)
    classical tragedy and 24
    as performance 77–8
Eumenides 2

Euripides
  Bacchae 16–17, 72, 115–16
  Christos Paschon 23, 24, 72
  Helen 15, 16
  Passion gospel according to 23
  preference for 71–2
  St. Jerome and 19
evangelism 23
Eve 57–61, 63, 156n.49
Everyman (play) 35
Exagoge (Ezekiel of Alexandria) 79
Expulsion from Paradise 57–8, 60–1, 156n.49
external goods 73, 75
Ezekiel, book of 23
Ezekiel of Alexandria, *Exagoge* 79

Fabris, Valentino 54
The Fall and Repentance of Mary (*Abraham*) (Hrotsvitha) 8, 132–3, 134, 135
Fall of Princes (Lydgate) 109, 110
farce 13
Farinata 105–6
Farsa de la Muerte (Sánchez de Badajoz) 40
Farsa del juego de cañas (the Farce of the Game of Canes) (Sánchez de Badajoz) 39–40
Fauvel 107–8
fear 44, 85
Feast of Fools 136
Feast of the Innocents (in liturgy) 116
Felski, Rita 114, 115
feminism, mystery plays (Passion plays) and 135–6
feudal revolution 103
fiction(s) 87, 96, 127
Fish, Stanley 62
Fleury playbook 117–18
Florence 105–6
Foley, Helene 115, 125
Fortuna (goddess) 37, 73, 74
Fortune 100–1, 106
Fortune's Wheel 36–7, 44, 52–3, 73, 79, 100, 107, 109–10, 129
Fourth Lateran Council 24
France
  Arras 38, 71
  audience discipline 13
  early fourteenth century 107
  Hundred Years' War 135–8
  Kermaria-an-Isquit 41
  late eleventh century 103
  morality plays 5
  Paris 2, 8, 51, 71

Franciscans 23
Freculf of Lisieux 21
Frederick II 106–7
Frogs (Aristophanes) 72

Galatians 84
Gallicanus (Hrotsvitha) 94–5
Ganelon 102
Gawain 25
Gemma animae (Jewel of the Soul) 24
gender
  gender identity 120–1
  Massacre plays and 115
  power and 21, 119, 121, 123
Genesis 57, 59, 60–1
genre(s)
  defined 50
  problems of 4, 5–8, 50
  tragedy as 52, 54, 56
Gertsman, Elina 40
Gervais du Bus (*Roman de Fauvel*) 107
Giles of Rome (*De Regimine Principum*) 104
Gilte Legende (Jean de Vignay) 8, 58, 59–60, 61
gladiators 82, 86, 89, 93
God
  Adam and 59, 61, 63, 157n.49
  blood sports and 83
  Christ's suffering and 87
  contemplation of 80
  Joan of Arc and 136–8, 140
  Job and 101
  as man 38
  mercy of 25, 45
  omnipotence of 74
  pleasing of 130
  Thérèse de Lisieux and 139–40
  will of 95
  women and 131, 133–4, 139
Golden Legend (Jacob de Voragine). *See Gilte Legende*
Goldhill, Simon 114
Goldsmiths' of Chester, Massacre of the Innocents play 119, 120–1
Goodland, Katharine 116
Gorgias 68
Gospel of Mark 86, 87
Gospel of Matthew 113, 117, 118, 125
gospels 4, 18–20, 23, 86, 88, 113, 118, 125
Gower, John 109
Grady, Hugh 114
Gratian 24, 150n.67
graves 23, 27, 30, 34, 41, 44, 47
Great Lavra, Orthodox monastery of 22

Gréban, Arnoul 38
   Mystère de la Passion 8
Greek, Attic 18, 115
Greek tragedy 17, 49, 87 (*see also* Athens)
Gregorian chant 70
Gregory of Cappadocia 20
Gregory of Nazianzos 18, 23
Gregory of Tours 20
Gregory the Great, Pope (*Moralia in Job*) 101
Gregory VIII, Pope 57
Guestin, Richard 136
The Guide of the Perplexed (*Moreh Nevuchim*) (Maimonides) 79
guilds 44, 60, 115, 120
Guo, Li 80
Guynn, Noah 85
Gwreans an bys 157n.49

hagiography 3, 6, 8, 13
   masochism of 85
   Roman torture and 95
   saints and 94
Hall, Edith 18, 115
Hall, Edward, *Chronicle* 136–7
Hamilton, Michelle 44
Hamlet (Shakespeare) 23, 30, 97, 117
Harrowing of Hell 8
Hecuba 85
Hecyra (Terence) 82, 95
Hegel, Georg Wilhelm Friedrich 9
Helen (Euripides) 15–16
Hellenism 17–18, 22, 71, 72
Henry of Marcy (Henry of Albano) 57
Henry V of France 109
Hercules furens (Seneca) 33, 54–7, 88
heresy 21, 106
Herod the Great 21, 86, 113, 116–24, 175n.47
heroes/heroines 127, 128, 138
Heywood, Thomas: *Apology for Actors* 97
Hiatt, Alfred 50
Hieronimo 97
Higden, Ranulf 57, 63, 119
high style, tragedy as 75
Hildegard of Bingen 71, 132–5
   The Play of the Virtues (*Ordo Virtutum*) 32, 132, 134–5
Hippolytus, Saint 89–91, 92
historians/history, Jewish 21, 44, 70, 76, 78–9, 86
historiography 8–11
The History of a Soul (Thérèse de Lisieux) 139
History of King Charles VII (Basin) 138
Holcot, Robert 57

Holsinger, Bruce 71, 91
Holy Spirit 83
"Holy Theatre" 34
Homer 20
Honorius Augustodunensis 24–5, 38, 150n.69
   De tragoediis 9
hope 10
Howard, Jean 115, 125
Hoxby, Blair 7, 114
Hrotsvitha (Hrotsvit) of Gandersheim 25, 93–6, 132–5
   The Conversion of the Harlot Thaïs (*Paphnutius*) 132, 133, 135
   The Fall and Repentance of Mary (*Abraham*) 8, 132–3, 134, 135
   Gallicanus 94–6
   Terence and 25, 94, 133
Hugh of Fouilloy 21, 148n.36
humanism 3, 53, 154n.16
humility 94, 135
Hundred Years' War, France 135–8
Hunter, G.K. 97–8
hypocrita, term 20

Iamblichus: *On the Egyptian Mysteries* 68–9
Ibn Dāniyāl, Muhammad 8, 78, 80
Ibn Gabirol, Solomon 70
Ibn Hazm 80
iconoclasm 22, 81
iconography 33, 34, 36, 40, 45–6, 64, 91, 97, 100
icons 22, 76, 78, 84, 91
Ideas and Forms of Tragedy (Kelly) 3, 26
identity(ies)
   Christian 72
   communal 78
   cultural 66, 72
   gender identity 120–1
   Greek 17–18, 22, 72
   performance and 76
   social 124
idolatry 96
Ikaros 22
image-making 79–80
immoral behaviour 67
"In Praise of Virginity" (Aldhelm of Malmesbury) 20–1
inclusion and exclusion, in communities 76
infanticide 2, 4 (*see also* Massacre of the Innocents plays; murder, of children)
Inferno (Dante) 75, 105–6
Isidore of Seville 32, 99, 127, 132
   Etymologies 5, 31, 52

Italy
    Florence 105–6
    humanism in 154n.16
    laudesti 71
    preaching in 23
    Rome 20, 33, 49, 68, 82–4, 88, 93, 94

The Jackass Conjecture 7, 10
Jacob the Deacon 130, 132
Jacobus de Voragine (*Legenda aurea*) 8, 58, 119
Jean de Meun 74
Jean de Vignay (*Gilte Legende*) 8, 58–61
Jerome 19, 23, 83, 84–5, 128–31, 149n.62
Jerusalem 28, 47
Jesus Christ
    Crucifixion of 21, 24, 37–8, 86–9
    death of Herod and 124
    Mary Magdalene and 29
    Passion of 16–17, 23–4, 32, 69, 72
        (*see also* Passion of Christ)
    Peace of 24
    Resurrection of 24, 44, 46–7, 72
    as a scapegoat 37–8
    Sermon on the Mount of 19
    suffering of 16–17, 77, 87
    violence rendered on the body of 16–17, 37, 77–8
Jeu de la Feuillée (Adam de la Halle) 36, 107–8
jeux-partis 71
Jewish Antiquities (Josephus) 119
The Jewish War (Josephus) 21, 119
Jews, Judaism
    anti-Semitism 8, 76
    casting of in a tragic mold 21
    Jewish chants 70
    Jewish funerary rites 44
    Jewish traditions, image-making and 79
    lamentable tragedy of 21
    persecution of 79
    piyyutim 70
    suffering of the Jewish nation 78–9
    theatrical representation and 80, 87
    violence against Christians 21
Joan of Arc 128, 135–8, 140
Joan of Arc Accomplishing Her Mission (Thérèse de Lisieux) 139–40
Job 79, 101
John of Lancaster 137
John of Salisbury 103–5
    Policraticus 35–6, 103, 170n.38

John the Baptist 21
John XXII, Pope 53
Johnston, Alexandra 28
jongleurs 25–6 (*see also* actors; minstrels; singing/song)
Joseph (Genesis 39) 21
Joseph b. Judah ibn' Aqnīn 79
Joseph (husband of Mary) 124
Josephus
    Jewish Antiquities 119
    The Jewish War 21, 119
    lamentable tragedy (*luctuosa tragoedia*) of the Jews 21
journals 23
Judeo-Christian narratives 21
judges 24, 44, 91
Judith (Marko Maruli) 8
Julian the Apostate, Emperor 17, 95
Julius Caesar 82, 108–9
justice 1, 10, 37
Justinian, Emperor 18, 131

Kaldellis, Anthony 18
Kantian aesthetics 114
Kelly, Henry Ansgar 3, 5, 26, 32, 52
Kempshall, Matthew 104
Kermaria-an-Isquit, France 41
Kerr, Walter 7–8
Killing of the Children (Digby) 1, 121–2
King Lear (Shakespeare) 10, 27
knowledge, cultural 20
koiné 18
Kolve, V.A. 77, 113
Kreitner, Kevin 42
Kress, Gunther 50
Kyd, Thomas: *The Spanish Tragedy* 96–8
Kyle, Donald 86

Lactantius 68
Lady Philosophy 100, 105, 129
Lai des Deux Amans (Marie de France) 13–14
Lalou, Elisabeth 6
Lancelot 26
Late Banns 120
Latin, challenges to the hegemony of 26
laude 71
laughter 13
Laurent de Premierfait 49
laws
    canon law 24, 102
    medieval sumptuary 122–3
    Plato and 12

INDEX

Laws (Plato) 5, 68
Lazarus 28, 29
Le Goff, Jacques 13
Lebègue, Raymond 3
Lefebvre, Henri 31
Legenda aurea (Jacobus de Voragine) 8, 58, 119
Leo I, Pope 21
Lerud, Theodore 76, 80
Liber Peristephanon. *See* Book of Crowns (*Liber Peristephanon*)
Life of Plato (Olympiodorus) 68
lingua franca 17
Lintilhac, Eugène de 6
literacy, lay 25
literary devices, emotion and 62
liturgy
    emotions and 70
    liturgical drama 3, 18, 38–9, 116–17
    liturgical festivals 32
    liturgical roles played by Christian clergy 24
    Mark's account 87
    as theater 93
    tragic drama and 49, 69
Livy (Titus Livius), *Ab urbe condita* 51
Llibre Vermell 31, 41–3
locus and *platea* staging 28–31, 34–5, 38
London stage 13, 81, 98
Louis X of France 108
Lucan
    as a cultural reference point 109
    Pharsalia 108–9
Lucian of Samosata 5
Ludus de Antichristo 84
lust 21, 90, 130, 133
Luther, Martin 23
Lydgate, John 41, 57
    Fall of Princes 109, 110
    Serpent of Division 109–10
    Troy Book 52, 53

Magnus Herodis (Towneley) 117
Mahābhārata 27
The Maid of Orleans: A Romantic Tragedy (Schiller) 138
Maimonides, Moses 78
    (*The Guide of the Perplexed* [*Moreh Nevuchim*]) 79
Malchus, Saint 84
Malory, Thomas: *Le Morte Darthur* 110
Manicheanism 10, 21

mappae mundi 28, 30
Marbod of Rennes 128
Marie de France 25
    Lai des Deux Amans 13–14
Marigny, Enguerrand de 108
Mark, Gospel of 86–7
Marot, Clément 11
Mars 106–7
Marsilion, King 102
Martial 86
martyrs
    actresses as 131
    Christian 86
    medieval martyr plays 96
    strength-in-weakness of 84–5
    the tragedy of martyrdom 88–93
Maruli, Marko (*Judith*) 8
Mary, Blessed Virgin. *See* Virgin Mary, Blessed
Mary 124
    The Fall and Repentance of Mary (*Abraham*) 8, 132–5
Mary Magdalene 28–9
Mary Magdalene (play) 28–9, 31
masculinity
    the English Innocents plays and 120
    late-medieval 122
    masculine power 119, 121, 123
    in medieval English guild drama 122
Mass (*see also* Communion; Eucharist)
    drama of 6
    as performance 77
    producing a Christian form of catharsis 24–5
    Prudentius' lyrics and 88
    as a tragic play 69
Massacre of the Innocents plays 88–9, 113, 115–19, 176n.66
    Chester (mystery) cycle 116, 118–21, 123–4
Matthew, Gospel of 19–20, 113, 117–18, 125
Mazouer, Charles 6
McNamer, Sarah 62
Medea 54
Medea (Seneca) 54, 88
media
    media landscape of 12th-century Europe 25
    mediation 16
    medieval 16–18
medieval English drama (Middle English drama, medieval English biblical drama). *See* drama

medieval sumptuary laws 122–3
Merback, Mitchell 36
Meriasek, Saint 79
metaphor 36
Metellus 84
Michael Psellus 72
Michael VIII, Emperor 17
The Miller's Tale (Chauser) 117
Mills, Robert 87
mimesis 86
minstrels 71, 103 (*see also* jongleurs; music; singing/song)
miracles 96
misery 99, 105, 110
misogyny 139
The Mission of Joan of Arc (Thérèse de Lisieux) 139
Monarchia (Dante) 108
monasteries 22, 41–2, 84, 139
monasticism, new monastic movement 18
monks 25
Monk's Tale (Chaucer) 36, 52, 74, 102–3, 109, 160n.62
moral authority 17
moral character 67–8
moral conduct, fortune and 74
moral function, of tragedy 51, 105
moral value, of tragedy 68–9
moral virtues, self-restraint as 66, 67
Moralia in Job (Gregory the Great) 101
morality plays
    crises of dislocation and 27–8
    East Anglian 30–1, 44–5
    English 32, 44–5
    Everyman 35
    France 5
    post-performance introspection 36
Mordred 110
Le Morte Darthur (Malory) 110
Mount Athos 22
Mozarbic/Visigothic, chant 70
murder, of children 1–2 (*see also* infanticide; Massacre of the Innocents plays)
Muses 135
music
    conflict and 71
    Dança general de la muerte and 42
    effect on human conduct 12, 69
    healing power of 70
    jeu-parti 71
    kinds of 69
    liturgical 22

music-drama 39
Neo-Platonists' views on 69
role of in the early Church 18, 70–1
saltatio and 5
spiritual value of 69
suffering and 71
from the *Totentanz* tradition 40
Muslim traditions
    image-making and 79
    Muslim funerary rites 44
    theatrical representation and 80
Mussato, Albertino 3, 7
Mystère de la Passion (Gréban) 8
Mystery of the Siege of Orleans 135–7
mystery plays (Passion plays) 6, 8 (*see also* saint's plays)
    Arras Passion 38
    Chester Plays. *See* Chester
    Corpus Christi cycles 80, 87–8, 135–6
    Coventry plays 121–2, 176n.55
    crises of dislocation and 27–8
    Digby plays 28, 118, 121–2, 175n.47
    feminism and 135–6
    Mystery of the Siege of Orleans 135–7
    N-Town plays 40, 88, 118, 156n.49
    received with frivolity 11
    scapegoating in 37–8
    Towneley plays 87, 117, 156n.49, 173n.16
    tragedy and 31
    York Plays 60–2, 78, 87n.52, 156n.49
mythology, transmission of classical 33

N-Town plays 40, 88, 118, 156n.49
Name of the Rose, The (Eco) 11
narratives, Judeo-Christian 21
Neal, Derek 122
Neo-Platonism 68–9
neoclassical unities 27
Nero 20, 83, 84
Neville, William 136
New Testament 18
Nicholas of Cusa 5, 9
Nicholas of Prato 52–3
Nietzsche, Friedrich 81, 83, 85, 86
Nimrod 103, 105, 171n.47
Nonnus 130, 132
Normington, Katie 77, 136
Norwich Grocers 156n.49
Novikoff, Alex 71
nuns 13, 94, 132, 134, 139

INDEX

Oedipus 21, 36, 71, 127
O'Hogan, Cillian 93
Old St. Paul's Cathedral, London 41
Old Testament 8, 21, 103, 118
Olivier (in *The Song of Roland*) 102–3
Olson, Glending 5
Olympiodorus, *Life of Plato* 68
On Music (Boethius) 69
On the Egyptian Mysteries (Iamblichus) 68–9
On the Eloquence of the Vernacular Tongue (Dante) 75
oral traditions, of tragedy and poetry 17
orators 22
order, chaos and 6
Orderic Vitalis 22, 149n.54
Ordinalia (play) 31, 38, 46–7
Ordo prophetarum 39
Ordo Virtutum. See The Play of the Virtues
Origo mundi 156n.49
Orleans 135
Orlemanski, Julie 50
Orthodox Church 22
Otto of Freising, *Chronicle* 101
Otto the Great, Emperor 25, 94
Ottoman Empire 17
Oxyrhynchus 15

Padua, *Representatio Herodis in nocte Epyphanie* 117
pagan culture
    Christians' adoption of 83, 88
    condemnations of 18
    pagan cult of heroes 88
    pagan literature 93, 97–8
    spectacles 32, 88
    of violence 91, 93, 98
paganism
    medieval drama/ritual and 18, 96
    pagan ritualism 22, 38
    tragedy described as pagan practices 31
pain 12, 81, 95 (*see also* Crucifixion; Passion of Christ; suffering)
Pambos 130
pantomimes 44
papacy 26, 107 (*see also* Roman [Catholic] Church)
Paphnutius 133
Pappano, Margaret Aziza 60
papyri, of Euripides' *Helen* 15, 16
Paris 2, 8, 51, 71
Parker, John 124

Paschasius Radbertus 21, 148n.38
Passion of Christ
    Christos Paschon (Euripides) 23, 24, 72
    Corpus Christi plays of 80, 87–8
    Mass and 69
    The Passion (biblical episode) 37, 38, 47, 86–7
    Passion of Christ (play) (*Passio Christi*) 31, 37, 46–7
    theater of 32, 78
    as a tragedy 6, 75–6, 87
The Passion of Saints Perpetua and Felicity 131
Passion plays. *See* mystery plays
Passion Sunday 26
Paston Letters 117
pathos 22
Patrologia Latina 19, 57, 125
Paul 84, 85, 155n.34
Paula 131
Pelagia 130, 132
penance 58, 60
La Penitance Adam 59
Pentheus, King 72
performance(s) 2, 7–8, 11, 13
    affective responses to 78
    in Anglo-Saxon England 70
    Christianity and 76
    in Church 24
    Eucharist as 77, 78
    identity and 76
    moving to churches, inn yards and city streets 87
    as a repository of spiritually suggestive images 80
    role of in the Middle Ages 65–6
    of tragedy 21–2
peripeteia 73
Perpetua 83, 131
Perran Round 33
persecution
    of Christians 83, 90, 94
    of Jews 79
Peter of Abano 105
Peter of Blois 25, 75, 150n.78
Peter the Venerable 25
Phaedra (Seneca) 91
Pharsalia (Lucan) 108–9
Phèdre (Racine) 127
Philip III of France 104
Philip IV of France 107–8
Philippians, Epistle to the 84

philosophy
  Aristotle and 66, 67
  consolations of 101
  Lady Philosophy 100, 105, 129
  Plato and 66–7
  relation to poetry 68, 69
  tragedy and 65, 68, 74, 75
Piero delle Vigne 106–7
pity 9, 12, 21, 25–6, 32, 67, 84–5, 100, 103, 110, 127, 138
Piyyut (liturgical poem) 70
platea 34, 44
Plato
  law/lawmakers and 12
  Laws 5, 68
  philosophy and 66–7
  Republic 67, 68
  tragedy and 68
Play of Adam and Eve (Chester Plays) 60, 63, 156n.49
Play of Saint Catherine 8
Play of Saint Theodora 13
Play of the Sacrament (Croxton) 8, 34, 35
The Play of the Virtues (*Ordo Virtutum*) (Hildegard) 32, 132, 134–5
pleasure 5, 11, 13, 21, 23, 31, 50, 81, 85–6, 123–30, 132, 134, 140
pleasure, pain and 12, 81, 85, 95
Pliny 82
plots 6–7, 29, 31, 36, 115–16, 118–20, 133, 135
poetic pastiche 23
poetics
  of medieval tragedy 31
  of medieval tragic place 32–8
Poetics (Aristotle) 4–5, 6, 22, 68, 75, 76, 114
poetry
  Christian 20
  Christian liturgical poetry 70, 88–9
  good and bad 69
  relation to philosophy 68–9
  tragic poets 17, 20, 32
Pole, William 136
Policraticus (John of Salisbury) 35–6, 103, 170n.38
politics
  Aristotle and 99, 104
  division and 109–10
  individuals and communities and 103–4
  political power 104
  political tragedy 99–100, 105, 109, 110–11

  violence and 103
  women and 115
Polybius 82
Pompey 108, 109
  theater of 20
populism 17
Porphyry the Phoenician 22
Potiphar's wife 21
power
  masculine 119, 121, 123
  political 104
  social and sexual 121
  spiritual and temporal 107
prayer(s) 24–5, 34, 42, 130
preachers/preaching 18, 22–6, 44, 84, 130, 132
Priam 85
pride 106, 110, 130
priests 9, 17, 24–5, 39
Princeton Encyclopedia of Poetry and Poetics 4
printing presses 18
Priscian 20
private sphere, women and 128
procession(s) 13, 33, 38–9, 41, 44, 47, 71, 118, 135, 137
Proclus 68
Procopius 131–2
production and consumption, of medieval drama 51
proscenium stages 28
Protestants/Protestantism, repurposing of Catholicism by 96
Prudentius 88–93
  Book of Crowns (*Liber Peristephanon*) 83, 88, 89, 91, 92
  Cathemerinon 88–9
  Psychomachia 45, 88–90
psalms 71
Psellus, Michael 72
Psychomachia (Prudentius) 45, 88–90
public life, women and 127–8, 132, 136, 139
Pulci, Antonia 13
purification, of emotions 69
Puritans 63

Quem quaeritis. See *Visitatio sepulchri*

Rabanus Maurus 20, 148n.33
Rachel 118, 119
Racine, Jean: *Phèdre* 127
rape 1–2, 91

INDEX

reconciliation, of conflicting emotions 9
redemption 94–5
Reformation 96
    Counter (Catholic) Reformations 24
rejoicing 24, 117, 118
relics 96
religion (*see also* Christians/Christianity; Muslim traditions)
    religious intolerance 76
    theater and 38, 66
Remigius of Auxerre 5, 38
Renaissance
    Carolingian 24
    Paleologan 17
    Renaissance theater 96
repentance 60
Representatio Herodis in nocte Epyphanie 117
Representation of Abraham and Isaac 8
Republic (Plato) 67, 68
Resurrection
    doctrinal function of the 38
    of Jesus Christ 24, 44, 46, 47, 72
retributive justice 37 (*see also* justice)
Revelation 118
revelation, deception and 135
rhetoric 5, 17, 19, 36, 94, 104–5, 110, 114
Rice, Nicole R. 60
Richards, I. A. 2–3, 7, 9–10
Richardus 2
Ristine, Frank 6
ritual
    Catholic 87
    medieval 96
    self-mortification rituals 37
Robertson, D.W. 6
Rodríguez Porto, Rosa María 33
Rojas, Fernando de 3
Roland 102–3. See also *The Song of Roland*
Roman (Catholic) Church 18, 21, 24, 25 (*see also* Catholicism; papacy)
    Franciscans 23
Roman de Fauvel (Gervais du Bus) 107–9
Roman de Troie 33
Roman Empire
    amphitheaters 32–3, 82, 86
    architecture 32–3
    Christianity in 33, 49, 82–4, 90
    eastern (Byzantium) 15–17, 22, 26, 71–2
    enthusiasm for spectacular bloodshed 82, 84, 86
    execution of Christians 90

    ironic play-acting 87–8
    Roman games 32, 82–4, 86
    theater and 82, 132
    theaters in 152n.17
    western 19–22, 72–6
Roman tragedy 17, 88, 97
romance(s) 23, 25–6, 33, 75, 111
romantic idealism 114
Romanus, Saint 89
Rome 20, 33, 49, 68, 82–4, 88, 93, 94
Romeo and Juliet (Shakespeare) 10, 27
Rosenwein, Barbara H. 70
Rosh Hashanah 44
Rouse, Richard 57
Rupert of Deutz 21, 148n.40
Russell, Willy: *Educating Rita* 6

sacramental drama 23
sacrament(s) 24, 77
sacred drama 96
sacrifice(s) 21, 26, 33–4, 38, 47, 70, 84, 100, 110
Saint-Maur-des-Fossés 2
Saint Catherine, Play of 8
saint plays
    early 93
    East Anglian 30–1
Saint Theodora, Play of 13
saints, two kinds of 94 (*see also individual saints*)
Salome 21
Sánchez de Badajoz, Diego: *Farsa de la Muerte*; *Farsa del juego de cañas* 39–40
satire 5, 19, 99, 107, 111
scaffolds 28, 31, 35, 45, 157n.51
scapegoating 31, 37–8, 47
Schiller, Friedrich: *The Maid of Orleans: A Romantic Tragedy* 138
schism 21, 90
scribal technologies, new 17
scribes 15, 49, 113
scriptures 24, 83, 93–4, 135
Sébillet, Thomas 5
self-mortification rituals 37
self-restraint, as a moral virtue 66–7, 85
Seneca the Elder 51
Seneca the Younger
    Christians/Christianity and 81, 83–4
    Hercules furens 33, 54–6, 57, 88
    Medea 54, 88
    Mussato's commentary on 7
    Nicholas of Prato and 53

ongoing popularity of 84, 94, 98
Phaedra 91
Prudentius and 88–9, 91
Roman blood sports and 86, 90–1
Senecan renaissance in England 96–8
spectacle and 81, 86
tragedies of 17
Trevet's commentaries on 51
Trojan Women 84–5
sentimental education 66
Sermon on the Mount 19
sermons 23, 36, 117
Serpent of Division (Lydgate) 109–10
Serre, Jean de 11
Seth 58
Sextus Afranius Burro 84
sexual assaults 1–2
sexual power 121
Shakespeare, William
    Hamlet 23, 30, 97, 117
    King Lear 10, 27
    median length of his works 27
    Romeo and Juliet 10, 27
    The Spanish Tragedy and 97
Shearmen and Tailors' Pageant 121–2, 176n.55
Sheingorn, Pamela 134
Sicard of Cremona 24
sin, suffering and 81
singing/song
    of the ancient theater 18
    clergy performing 18
    Dança general de la muerte 31, 42
    deacons excused from 24
    emotion and 72
    in *Hercules furens* 56
    jeu-parti 71
    of jongleurs 26
    liturgical songs 88
    from the *Llibre Vermell* 31, 41, 43
    The Monk's Tale 103
    in praise of God 70
    sacred songs 24
    singing Innocents 118
    Song of Roland 8, 102–3, 169n.23
    Song of Songs 20, 131
    Song of Sybil 31, 39–40
    spectacle and 7
    Totentanz 40
    tragedy and 5, 23, 52, 56–7, 99
    tragic poets and 32
Skoda, Hannah 13

skulls 23, 26
slavery 93, 94–5
Smalley, Beryl 51
social contract 21
social function
    of theater 65–6
    of tragedy in Byzantium 71–2
social identity 124
social mixing, at Roman games 92–3
social power 121
social roles, performed by female characters 115
social status 122–3 (*see also* class; elites)
Socrates 66
Socrates Scholasticus 130
Song of Roland 8, 102–3, 169n.23
Song of Songs 20, 131
Song of Sybil 31, 39–40
sophists 66
Sophocles, *Antigone* 29
Sophonisba (Trissino) 127
soul (*anima*) 134
space(s)
    absolute space 31
    medieval concept of 30
    performance spaces 34
    phenomenology of 34
    time and 27–8
    value of peripheral 30
Spain
    Blessed Virgin Mary of Montserrat 41, 42, 43
    Catalonia and Castile 39–40, 44
The Spanish Tragedy (Thomas Kyd) 96–8
spectacles
    Aristotle and 7
    of death 81
    after the fall of the Roman Empire 87
    pagan 32, 88
    Seneca and 81, 86
    of suffering 78, 81–98
    women as 130
Sponsler, Claire 3, 4, 76, 123
St Meriasek 79
Staines, David 116
Steiner, George: *Death of Tragedy* 2
stoicism 83, 100
Stone, Donald 10
stytelers 28
subversion 13, 123
Suetonius 92
suffering
    of Christ 77, 87
    by the entire Jewish nation 78–9

human 76
of Job 101
meaning and 85
music and 71
the Romans and 82–4
shadow plays and 80
sin and 81
spectacle of 78
Swartz, M.D. 70
Swift, Christopher 7
Symes, Carol 11, 31, 49–51, 57, 70–2, 76, 94n.88, 113–14, 124–5
synagogue 19, 21, 70
Syria, Apamea 68

T-O maps 28
Talbot, John 136
tales 8, 25, 101
tears 11, 13, 23, 25–7, 108, 127
technology
    scribal 17
    printing press 18
Templars 107
Terence
    Ælius Donatus and 19
    Hecyra 82, 95
    Hrotsvitha and 25, 94, 133
terror 2, 12, 28, 83, 85, 122–3
Tertullian (*Ad martyras*)
    Christians and 82–3
    De spectaculis 32
    negative references to tragedy 19
    pagan literature and 98
    tragedy and 49, 67, 68
    women and 129
textual transmission 15–18, 114
Thaïs 133, 135
theater(s) (*see also* drama)
    actresses in 130–2
    amphitheaters 32–3, 82–6, 87
    change in West 87
    Christianity and 18, 135
    circular arena of East Anglia and Cornwall stages 31
    Elizabethan public 31
    falling into disrepair 87
    function of place and time in 27
    "Holy Theatre" 34
    liturgy as 93
    locus and *platea* staging 28–31, 34–5, 38
    medieval biblical 113, 115
    medieval outdoor 28

pagan ritualism and 38
performance spaces of 28
proscenium stages 28
Renaissance 96
Roman 17, 31, 32, 82, 86
social function of 65–6
subversive potential of medieval theater 123
theater-in-the-round settings 39, 46, 79
theatrum mundi 35–6
transvestite or cross-dressed 123
theatrocracy, of Plato 12
Thecla 131
Theoderic the Great 20, 100
Theodora 131–2
Therapy of the Soul (*Tibb al-nufūs*) 79
Thérèse de Lisieux 138–40
    The History of a Soul 139
    Joan of Arc Accomplishing Her Mission 139–40
    The Mission of Joan of Arc 139
Thucydides 22
time 11, 27–8, 124–5
Timothy, Second 84
Tolmie, Jane 116, 123
tombs, theatrical primacy of 29
torture 1, 37, 78, 87, 95
Totentanz 40
Towneley Plays 87n.51, 156n.49, 173n.16
    Magnus Herodis 117
Tractatus Coislinianus 22
Tractatus de peregrinante civitate Dei 57
trade 25, 96
tragedy
    as an ancient genre 21
    death of, alleged 3, 49, 81, 114
    defined 4, 5
    meaning of 73
    medieval renascence of 93–6
    medieval suppression of, supposed 15
    in the Middle Ages 15, 65, 81, 86–7
    origin of 57–64
    term 125
    theories of 17–18, 66–9, 72–6
tragic poets 17, 20, 32
tragicomedy 3, 5, 6, 25
transvestite or cross-dressed theater 123
trauma, Jewish communities and 79
travel, long-distance 25
Treaty of Troyes 109
Tres Clerici 8
Tretise of Miraclis Playinge 13

Trevet, Nicholas 33, 51–6, 64
Trevisa, John 57, 119
Trinity 81
Trinity Sunday 78
Trissino, Gian Giorgio, *Sophonisba* 127
Tristan 25, 26, 110
Troilus and Criseyde (Chaucer) 52
Trojan Women (Seneca) 84–5
Troy 108
Troy Book (Lydgate) 52, 53
Trullan Synod of Constantinople 22
Tydeman, William 33
tyrants 103–4, 118, 170n.38, 170n.41
Tzetzes, John 72

Ulysses 21
Unity of Time 27
Urban IV, Pope 78
urbanisation 26

vernacular(s)
   European 19
   the rise of written 25
   translations of the Eucharist 24
   vernacular drama 57, 113
   vernacular saint plays and passions 87
Veroli casket 33
vice 28, 30, 36, 74, 85, 128, 133, 140
vices, the 40, 45, 88–9
Villon, François: "Ballad of Ladies from Yesteryear" 138
violence
   aesthetic of 85, 87, 89
   art and 91
   domestic 1, 7
   Jewish against Christians 21
   of pagan Rome 91, 93, 98
   politics and 103
   rape 1–2, 91
   rendered on the body of Christ 37, 77, 78
   repurposing of pagan 87
   sexual assaults 1–2
   torture 1, 37, 78, 87, 95
virelai 42
Virgil, *Aeneid* 67, 108
Virgil (character) 106
Virgin Mary, Blessed 2–4, 13, 43, 124, 130–1, 136
Virgin of Montserrat 41, 42, 43
virginity 130, 131, 133, 134
virtue 25, 32, 45–6, 40, 66, 69, 75, 78, 83–5, 88–9, 91, 101, 123, 128, 131–40
virtue, tragedy and 78

Virtues, the 134–5
Visitatio sepulchri (*Visit to the Sepulcher*) 3, 28
Vita Adae et Evae tradition 58
Vives, Juan Luis 11

Walsingham, Thomas 57
Warning, Rainer 38
war(s)
   of Christ 26
   civil wars between Julius Caesar and Pompey 82, 108
   France and England (14th-century) 107
   Helen of Troy and 128
   Hundred Years' War 135–8
   Mars and 106, 107
Weimann, Robert 116, 117
wheel of fortune. *See* Fortune's Wheel
Wickham, Glynn 79
William of Blois 25
William of Conches 6–7, 52, 74, 102
William of Malmesbury 21, 149n.51
William of Moerbeke 75
Wilson, Grace G. 54
Wittenberg, University of 23
Wolberus of St. Pantaleon 57
women
   actresses 130–2
   banning of from Roman games 93
   Church Fathers and 129–33
   elite 17
   eroticism and 130–1
   fallen 135
   God and 131, 133–4, 139
   politics and 115
   public life and 127–8, 132, 136, 139
   as spectacle 130
   spread of Christianity and 93
   tragedies of Euripides and 19
   tragedy and 127–8
   unruly 135–6, 137
"Women on Top" 135

Yahlom, J. 70
Yehudah ha-Levi (Judah ha-levi) 70, 78
Yom Kippur 44, 70
York
   Feast of Corpus Christi 60
   Great East Window in York Minster 60–1
   scaffolds 157n.51
   York Plays 60–2, 78, 156n.49
   York Register 60